JOHN PHILIP
(1775–1851)

JOHN PHILIP
(1775 – 1851)

Missions, Race and Politics in South Africa

Andrew Ross

ABERDEEN UNIVERSITY PRESS

First published 1986
Aberdeen University Press
A member of the Pergamon group
© Andrew Ross 1986

British Library Cataloguing in Publication Data

Ross, Andrew
 John Philip : Missions, Race and Politics in
 South Africa
 1. Philip, John   2. Missionaries—South Africa
 —Biography
 I. Title
 266'.0092'4   BV3557.P4/

 ISBN 0 08 032457 6
 ISBN 0 08 032467-3 (Pbk)

PRINTED IN GREAT BRITAIN
THE UNIVERSITY PRESS
ABERDEEN

Contents

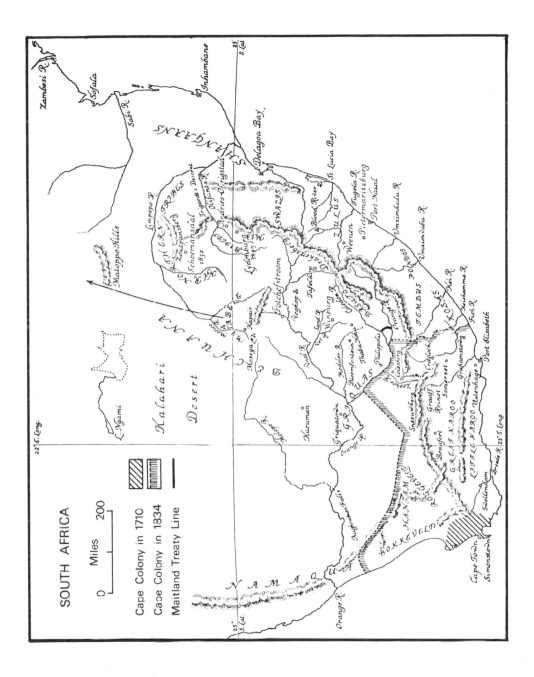

SOUTH AFRICA

Miles

0   200

Cape Colony in 1710
Cape Colony in 1834
Maitland Treaty Line

Introduction

A tall, dark, strongly built Scottish preacher, John Philip (1775–1851) has so indelibly left his mark on South African history that Prime Minister Johannes Strydom could use his name as an immediately recognisable symbol: when advising missionaries not to follow in the footsteps of Fr Trevor Huddleston, he warned them 'not to do a Philip'. Yet Dr John Philip of the London Missionary Society, one of the truly outstanding Scotsmen and missionary leaders of the nineteenth century, is unknown in his native Scotland except to students of South African history.

In the specifically ecclesiastical scene in Britain as a whole, John Philip is no better remembered. His name was not deemed important enough to merit an entry in *The Oxford Dictionary of the Christian Church*, while many who made a far less significant impact did have entries. For example, from the southern Africa of Philip's own era, Robert Moffat has a substantial entry in the *Dictionary*. This reflects popular understanding and knowledge of church history. In any lively congregation interested in missions, the name of Robert Moffat is known, while it is unusual to find someone who knows the name of Dr Philip.

Certainly Robert Moffat's career in South Africa was a distinguished one and a very long one, from 1817 to 1870. Yet, despite his massive achievement in translating the Bible into seTswana and the importance of his relations with Lobengula, the king of the Ndebele, Moffat's role in the planting and development of Christianity in southern Africa was a limited one. As for his significance in the general history of South Africa, it cannot be estimated as anything more than marginal to that history.

In stark contrast, John Philip was the central figure linking all the Protestant missionary societies in southern Africa, except the Methodists. He persuaded the Paris Mission to begin work there and was their agent at Cape Town. His role in influencing the Rhenish Mission and the American Board Mission to come to South Africa was crucial and he continued a close association with them for the rest of his life. His relations with the Scottish missionaries in the eastern Cape was not so central as with these others, but it was still an important element in the history of the Scottish mission.

In any general history of South Africa, Philip is a figure that has to be discussed. Indeed, this is so even in the more specialised histories of the Afrikaner people, of the Cape Folk, the Griqua, the English settlers, the Sotho and the Xhosa peoples.

What is the cause of this dramatically inappropriate disparity in the recognition granted to these two men, both in their native Scotland and in the United Kingdom as a whole?

Answering this question thoroughly would entail an elaborate

investigation of British ecclesiastical historiography, which is not possible
here. However, one important element in any answer was the impact of the
flood of popular missionary literature, consisting primarily of biographies,
that swept Britain from around 1880 until the 1920s—a literary genre which
retained some popularity in Scotland and Northern Ireland as late as the
1940s.

During the period of popularity of this literary form, thousands of young
people received such books as prizes, not only in Sunday school but in the
ordinary day schools as well. In addition, certainly until the Great War,
these books had a significant sale among adults.

John Philip, who died thirty years before this minor industry got going,
was never taken up by it, while Moffat was. This is not simply a matter of
chronology, though Moffat's living until 1883 is not irrelevant. Much more
important was the fact that Moffat's life and work fitted into the model
scenario within which these writers operated. He worked far from any area
of significant European presence and he did pioneering work with
Lobengula and his Ndebele, a war-like people, made notorious by Rhodes'
propaganda efforts related to his 'drive to the North' in the 1890s. Moffat
was the epitome of the self-sacrificing missionary, cut off from the
comforts of European civilisation far in the interior of the 'Dark
Continent'. This was the pattern that was believed to sell. It was the pattern
of life of Mary Slessor, the ex-mill girl from Dundee, alone in the
mysterious rain-forest of eastern Nigeria; of David Livingstone, who, in
that period, was remembered primarily as the lone venturer 'lost' in Central
Africa. These, and others including Bishop Hannington, martyred on the
shores of Lake Victoria, were the stuff of the missionary heroism that these
books aimed to portray.

In addition, these missionary figures, as they were portrayed, presented
no challenge to the imperialism current in the Britain of that time. To
achieve this portrayal, some aspects of their lives and their principles had to
be ignored or glossed over, particularly so in the case of Livingstone.[1] In the
same way, the ecclesiastical conflicts in which many of these strong
personalities were involved, were also delicately avoided or played down.

John Philip simply did not fit the bill. He lived most of his life in Cape
Town, the only 'European' city in Africa; he was not a lonely pioneer, and
if his controversies—political, social and missionary—are avoided, what is
left to write about?

Whether Philip was omitted from this missionary literature for these
reasons or not, omitted he was, and this undoubtedly has contributed to his
'invisibility' in Scottish and British ecclesiastical historiography. As a result
he has been written about by historians of South Africa. Understandably
these writers have paid little attention to the particular Scottish background
and the form of evangelicalism that shaped his life and thoughts.

His Scottish background was that of Scotland's intellectual Golden Age,
the Enlightenment, when Edinburgh was a key centre of European thought.
His youth and young manhood coincided with a rare period of comparative
prosperity in Scotland, a prosperity that affected particularly the skilled
artisan class to which he belonged.

Perhaps even more important, for a man who was going to leave Scotland to work in the Cape Colony, was the fact that Philip grew up in a Scotland that less than fifty years before had seen the crushing of the last major war-like tribal culture in Europe. Philip grew up among people who had, in their youth, lived in an uneasy proximity to the cattle-raising and cattle-raiding Highland clans. As a young man he saw the sons and grandsons of the warriors defeated at Culloden take their place in Scottish society as doctors, lawyers, teachers and ministers, through the transforming power of the parish school and the democratic university system of Scotland. If the sons of Lochiel could be so transformed, why not sons of Ngqika?

As Philip's Scottish background has not been considered in the literature, so his particular evangelical background has also remained unexplored. It certainly cannot be subsumed under the phrase 'city-bred liberalism' used by de Kiewiet.[2] It cannot be so subsumed because the brand of evangelicalism which profoundly shaped John Philip was one which was at serious odds with society, both in the United States and the United Kingdom where it developed.

All Protestant missionaries and mission supporters of that era were evangelicals, but there were as important differences among evangelicals then as between, for example, Marxists today.

All evangelicals shared a nominal opposition to slavery, that is until around 1830, when, in the States that would later form the Confederacy, an evangelical defence of slavery was developed. However, this agreement on opposition to slavery went, in many cases, with a horror of doing anything that could be construed as being 'political'. This led to preaching against the wickedness of the Institution coupled with a refusal to be involved in any kind of action against it. Even among those who were willing to campaign against the institution, there were many who showed little or no concern for the plight of free Blacks and who doubted their capacity for integration into a civilised society.

The particular strain of evangelicalism to which Philip belonged was decidedly different from this. His tradition insisted that the Gospel had a bearing on all aspects of society. It believed that the expansion of the Gospel message throughout the world was part of God's plan for greater justice and a more humane society and it firmly asserted the oneness of all humankind. One of the most succinct expressions of this tradition comes in a sermon by Richard Watson, one of the leading evangelicals in England. Of God he said

> His design is, that truth, the truth of the Gospel, shall be freely and universally proclaimed; that Christ shall be universally believed in and adored; that the purity, and justice, and kindness of his religion shall influence all the institutions of society; that all public vice shall be suppressed; that all public oppression and wrong shall be removed; that all nations, in a word, shall be blessed in Christ, that is be brought into an enlightened, a holy, and a happy condition by the influence of the Gospel.[3]

Although this strand of evangelicalism was a numerical minority within the general movement, it was of enormous importance because of the many outstanding men and women who belonged to it. They ranged from the comparatively conservative Wilberforce, through John Smith of Demerara[4] to John Brown of 'John Brown's Body' fame. Their influence was great on both sides of the Atlantic, so great, indeed, that some US historians have insisted that the differences between the North and the South could have been settled without war but for their 'fanaticism'.[5]

Perhaps the outstanding figure in this branch of evangelicalism was Theodore Weld, whom Professor Brauer[6] suggests did more for the Abolitionist cause than even William Lloyd Garrison. Weld, while still a student at Lane Seminary in Cincinnati, led a rebellion by the students against the Seminary Board of Governors and the local churches, criticising them for their lack of commitment to the anti-slavery cause and the plight of the free Blacks in that 'border' city. They even opposed that great leader of American evangelicalism, Lyman Beecher, the President of the Seminary. Beecher's sermons were strong on the slavery issue but he was very nervous of political action and he appeared indifferent to the problems of the free Black population. So disappointed by all this were Weld and his fellow students that they looked elsewhere for their spiritual home and found it among the freemen and escaped slaves of Cincinnati. As Weld wrote later

> While I was at Lane Seminary my intercourse was with the Coloured people at Cincinnati, I think I may say exclusively. If I ate in the City it was at their table. If I slept in the City it was at their homes. If I attended religious parties, it was theirs—weddings—funerals—theirs—Religious meetings—theirs—Sabbath schools—Bible classes theirs.[7]

These divisions among evangelicals were reflected among the missionaries who came to serve in southern Africa, among whom John Philip was the most important exponent of the minority radical view. He should also be seen as one of its leading figures in the world. Along with people like Theodore Weld, he is one of the outstanding exponents of an understanding of the purpose of evangelical Christianity most pointedly expressed in the words, sung by thousands of young men in the blue of the Union army,

> In the Beauty of the lilies
>   Christ was born across the seas
> With a glory in his bosom
>   That transfigures you and me
> As he died to make men holy
>   Let us die to make men free
> His truth is marching on
>   Glory, Glory, Halleluia,
> His truth is marching on.[8]

John Philip was a man produced by a Scotland going through a particularly exciting and dynamic period in its history. He was someone profoundly influenced by a radical brand of evangelicalism. If these two formative influences upon him are not brought into consideration of his life and work, he cannot be understood. Without such consideration, his controversies with his missionary colleagues, his clashes with the colonial government, with the trekboers and the English settlers, are reduced, too readily, to the level of problems of personality, even of eccentricity.

The aim of this study of Philip's career in South Africa is to attempt to relate his Scottish roots to what he said and did. It is also to place him as one of the leaders of a worldwide evangelical crusade, a crusade that was mounted from New York to New Zealand,[9] to ensure, as Watson put it, 'that the purity, and justice and kindness of his religion shall influence all institutions of society; . . . that all public oppression and wrong shall be removed'.

If it had been possible, it would have been good, in addition, to show John Philip in a more private and personal light. Unfortunately, the fire which destroyed the collection of Philip papers in the library of the University of the Witwatersrand, upon which Professor Macmillan and his assistants worked, has made this almost impossible. The vast number of Philip letters still available in the Library of the School of African and Oriental Studies in London reflect his public life in South Africa. However, some hints of what Dr Philip was like as a man can be gained from contemporary publications and the remaining small fragment of the originally large correspondence between him and his family. These are to be found in the Cullen Library at Witwatersrand and in the Pringle–Fairbairn correspondence in the Library of Parliament at Cape Town. There is also a collection of over fifty family letters recently donated by Mr Peter Philip to the Jagger Library of the University of Cape Town.

There has been no serious attention paid to these fragments. As a result Philip has been discussed always in terms of his public activity. Theal's judgement of him, which was not based on any knowledge of his letters and journals at all, has tended to dominate all subsequent discussions. Even writers, basically sympathetic towards Philip and the causes which he supported, have tended to explain the antagonism to him in terms of flaws in his character without any reference to the few personal insights that can be gained from the extant material. A good example is the entry under Philip's name in *The New International Dictionary of the Christian Church*, where the author says

> His aggressive and intolerant manner did harm, as did his unwillingness to admit mistakes and his unsympathetic attitude towards colonists.

Less sympathetic authors have added pomposity and arrogance to the list of character flaws in the missionary leader. John S. Galbraith even goes so far as to say that he was a 'moral totalitarian' and that his life and work are simply not susceptible to judgement in rational terms![10]

How could such a man have had so many friends who gave him life-long affection? How could such a man have raised a family of spirited sons and daughters and retained their affection and respect? John Philip did have such a family and did attract such friends.

From the vast public correspondence and the few fragments of private correspondence that are available, and, making use of some personal references in the writing of contemporaries, some tentative features of John

Philip as a private individual can be built up to set alongside the public figure.

When we begin to do this, it becomes immediately clear that he cannot be seen apart from his wife, Jane Ross. She was the daughter of an Aberdeen family converted to evangelical Christianity by Philip. John and Jane were married in October 1809, and from then on she played a vital role in his life. She became an additional administrator for the London Missionary Society in South Africa, she helped with the work he did for the other Protestant societies that used him as their agent, she ran the office single-handed during her husband's long treks throughout the Colony and beyond. Jane also acted as John's amanuensis when his handwriting, never easy to read, became completely illegible due to ill health. She brought up their seven children and, until her death, kept up a close correspondence with them all. She made their homes in Aberdeen and in Church Square, Cape Town warm welcoming places for a host of visitors. She was in every sense his partner, his comrade.

In Aberdeen, Jane bore four children and still held open house for the host of young people attracted by her husband's preaching. One of these, a student at the University, Robert Philip (no relation) has left us the only substantial personal picture of John Philip. This was a pamphlet he had published to mark his old friend's death.[11]

In this pamphlet, Robert Philip gives us a warm picture of a man who gained great popularity as a preacher, in great demand throughout the Northeast of Scotland, a man who became a public figure, prominent in the affairs of Aberdeen and the surrounding districts, yet one who gave of himself to the young people who gathered around him.

Every Sunday, young people, students and townsfolk gathered in the manse to discuss religious and moral issues. In these 'seminars' they were encouraged to express themselves on these issues, girls as well as boys. This is in marked contrast to the authoritarian stance of the Scottish pulpit and lecturer's desk of the day. Years later, many of these men and women looked back to these evenings in the Philip manse as the formative influence on their lives, both spiritually and intellectually.

This style with young people, where they were guided intellectually and spiritually without being dragooned, seems to have been the style Jane and John Philip used in bringing up their own children to adulthood. Of these children, Mary (b.1810), Elizabeth (b.1812), William (b.1814) and John (b.1816) began life in Aberdeen. After the family's arrival in Cape Town in 1819, three further children were born. Durant was born in November 1819 and in 1825 a daughter, Margaret, was born, who died young, and then, in December 1829, Wilberforce Buxton, the baby of the family was born.

The children all grew up to be individuals with strong personalities and decided opinions while remaining close to each other and to their parents. This is clearly reflected in the fragments of family correspondence that remain.

The early adventures of William, the oldest boy, are firm evidence that, in his personal relations at least, Philip was no moral totalitarian. On the contrary, this episode points to his being a more understanding and considerate father than the style of fatherhood reflected in Victorian literature.

William accompanied the rest of the family to the United Kingdom in 1826 and furthered his school education there. In 1829 he enrolled as a 'fresher' in the University of Aberdeen. However, he got into some sort of difficulty before his first year was completed. What it was is not recorded in any of the sources left to us. His solution to the problem was to run off to sea. He wrote to his guardian, Mr Foulger[12]

> I am not particular on what vessel I go so that I have a place where I occasion nothing but trouble and [illegible] to my friends. I would rather go on a trader to the East Indies that I might have an opportunity of seeing my Father and tell him my real story.[13]

William, according to his brother Durant, signed on before the mast on a vessel of the Royal Navy. This presented Mr Foulger with a very difficult problem. He did not want to dissuade William from going to sea but felt that service of this sort in the Royal Navy was not for him. However, after a great deal of negotiation he finally persuaded William to sign on as an apprentice officer with the merchant service and also to persuade the Royal Navy to release the lad.[14]

This performance would have gravely disturbed any father. However, there was no melodramatic outburst from the 'moral totalitarian'. John and his wandering son kept in touch and there are many references to what was clearly a regular correspondence between William, his mother and his sisters.

After four adventurous years,[15] William decided, while on a voyage in the Indian Ocean, to give up the sea. He also appears to have, at that time, decided that he had a call to the ministry. He returned to live with the family in Cape Town some time in 1833.

The other boys were all sent to the United Kingdom for secondary education at Mill Hill school. During the school vacations they stayed with the Foulger family. When John Ross Philip, the doctor's second son, left Mill Hill, he returned to the Cape where he entered the printing trade. In 1845 he became one of the co-founders of the *Eastern Province Herald* based in Port Elizabeth. Durant, son number three, went to Glasgow University when he finished school in 1836. He had as a classmate his oldest brother William. They were both preparing to enter the Christian ministry and the service of the London Missionary Society. At Glasgow they followed the four years Arts course leading to the Glasgow MA, on the completion of which William proceeded straightaway to the Cape, while Durant went to England for specific missionary training under the auspices of the Society. In 1844, Durant sailed for the Cape just as the 'baby' of the family, Wilberforce, arrived in Britain to begin his secondary schooling and subsequent training for the ministry, which brought him back to the Cape and service with the London Missionary Society.

As for the two girls in the family, the elder, Mary, married George Christie, a young Congregationalist minister, who had served the London Missionary Society in India from 1830–32, and whom she met on a visit to

England. He came later to serve the London Missionary Society in the Cape, but he and Mary, unlike the rest of the family, did not stay in South Africa, and returned to the United Kingdom some time after the doctor's death. The second daughter, Elizabeth (she was always called Eliza within the family) married John Fairbairn, Philip's close friend and political ally.

Both young women were lively and intelligent with many close contacts within humanitarian and evangelical circles in England as well as with most of the leading figures in Cape society. The few remaining letters between them, which are preserved in the Cullen Library and the Library of Parliament, are clearly a part of a much larger and systematic correspondence. The contents of this fragment show only too well how much of a loss to historians was the 'Wits' fire. An example of this is some of the letters between the two during the family's stay in the United Kingdom while both Fairbairn and Philip were there to give evidence before the Aborigines Committee.[16]

This was a crucial period for Philip's relations with his fellow Directors of the London Missionary Society. When he returned to South Africa after this visit he never again enjoyed either their confidence or their support in any controversial matter. From the official correspondence of the Society this development is clear but how exactly it came about is not.

Mary and Eliza's letters give us a unique glimpse of the situation. They were both concerned about their father, and, from their many associations in evangelical circles, they built up their own understanding of what was going on. They believed that Mr Hankey,[17] one of the outstanding organisers of the Society, was deliberately attempting to isolate Philip and cut off his support, and, they also believed, that he was using Ellis, the Treasurer, and Freeman[18] as his pawns. The latter two, the girls felt, were not really aware of how they were being manipulated.[19]

If more of the correspondence had survived we might have obtained fuller insight into a crucial period in Philip's life and in the history of the Society. As it is, we are left with a few glimpses which might have been prejudiced gossip or important insights unavailable elsewhere.

John Philip was someone to whom young people were drawn, and with whom he was able to establish lasting friendship. He did this with his own children (not all fathers do so by any means), as well as with many others. One particularly moving example is his relationship with the two daughters of the Foulger family, Emma and Mary Anne, who continued to correspond with him long after their marriages. Mary Anne married a young clergyman whom, she feared, was in danger of being persuaded by Dr Philip to volunteer for service at the Cape. She wrote to Philip explaining how this was not how she saw their future. Fearing his disappointment, she ended her letter

> Forgive me, my father, my friend, caution me, guide me, reprove me, but let me still be acknowledged as your fondly affectionate attached child.[20]

She need not have feared, for as with the erring William, the relationship remained unbroken.

John Philip also gained the affection and respect of many who first came
to know him when they were already mature adults and not as teenagers,
who, some might suggest, are more easily impressed.

The Philip house in Church Square, Cape Town, was always full of
visitors, even more than the manse in Aberdeen. Missionaries proceeding
up-country or returning to Britain stayed there, not only the London
Missionary Society men, but also those returning to Germany or France
from the Paris and Rhenish missions. In addition, missionaries going to, or
coming back from, the east stayed in Church Square as their vessels often
docked at Cape Town for some considerable time and the throng was often
added to by visitors to the Cape who had evangelical connections like James
Backhouse.[21]

An important description of life in the Philip house comes from one of
these visitors, Eugene Casalis, the outstanding figure in the early years of
the work of the Paris Mission among the Sotho of Moshweshwe. Of his
arrival in Cape Town he wrote

> Dr Philip received us with a kindness truly paternal. He was entertaining at this
> time several missionaries, coming, one from the interior of Africa, others from
> India and Madagascar.
> We were struck from the first hour with the heartiness and good humour
> which reigned at his table. I had rarely heard men laugh so heartily. This
> shocked us a little at first, being still full of the emotions of a first arrival.
> Young recruits, we were entering the camp with a solemnity perhaps a little
> exaggerated.[22]

Perhaps the most revealing letter, from a new visitor to the Philip
household, is one written by David Livingstone. It was addressed to a
colleague, Thomas Prentice, who was still awaiting a posting with the
Society. It reveals the anti-Philip lobby in London as a fact, whatever the
correctness of the Philip girls' suspicion of how it was organised. The letter
also points to the division among evangelicals on the issue of politics
already considered.

Livingstone wrote:

> . . . first of all I want to set you right with respect to Dr. Philip concerning
> whom I was entirely wrong when in England. I came to the Cape full of
> prejudice against him but after living a month in his house and carefully
> scrutinising his character that prejudice was entirely dissolved and affection and
> the greatest respect took its place. . . . He has been the means of saving from
> the most abject and cruel slavery all the Hottentots and not only them but all the
> Aborigines beyond the Colony. The Boers hate him cordially. They have an
> inveterate hatred to the coloured population and to him as their friend and
> advocate, you can't understand it, it is like caste in India. Can you believe it?
> Some of the missionaries have imbibed a portion of it. I name none but you find
> none amongst the friends of Dr. Philip. I am now heartily sorry I ever retailed
> anything said to me by missionaries whilst I was in England. I am no partizan
> but I am and always have been on the side of civil and religious liberty.[23]

Before Livingstone left South Africa for the North in 1851, he did express
strong disagreement with Philip on the latter's attitude towards the

independence of the missionaries among the Tswana, but he never ceased to admire and respect him.

It would be quite wrong to suggest that John Philip was someone whom everyone, except for the perverse and wicked of this world, liked and admired. He was the leading spokesman in South Africa of a radical minority stream within evangelicalism, a cause that was bitterly unpopular among many evangelicals let alone among the many for whom evangelicalism itself was unpopular. He was a man of deeply held convictions and of passionate feelings. This often led to situations where decent men of goodwill, let alone opponents, felt him to be unnecessarily aggressive, but for him decency was not enough. To those whose understanding of humanity and the purpose of the Gospel were different from his, many of his actions appeared wrong and, at times, dangerously so. It has also to be admitted that his very virtues of persistence and commitment to causes in which he believed, led him into condemning, with great severity, those who saw things differently. Because he was willing to believe what Africans told him he has often been condemned as an unreliable witness.

His critics have, for the last hundred years and more, made much of this, indeed at times, too much. What has been absent from the vast amount of references to him in South African historiography, even in work by sympathetic authors like W M Macmillan, has been any discussion of the influences that created him and what he was like as a human being.

Before embarking on this study of his public life in South Africa with all its significance for the secular as well as the ecclesiastical history of the area, it is important to be reminded of John Philip, the genial host, the loving and understanding father, the man who could charm others, even those already prejudiced against him, and make them lifelong friends.

1

The Cape Colony in 1819

In 1819 the Cape Colony was South Africa from a European point of view. The two words referred not only to a much smaller area than they do today, but, more importantly, they conveyed a very different image. For even the informed members of the British public, South Africa was a little-known and rarely discussed colony, deemed to be poor and offering no apparent commercial opportunities of any kind. Indeed, it was only the importance of Cape Town and Simon's Bay to the Royal and merchant navies of Britain that justified its retention after the end of the Napoleonic wars.

It is very important to keep this in mind when discussing any period in the history of South Africa before 1870, when, first diamonds, then gold and the 'Scramble for Africa' changed this situation dramatically. After 1870, serious debate in Britain about policy towards South African colonies and their neighbours was common in the serious journals and in Parliament and, at times, became a matter of widespread public concern.

In stark contrast, during the lifetime of John Philip, one is hard put to find anything that could be called a positive policy towards South African affairs; that is, except the firm resolve that the Cape be maintained as a vital staging post on the route to India and that the Colony should cost the Exchequer as little as possible. There was so little interest evinced in Britain with regard to South Africa, that years passed during which there was no reference at all to South African affairs in the House of Commons, despite the fact that in South Africa events occurred of enormous importance to the peoples of the area.

As a result of this, the destiny of the various peoples living in the area in the first seventy years of the nineteenth century was very much in their own hands and those of the British officials in the Colony. The power of the British presence guaranteed that Whites were going to live there and not be driven out. Beyond that, the nature of the society in the Colony, and, to an extent, the geographical limits of the White presence, were in the hands of the people of South Africa. The London Government did, from time to time, intervene, but, except for the abolition of slavery, this intervention was always provoked by the actions of people in South Africa and not as a result of initiatives from London based on any policy of how South Africa was to develop or not develop.

So the principal actors acted out their dramas very much on their own, but they acted out dramas that created massive problems for the British later in the nineteenth century and for the world in the twentieth.

What was the extent of the colony in 1819? It stretched from Cape Town along the south coast for 450 miles to the Fish River and from Cape Town northwards along the west coast to the edge of the Bokkeveld about one hundred miles short of the Orange River mouth. Inland the boundaries are a bit more difficult to describe. Roughly they went from the northernmost point of the Bokkeveld eastwards in a line that dipped in a southerly direction towards the Sneeuwberg Mountains but swept up again to take in the good grass veld between the Sneeuwberg and the Orange, meeting that river about fifty miles south of its junction with the Modder. The boundary then followed the course of the Orange to its junction with the Caledon and then ran almost due south to the estuary of the Fish River.

These boundaries were important for government officials and for official documents but they had little practical significance to most people, White or Black, in or out of the colony.

Who were these people? When the Dutch first came to the Cape they referred to the peoples they found there as Hottentots and Bushmen. These peoples are now usually called by scholars Khoi and San. These were light skinned peoples who have often been divided, in academic studies, along very simple lines which say that the San were primitive hunter/gatherers while the Khoi were more 'advanced' pastoralists. However, the lines of division are in reality much more complex. It is impossible to distinguish between these people, either by language only, or, by life style only. For example, most of the hunter/gatherers in Angola, Namibia and Botswana speak a Khoi and not a San language.

However, in this study we are concentrating on the Cape area where the pastoralists did all speak Khoi. These Khoi had long established patron/client relationships with the hunting groups, who were predominantly San. The two types of society apparently fitted together amicably and peaceably enough. What was essential to this amity was the large area in which they moved, the plentiful supply of game and the fact that both populations were small.

The coming of the Dutch East India Company, which founded Cape Town in 1652, began to change all that. Initially the Khoi pastoralists traded with the newcomers and many established a form of client/patron relationship with Whites. The terrible waves of smallpox that devastated the Khoi in 1713, and again in 1755, broke the strength of many of the Khoi groups and facilitated the advance of Whites into their lands. As a result, in 1819 most Khoi were not any longer members of independent tribal groups following a traditional way of life. They were reduced to being a servant class among the Whites, or lived as tolerated 'squatters' on White ranches.

These dependent Khoi were an increasingly vital element in the White society of the Cape during the eighteenth and early nineteenth centuries. This is summed up by Daniel Neumark in his seminal study of the Cape economy in the eighteenth century.

> The first European colonists were very fortunate in having found in the Cape the long horned cattle which served as draft oxen. But what was of no less importance was the fact that the colonists had found in the Hottentots careful shepherds and herdsmen. The Hottentots also proved to be skilled trainers of draft oxen. Indeed it was with the assistance of the Hottentot herdsmen and shepherds, trainers of draft oxen and wagon drivers, that the vast territories of

the interior could be utilized. Without the Hottentots no such rapid expansion of the colony could have taken place.[1]

On the eastern frontier, things were a little different. In 1819, the trekboers had been living for decades in uneasy contact with the Xhosa people. There some independent Khoi groups did survive, but only because of their earlier relationship with the Xhosa. The two groups that had some political independence and were still, in some sense, Khoi, were the Gona, who had absorbed a significant number of Xhosa into their society, and the Gqunukhwebe. The latter are somewhat ambiguous. They were clearly Khoi in origin but they had been so influenced by the Xhosa and had so long intermarried with them that they spoke seXhosa and were regarded by the Xhosa as, in some sense, a Xhosa group.[2]

The hunting groups, the 'bushmen' of the older literature, had resisted much more stubbornly and persistently. A few became herdsmen to frontier graziers but the majority fought on as they retreated northwards, towards the desert country or into the Sneeuwberg mountains. In the 1780s they mounted a massive attack across the whole northern area of the Colony. Since the San lived in small individual family groups, it is unlikely that this was a formally concerted military campaign, yet the colonial records show that the persistence of the raids was such that the Government at the Cape was forced into supporting the trekboer of the northern frontier area in a formal campaign to eradicate what was seen as a major threat to the security of the Colony. This was the last appearance of the San as a significant element in the politics of the Cape.

As we have seen, in the eastern frontier area of the Colony, the White cattle ranchers, the trekboers, were in contact with the westernmost groups of the Xhosa people. The Xhosa are one of the Nguni peoples of southern Africa. The Nguni speak closely related languages which form a sub-group within the Bantu family of African languages. The Nguni languages are unusual because they contain the non-Bantu 'clicks' of the Khoi family of languages.

The Nguni peoples stretch in an arch round the coastlands of southern Africa from the Swazi, inland of Delagoa Bay, throughout the Zulu, Mpondo, Mpondomise, Thembu and other smaller groups to the Xhosa in the eastern Cape. These people are distinct linguistically from the Tsonga, Tswana and Sotho people who occupy the rest of southern Africa.

Popular folk history among White South Africans has held that the Bantu-speaking peoples, both Nguni and non-Nguni, were recent arrivals in southern Africa. They were believed to have entered from the north in the seventeenth century, roughly the same period as when the Whites entered from the south. Formal historiography, based on Theal and Cory,[3] has generally operated with a similar understanding of the past. As late as the work of J S Galbraith in his *Reluctant Empire* traces of this theory are still present. He talks of the Nguni as 'trekkers' in the same way as were the trekboer with whom they came into contact in the 1770s. He also says that they were long established in the lands where the Whites found them, suggesting that the Xhosa arrived in that area 'in the last quarter of the seventeenth century, perhaps earlier.[4] This times their arrival in the eastern Cape at about the same time as the Dutch arrived to found Cape Town.

This is a surprising conclusion in a book which is otherwise so carefully researched. It runs contrary to a vast body of work which has gone on since the 1950s on Nguni history and culture. This work, while it still has gaps and areas of controversy, has reached a consensus that the Nguni reached the lands between the Drakensberg and the sea a very long time ago indeed, much earlier than the middle of the seventeenth century. Monica Wilson calls their occupation of those lands 'an ancient one'.[5]

The argument for this ancient occupation can be summarised briefly. The first point is that there are no groups north of the Drakensberg speaking an Nguni language except those groups whom we know migrated northwards in the nineteenth century. There are no linguistic traces remaining of any southward movement by the Nguni, although it is clear that at some time in the distant past they did migrate from the north.

The second element in the argument is that in the Nguni languages there are present the 'click' consonants that are non-Bantu, coming from Khoisan languages. This again points to a long and close relationship with the Khoisan peoples of South Africa. There are no Nguni folk-tales or legends referring to how the 'clicks' came, a usual phenomenon in Bantu culture to explain 'strange' phenomenon.

Third, the genealogies of various Nguni chieftaincies, many of them recorded as early as 1820 and going back for some 300 years, have no reference to any 'Moses' figure bringing them south, or any other similar reference. This is usual in all genealogies of peoples who have moved within the historic memory of the people, which, in non-literate cultures, is a long memory indeed.

Although serious archaeological work has not yet amassed a great deal of evidence, what evidence there is all points towards Wilson's 'ancient occupation' theory.

For the purposes of this study, the culture of the Xhosa-speaking people only will be discussed. This is because they, and the other Nguni peoples, together with the other non-Nguni peoples, Tsonga, Sotho and Tswana to the north, all share a common culture. Although there are differences, and, for some purposes these differences are important, in comparing them with European-based cultures, what they share is much more important than the differences in detail.

The Xhosa were a cattle-herding people who also carried out extensive hoe agriculture. Their lives were controlled by a sophisticated network of social and political relationships which were, both quantitatively and qualitatively, on a scale much more complex than those of the Khoi and the San.

Basic to the Xhosa way of life was an undergirding religious understanding of reality. As with all Bantu peoples, this religious understanding was a total world view encompassing all aspects of life. This is a world view markedly different from the understanding of reality among Western

Europeans in the nineteenth century. This world view, created in the West by the Renaissance and the Enlightenment, compartmentalised life into areas like secular, sacred and so on. These divisions are not helpful categories in any attempt to understand Xhosa culture.

We cannot discuss this culture in detail but some matters need to be noted. Despite what was often asserted by White observers, some of the early missionaries among them, the Xhosa shared with the other peoples of Bantu culture a belief in a one Creator God. It was His name that was used for the God of the Bible when the Bible was translated into seXhosa. Xhosa tradition saw this Creator as being distant from the life of man so that direct worship of Nkulunkulu was extremely rare, which partly accounts for early European observers saying that they had no religion, merely a jumble of magical beliefs.

However, just as one would approach a great chief via an elder, so one could reach God by talking to what Professor Wilson, in the *Oxford History*, calls 'the shades' and what some African Christian theologians call 'the living dead'. The living dead are of constant importance to any man or woman. The individual human is defined, in Xhosa culture, by his or her relationship with them, to his or her contemporaries, old and young and to the generations yet unborn. The good person is defined as such, by their successful fulfilment of the duties and obligations imposed on them by these relationships which define their being.

Evil happenings were explained by either seeing these happenings as someone receiving their just deserts from the living dead or even occasionally from God Himself, because of their obvious anti-social behaviour, or, what was much more common, the evil was held to result from the malice, hatred, envy in some human heart which through the power of sorcery brought about the evil.

Despite what is said almost universally in nineteenth-century literature, Nguni religion then was not magical animism, but a logical and consistent system which saw God and man as the only actors in life. This understanding was so woven through their whole culture that family clan and chiefly relations cannot be understood apart from this 'religion'.

Among the Xhosa, as among all southern Bantu peoples, there were no great 'kings' or 'paramount chiefs' with executive authority spreading over a wide area and a large population. The development of a centralised military structure with a royal figure of great authority at the centre by the Zulu and the Amandebele Nguni was a very unusual phenomenon. It so fascinated Whites, both British and Afrikaner, perhaps because it fitted their assumptions, that they held this pattern to be the norm of African political structures.

The Xhosa were typical of southern Bantu peoples in that each political unit among them numbered only a few thousand individuals. Within this unit the chief could only act with the advice of his elders, and 'the chief-in-council', as it were, could only act effectively if they had agreed rightly what the people wanted, or would, at least, tolerate. Tradition did give dignity to certain hereditary figures, but power was always democratic because in an effective, not just a theoretical, way the chief's authority depended on the agreement of the people.

There were certain chiefs who were honoured above others for hereditary reasons. They were used as a court of appeal in the case of unresolved disputes among other chiefs, but this was far from kingship as in Ashanti or among the Yoruba, or even paramountcy, the term used elsewhere in Africa by later British colonial authorities for chiefs who had wide-ranging executive authority. This was not at all understood by the various White authorities, Batavian, British and trekker. They continually referred to some chief or other as the paramount of the Xhosa and blamed him for failing to control people, over whom, in fact he had no control at all.

Another 'democratic' feature of Xhosa, as well as other 'Bantu' societies, was that the land belonged to the whole people—no chief could sell it or permanently dispose of it. A chief could, with the agreement of his elders, allow someone to use the land for a time, be they kin or stranger, White or Black, but he could not alienate the land. Again this was an area ripe for conflict with the incoming Whites.

Who were these incoming Whites with whom the Xhosa were attempting to find some *modus vivendi* in 1819? The Dutch East India Company's rule had been replaced by that of the British in 1795, to be replaced by a short-lived Batavian regime, 1803–05. When the British replaced the Batavians in 1806, this wartime occupation was not intended to be permanent. It became so at the Congress of Vienna in 1815; its importance to the sea route to India was such that Britain could not let it go. This change of status had, by 1819, made little difference to the composition of the White population of the Colony.

The White population of 1819 can be divided, in general terms, into three sections. First, the population of Cape Town, which was made up of Government officials, merchants, hotel keepers and some artisans. Although the senior officials and some merchants were British, a majority of the White population was still Dutch speaking.

The second main group was the stable element in White society in the Colony; the farmers of the 'western' Cape, an area which is geographically and ecologically defined. It is the area of 'Mediterranean' climate at the southwest corner of Africa, an area untypical of the Colony and indeed of southern Africa, above all else, because of the regularity of its rainfall. From almost the beginning of the Dutch East India Company's occupation of the Cape, men had left the Company's employ and gone to farm for themselves in this beautiful and fertile land. Apart from the coming of the Huguenots in 1688, there had been no systematic attempt by the Company to settle Whites at the Cape, but time-served soldiers, German as well as Dutch, together with disillusioned functionaries and the sons of Company servants, all went to create this new people and this new land. Solidly built farmhouses, some of them of real elegance and most of them of manorial proportions, dotted the landscape; a landscape which was, by 1819, a settled one of vineyard and wheatfield, of market garden and milk-herd pastures. This beautiful and fertile district prospered enough so that by the beginning of the nineteenth century there had developed a number of small towns or dorps. The focus of each of these communities was the Church and the school, which accurately reflected the loyalty of these people to the Dutch Reformed Church. These dorps, however, had populations which did not rise above 3,000 so that Stellenbosch, Paarl, Tulbagh, Worcester and Swellendam were only villages by the standards of Britain or the Netherlands.

This society was therefore dramatically unlike the Netherlands, that quintessentially urban society. Outside the one real town, Cape Town, the farm was the basic unit of society.

These farms were like medieval manors in many ways. The head of the house presided in seigneurial fashion not only over his own, usually large, family, which often included married sons with their families, but also a large retinue of slaves and Khoi servants. Like the medieval manor, the Cape farm tried to be as self-sufficient as possible. It produced its own food, and slave craftsmen made most of the artifacts used.

However, these farms existed economically to supply the Cape Town market which consisted not only of the inhabitants of the town but the large market created by visiting ships which not only took on fresh supplies there, but usually stayed for a considerable time, with their passengers living in hotels and boarding houses in the town. This market increased in size during the second half of the eighteenth century, particularly during the Napoleonic Wars. The farms in this area, therefore, were primarily units in a market economy and not engaged in subsistence agriculture.

These settled Boers within seventy miles of Cape Town came to be known as akkerboers in contrast with the grazier or rancher Boers who went much further afield gaining themselves the name of trekboer.

All Boers continued to use the classic Dutch of the Netherlands for worship in church, for legal business and the Dutch Bible was almost the only book regularly read by this literate people. However their normal speech took the form of what had become, even as early as 1819, a new language. It was a form of Dutch with simplified grammar and syntax but with an increased and increasing vocabulary drawn from the slaves and the Khoi. All the members of this farming society spoke it, White and Black. The 'taal', as it was called, was the foundation of modern Afrikaans.

The third main division into which the Whites of the Cape Colony can be divided, were the trekboers of the northern and eastern frontier areas. From the beginning of the eighteenth century there had been a small but steady stream of families who climbed through the mountain passes out of the settled landscape of the western Cape onto the Bokkeveld and Roggeveld to the north and the Karoo to the east. These families became the trekboers who created yet another way of life for Whites in southern Africa.

In the eighteenth and nineteenth centuries, these trekboers were not seen in a particularly idealised or heroic light, either by the British or by the Boers of the Western Cape. However, in the twentieth century the trekboers have supplied official Nationalist propaganda with its first heroes. Nevertheless, the trekboers are not an heroic people to the propagandist alone. Many writers, American and British, have treated them as something special and invested them with a romantic glow. A recent popular, though respectably researched book begins

> By the end of the eighteenth century a new breed of men had evolved in South Africa—the trekboers. No people quite like them had ever existed before.[6]

A few pages later, the same writer says

> The trekboers' slow advance through the extremity of Africa may have been sporadic and casual but it went on with the inevitability of an incoming tide, each individual trekker party representing a wavelet which lapped across another section of the wilds. These pioneers were not inspired by the explosion of an ambitious will, by the lure of a rich country's plunder, or by the drag of newly discovered gold. Their advance was the communal quest for increased freedom combined with a feeling for seclusion, a resentment of authority and an abiding curiosity about the veld which lay beyond the next line of hills.[7]

This is not so different from the words of the distinguished academic historian John S Galbraith:[8]

> Rain usually comes to this thirsty land in storms of great intensity; dry gullies become torrents, and the rush of water tears deep gashes in the land and washes away the soil the drought has laid bare. The Orange River, which in the dry season sometimes is little more than a string of stagnant pools, becomes in a rainy season a torrential flood, sweeping the soil of Africa into the ocean. In this vast wilderness of the interior plateau a new species of humanity came into being, the cattle Boers, children of the Karroo just as the thorn bushes that dot the landscape.

Throughout the eighteenth century these trekboers had gone further and further away from Cape Town and from any close relationship with the colonial authorities. From time to time the Company administration made gestures that implied that they ruled wherever the trekboers went, but this was not so. The Company had neither the resources of men and money to attempt this, nor any real inclination to do so.

The trekboers were pastoralists and their way of life was not so dissimilar to that of the forebears of their Khoi servants. The basic attitude to life among these people has been characterised as 'trekgees', a restless spirit that wants solitude and freedom, but, usually the solitude and freedom that can only be found beyond the next mountain or across the next river. They appeared to have a passionate love of the great open spaces of Africa, but no particular affection for any one spot. Home to the trekboer was his family, his wagon, his flock and his servants. Houses were sometimes built by trekboers. Very often they were simply sod-walled, single-roomed cabins, with thatched roofs. In the eastern districts they built round daub and wattle huts similar to those of the Xhosa. If they decided to settle, then more permanent houses were built but otherwise any buildings were supplementary to the trekboers Cape waggon.

However, as Neumark has convincingly shown, the trekboers were always linked to the Cape economy. They produced no cash crops but lived by cash flocks, which they raised, and increasingly in the eighteenth century they obtained these herds by trading with the Xhosa. This situation was to cause far-reaching problems for the Cape administration in the nineteenth century.

At the very edge of the trekboer movement there were those who were hunters and adventurers. For some of these it is very difficult to decide where the trekboer community ends and where the frontier banditti begins. These latter were made up of runaway slaves, broken remains of Khoi clans, so-called 'Bastards' who had up and left their master taking a gun and horse, together with deserters from the Company forces and others.

However, the vast majority of trekboers kept contact with Cape society, indeed they were part of it.

Trekboer family groups were usually large, married sons often remaining with their parents. Also there were always a number of Khoi servants, even San servants sometimes; if the latter were caught young enough they could be denatured so as to accept this role. Legal slaves were less common in trekboer society than in akkerboer society. These servants were usually closely involved with the Whites, and there was a pattern of concubinage followed as well as the more casual sexual exploitation of females that is found in any such 'feudal' social structure. Many of the children so produced, not exactly family but not exactly servants either, were often trusted members of the group. In times of danger the men rode with their guns alongside their 'ou baas' on commando. It was also not unusual for such men to leave with wife and children, horse and gun, and go to swell the fringe society of marginal men to the north of the Colony.

How did the trekboers keep their links with Cape Town? They maintained it by continuing to register their land claims with the authorities in Cape Town, however far away from Cape Town they reached. The new 'farm' was measured by walking a horse for half an hour along each of the four main points of the compass from a chosen spot. The trekboer then paid to the authorities an annual sum, 'recognitiegeld' (recognition money), for his 'leeningsplaats' (the place licensed to graze). Theoretically the government could refuse to renew the grant the next year without any recompense, except for any homestead buildings raised, but, in practice, they never did.

To the trekboer the land seemed to stretch endlessly ahead, with only a few remaining Khoi and San groups with whom to compete for it. So the trekboers believed that they could move at will and their 'lekker lewe' (sweet life) would go on for ever. That was until they ran up against the Xhosa in the east. However, during all this time of expansion to the north and east, the trekboer maintained their connection with the authorities in Cape Town though those authorities had little or no power with which to influence events outside the western Cape, that is, until the arrival of the British in 1795. By that time, the trekboers in many areas were years behind in the payment of their recognitiegeld, and many had not registered their places at all.

When first the Batavians, and then the British, began to attempt to make Cape Town authority effective throughout the area of White occupation, the trekboers did not like it, but, for the most part, they accepted it. This was because of the second vital link between them and Cape Town, which was economic. Their way of life depended on their being able to reach a market for their products so that they could obtain their essential supplies of shot, powder, coffee, tea, brandy, sugar and tobacco.

Undoubtedly, trekgees and the desire for the lekker lewe were fundamental to the trekboer way, but so was this economic link to Cape Town. It was as necessary to maintain their life style as was the availability of land and game. In the last decades of the eighteenth century and the first two of the nineteenth, the demand for the product of the frontier ranches was increasing dramatically and it has been suggested that these ranches were more consistently profitable than those of the farms of the akkerboer.[9]

Cape Town had an almost inexhaustible demand for meat, both mutton and beef, during this period and it could only get these in the quantities desired from the trekboers. In addition, the Cape market also paid well for tallow, hides and butter as well as for goods that could only be produced on the farthest limits of white expansion either by hunting, or by trading ivory and ostrich feathers with the Xhosa.

The third link with the Cape, in addition to the governmental and the economic, was one which the trekboers maintained on their own initiative and usually wished to strengthen, unlike their relationship to the government; this link was that with the Church. Along with the taal, this was one of the few things they shared with their compatriots, the akkerboer of the 'western' Cape. The link with the Church was the only link these two communities had with their cultural past in Europe. As de Klerk says of them

> Cut off from the brilliant academic life of the Netherlands, with no intellectuals, inadequate schools, no professional or merchant classes, hardly any public institutions, not a single publication of their own, the colonists were culturally severed from their own background. Only the church afforded them some relief.[10]

In the settled district, although even there distances were considerable, attendance at the kerk in the nearest township, be it Stellenbosch or Paarel, was normal for the family, together with those slaves and servants who had been baptised. However, in over three-quarters of the land area of the colony where the trekboer lived, there were no townships and there were no church buildings. From time to time, ministers went out into the trekboer areas and the families of the district where they visited would meet for the nagmaal. This was a communion season like that of the same period in the highlands of Scotland. The families gathered for a period of days and there were marriage and baptisms as well as the actual Holy Communion services. For the trekboer these were of great social and spiritual importance, but these rare meetings with a minister of the Church did not profoundly affect the character of their ministerless religion. Indeed, for most of the eighteenth century the nagmaal had been held most infrequently, and it was only after 1792 that regular attempts at itineration were made.

Any kind of regular contact with a properly educated and trained minister only became an integral part of the life of most trekboers after 1815, when a scheme of recruiting pious evangelical Scots divinity students began to make the D.R.C. establishment adequate for its task.

A deeply religious people the trekboers certainly were, but were they a firmly Calvinist people as is so constantly asserted by almost every authority? They were not, if by Calvinist is meant anything comparable to the Christian life of the Netherlands, Scotland or New England. In these places, the tradition of the Calvinist churches was maintained, which was of a people under the close care of academically well-trained ministers, and the spiritual guidance of the kirk-session which produced a strong communal social discipline. The presence of schools and universities in intimate relationship with the Church maintained the pattern created by Calvin in Geneva, where the ability to pass university exams was seen as much as a part of God's calling to the ministry as other phenomena which many, not acquainted with the holy secularism of Calvinism, would deem more spiritual and appropriate.

Calvinist churches flourished in urbanised societies, or in societies where the population was dense enough and where all these necessary elements could flourish. New England Calvinism, for example, was simply unable to cope with the rapid and massive expansion of the population westwards in the early decades of the nineteenth century.

Trekboer society could not be further from the society of the Netherlands, Switzerland, Lowland Scotland or New England. Even in the more settled area of the western Cape and in Cape Town itself, there was never any attempt to develop the school and university system so characteristic of Calvinism when it is alive and well. After all, the Massachusetts Bay Colony was only six years old when that community founded Harvard University![11]

Coming from genuine Calvinist roots in the Netherlands, the Rhineland and France, the religion of the trekboers was not essentially Calvinist but a folk Christianity formed and shaped by their experience of life in Africa. For 150 years this religious life received no fresh injection of theology from Europe and even the classic texts of Calvinism were unknown. The only books known to the trekboer were the Bible and some popular commentaries on the Confession of Dort. The majority of the trekboers were certainly religious people, often displaying a deep Christian piety. For them, however, worship was not the regular attendance, Sunday by Sunday, to hear a learned preacher, but it was daily Bible reading with prayers, led by the head of the household. Cut off from other references, it was their experience as trekking cattle herders which came to dominate their understanding of the texts read to them. In this understanding, the Old Testament came to play what some would consider an inappropriately large role. This was partly a function of size in a situation when a leader read the Bible through from the beginning to the end and then started at the beginning again but also because they found so much in the Old Testament with which they could readily identify.

The strange isolated trekking life style of this people, cut off from the preaching of a properly trained ministry (indeed of any formal ministry), unsupervised by a kirk session, cut off from schools and university, cut off that is from all the essential characteristics of a Calvinist Church, created a deeply felt and genuine religious life, but one which was not Calvinist.

This is so manifest that one is puzzled by the use of 'Calvinism' as a key explanatory category by so many historians and political scientists who write about the development of the Afrikaner people. From writers of the period such as de Kiewiet and Keppel-Jones, on through Eric Walker and on to contemporary writers such as Dunbar Moodie and de Klerk, Calvinism appears as the key. The Afrikaner volk has been a religious people since it came into being and that form of Christianity which it has shaped and by which it has been shaped does merit investigation. Referring to this dimension in the history of the Afrikaner people as Calvinism is inaccurate as a description and explains nothing at all about them.[12] This folk form of Christianity was the intellectual framework within which the people found meaning for their individual lives as well as for the history and future of their people. It was taken into Africa, beyond the Colony by the Voortrekkers and continued as their pattern of belief.

The steady expansion of the trekboers to the north and east together with an easy enjoyment of the lekker lewe, came to an end after 1780. From then on the way was blocked. In the north, this was due to the massive raids of the San already referred to; in the east the trekboers met up with western elements of the Xhosa. These checks led to the trekboers appealing to Cape Town for help with these problems. Just what the administration in Cape Town, be it Company, Batavian or British, was to do about the frontier became one of the main problems facing colonial policy makers for the next hundred years. To understand the situation facing John Philip when he arrived in the Colony we have to look at how frontier policy developed during the previous thirty years.

Although the Dutch East India Company was nearing bankruptcy when the initial appeals for help arrived at the Cape, they were able to supply additional war material to aid the trekboer commandoes. Against the San in the north this did work. In the early 1790s three large commando sweeps (half the riflemen were 'Bastards and Hottentots' according to the records) broke the effectiveness of the San, though some raiding on a much smaller scale did continue for some years.

The commando system simply did not work so effectively against the Xhosa. The Company sent a landdrost and established a post at Graaff-Reinet to try to bring government to the whole vast northeast and eastern frontiers. However, the landdrost had no regular troops with him, since this was beyond the financial powers of the nearly bankrupt Company. He therefore had to rely on the burgher commando which presented him with a further acute problem—on which frontier were they to be deployed? Who would look after a man's herd in the face of attacks by the San, if the commando had all the men away fighting the Xhosa or vice versa? This tension created deep divisions between the trekboers and the authorities at Graaff-Reinet.

Before the post at Graaff-Reinet had been set up in 1785, Governor Plettenberg had paid a visit to the frontier districts, a unique visit in the history of Company rule. There, on the middle reaches of the Fish river in 1778 he had met with some Xhosa chiefs and made an agreement to which they added their marks, that the Fish should be a firm frontier between the Whites and Xhosa. It is from here that the classic divisions among historians begin as to what actually happened on the frontier problem between Boer and Xhosa.

Hardly anyone who writes about this frontier problem does so with the calm disinterest of, say, a discussion of the authenticity of Yorkist claims during the Wars of the Roses. Like French writing on the Revolution or American writing on the Civil War, writers on the problems of the eastern frontier of the Cape Colony are involved in discussing problems that still have relevance to their own political and social situation.

The interpretation of these events on the eastern frontier, as they were understood by the men and women who set off on the Great Trek in the 1830s, has been well described by Eric Walker in the third chapter of his classic study, *The Great Trek*. What is remarkable is that it was this understanding, portrayed with a good deal of historical sophistication, that was developed by G. M. Theal. It was refurbished and produced once more by V. T. Harlow in *The Cambridge History of the British Empire*, volume VIII, chapters 7 and 8. The same fundamental understanding of the beginnings of the frontier problem then re-appears in the well-received and much read work by de Klerk, *Puritans in Africa*.

Briefly, the story goes that despite the Plettenberg treaty, the Xhosa continued to invade the Zuurveld between the Fish and Sunday Rivers. They raided the herds and burned the property of the trekboers who occupied the area which the Xhosa had agreed with Plettenberg, was part of the Colony. The trekboers again requested the authorities in Cape Town to take action to help them to drive the Xhosa back to their side of the Fish river. The landdrost of the area agreed with them and decided to raise a general commando in order to accomplish this necessary task. However, the authorities in Cape Town said no and insisted that some sort of peaceful agreement could be reached with the Xhosa. A new and enthusiastic official, Honoratus Maynier, was sent to Graaff-Reinet, first as secretary to the landdrost, then as landdrost. He simply appeased the Xhosa chiefs, allowing them to stay on territory they had wrongfully occupied and doing nothing to protect the trekboer. Then Adriaan van Jaarsveld, a popular local trekboer leader, formed a commando which chased Maynier back to Cape Town. The angry cattlemen then set up their own republic. Following their example, the men of Swellendam district (the only other drostdy for the vast area outside the 'western' Cape) did the same. The supporters of the new Republics, who wore tricolour favours and talked of liberty, also bitterly complained of the weak government that had led to chaos on the frontier, a chaos they could have put an end to quickly enough had they been allowed to act independently. After all, before the coming of a landdrost to Graaff-Reinet, had not a commando under van Jaarsveld cleared the Zuurveld of Xhosa and pursued them beyond the Fish? However, their independence was brief because the British, under General Craig, took over the Cape. Redcoats and a new regiment, the Cape Corps, recruited from among the Khoi, combined with effective diplomacy from the senior British officers, brought any resistance to an end.

The British then did try to use these troops to clear the Xhosa invaders from the Zuurveld, but it was not pressed home thoroughly, so life continued to be precarious for the trekboers of the Zuurveld. The Batavian administration, which followed briefly, contributed little to the solution of the trekboer difficulties, although they got Ngqika, the 'paramount' of the Xhosa to agree to the Fish as being the eastward boundary of the Colony. When the British took over again, the eastern frontiersmen got some effective support at last when in 1809 Colonel Collins visited the frontier. Harlow says of his visit

> The reports which he submitted on his return embodied the most constructive scheme of frontier policy that had yet been devised.[13]

Collins accepted the Fish as the colonial boundary but recommended that between the Fish and the Keiskamma, no Xhosa kraals were to be allowed, though Xhosa sovereignty over the area was to be recognised. The Zuurveld was then to be heavily settled by Whites. They were to be set down close together on small farms, not the huge leeningsplaats of the trekboer, thus forming an effective barrier against Xhosa invasions.

Although Lord Caledon, to whom Collins reported, did nothing, the succeeding Governor, Sir John Cradock did. In 1812 he sent Colonel John Graham to the frontier to settle the business. Graham, his redcoats backing a strong force of Cape Corps and trekboer commando, swept the Xhosa, or most of them, back across the Fish where they belonged. He then set up a chain of military posts along the line of frontier to make sure that they remained there.

There are a number of significant objections to this version of the history of the Cape during these decades which ended the eighteenth and began the nineteenth century.

The first is that the consistent imagery of constant tribal invasions into a clearly defined and well-demarcated area of White settlement, which runs throughout this version of events, is somewhat less than accurate. It is clear from the colonial records themselves that as the trekboers entered the Zuurveld there were Xhosa groups already there, and it is also clear that the two communities coexisted in the area for some time, albeit somewhat uneasily.

The story of chief Langa is a good example illustrating the reality of that original situation. When Langa appears first in the colonial records, he is already herding stock on the western bank of the Bushman's River. He appeared ready to admit that the Whites had some authority there, but if a frontier existed for him, it was the Bushman's River not the Fish.

> The said Rensburg further reported that the Kafir Captain Langa had voluntarily sent back 109 head of cattle and four horses, which had been

restored to the owner by the said Field Corporal. Further that Langer [*sic*] had asked permission to be with his cattle on this side of the Bushman's River for three days, but though this time had long elapsed, he would not remove, and that therefore they would require a large and respectable force.[14]

The records of the time are full of information about tension between trekboer and Xhosa who are clearly neighbours, as well as of raids in both directions across the Fish.

The second objection is to the way the description of these uneasy, and, at times violent, relations are described. Although 'Who started it?' is in some ways a rather childish question, when writers consistently imply that violence was always initiated by one side, a very false picture of the situation does finally, and all too definitively, emerge. From Theal to de Klerk the picture is consistently of Xhosa aggression. Yet in the Colonial Records, for all to see, there are many reports of aggression where the initiative had been taken by the White ranchers. For example, this report by the landdrost of Stellenbosch to Governor van Plettenberg on 11 November 1780, in which the official doubts if it would be politic for the Governor to prosecute some trekboer despite the

incontestible and evidently wilful and in every way culpable conduct of the said inhabitants on the face of the report, as well as with respect to their taking the field against the Kafirs, as their offensive operations against them, with the result that a great number of them were killed, and the arbitrary division amongst themselves of the large quantity of cattle captured.[15]

Or again the letter of 13 March of the same year from the landdrost to the Governor, where it is reported,

From the first letter the Council will perceive that these hostilities are chiefly caused by the violence and annoyances commited against the Kafirs by the inhabitants, with respect to which they had complained to the Field Sergeant, that Willem Prinsloo, sen., had taken possession of some of their cattle and also of Martin Prinsloo, by whom or some of his companions during a journey into Kafirland, one of the subjects of Captain Gaggabie had been killed.[16]

This record of agression on the part of the White farmers is simply not reflected in the historical tradition of Theal, Harlow and others.

Third, these records also reflect an intimacy between Xhosa and trekboer which is not presented by this tradition. Alien invading tribesmen do not go to the Field Sergeant and complain of individual trekboer whom they can name. This same intimacy is also made clear in another, often ignored, element in the history of the time; in both the early trekboer rebellions against the authority of Cape Town, whether that authority was British or Dutch, at Graaff-Reinet in 1795 and Slagter's Nek in 1815, the White rebels asked, in each instance, for the help of the Xhosa against the colonial authorities!

The relationship of trekboer and Xhosa was therefore clearly not the simple Black and White one, in every sense of these words, that has so often been suggested.

The last, and perhaps the most important, complaint about the accuracy of this traditional history, centres on Plettenberg's famous treaty which made the Fish river the official boundary of the Colony. In the first place, it was made with a number of Xhosa chiefs, but that decision could only affect them and according to Xhosa custom, had nothing to do with other chiefs.

More important is to discover what the line of frontier was that Plettenberg and these chiefs agreed upon, because this line is the basis of complaint and action from then onwards.

The Fish River runs north–south from its mouth for about forty miles. It then bends and runs along an east–west line towards the west for sixty miles before turning again onto a north–south line. It was on this latter north–south line that Plettenberg met the chiefs. The line of the frontier of the Colony that was then agreed was that line of the river which, projected southwards, reaches the sea approximately at the mouth of the Bushman's River which coincides with chief Langa's understanding noted above.[17] Unfortunately, by around 1800, most Whites believed that the agreed line was a projection northwards of the north/south channel of the Fish at its entry to the sea. This was understandable since all that people knew was that Plettenberg had got the Xhosa to agree to the Fish as a boundary. This wrong interpretation, however, took in, as part of the Colony, a vast area of land that had long been Xhosa and had been recognised as such by the trekboers including leaders like van Jaarsveld. What is less understandable is that this very important shift is not recognised for what it was in the traditional history as represented by the work of Theal, Harlow and de Klerk.

The coming of the British as the permanent rulers of the Colony meant a dramatic change in situation for all its inhabitants and neighbours. Unlike the Dutch East India Company, the British did not let things drift. What did the coming of this new vigorous regime mean for the Khoi, the trekboer and the Xhosa?

As we have seen, the Khoi were divided into two categories by the beginning of the nineteenth century. The first group was made up of those who had become detribalised and lived as a servant class under the patronage of the akkerboer and trekboer communities. The second category were those who still retained some independence and autonomy. The Gona allies of the Xhosa chief Ndhlambe are perhaps the best-known example of this category. However, in the northern frontier area a new sort of independent community had been growing up out of Khoi origins. There certain Khoi families had gathered around them communities made up of people from a variety of backgrounds. As well as other Khoi there were runaway slaves, the odd trekboer adventurer, deserters from the Company army and so on. These communities, like the first category of Khoi, spoke die Taal, they wore Boer clothes and used as many guns and horses as they could obtain. They were cattle herders, but they were also cattle raiders, raiding into the Colony for guns and horses occasionally, more usually raiding the Tswana groups to the north for both cattle and grain.

These groups appear in the historical records of the Colony under a variety of names—Coranna, Bergenaar, Griqua. Two communities of long-term importance grew up round the Kok and Waterboer families. They were the Griqua. They came to have a close relationship with the London Missionary Society after it began its work in South Africa. So successful was this relationship that John Philip came to see them as the prime example of what Christianity and civilisation could achieve among an Africa people, independent of White settler or governmental power.

However, the vast majority of Khoi lived within the Colony as servants of the White community. They lived in a strange limbo for, unlike the slaves whose status was clearly defined in law, their existence was scarcely recognised in a legal sense. The Batavian regime had just begun to deal with this problem, stating that they were a free people (whatever that meant exactly) when they were replaced by the British.

The first British governors, from Baird to D'Urban, were all soldiers, men of action, used to command and were all old-fashioned Tories. They were in no way the vanguard of liberalism, the spearhead of the advance of new urban values into colonial society, as has so often been suggested.[18] As traditional high Tories they were the opponents of these very values of liberalism and urban humanitarianism. They were however, efficient British officers who were not going to tolerate the semi-anarchy which, under the Company, had reigned over much of the Colony.

They did a number of things to attempt to bring effective government into the large area outside the settled vineyards and farms of the western Cape. The legal changes they made which concern us were the Vagrancy Proclamation of 1809, the institution of Circuit Courts in 1811 and the Apprentice Proclamation of 1812.

Judges from Cape Town, moving on circuit around the drostdies of the Colony every year, brought a new dimension to law and order. Cases were heard locally with all the authority of the High Court in Cape Town and everything was not left to the landdrosts, usually themselves local ranchers, and the field-cornets, who were always locally elected by the trekboers from among themselves.

The Vagrancy and Apprentice Proclamations were one in giving the Khoi a clear status in law. Labour contracts had to be made with them, and they could bring their masters to court over the contract or over what they considered ill-treatment. Without the Circuit Courts they would never have attempted any such thing, whatever the law allowed. When one remembers that, apart from some general statements by the Batavian authorities about the Khoi being a free people, their status in law had, in effect, been non-existent since they could neither be witnesses in a case nor could they bring a case, these Proclamations by the British could be seen as a victory for philanthropy.

However there was another side to the Proclamations. The Vagrancy Proclamation meant that all Khoi, at all times must 'belong' to someone White. If found on the road by a White, unless they could produce a letter from a master explaining who they were and what they were doing, they were then taken to the nearest landdrost or field-cornet. The officer then appointed them to serve a farmer, or work on local government work. This Proclamation, and that of 1812, which gave the farmer the right to the labour of all Khoi children on his farm from the age of eight years, laid down the details of the labour contracts between the farmers and their Khoi servants, and amounted to a kind of slavery. It could be suggested that this legislation, together with the decision to bring to an end, once and for all, the chaotic conditions on the eastern frontier, was an attempt by the British to gain the favour and cooperation of their new White subjects.

However the new system had an opposite effect. This was a result of the initiative taken under its terms, by two missionaries of the London Missionary Society, Dr Johannes van der Kemp and James Read. They encouraged Khoi who felt they had a case against their present or former masters for physical ill-treatment or for cheating on contacts. The wave of cases brought against them deeply disturbed the White community of the Colony. The whole social structure upon which life on the farms and ranches had been built was being threatened by this development. Although many cases brought to the Circuit Courts in 1812 resulted in farmers being found not guilty, a number were convicted and punished by the courts. De Kiewiet said, 'The sentences which the court pronounced against White masters shook the colony with indignation.'[19]

In the traditional understanding of the past, already referred to, this imposition by the British of a severe and alien system of law and procedure drove the trekboer into a state of rebelliousness which culminated in the Slagter's Nek rebellion. This rebellion was put down by the British using the Cape Corps. The ringleaders were eventually hanged in the presence of these troops, a deliberate encouragement by the British of Khoi aggression against their masters. In the twentieth century a memorial was raised to the men of Slagter's Nek as forerunners of Afrikaner nationalism and independence.

The reality would appear to have been somewhat different. Certainly the men of Slagter's Nek wanted freedom and independence, but it would seem that it was freedom from any authority other than their own. The whole affair began with a frontier trekboer, Frederick Bezuidenhout, refusing to answer a summons from his own landdrost to answer a charge of ill-treating a servant. He threatened his elected field-cornet when the latter came to bring him to the landdrost. This was seen as intolerable behaviour by the heemraad, the locally elected council of trekboer who advised the landdrost. It was with their agreement that Cape Corps troopers went to make the arrest and killed him in the ensuing gun battle. This happened late in 1814 and as a result, early in 1815, a small force of trekboers came together in rebellion against the Cape Town authorities. They were led by members of the Prinsloo and Bezuidenhout families, and though they canvassed widely among the local trekboer population, only a handful rallied to them. What is very important to note is that these men, far from being proto Afrikaner nationalists, were eager to gain Xhosa help against their enemies, their fellow Afrikaners as well as the British. They appealed to Ngqika to help them, but he refused their request. Their behaviour becomes perfectly understandable if one views these men as fiercely independent frontiersmen who prized their own freedom above all else, and do not impute to them later ideologies of race and nation.

The little group of malcontents then assembled at Slagter's Nek, near where the Baviaans enters the Fish. The landdrost, Colonel Cuyler, with a trekboer commando, aided by redcoats and Cape Corps, went out to suppress this revolt. Most of the rebels came forward and surrendered to him without serious resistance. A handful did not surrender, but fled, pursued by horsemen from the Commando and the Cape Corps who rounded them up, killing Hans Bezuidenhout in the process. Finally, after due legal process, the six leaders were hanged in the presence of the Cape Corps soldiers and the Commando that had captured them. The fact that the scaffold collapsed, leaving five men alive who had to be hanged again, is a horrible fact, but does not alter the main joint of the story.

So far we have seen the impact of the British on the Khoi and the trekboer, but what was the result of British control of the Cape for the Xhosa frontier? We have seen that Collins had gone to the frontier to try to sort out a feasible and fair boundary between the Xhosa and the colony, and his misinterpretation of the meaning of the Plettenberg Treaty. When he had gone to the frontier, the Xhosa with their Gona allies had been pressing the trekboer community hard, forcing many to withdraw from the Zuurveld. The result was that Collins decided that there must be an effective barrier set up between the Xhosa and the Colony and no intercourse between the two societies be allowed. Collins said

> I consider as a maxim of the first importance to the Colony of the Cape of Good Hope, that all intercourse between the settlers and the Caffres should be scrupulously prevented, until the former shall have increased considerably in numbers and are also much more advanced in arts and industry. The efforts of philanthropy may then, I hope, be safely and usefully exerted for the advantage of that people; but they would now, I fear, be productive of great inconvenience and danger. In consequence of these opinions formed by such observation and reflection, it appears to me that the steps necessary to be taken for the permanent tranquillity of the eastern districts, are to oblige all the Caffres to withdraw to their own country; to oppose insurmountable obstacles to their return to the colony; and to remove every inducement to their remaining near the boundary.[20]

He went on to suggest, tentatively, that the Xhosa might even be forced to retreat eastwards over the Keiskamma, leaving an empty zone between them and the Fish River.

In any case, he insisted that the land on the western side of the Fish should not be parcelled out as large grazing ranches, the traditional leeningsplaats of the trekboers. For the first fifty or so miles inland from the sea, the land was good enough for arable and vegetable farming. It could therefore be divided into small farms of one hundred acres or so, an adequate size for the type of farming envisaged. The result would be a density of White population that would be an effective barrier to Xhosa infiltration back across the river.

However, the trekboer population was not suitable for this development, partly through their having no desire to undertake such farming, partly because there were not enough of them anyway. For the scheme to succeed it was vital to bring immigrants from Europe. In 1820, the British settlers, the first new element in the permanent White population of the Colony for over one hundred years, were called on to fulfil this role.

Further north the land on the west of the Fish was certainly only fit for cattle ranching, Collins conceded. How then was the line of frontier to be made readily defensible? Collins' solution was simple—move the frontier, eastwards, of course.

> The country between Agter Bruintjes Hoogte and the Konaba River abounds in excellent fountains. The soil is good; and the timber growing on the mountains that border it on the north is superior to any within the Colony. The acquisition of this tract would strengthen the frontier, not only by the great number of the inhabitants that would be brought together in consequence of the land being granted in small portions, but also by affording the advantage of a shorter line of defence, and the consequent greater facility of communication and support. The loss of this part of the territory would occasion no inconvenience to the Caffres, for they have not a single hut in its whole extent, and they have always been averse to inhabiting it, on account of its being an open country; a circumstance that would enhance its value as a colonial frontier possession. I do not think that much objection would be made by that people to its occupancy, but they would at all events be easily induced to transfer their right to it for an adequate payment in cattle.[21]

This last paragraph shows such a profound misunderstanding of the Xhosa attitude to land as to bode ill for British/Xhosa relations. In addition to his lack of understanding of the fact that land was inalienable in Xhosa tradition, how did he come to believe the Xhosa would so readily give up this land, never, heretofore, claimed by Whites? Particularly when they had been stubbornly insisting for the previous forty years, at great cost, on their rights over the Zuurveld to the west of the Fish. Did Collins really believe that they would give up what was universally recognised as their land to the east of the Fish as a straight business deal?

As we have noted, Lord Caledon was not willing to become involved in the massive military effort needed to remove the Xhosa and the Gona across the Fish, but his successor Cradock was. In 1811, he transferred his whole force of British regulars to the frontier along with the Cape Corps. He then called out the trekboer on commando and put the whole force under Colonel Graham with carte blanche to clear all the Africans from the Zuurveld.

Graham began a ruthless campaign which, he insisted, however unpleasant it might appear, was necessary. He characterised it as 'destroy and lay waste'.[22] The Xhosa chiefs said they would go peacefully if they were allowed to wait and harvest their crops which were nearly ripe. This was refused, part of the whole point of the operation being to destroy the crops. This total war was something new to the frontier, new to the trekboer as well as to the Xhosa, but it was the Xhosa who suffered from it. It is quite difficult for anyone today to imagine the impact this campaign had on the Xhosa people. The experience of being attacked in this way was something, so different as to challenge their traditional understanding of reality. This ruthlessness on the part of authority was certainly something new that the British brought to South Africa; it could hardly be seen as liberalism or urban humanitarianism.

This deep shock that the Xhosa received helps to explain the rise to fame and authority of two great Xhosa prophets, Nxele and Ntsikana. They had both experienced the deep spiritual change that many had undergone in the past while becoming the mouthpiece of God to the people. These two were different in that they incorporated much that was biblical and Christian in their experience and their message. Ntsikana had far less impact at the time than Nxele and is remembered mostly now for his magnificent hymn which is still sung by Xhosa-speaking Christians. Nxele had a very wide appeal. His appeal was that his new teaching linked the new and old in a way that made sense of the new to the Xhosa.[23]

Despite the success of Graham, his line of forts did not keep the Xhosa out for long, How could it? since the scheme demanded Collins' densely packed White farming population for it to work. Instead there were only the thinly scattered trekboer ranches, each of whose hundreds of acres left plenty of room for Xhosa groups to slip back into the land they claimed as their own. Cattle raiding now became worse than ever and the trekboer were soon complaining of the intolerable conditions under which they had to try to survive.

The whole situation was made worse by the fact that the British insisted on treating Ngqika as the paramount of the frontier Xhosa when, in fact, he had only a small following and was very unpopular. Most Xhosa of the area looked to Ndhlambe. On a number of occasions Ndhlambe attempted to approach the British for some kind of treaty or agreement but he was always repulsed. The British were committed to a 'good Ngqika, bad Ndhlambe' scenario.

In October 1818, Ngqika was massively defeated by the combined forces of many chiefs under Ndhlambe's leadership. The latter sent messages to the British that he had no quarrel with them, that his actions were not in any way against the Colony. However, the British saw his actions as an attack on their ally and therefore on them. As a result Colonel Brereton marched into Xhosa territory on a massive punitive raid, a raid that Stockenstrom, Stretch and others in their evidence before the 'Aborigines Committee', declared to be one of the most massive errors committed by the British in their relations with the Xhosa. Brereton came back with, it was said, 23,000 head of cattle.[24]

The Xhosa now swept into the Colony in a massive invasion. It is often said this was inspired by Nxele. There is no doubt that for the previous three or four years his influence had grown enormously and he played a leading role in the invasion. However he did not provoke it. He did not need to. As Pringle said

> The great majority of the Amakosa tribe had not only been wantonly exasperated by an unprovoked attack, but were absolutely rendered desperate by thousands of them being deprived of their only means of subsistence.[25]

The Xhosa even attacked Grahamstown in broad daylight and almost took it. However the tide of war soon turned. Once and for all, the British decided, the Xhosa were going to be dealt with. All of them, 'allies' as well as the enemy, were driven back across the Fish. The destruction was terrible with women and children being killed as well as warriors.

Lord Charles Somerset dictated treaty terms to the Xhosa. The Fish was once again asserted to be the frontier of the Colony, but now between the Fish and the Keiskamma the land was to be neutral, no one to occupy it except a British garrison at Fort Willshire, who would patrol the area and, at last, the raiding and bickering would end.

At the peace conference with Somerset, one of Ndhlambe's elders made the following speech, as it comes, in translation, from Pringle.

> We lived in peace. Some bad people stole, perhaps; but the nation was quiet—the chiefs were quiet. Gaika stole—his chiefs stole—his people stole. You sent him copper; you sent him beads; you sent him horses—on which he rode to steal more. To us you only sent commandoes.
>
> We quarreled with Gaika about grass—no business of yours. You sent a commando—you took our last cow—you left only a few calves, which died for want, along with our children. Without milk—our corn destroyed—we saw our wives and children perish—we saw that we ourselves must perish; we followed, therefore the tracks of the cattle into the Colony. We plundered and we fought for our lives.[26]

So, in the year that John Philip came to the Cape to begin his career as resident Director of the London Missionary Society, the British believed that they had, at last, solved the frontier problem that had bedevilled colonial administrations for fifty years.

Thomas Pringle, writing in 1834 of his life in South Africa, summed up the situation rather differently.

> By this iniquitous act, nearly 3,000 square miles of country were added to the colonial territories already far too extensive; while the native inhabitants were driven back upon a population for which, in their pastoral state, the land is greatly too narrow.[27]

The British actions were certainly decisive and dominated colonial/Xhosa relations from then on, as Hermann Giliomee has pointed out in his article 'The Eastern Frontier, 1770–1812'.[28]

Xhosa and trekboer had lived together for some time, struggling to find some *modus vivendi*. The Xhosa had to learn that the trekboer could not be gradually absorbed as had been the Khoi, though the Xhosa did try this approach for some time. The trekboer, for their part, had come to learn that the Xhosa were not going to simply go away or become servants as had the Khoi. What the outcome might have been cannot be concluded now. The British changed that situation completely. It was the firepower of the British regulars, redcoat and Cape Corps, when combined with British ideas of clear-cut frontiers, that transformed the whole situation. Tragically, it was a situation that the Xhosa could not accept.

2

The London Missionary Society and the Cape before 1819

The birth of the Protestant missionary movement was an overdue delivery. From the beginning of Protestantism in the sixteenth century until the last quarter of the eighteenth century, there was no significant Protestant attempt to preach the Gospel to non-Christians. That Protestant missionary activity did emerge when it did, so that it appeared to coincide with the economic and political emergence of Britain as the dominant power in the world, has encouraged the simple identification of Christian missions as the cultural and spiritual arm of European Imperialism. This can be seen reflected in Klaus Knorr's *British Colonial Theories* and K. M. Pannikar's *Asia and Western Dominance*, as well as in many other less perceptive and less scholarly works. However, this approach ignores the fact that from the days of St Paul until the Reformation, missions to non-Christians were an integral part of what made up Christianity. The level of missionary activity varied from time to time, from high spots like the Celtic expansion of the sixth century, Boniface in Germany in the ninth, the bold Franciscan assault on China in the fourteenth to the nadir, the crusades of the eleventh and twelfth centuries. However, the missionary drive never died out and, from the time of the Reformation, the Roman Catholic section of divided Western Christianity carried on the tradition. Indeed at the height of the Reformation struggle, Francis Xavier initiated the brilliant Jesuit thrust of the sixteenth and seventeenth centuries into India, Indonesia, Japan, China and Canada. The Catholic Church's efforts did falter dramatically in the eighteenth century but the effort grew rapidly again in strength and geographical extent after 1850.

It is not our task to answer the important question raised by these facts—Why was Protestantism bereft of any effective missionary concern during this long period? It deserves to be considered, however, with much more seriousness than hitherto, by both historians of Christian thought and by theologians.

In the first decades of the eighteenth century, not only was there still no Protestant missionary concern, but the level of spiritual or any other kind of activity in Protestant Christianity was at a particularly low ebb. In some respects, official churchly Christianity was more weak then than at any other time in the West since the Dark Ages. However in the middle of the eighteenth century, both in New England and in Britain a new development took place which is generally known as the Evangelical Revival. This dramatic awakening brought life into the old churches, dissenting as well as established, and created a new one, Methodism. A similar, yet in some important respects different, movement called pietism brought fresh life to Protestantism in Switzerland, Germany and the Netherlands.

The differences between pietism and evangelicalism are theological, sociological and cultural, but the relevant area of difference, for this study, is in the area of the relationship of the Gospel to political and social issues. Pietism was essentially quietist in this area, evangelicalism was not.

From convictions that were fundamental to the pietist position theologically, the movement held that political and social change were of no concern to dedicated Christians. Of course, just as hurricanes and famines produce suffering among people which the good Christian must try to ameliorate as best he or she can, so with the results of political and social injustice. However, to be concerned over bringing about the amelioration of social or political conditions was to stray from the path of Christian dedication, and was, in any case, pointless because of the fallen state of this world.

On the other hand, evangelicalism was open to a belief that social and political issues were central to the concerns of a Christian. Evangelicals were open to the belief (it was not fundamental) in the sense that there were many evangelical men and women who were unaffected by these issues and unconcerned about the problems they raised. Yet in another sense, concern about social and political change was central, in that so many of the outstanding leaders of the evangelical movement were so concerned, on both sides of the Atlantic. These men were outstanding both for their religious impact on Protestant Christianity as well as for their political activity. Two notable examples are Timothy Dwight and William Wilberforce. Dwight was the President of Yale during the first two decades of the nineteenth century. He turned Yale into a centre of revival which affected the whole of the area which became the North in the era of the Civil War. He was also one of the leading politicians in Connecticut at a crucial time in US history. Wilberforce is well known as the leader of the anti-slavery movement, as an MP, friend of William Pitt and strangely, also a friend of Charles James Fox. Yet Wilberforce had more impact on English evangelicalism than any theologian or clergyman of his day through his book. *A Practical View,* which became the spiritual handbook for a majority of evangelical men and women in Britain.

The anti-slavery movement, in Britain as well as the United States, was supported, funded and staffed primarily by evangelicals. However, there were also evangelicals who were opposed to the politics of anti-slavery and others indifferent to them.

It is then important to insist that political and social reform were seen as part of, or adjuncts of, the Gospel by many evangelicals but not by all. Although there was, for example, a close interpenetration of the leadership of the anti-slavery movements and the missionary movements in both Old and New England, many committed to missions were not committed to anti-slavery activity, nor to a concern for social righteousness. It was this concern, which Wilberforce called quaintly 'the reform of manners', which led him to join forces with the other distinguished evangelicals who were to become known as the Clapham Sect.

These men were of such distinction both socially and politically that it is easy to see them as integral to the British Establishment and the British way of doing things. This explains, at least partly, why so many writers on South Africa see the arrival of British authority at the Cape as the arrival of 'philanthropy'. Yet Wilberforce's attempts at change were rejected for decades. Indeed the Clapham Sect's attempts to interfere with the slave trade, let alone free the slaves, were seen as profoundly dangerous. In the eyes of the British Establishment of the Napoleonic era their campaign challenged the rights of private property, the foundation on which the whole fabric of civilisation stood. As a result we have the, preposterous in modern eyes, identification of the anti-slavery movement with Jacobinism and republicanism in high Tory circles. Because the missionary movement also came under the direction of the Clapham Sect, who between them dominated the Boards of Directors of the rash of missionary and Bible Societies that sprung into being between 1790 and 1815, missionaries were suspect in the eyes of British colonial administrators as well as in the eyes of many in the United Kingdom, including leading churchmen. For example, when the Scottish Missionary Society began its activities as an auxiliary of the London Missionary Society this led to some mission supporters raising the issue of missions in the General Assembly of the Church of Scotland. During the debate which ensued, and which ended with the motion for the initiation of such activity being defeated, Principal Hill of St Andrews University, a most distinguished churchman, spoke against the Motion. He used many of the classic arguments that had been used by mission opponents in England but went on to indicate that he believed that the missionary societies were dangerous and subversive organisations acting as a holy cover for the ideas of Jacobinism and Tom Paine.

A little later in the *Edinburgh Review* of April 1808, that brilliant Anglican man of letters, Sydney Smith, wrote a caustic attack on the missionary movement. He had noted a fact that many commentators since have not, that at this time the movement, despite its aristocratic leadership, was one which was fundamentally rooted in the lower middle class and the skilled working class. He rounds on the members of the movement thus

> Are we to respect the poor when they wish to step out of their province and become the teachers of the land—when men whose proper 'talk is of bullocks' pretend to have 'wisdom and understanding', is it not lawful to tell them they have none? An ironmonger is a very respectable man so long as he is merely an ironmonger,—an admirable man, if he is a religious ironmonger; but a great blockhead, if he sets himself up for a bishop or a dean, a lecturer in theology. It is not the poor we have attacked—but the writing poor, the publishing poor—the limited arrogance which mistakes its own trumpery sect for the world. . . .

These are the same class arguments that were hurled at the Levellers and at the Quakers, and later in Africa against the 'cheeky mission kafir'.

It was only after 1860, when a certain, and it could be argued, a somewhat distorted version of evangelicalism became the folk religion of the English middle classes, newly made powerful by industrial growth and the reform of the franchise, that evangelical Protestantism became part of the 'establishment' in Britain.

Thus during the years from the arrival of the first LMS missionaries in the Cape in 1799 till Philip's death in 1851, the attitude of the British upper-class officials who ruled the Colony was similar to that of Sydney Smith, though perhaps not as extreme as that of Principal Hill. They did try to use the missionary presence to support their aims where they could, and constantly tried to turn them into government parsons like their country rectors back home. They certainly did not see them as allies in the same struggle. It is true that in the long view of African history, the missionaries played a part in the 'Westernisation' of African people and, at times, for their own reasons, aided the growth of British authority. That is quite different, however, from seeing missionary and the Cape authorities as in any way conscious allies. In the last fifty years of the nineteenth century, the growth of the university-educated middle-class's participation in missions changed things. By 1900, missionary and District Commissioner in African Colonies were often drawn from the same class and had gone to the same public school and university. At that time they often did see themselves as allies in a great civilising task, but this was not so between 1799 and 1850.

During the first fifty years of Protestant missionary activity in Africa, in West Africa as well as in the Cape Colony and its environs, missionaries and officials were drawn from radically different classes. These classes were sometimes linked by paternalist benevolence on one hand and a fawning response on the other, but they were also, as in the United Kingdom, as often divided by suspicion and at times by aggressive antagonism. In terms of culture, education, concerns and principle, missionary and official had little in common except that they both were British.

Yet historians as distinguished as de Kiewiet suggest that the arrival of British rule and British missionaries was the two-pronged attack of modern urban philanthropy on the old-fashioned conservative society of the Boers. This kind of assertion is explained by the mistakes of talking as if the last analysis of ultimate effect was the same as the actual detailed events of history, and by a telescoping back into the period before 1850 of the cultural alliance of the late nineteenth and early twentieth centuries.

As was suggested in the last chapter, British rule brought more effective government to the Cape, something the trekboers resented. This government was, however, not 'liberal' or philanthropic. It was autocratic in the extreme. It placed enormous personal power in the hands of Governors drawn from the class who were resisting change in Britain, and who were in no way part of the new industrialised urban middle-class Britain which was only struggling into existence at that time.

Yet still it is possible in a recent highly praised book for us to find this written about episodes we have been considering:

> Caledon was not only determined to enforce positive respect of law, but considered it unquestionably necessary that 'British ideas', especially those which had become fashionable due to the activities in England of Wilberforce and other members of the Clapham Sect, should be inculcated into the

Africaners. His successor, Sir John Cradock, took the cue and declared: 'I therefore anxiously hope that, in whatever Directions we may receive from Home . . . there will appear the Desire to assimilate the institutions of this country to those of England.'[1]

This assertion by de Klerk can only be described as bizarre. Caledon, Cradock and Somerset were the kind of Tory that saw the Clapham Sect as dangerous 'enthusiasts', who were only one degree better than Jacobins. They wanted to assimilate the Afrikaner people and their institutions but it was to their England of aristocratic autocracy, not an England of humanitarian philanthropy.

Let us look more closely at the missionaries and at the movement which sent them. 1792 saw the formation of the Baptist Missionary Society, the result of the eager and effective campaigning of William Carey, who went himself to India as one of its first missionaries. Carey had been the centre of a propaganda and lobbying campaign among dissenting circles in England, which was paralleled by a related movement in New England. This movement had some effect among Anglican evangelicals as well as in some circles in Scotland. The result was that there came into being a dedicated minority of Christians in New England as well as Britain committed to missions. There was a spin-off also into Europe where British evangelical promptings found a ready response in pietist circles. This activity was channelled through a large number of societies for mission both at home and abroad—the London Missionary Society in 1795; the Netherlands Missionary Society in 1797; the Church (i.e. Anglican) Missionary Society in 1799; the British and Foreign Bible Society in 1804; the American Board of Commissioners for Foreign Missions in 1810; and the Basel Mission in 1816 being perhaps the most important.

The London Missionary Society was intended from the beginning to be entirely inter-denominational. This is a characteristic which is often held to be integral to early evangelicalism, but like the commitment to social and political righteousness it clearly was not a central belief for many evangelicals as the existence of the denominational societies shows. However, the radical nature of the LMS commitment was made quite explicit at its second Annual General Meeting in May 1796. At that meeting the Society passed a statement that became known as the Fundamental Principle.

> As a union of God's People of various Denominations, in carrying on this great Work, is a most desireable Object, so, to prevent, if possible, any cause of future dissension, it is declared to be a fundamental principle of the Missionary Society, that our design is not to send Presbyterianism, Independency, Episcopacy, or any other form of Church Order and Government (about which there might be differences of opinion among serious Persons), but the Glorious Gospel of the blessed God to the Heathen: and it shall be left (as it ever ought to be left) to the minds of the Persons whom God may call into the fellowship of His Son from among them to assure for themselves such form of Church Government, as to them shall appear most agreeable to the Word of God.[2]

This statement was hailed at the time as the death-knell of bigotry but, in fact, by the 1840s the main thrust of missionary activity was through those missionary societies attached to specific denominations, or through official church missionary committees like those of the Free Church of Scotland, the Church of Scotland and the American Presbyterian Church. Even more important, the other radical part of the Fundamental Principle, which showed such trust in the new Christians who were to be called to make up the new churches, was an attitude that gradually disappeared during the nineteenth century, with a few outstanding individual figures excepted, to reappear only after the First World War.

The movement, which produced these societies in Britain, was essentially a layman's movement. A certain number of English dissenting ministers took part and a handful of ministers of the Church of Scotland, but the main thrust of action came from laymen. What was even more marked was their social class which, as we have seen, made them so objectionable in the eyes of Sydney Smith. Although invaluable leadership was given by socially and politically important figures like William Wilberforce, the majority of activists at home were lower middle class or skilled working class. Indeed the skilled working class (Carey himself was a cobbler long before he was a preacher and worked at both trades until he went to India) were the core group from which the missionaries themselves were drawn. In the early development of the Industrial Revolution, although the new urbanised working class as a whole suffered a great deal of hardship, men with skills, which were at a premium, did do well compared with their fellows. These skilled men, the artisans, the later 'aristocracy of labour', were a group significantly influenced by evangelical Protestantism. These families were the same group from which early trade unionism developed and they were also the population pool from which sprung the new lower middle class groups that came into being in the developing towns and cities.

The lay dominance in the movement in Britain and the indifference of the traditional establishment towards missions are borne out particularly clearly in the early history of the Church Missionary Society. Wilberforce and other evangelical leaders who were Anglican formed the society to provide a specifically Anglican channel of activity. From its foundation in 1799 until 1830, the society was unable to find a single Anglican clerical volunteer for service, nor was it able to find a bishop in England who was willing to ordain a man for service abroad with the Society. During these first thirty years then, the CMS staff in the field consisted of English artisans and German pietist pastors whose Lutheran orders were accepted as valid by Anglican church law.

The LMS Arrives at the Cape

The work of the LMS in South Africa and the career of John Philip there are inextricably involved with an extraordinary Netherlander, Dr Johannes Theodore van der Kemp. He approached the Society in 1796 when they had just begun to consider whether South Africa would be a suitable area of activity. It is not very clear from the records why they considered South

Africa at this time. The temporary British occupation of the Cape in 1795 may have drawn it to their attention—they certainly were in close contact with the Moravian Brethren who had re-started a mission there in 1792, after an initial attempt in 1737. In any case, whatever the reason, South Africa was being considered and van der Kemp volunteered. He had been an officer in the Netherlands Dragoon Guards, had retired early and completed a medical degree at the University of Edinburgh. He then returned to the Netherlands where the tragic death of his wife and only child had a profound effect on his life. He became a fervent Christian and began to read and study so that he became, for his time, an outstanding scholar in the Biblical field. When Henry Martyn, the saintly Anglican, called at the Cape on his way to India, van der Kemp gave him a Syriac New Testament as a memento!

He first approached the Society after having read some of their propaganda material which had been translated into German. He asked to be kept in touch with such material as he could translate into Dutch and use it to try to stir up activity in the Netherlands. He was kept supplied with material and the same year, 1797, saw the inaugural meeting of the Netherlands Missionary Society (NMS). He then offered himself to the London Missionary Society to head their new Mission to the Cape which the NMS offered to help support in men and cash. (This support ended in 1810.) After careful consideration the Society appointed van der Kemp as superintending missionary in their new venture. He tried to evade any such role, insisting that there should be no superintendence but the Society insisted that there should, and he finally accepted.

Along with him there were appointed J J Kicherer, a divinity student from Utrecht and two English artisans, John Edmonds and William Edwards.

Just what they were to do in South Africa was left in the hands of van der Kemp and his colleagues, which seems a strange idea to modern eyes but was normal for the LMS in those days. Only when men were on the spot could they really judge what had to be done. Van der Kemp decided that the task to which they were called was to preach to the Xhosa people outside the colonial frontier.

This intention was one which he soon had to postpone, though his concern to remain in contact with the Xhosa and keep lines of communication open with them affected his conduct and policies until his death in 1811. The postponement of a permanent Xhosa mission was the result of the state of the frontier region at this time. After all, van der Kemp arrived in the Cape when the troubles on the frontier had reached a particular peak, with the frontier Khoi allying themselves with the Xhosa, and various trekboer groups threatening rebellion against the British. The incidents with the Xhosa, which lasted until 1803, came to be known as the Third Frontier War. Van der Kemp did make three visits to the Xhosa territory beyond the colonial boundary, the first of only a few weeks but the second and third each lasted several months. During these he managed to establish a relationship with some of the leadership of the Rarabe Xhosa and their chief Ngqika. In August 1801, in company with James Read, one of the new staff who had arrived that year, together with the son of the infamous (in Boer eyes), Commissioner Maynier, he paid a final visit to the kraal of Ngqika. However this only confirmed the impossibility of a permanent missionary presence at that time.

So van der Kemp was open to the suggestion, made by an officer on General Dundas's staff, that the LMS should open an institution for the frontier Khoi similar to that of the Moravian brethren at Genadendal in the western Cape. Van der Kemp was all the more enthusiastic about this when he saw the positive response on the part of the Khoi to the work of the missionaries at Graaff-Reinet, which had been their base during the frontier troubles. Indeed from May 1801, he had begun deliberately to build a Christian community among the slaves and Khoi who had gathered there during the troubles. As well as worship services, prayer meetings and instruction sessions of a catechetical nature, van der Kemp added, with Read's help, formal schooling for young and old.

Thus, after the discussions with his colleagues, van der Kemp sent a long letter to Dundas suggesting that the Governor assign land for a settlement of Khoi under missionary auspices.

It seems clear that the British authorities were interested in the creation of such a station as part of their attempt to deal with the frontier situation. First they wished the Xhosa kept outside the colonial area and as little intercourse between Xhosa and colonials, White or Black, as possible. The Khoi who had taken up arms against the colony, as well as those who stayed with their masters or fled to Graaff-Reinet, were all similarly upset by the frontier situation. Might a missionary institution of their own be one means of reconciling them to the colonial government? A centre for the Khoi, which was under some kind of government patronage, would help. The missionaries, if they were to become identified with the Khoi, would be a useful peace-keeping tool in the hands of the administration. That this was their attitude is partly confirmed by their interspersing their correspondence with van der Kemp about the setting up of the Institution with letters seeking to use him as a go-between with Klaas Stuurman, a leader of the rebel Khoi.

It is as well to notice in passing, that, in this the British authorities continued the same kind of error as their Dutch Company predecessors had, both with the Khoi and the Xhosa. Just as both administrations treated Ngqika as if he were administrative head over all the Xhosa of the frontier, which he at no time was, so they treated Klaas Stuurman as if he had authority over the rebel Khoi. He had no such authority; he led his band of people, others followed because of his daring and his fighting ability. When he chose to do something they did not want, he had no authority, moral, legal or physical to make any, except his own immediate band, follow him.

On the eve of the British departure, a site was agreed on near Algoa Bay, Botha's Farm. The farm was vacant because the previous occupier had been one of the trekboer rebels and was being held in Cape Town. It was not a particularly fertile spot and was not suitable for the support of the large community planned—it really was only of use as a stock ranch. However, van der Kemp and Read led over a hundred Khoi from Graaff-Reinet to Botha's Farm in July 1802.

It is significant that immediate opposition was expressed by the trekboers to this new Institution. Their principal complaint was that it was depriving them of a pool of potential servants. They also insisted that such a concentration of Khoi, so near the Xhosa frontier, was a danger to the security of the frontier. They had already shown their dislike of Read and van der Kemp while they were still at Graaff-Reinet. Originally Maynier had let the missionaries use the Dutch Reformed Church at the Drostdy, with the agreement of the local church elders. However, later the Boer community complained of this, and part of the price that the Government had to pay to achieve peace with the trekboer malcontents was to have the whole church washed and scrubbed clean. This was a quite extraordinary demand. After all, any trekboer household included Khoi servants, and at family prayers which were held daily, they attended. Again there were many fringe members of trekboer groups who were of mixed race, and they, as well as some unmixed Khoi, rode with gun in hand on commando with their 'baas'. Racial domination was what they believed in, or if that is too intellectualised a way of putting the matter, racial domination was an essential part of their life style, not racial segregation, most certainly not of the kind that would demand this extraordinary, almost ritual, scrubbing out of the church building.

Was it the way the missionaries and the members of the slave/Khoi congregation behaved that so shocked them and forced them to make this demand? Antagonism to the missionaries there certainly was, there simply is not enough evidence available to let us give a confident explanation of their behaviour. Whatever the explanation, antagonism to the LMS missionaries was already widespread among the trekboer community by 1802.

Before any significant developments could take place at Botha's Farm, the British began their withdrawal from the Cape in favour of the Batavian Republic and the situation changed. In view of the continuing violence in the frontier region, Dundas suggested to Read and van der Kemp that they withdraw to Cape Town until such time as the new administration made its rule effective. If that was not acceptable they should at least withdraw into Fort Frederick where Khoi soldiers of the Cape Corps were remaining. The missionaries refused these offers but were soon forced into the Fort along with their people, because as soon as the British regulars withdrew, the Institution was raided by both Xhosa and Boer raiding parties and all their stock was stolen. Indeed, after they were safely in the Fort, their few buildings at Botha's Farm were burned down by a trekboer commando.

The new Batavian administration decided to continue the old line in the matter of the frontier; pacify the trekboer, reconcile the Khoi to the Colony and draw a firm line of demarcation between the Xhosa and the Colony. The new Governor, Janssens, therefore decided that the LMS should have its Khoi Institution. A site had to be chosen and again the mission was offered a site that was not suitable for the growth of vegetables and cereals on a significant scale. There was however, no better alternative offered so the community left Fort Frederick to go to their new site, which they called Bethelsdorp. This was in June 1803. Van der Kemp and Read, it seems, thought they were giving the site a trial and they might be able to obtain a better one if this proved unsuitable.

This arrangement with the LMS was clearly part of Janssens frontier policy. Klaas Stuurman was also granted a 'farm' for his people and various similar arrangements were concluded with various Khoi captains and the Gcaleka Xhosa chiefs, Ndlambe and Tuli and their Gona ally, Cungwa. It is again worth noting that these chiefs were all declared by the documents to be chiefs west of the Great Fish River without any further remarks about them being illegally within the Colony.

Relations between the missionaries and the Batavian administration did not remain at the initial amicable level. One source of trouble was that Janssens and his principal officer de Mist both rapidly became of the opinion that to reconcile the trekboers to the Government was the primary aim of their policy. They changed from their initial attitude, which was that these same trekboers were to be brought to heel, and justice be made available to the Khoi population. They continued to hope that the Boers would learn the lesson that a well-paid and justly treated workforce was to their own benefit as well as to the benefit of the Khoi, but this was a secondary point; the reconciliation of the trekboer to the administration was the main aim of the Governor's policy.

So when the trekboers continued their complaints about the mission as a place where potential members of the workforce vital to the frontier economy lived in idleness, where these Khoi were being trained in a way quite unsuitable for their status, Janssens and de Mist listened. Their attitude to Bethelsdorp is summed up by van der Kemp's biographer thus

> Governor Janssens and his advisers planned Bethelsdorp as an aid to the farmers. Vanderkemp was to keep it going with just a modest amount of religious instruction, not overmuch, for religion was a medicine to be taken in small prescribed doses. Of industrial instruction there was to be a more generous allowance, because things seen and temporal have earthly values. . . . The main concern was that neighbouring farmers should be able to draw upon the place for obedient servants. In short, Bethelsdorp was to be a factory turning out useful black tools for white hands. Under such circumstances it was not even desirable that there should be very great prosperity at Bethelsdorp. The bleakness and barrenness of the place were perhaps a safeguard against the inhabitants becoming too much at ease in Zion.[3]

The Cape records do not let us see anything written by Janssens or de Mist which explicitly confirms this assertion of Martin's but it reflects how van der Kemp and Read understood the Governor. They came to feel that the cruelty and injustice meted out to the Khoi, employed by the local colonists, was utterly unacceptable to a Christian conscience and was being connived at by the Government. So in their report to the LMS in 1804 they asserted

> We thought it our duty to declare, in a letter written April 18th to the

Governor . . . that our consciences would not permit us any longer to observe the hard article of the settlement granted to our institution, by which we were recommended to encourage the voluntary engagement of the Hottentots into the service of the Colonists, on account of the cruelty and injustice with which those who entered into service were treated, without any justice being done to them by Magistrates. In answer to this the Governor ordered the landdrost of this district to take the necessary steps. This not being done, and the oppression of these inhuman wretches, who call themselves Christians, for the greatest part continuing unpunished, we find ourselves constrained to persist in our declaration.[4]

One can understand how the authorities at the Cape came to be somewhat exasperated with Bethelsdorp and its missionaries.

However, it is clear that Janssens was willing to accept that injustice was part of the normal pattern of master–servant relations on the frontier and though he did punish a few extreme examples, he turned a blind eye in general to the problem. He did so because he felt the need to pacify the frontier and gain the active loyalty of the frontier boers. The Bethelsdorp complaints were therefore unwelcome to Janssens, as was van der Kemp's unwillingness to give up teaching the Khoi at Bethelsdorp to write. Janssens felt that if they learned to read and learned some agricultural skills, that was quite enough for them at their stage of civilisation. Janssens also turned against Bethelsdorp because of the missionaries' insistence on their right to maintain contact with the Xhosa. This was represented as making them a danger to the Colony by their relations with enemies outside it. Yet the administration tolerated some Xhosa within the 'frontier', for example a group of Gcaleka Xhosa under their headman Tsatsu lived on land neighbouring Bethelsdorp and indeed herded some of their stock on mission land. The son of the headman, later baptised Jan, became attached to van der Kemp and attended the school run by the old man and by James Read.

At the time when it became clear to Janssens that the British threatened to again occupy the Cape, his exasperation with Bethelsdorp and its recalcitrant missionaries was at its height, especially since they had taken to complaining about the lack of care taken by his administration of the families of Khoi, from Bethelsdorp and elsewhere, who had been called for service with the Cape Corps.[5] At a time when he needed the maximum loyalty he could muster in his small garrison, he naturally wished to quieten two men who might threaten the loyalty of the Cape Corps and certainly exasperate the colonists whose support was necessary for the defence of the eastern part of the Colony. In April 1805, Janssens ordered van der Kemp and Read to Cape Town, where they remained until the British occupation in January 1806.

Baird, the new British Military Commander, allowed van der Kemp and Read to return to Bethelsdorp. As a result of his interviews with Baird before he returned to the mission, van der Kemp had come to the conclusion that a new era was opening in the history of the Khoi. He felt the new administration shared his sympathy with the sufferings of the people and would begin to rectify them.

However, initially little seemed to change and the same old complaints from Bethelsdorp, which had so annoyed Janssens, also began to flood onto the desk of the new British Governor.

Despite the apparent sameness of affairs, from 1806 onwards there was a slow but well-defined improvement in the prosperity of Bethelsdorp. The herds of the inhabitants brought them more profits, but more important, the various skills that the staff were imparting to the inhabitants began to pay off. It must be insisted that this was so despite the fact that Lichtenstein's famous criticism of the mission for totally neglecting this type of education is sometimes still believed to be true. It gained acceptability by its repetition in the classic works of Cory and Theal. Technical skills were imparted to the Khoi—salt making, carpentry, wagon making and wagon driving. More and more families at Bethelsdorp during this period gained a modicum of prosperity through the pursuit of these trades. Indeed some men became small-scale entrepreneurs; as salt sellers, carpenters and as carters they played an increasingly vital role in the economic life of the colonists. In many ways this increased prosperity and independence served to worsen relations between the mission, the colonists and the authorities at Cape Town. Fewer inhabitants of the Institution were willing to hire themselves out as herders and shepherds to the colonists, and the burden of public works for the landdrost and service in the Cape Corps became exceedingly irksome to men for whom it interfered with more profitable undertakings. On the side of the colonists, the abolition of the slave trade by the British Parliament meant that Hottentot labour became increasingly important. Indeed the colonists found labour to be in such short supply that they began to hire Xhosa labour both from within and from without the Colony.

Although van der Kemp and Read continued to pass to the Governor on behalf of their people, the traditional complaints of a lack of justice from the landdrost, there were some attempts to change things. The new British administration did make certain changes in the law with regard to the Khoi. Lord Caledon in 1809 and Sir John Cradock in 1812 passed ordinances to better order the treatment of Hottentot labour. As we shall see in Chapter 4, these laws can be seen as binding the Khoi even more firmly to the status of an unfree labour force for the colonists. However they did give the Khoi legal status in the Cape and obliged their employers to make and fulfil contacts with them. This would have been worse than useless had the enforcement of these laws been left to the traditional local administration, which was simply part of local White society. However Sir John Cradock in 1811 also set up a system of Circuit Courts. By this measure Judges of the High Court at the Cape went on circuit throughout the Colony to hear cases. Under the new legal dispensation, Khoi could bring their masters to court for breach of contract but also, and even more important, their new status in law allowed them to bring charges against Whites for assault.

The possibility of gaining the justice, long sought for their people, now lay open before Kemp and Read. They began immediately to aid the Khoi of Bethelsdorp and many others scattered throughout the eastern frontier districts to raise their complaints with the new Circuit Court. These cases were heard during the infamous (in White eyes) Black Circuit of 1812. By the time the justices embarked on their circuit, Johannes van der Kemp was dead but Read did his utmost to help the many complainants bring their cases to court.

The Black Circuit looms large in South African history and is a vital element in the view taken of the LMS by British administrator and Boer, both at the time and subsequently, a view which has continued to be reflected by historians into the third quarter of the twentieth century. Professor de Kiewiet says of this episode

> The Circuit Court, freshly created in 1811, announced a new era by making itself accessible to the Hottentot as well as the European population. Of the cases promptly brought against European masters many were malicious, collusive and false. Certain missionaries undoubtedly overreached themselves in trying to strike a blow for their proteges. But other accusations were proven. The sentences which the court pronounced against white masters shook the colony with indignation. The action of the court was a declaration that the protection of the law extended to servants as well as the masters. The social revolution had begun. It was the achievement of Dr. John Philip and the Philanthropic movement to carry it significantly farther.[6]

From Cory and Theal's monumental works up to de Klerk's *Puritans in Africa* published in 1975, great emphasis has been placed on the large numbers of the accused who were found not guilty and on the fact that the Judges found that, as de Kiewiet says, many accusations 'were malicious, collusive and false'. Decent respectable people had been maliciously accused and forced to travel long distances to court at a time when their districts were in a very unsettled state. The volume of the cases were used to malign a good people who looked after their folk with care and understanding. That these cases have been used over the last 170 years by some commentators as a stick with which to beat the Afrikaner people is undoubtedly true. It is also true that many Boer households contained loyal and devoted Khoi servants. This is clearly attested by the large number who trekked with their masters on the Great Trek, and the many commandoes of the period, where as many as half the mounted riflemen were Khoi or Bastards.

However, if there had been in existence a similar system of Circuit Courts during the previous decade, then the number of cases in 1812 would not have reached such massive proportions. There had been no avenue of seeking justice for ill-treated servants until then, so when the opportunity came in 1812 a flood of cases burst out, many of which were related to incidents dating back over several years. It is also essential to point out that it was the Khoi who brought the complaints, not missionaries, such as van der Kemp and Read, who encouraged them to venture boldly into this unknown territory of litigation, but the missionaries did not 'overreach themselves on behalf of their proteges'. It was die Kaapse Volk, as their descendants now call themselves, who brought the charges.

What of the many-times repeated complaint, that of the accusations

made, 'many were malicious, collusive and false'? It is undoubtedly true
that the newly appointed Judges thought them so. In addition, the novelty
of this extraordinary situation of being able to bring a master to court, may
have been too good an opportunity to miss for some people. Just as it is
clearly unbalanced to see the Boers of the eastern frontier as a collection of
Simon Legrees, it is equally foolish to view all the Khoi of the same district
as free from the human sins of hatred and vengefulness. Although it is now
quite impossible to confirm the details of any particular case, it is
reasonable to believe that some cases were indeed brought from motives
other than the seeking of justice.

However, many of the Khoi witnesses must have been overawed and
confused in the novel and frightening situation of the new courts, and so
appeared to be unreliable witnesses. In addition, in a number of instances,
given the troubled state of the eastern frontier areas, corroborative
witnesses for incidents dating back some years could not be found. Thus, it
is reasonable to suggest that many of the cases which failed were by no
means necessarily based simply on malicious accusations.

Be that as it may, what cannot be got round was that a significant number
of masters were found guilty of grossly ill-treating their servants and other
Khoi. The sentences, meted out to those found guilty, which de Kiewiet
suggests 'shook the colony with indignation' could on the other hand also
be viewed with astonishment because of their trifling nature.

A D Martin writes

> One charge concerned a Hottentot servant named Katharyn Stephen. Ten
> witnesses gave evidence that this child—she was but fourteen and a half years
> old—had been stripped and laid on the kitchen floor and there held while she
> was flogged till the blood came. Her offence was taking a bowl of victuals
> before it was given to her. Dr. van Colff testified as to the severity of wounds
> inflicted. The two culprits involved in this case got off with fines of £12 plus
> costs.[7]

It is quite clear from historical sources far-removed from 'philanthropic
circles' that this kind of ill-treatment was not unknown in the frontier areas.
Colonel Collins, a man sympathetic to the colonists, no friend of
missionaries and a British soldier well used to the harsh discipline of the
British Army of his day, could still write in his famous report on the frontier
in 1809

> The establishment of a drostdy in the eastern part of Swellendam is exclusive of
> exterior relations, if possible more necessary than on the banks of the
> Ghamgha. There are many respectable persons now residing there who deplore
> the evils that exist, and anxiously wish for their removal by a less distant and
> more efficient control. The landdrost complains that in consequence of
> connexions of partialities, the most important occurrences are either totally
> concealed from his knowledge, or else so misrepresented as to render it
> impossible to form a just opinion upon the merits of any case. Authority is not
> respected, the laws are disregarded, *and the most atrocious crimes have been
> committed there with impunity.*[8]

Or again if we consult the journal of Dirk van Reenen, a Boer who served as an official with the Batavian administration. In reporting his negotiations with Klaas Stuurman on behalf of the Governor he said of the Khoi recently displaced by the trekboers who had been granted leeningsplaats by van Plettenberg:

> This action caused poverty among the Hottentots, who no longer had grazing for their cattle and found themselves compelled to enter into service with the inhabitants. They no doubt had to take their few head of cattle with them and now all depended on whether they took service with people who were fairminded enough to protect and respect their scanty property or with folk who, with greedy eyes, sought to appropriate the little still remaining to these poor creatures. This was also the predicament of other natives who hired themselves to Colonists. If they were ill-treated they could not say 'I am going to another master who will treat me better, or back to my possessions'—they had to remain there. Thus was poverty riveted in chains. Little attention was paid to the treatment, whether bad or otherwise meted out to these natives.[9]

There are many other similar sources confirming the bad treatment of Khoi servants in the frontier zone. This simply confirms what Read and van der Kemp said. Not that all trekboers were evil people and cruel employers, but that some did commit crimes against their servants and until the time of the Circuit Courts little was done about it. The veld-cornets were unpaid, elected burghers from among the number of the trekboers, who, out of partiality or connection, as Collins said, had done nothing about crimes they knew had been committed. The missionaries saw it as part of their task to help these afflicted people receive justice. They did not condemn or seek to condemn the trekboer as a nation. However, the response to their action was that the trekboer as a whole felt threatened. This was not because of the accusations brought by the Khoi (again it must be insisted against what is said in so many even current textbooks). What disturbed them was that their autonomy was now threatened and their old freedom was gone because of the exertion of effective government control over the frontier zone for the first time. It was government from the Cape they feared and disliked in the very depth of their beings.

After the Black Circuit and the Death of van der Kemp

The years between the death of van der Kemp and the arrival of John Philip were particularly difficult ones for the LMS in South Africa. James Read was left as superintending missionary in place of van der Kemp but did little to fulfil this task since he was busy until 1814 with aiding Khoi and slaves whose cases against their masters were still brought to court. In addition he had the onerous task of leading the Bethelsdorp Institution. The missionaries stationed elsewhere were left very much on their own to get on with the task. The main areas where the other LMS missionaries worked were among the Namaqua Khoi to the north of the Colony, among the Griqua beyond the frontier, where William Anderson, who had arrived in the Cape with Read, had established himself with the Waterboer family, and at various points in the colony where Khoi and slaves could be approached readily.

From 1812 to 1814, the Reverend John Campbell came out as a Director of the Society to supervise the work. Under his aegis some new tasks were undertaken. The first was to negotiate with Tswana people around Lattakoo, north of the colonial frontier. The chief agreed to accept a missionary to work with his people. It was there that Robert Moffat went to carry out his life's work after a short apprenticeship among the Bastards of Afrikaner, a group of pacified banditti along the Orange River. The second was in the area of the Zuurveld recently 'cleared' of Xhosa by Cradock's aggressive forward policy. Another Khoi Institution was set up on land given by the government, called Theopolis. Also a missionary was stationed at a place, later named after him, Pacaltsdorp, at the kraal of a still-independent Khoi clan. Campbell left South Africa in February 1814, leaving behind as Secretary of the missions in South Africa, George Thom, an Aberdonian who had come to South Africa with him but had spent most of his time in Cape Town and worked there as pastor of a White congregation.

After Campbell's departure, only one new venture was initiated, but a venture with enormous importance. The Government finally allowed the LMS to open up work with the Xhosa beyond the frontier. This was after years of trying to keep 'colonial' and Xhosa separate and even trying to get van der Kemp and Read to send to the drostdy as prisoners, any Xhosa who came to Bethelsdorp, something they had consistently refused to do. In 1815, Joseph Williams accompanied by Chief Tsatsu's son, now baptised Jan, as an evangelist together with some Khoi teachers, settled among the Xhosa on the Kat River. The Govenment undoubtedly allowed this mission as a possible counter to the influence of the rebel Boers, who were trying to seek Xhosa help against the Colony. The British officials were not so enamoured of the LMS, but they were well aware that the mission and the rebellious frontier trekboers were fundamentally opposed, so the missionary presence in the Xhosa frontier area was a neat way of counteracting the rebels without any cost to government or any commitment by the British to the Xhosa.

As they did with Anderson amidst the growing unity and power of the Griqua peoples on the Orange River frontier, the British tried to persuade Williams to be a direct agent of Government. Like Anderson, he politely but firmly refused. This was extremely annoying to the British officials and increased their growing dissatisfaction with the LMS. This dissatisfaction we have seen was primarily based on the twin pillars of class difference between the officials and the missionaries and the Government desire to pacify and conciliate the trekboer population who profoundly disliked the LMS. This situation became increasingly tense after Campbell's departure. The leadership of the mission, divided between James Read and George Thom, simply did not work. Dissatisfaction and tension among the missionaries grew apace and in 1817, George Thom took the arrival of some new missionaries in Cape Town as an opportunity for setting the mission onto a new track. He called on the Colonial Secretary for permission for the new missionaries to go to work beyond the colonial frontier. We have seen Somerset's attitude and, in keeping with it, Colonel Bird refused such permission. Bird then went on to condemn Theopolis, Bethelsdorp and Anderson's work among the Griqua as irregularly conducted and inimical to the well-being of the colony. He also attacked the moral character of some of the missionaries, including James Read. George Thom, whose work had kept him in Cape Town and close to the British Establishment, was very alarmed by this. In addition it does seem that he also saw this crisis as an opportunity for dealing with Read and other mission staff of whom he disapproved.

He called a 'Synod' of missionaries to review the situation, brought to their notice in such a forcible way by Colonel Bird, and to attempt to find a resolution of these difficulties. Thom's actions were irregular in the extreme. First, he called to the meeting only those close to or in Cape Town, which meant that only those who had been in the settled western area of the Colony attended, along with the new missionaries, who had no experience of the situation at all. Second, even if all the missionaries could have been present, such a meeting had not any legal status whatever. The LMS regulations were clear that there was a superintending missionary who alone was in charge and responsible to the Society, the only other authority allowed was one that would be set up by the new indigenous Christians as the form of government of their new Church. Thom's meeting was incomplete in a most significant way as a conference of missionaries and had no status at all as a church 'court', since the infant churches among the Khoi and Griquas had certainly not called the meeting, nor did they even know about it.

Thom's 'Synod' has played an important, if minor role, in South African historiography, since its records have been taken as a confirmation of official and colonist views from within the LMS, notably the condemnation of those persons and institutions most disliked by both the officials and the frontier Boers, that is, Read, Anderson and Williams together with Bethelsdorp, Theopolis and the Griqua mission.

Read, Corner and Wimmer were arraigned on accusations of fornication. The arraignment cannot be disputed though the validity of their condemnation is open to dispute. However, Read was also condemned for sending missionaries beyond the frontier without Government permission.

It is evident from Thom's correspondence with George Burder of LMS headquarters in London, that to him and his circle, Read was the focus of the trouble with the mission. Read's anti-Government behaviour was bad and his having married a Khoi wife in itself showed his sexual depravity, so that the charge of fornication was no surprise, indeed it was almost to be expected. The Synod's actions gave further impetus to the anti-LMS gossip of the day among British officials and Boers alike. How were the mighty fallen—Read, the righteous accuser of good burghers on behalf of their servants, was shown up to be unrighteous.

How deeply these accusations took root is shown in J S Moffat's

biography of his father and mother published in 1886. He passes over the
matter of Thom and the Synod briefly enough but he still damns a number
of nameless missionaries. Yet to South African readers it would be quite
clear about whom he was talking. James Read had died only thirty years
before and his sons were ministers in the Congregational Union, the Cape
Coloured Church that had grown out of the old Khoi missions. J S Moffat
wrote

> In the year 1816 the Missions in South Africa had fallen into a state of grievous
> disorder. The numbers of stations was large, they were scattered far apart.
> Some of the men who had been sent out had proved themselves unworthy of
> their trust, and had not maintained even an ordinary standard of Christian
> conduct. On the arrival of Robert Moffat and his colleagues they were
> astounded to find themselves associated in the Service of the Society with men
> who had brought shame on the very name of Christian, and whose reputations
> were a by-word to the ungodly.[10]

Corner and Wimmer were relatively unknown in their own day and long
forgotten. Both at the time, and later, the whole focus was on Read. The
focus was on him because he had been the agent through whom the Bastard
and Khoi servants had brought their charges to Court against their masters.
Read's actions in this area were what mattered and the sexual accusations
were a useful stick with which to beat him. It was then and is still a stick
with which to beat the LMS activity as a whole, especially the stand made
on behalf of the non-Whites within the colony by van der Kemp and Read.
J S Moffat in 1886 was reflecting his father's antagonism towards the
activity of van der Kemp and Read and, despite some praise for him in the
book, of John Philip also.

The Synod members were also unhappy with Anderson for refusing
Government demands for him to return to the Colony people who had fled
to live with the Griqua, and at other times for failing to deliver up a quota
of Griqua for the Cape Corps as if Griqua Town was a station in the colony
like Theopolis. The mind boggles at the misunderstanding of Anderson's
position that is revealed by these demands by the Government. He lived as a
dependant of the Waterboer clan, an important dependant certainly who
helped Waterboer and his associates build a viable political unit, a new
state, out of a strange mixture of Khoi, Bastards, ex-slaves and various
Tswana and Sotho families. In no way had Anderson any independent
authority; he had influence and power, but as one powerful figure among
many on the Griqua social and political stage. This was to be the role of the
French Protestants among the Sotho of Moshweshwe, the CMS in
Buganda, the Scots Presbyterians in Malawi—interestingly, all places where
Christianity became rooted among the people and was to flourish later in
indigenous forms. It gave him no power whatever of a kind that would
enable him to fulfil the demands placed on him by the colonial authorities.

This whole episode of Thom's 'Synod' threatened the continued existence
of the work of the Society in South Africa. A number of the staff resigned
in order to take up positions as pastors of Dutch Reformed parishes,
notably George Thom and John Taylor, while Brownlee, another of the

new missionaries who had arrived with Moffat, became a 'government missionary' among the Xhosa of Ngqika. Government missionary is a very strange invention indeed, especially since Lord Charles Somerset, the Governor, had been inveighing, until only a few months before, about the missions and what a disaster they had been beyond the frontier. Government thinking seems to have been that since it seemed impossible to prevent missionaries from crossing the frontiers, it would be as well to have one's own who would perform the function that the LMS staff would not; Thom's Synod had made it clear that there were missionaries around that were potential material for such a venture. Just how strange a 'Synod' this had been is seen in that it was not able to produce an unequivocal condemnation of slave-owning, simply stating a missionary should not 'buy or sell slaves'!

As a result of these resignations plus the suspension of James Read by the Directors in the UK on receipt of the reports from Thom, the staff of the mission was much depleted and without any clear leadership. The Government in the United Kingdom also approached the Society about the situation of the Society in the Cape. The Directors agreed to send out two of their number to inspect the work of the Society within and without the Colony, in order to reorganise it and put it on to a secure footing. They chose two Scots, Dr John Campbell and Dr John Philip of Aberdeen. Campbell had performed a similar task in 1812, which leaves one a little puzzled about his choice for this venture so soon after his previous attempt which appears to have achieved something less than success.

It was decided that, while both were to carry out an investigation, Dr Philip was to stay on in South Africa as a Director in residence to make sure that the reorganisation of the work was effectively carried out. He was also to act as the only intermediary between the Mission and the Colonial Government, with the responsibility of eliminating the deep distrust that had grown up during the previous decade. The post of Superintendent was abolished. John Philip arrived in Cape Town as a full member of the Board of Directors of the London Missionary Society, differing from the others in that he was to be resident in South Africa. Strangely, the title of Superintendent of Missions was resurrected and Philip did use it of himself. Indeed on his parents' tombstone, erected by John Philip in Kirkcaldy Old Churchyard, he refers to himself as 'Superintendent of Missions'. He also uses the original spelling of the family name Philp. However, he always remained a director of the Society and as such, had a position no other Superintendent, before or after, had.

3

John Philip in Scotland

The Agricultural Revolution of the generations after 1760 enclosed the Scottish fields, broke down the rigs, consolidated the strips, drained the stagnant mosses, took in the common, changed the crops and the rotations and destroyed forever the traditions of husbandry which, hallowed and inefficient though it was, had dictated the framework of life for most Scots for as long as our knowledge of agrarian history goes back. In doing so it sundered for ever a peasant economy that had been mainly dedicated to producing enough for itself in a largely rural world where most people were themselves producers: there arose instead a society in which capitalist farmers and landless labourers worked mainly to produce for great towns filled with consumers, and who did their task so well that the farming system in many parts of Scotland became the envy of Europe.[1]

It cannot be overemphasised that in 1780 as a result of this process and the first stages of the accompanying Industrial Revolution, Scotland had become a new country in a dramatically short space of time. In 1740, in the lifetime of Philip's parents, the pattern of life had been, for the vast majority of Scots, little different from that of 1640 or 1540. One additional factor has to be added to Professor Smout's succinct description. The older Scottish society had had to live through these centuries with a fiercely warlike and thoroughly tribal society constantly threatening it, that of the Highland clans, whose last desperate fling had ended in the bloody disaster of Culloden Moor as recently as 1746. The situation of the Cape Colony, so alien to the vast majority of Englishmen, had been similar to that of the Lowland Scots up until a brief twenty-nine years before Philip's birth.

By 1760, the Celtic clans had been pacified once and for all, the fundamental Agricultural Revolution was well begun and the Industrial Revolution, which was to complete the total transformation of Scotland, was underway. These changes, although they created a large landless labouring class, did not cause an impoverishment of the people of Scotland. On the contrary, from 1760 until 1780 the general standard of living rose dramatically and remained high, with a few localised and temporary dips, until the troubled times after the ending of the Napoleonic Wars.

The initial major industrial developments in Scotland were centred on the textiles—flax, linen and cotton. Scotland's second Industrial Revolution which produced a massive development in coal, iron and steel did not come to dominate Scotland and her economy until after 1830, when Central Scotland became one of the world's greatest centres of heavy industry.

The creation of a powerful textile industry brought prosperity to a large segment of the Scottish population. Many people found jobs in the new industries as weavers and spinners, which in turn caused many skilled workmen in ancillary trades to prosper as well as bringing profit to entrepreneurs and merchants. Arkwright's and Crompton's mechanical inventions soon began to move to concentrate spinning in newly built factories but weaving remained a handloom craft based on the weaver and his family working in the family home. These weavers, in particular, knew a period of great prosperity from the 1770s into the first decades of the nineteenth century. They continued to dominate the industry even after the beginning of profitable factory weaving. As late as 1831, when the flood of Highland and Irish immigrants into the trade had far more effectively diminished their prosperity than had the competition of the new factories, a survey of the weaving industry in the Glasgow area indicated that handloom weavers still outnumbered those employed in factories.

The spinning of fibre, whether cotton, linen or flax, developed differently from weaving and after 1770 developed rapidly as a factory-based activity. However, these factories were not concentrated in a few urban areas but were spread over much of Lowland Scotland. Some developed in the old burghs like Paisley or Kilmarnock while entrepreneurs like David Dale built model industrial villages along with the new factories in places like New Lanark, Catrine or Stanley. These villages were very similar to the model villages deliberately and carefully planned by the 'improving' landlords of the previous generation.

John Philip, who was born in Kirkcaldy in April 1775, grew up then during this period of dynamic change, a phase of development categorised by the noted economic historian W W Rostow as that of 'take-off'. These developments brought about widespread prosperity, shared in varying degrees by many in the population, but it did not create the massive urban slum conditions which were to become the mark of Victorian and Edwardian Scotland.

There were areas of slum conditions, in the Old Town of Edinburgh, in parts of Glasgow and elsewhere, but these were not characteristic of the urban growth of the period. On the contrary, prosperity and the industrial as well as agricultural development that created it, were spread throughout the Lowlands in this period of rapid growth between 1760 and 1815.

This period saw the growth, for the first time in Scotland, of a significant middle class. This class consisted of increasingly prosperous entrepreneurs in the burghs, of farmers, who in the east from Aberdeen to Berwick were building houses for themselves which would have pleased a middling laird in 1750,[2] as well as doctors, lawyers and teachers. This burgeoning class was spread throughout the burghs of the land and not concentrated in Glasgow and Edinburgh. Fine new terraces and squares of 'Regency' houses, smaller versions of Edinburgh's New Town, were built in Dundee, Perth and Aberdeen as well as in smaller burghs like Cupar, Dumfries, Kirkcaldy, Paisley, Ayr and several other places.

Intimately related to this expanding of middle class, and the prosperity of the skilled artisan which accompanied it, was the rapid growth of the 'academies'. These were new or revived secondary schools created for the

post-elementary education of the newly prosperous groups in Scottish
society. They were the foundations of a phenomenon which was to mark off
Scottish society from that of England until well into the twentieth century,
the free burgh high school. A few of these schools, like Perth Academy,
briefly aspired to provide an alternative to the Arts course of the universities
but that experiment soon ended.

This dramatic expansion of education was based on the new prosperity
together with the concern and respect for education, long a part of Scottish
life. By the middle of the eighteenth century the dream of John Knox of a
school in every parish had come close to fruition outside the Highlands.
Indeed as late as 1833, when Irish and Highland immigration had
dramatically altered the balance of the Lowland population, and in the new
densely populated centres growing round the developing centres of heavy
industry the parish school system had collapsed, still 93 per cent of the
workforce could read and 59 per cent could write.

In this brief heady period of expansion and prosperity, the old class
system of the predominantly rural and feudal Scotland was dramatically
challenged and the new hard and bitter class divisions of Victorian Scotland
had not yet developed. A very large number of the population of the land
were drawn into a social grouping which was both prosperous and clearly
middle class at one end and was reasonably well-off and unquestionably
working class at the other. However there was in this period as yet no clear
dividing line within the group. Of this massive new element in Scottish
society Christopher Smout writes

> . . . the middle class also contained a great many who were on the edge of what
> we would now call the working class, especially those described in contemporary
> directories as 'mechanic'—the artisans and craftsmen who were part employers
> of journeymen and apprentices and partly workers dependent on the skill of
> their own hands and eyes. Take, for example, the calling of shoemaker. About
> 1790 there were in Dumfries 110 shoemakers in the incorporated guild,
> employing eighty-four journeymen and forty-two apprentices: the ratio of
> master to men is so low that both obviously had a near working-class character,
> but with many of the journeymen and apprentices still hoping to become
> masters one day. In Kilmarnock at the same date, however, there were fifty-six
> 'master shoemakers' employing 408 journeymen: the calling of shoemaker was
> here that of a small middle-class employer, but few of the journeymen could
> here hope to reach the status of master.[3]

In effect, during this period it is difficult to define the limits of what were
the middle and working classes. Moreover, people's self-understanding did
not conform either to the old class structures or to the new that were soon to
develop. In retrospect we can see David Dale, owner of three mills and their
attendant model villages at New Lanark, a schoolmaster at Perth Academy
and a master shoemaker in Kilmarnock, some of whose apprentices still
slept in his house, all as middle class. At the time, however, they did not feel
that they had much in common, except negatively; they all knew that they
were not of the nobility, they certainly were not 'labourers', nor yet were
they 'lairds', though a number made the move into the latter class by buying

small estates. Similarly with groups that we would today insist were elements of the working class. The handloom weavers, though prosperous, were clearly working class, but felt little, if anything, in common with the spinners who worked alongside their wives and children in the new mills and lived in the company village, and certainly both groups felt that their situation was wholly other than that of the Lothian miner whose status ceased legally to be one of serfdom only in 1799.

Scottish society in the last decades of the eighteenth century was one of dynamic movement and change. A centuries-old agrarian society with a small urban periphery had changed after 1760 with immense rapidity into one of new-found wealth based on the most advanced agriculture in Europe and dominated by a network of prosperous burghs based on new industry which spread across the whole of Lowland Scotland and the Northeast. We must not overlook the tremendous sense of freedom, prosperity and new possibilities that this opened for many, simply because we know how drastically these opportunities would be curtailed from the second quarter of the nineteenth century onwards.

John Philip was a typical product of this rapidly changing and confident society. His father, a handloom weaver, was both prosperous and literate. He appears to be typical of this group of men who produced during the period poets of some real distinction and writers of some standing on a number of subjects. As far as we know, Philip senior was neither poet nor authority on the bird life around his home town, Kirkcaldy, but he was a lover of books. John had available to him, in his father's house, books by Bacon, Swift, Johnson and Newton.[4]

This list was not remarkable for a weaver's library at that time except for the absence of theological works which were very common in similar households. Drummond and Bulloch in the most recent and best history of Scottish Christianity write of the weavers that their ranks

> contained many men of native intelligence. He the weaver often bought many books, especially of poetry and religion, was independent in his churchmanship, and often was concerned with some small independent sect. Of the minor poets who came from his background, Robert Tannahill of Paisley was longest remembered. Weavers became amateur students of botany, ornithology and geology and were known for enduring minds.[5]

The handloom weavers were prosperous but they had to work hard for their prosperity. This hard work usually involved their wives and families as assistants. However, the pattern of their activity had a number of features which kept them in the craftsman tradition of labour and marked them off from the factory spinner and the miner, despite the latter's skills. Perhaps the most important of these features was that the weaver and his family chose the rhythm of their work. He took his breaks when he wanted to—if a visitor arrived he could stop and chat; he could, if he so chose, work for eighteen hours at a stretch in order to have what we would call a 'long weekend'. His family shared this self-determined pattern of work and leisure typical also of the traditional trades of carpenter, mason, shoemaker and so on, but in stark contrast with the lives of the spinners and miners, the harbingers of the relentless patterns of work of nineteenth-century heavy industry. The spinners—men, women and children—were bound by the rhythm of the loom and the need of the owner to maximise the efficiency of his machinery by regular and consistent use. Mill life was like pit life, one of inexorable daily toil, six days a week, 52 weeks a year with a few breaks of two or three days' duration decided by management. This pattern of drastic factory discipline could hardly be more different from the self-regulated regimes of the traditional crafts.

Compared with the harsh poverty which was the lot of most Scots during the previous centuries, even the spinners and to a lesser extent the miners did financially prosper during this period. However, in contrast with the traditional crafts and above all the massive new workforce of handloom weavers, the spinners and miners were caugh in a monotonous drudgery and a humiliating factory discipline which left little leisure. Foreshadowing the general pattern of the future, it was prosperity combined with leisure time that allowed the newly prosperous craft working class to play their part in the life of Scotland. They produced not only poets, amateur geologists and botanists, but also popular support for the movement seeking Parliamentary and local government reform. In the ecclesiastical world, the religious liveliness of this class profoundly altered the patterns of Scottish Church life.

This appears almost inevitable, because these large new prosperous groupings of middle class and working class folk with their leisure time and literate interests did not fit well into the Scotland of the Moderates.

The Moderates were a party of laymen and ministers, who, after the Act of Union in 1707, came to dominate Church and State in Scotland. They brought peace to a country which throughout the seventeenth century had been riven by bitter divisions often leading to bloodshed, kept constantly at fever heat by religious 'enthusiasm' and its attendant ecclesiastical and theological disputes. Central government at Westminster had little impact on Scottish life except in the Highlands during, and briefly after, the 1715 and 1745 rebellions. Scottish life was dominated in almost all of its aspects by the Kirk session and the lairds in the country and by the Kirk session and the burgh councils in the towns. The latter institutions were self-perpetuating oligarchies playing the same role in burgh life that lairds did in the countryside.

Under the sway of the Moderates, the Presbyterian form of church government of the Kirk, an institution which was both popular and national, became a tool for the control of local communities, when in the seventeenth century it had been a vehicle for the expression of local popular feeling. The Moderates made shrewd use of the Patronage Act of 1712, which ended the popular election of ministers and replaced it with appointment of ministers by the 'heritors', a laird or group of lairds in the countryside and the council in the burghs.

By the second half of the eighteenth century, Church and State seemed to have worked so well together under the skilful leadership of the Reverend Dr Robertson, Principal of Edinburgh University, and Henry Dundas, a principal member of Pitt's Administrations, that Scotland became an area of political peace and a source of consistent support for the Administration.

The spirit of 'enthusiasm' and sectarian radicalism which had been so characteristic of Scotland was effectively defused by the moderates. Where this enthusiasm still existed it was in the 'seceder' churches, groups which had withdrawn from the Kirk to form their own denominations on essentially seventeenth-century ecclesiastical and theological issues. These groups had gravely disturbed the peace of Scotland in the past, but by the second half of the eighteenth century their aggression was inward looking and had little impact on contemporary society. Robertson and Dundas would seem to have effectively drawn their teeth while still allowing them to growl occasionally.

The rule of the Moderates in Scotland, however, was far from being a purely negative force in Scotland. It was under their aegis that the universities of Scotland, particularly Glasgow and Edinburgh, flourished as they had never before, and the country entered her cultural 'Golden Age' of the Scottish Enlightenment. This period of rich intellectual activity was one in which the newly prosperous classes created by the Agricultural and early Industrial Revolutions, fully entered. Indeed, without the economic changes of the period there probably would have been no Scottish Enlightenment. As Professor Smout has pointed out[6] every important figure in that period of intellectual ferment came from the new middle class. The patronage of the great landowners and even of lairds was not unimportant in the careers of some of these men but the old Scottish class of wealth and power produced no significant figures in the intellectual world. The universities played a major role in this age and these were universities whose student bodies largely came from this new middle class together with a not inconsiderable minority from the ranks of the skilled artisans. The foundations of literacy, well laid by the educational policies of the Kirk, now had the essential input of prosperity enabling this period of intellectual excitement and activity to take place.

The new prosperous groups in Scottish society found a place for themselves in the universities and the new intellectual ferment associated with these institutions, but they found no other place for themselves in the Scotland of the Moderates. In the countryside they were not heritors, so had no voice in Church and State. Again in the burghs, where their strength lay, the self-perpetuating oligarchies that controlled both the burgh councils and the Kirk excluded them equally effectively.

Some found a place in which to both exert and assert themselves in the old secession churches, where, as leading laymen, they were able to exercise a dominant role in these small communities. In these denominations the Kirk Sessions were elected as was the minister through the system of 'call' by the congregation. David Dale, the founder of New Lanark, was typical of many when he left the Kirk and became an elder in a congregation of the Relief Synod. He was also a harbinger of what was to come when he left the Relief Kirk and joined a wholly new ecclesiastical venture, initiated by three ministers who broke with the national Kirk. John Barclay of Fettercairn,

James Smith of Newburn and Robert Ferrier of Largo together founded a number of congregations across central Scotland based on congregationalist principles in the late 1760s. Their support came entirely from newly prosperous middle-class and skilled artisans. From 1769 until his death in 1806, Dale served as an elder in one of their Glasgow congregations, taking part in pastoral care but also playing a leading role as preacher and organiser.

This development was one of the first signs of the Evangelical Revival brought about by the Wesleys and Whitefield in England having its effects in Scotland. The literate prosperous classes we have been discussing provided a ready-made and eagerly receptive audience for the new approach to Christianity. Methodism, as a denomination, did not grow in Scottish soil, but its offshoot, evangelicalism, did take root and flourish. This new growth took two forms. The first was the creation of new churches. These were not divided from the Kirk on the old dead Covenanting and Calvinist issues, but came into being to satisfy the needs of men and women for whom Kirk structures, so deeply involved in the old Scotland which was now socially and economically dead, gave little opportunity for self-expression. The second form was the creation of a party within the Kirk dedicated to reform, in particular to the abolition of patronage and the return of what was, in effect, the popular election of the parish minister thus ending the power of the heritors and the burgh councils.

It was the very social groups we have been discussing who took the lead both in the creation of the new Baptist and Congregational Churches and the reforming movement in the Kirk. In the last two decades of the century, these same groups also produced the new movement for burgh and parliamentary reform. Given the relations of Church and State, these issues could hardly be disentangled in any case, but they were entwined especially deeply because it was often the same people seeking both. The Moderates had effectively tamed the old Scotland, but the new Scotland of the prosperous burghs and the best agricultural system in Europe, could no longer be confined by a system which effectively excluded the dynamic new groups created by the economic revolution. These groups in Scottish society took up the support of new churches, of reform of the Kirk, the abolition of slavery, the new call to overseas missions, parliamentary and burgh reform, all of which, in different ways, presented a challenge to the cosy, quiescent Scotland of the Moderates.

It was two of the most important leaders of this new stirring in Scottish life who directly affected John Philip and the direction his life took. They were the Haldane brothers, Robert and James. Robert inherited a small estate but his brother made a very profitable career with the East India Company, which was typical of a significant element in the Scottish middle classes. The brothers were awakened by what, to late twentieth-century eyes, was a somewhat bizarre concatenation of events; the founding of the Baptist and London Missionary Societies in 1792 and 1795 respectively and the French Revolution. In fact, many in both England and Scotland who responded to evangelicalism and its concerns over slavery and missions were also deeply affected by the Revolution. So much so that conservative circles in both countries saw the abolitionist and missionary movements as covert forms of Jacobinism!

Robert Haldane was quite explicit about the fact that it was the Revolution which awakened him to a new view of life. At first he agreed with Burke's *Reflections* but was convinced that Burke was wrong by a brilliant reply to that famous work—James Mackintosh's *Vindiciae Gallicae*. Mackintosh was a Scot resident in London but a product of Aberdeen and Edinburgh Universities. In response to Mackintosh and some more ephemeral pamphlets sympathetic to the Revolution, Haldane wrote

> Although I did not exactly agree with these writers, a scene of amelioration and improvement in the affairs of mankind seemed to open itself in my mind which I trusted would speedily take place in the world, such as the universal abolition of slavery, of war, and of many other miseries that mankind were exposed to, and which appeared to me wholly to result from the false principles upon which ancient governments had been constructed. I exulted in this prospect, from motives of benevolence, and, as far as I know, without any allowed mixture of selfishness. I rejoiced in the experiment that was making in France, of the construction of a government, at once from its foundations upon a regular plan, which Hume in his essays, speaks of as an event much to be desired.[7]

He went on to insist that the terrible happenings that occurred in France as the Revolution developed were due to the degraded state of the people which could directly be attributed to the Ancien Régime. Neither he nor his brother joined any of the new radical groups calling for burgh and parliamentary reform such as 'The Friends of the People' or 'The United Scotsmen', but he continued to assert that

> The French were making the experiment upon themselves; from them I wished to see its effects. I thought these would be so good as soon to convince other nations, and make them willing to follow their example; and I hoped that this might one day take place, without either bloodshed or loss of property.[8]

Despite gaining for himself some unpopularity by expressing these ideas he soon became the central figure in a discussion group, made up mainly of local ministers, which met regularly in his house near Stirling. The times were so tense that these ministers were advised by many of their friends, and more important, by their patrons, that this was a most unwise venture. It was during the course of these meetings that Haldane decided that it was only the spread of evangelical Christianity that could bring about the amelioration of the human condition, the concern that had been awakened in him by the Revolution.

His initial response to this new understanding was to begin the planning of a missionary venture to India which he intended both to lead and to finance. Permission to embark on such a venture within the territory of the East India Company was refused, despite his attempts to gain Dundas's help to persuade the Directors. In fact it was Dundas who warned the Directors to give no such permission.

Frustrated over his desire to go to India, Robert decided instead to dedicate himself to the spread of evangelical Christianity in Scotland. In this venture he had the enthusiastic support of his brother James. Robert organised the financing of the campaign, while James took up itinerant preaching himself in the Wesley tradition. The brothers decided fairly rapidly that the work should be put on a proper institutional and organisational footing. They set up 'The Society for the Propagation of the Gospel at Home'. This was a society which was a replica of the Baptist and London Missionary Societies for work abroad, and like them, although having the support of a small number of clergy, was essentially a lay movement detached from any formal connection with any church, established or dissenting. Also in the manner of the London Missionary Society, the Haldanes' new Society began to set about the training and the employment of its own missionaries.

The Haldanes used the well-tried techniques of open-air preaching and the distribution of specially prepared tracts and pamphlets. However, the main thrust of their activities was through the setting up of Sunday Schools for adults as well as children. They concentrated these activities in urban areas and in the Highlands where parochial pastoral care and parochial education were ineffective. In 1797, James Haldane undertook one of his most important tours. This was to Argyll, where together with his assistant John Campbell[9] he set up sixty new Sunday Schools.

Although the London Missionary Society had set up auxiliary committees in Glasgow and Edinburgh with a modicum of support from the evangelical wings of the Kirk and the Seceders, it was not at all popular and was viewed with suspicion by the establishment. This suspicion was increased by this new outburst of lay religious enthusiasm on the part of the Haldanes' new organisation. The source of this suspicion would seem to lie, not simply in the tense atmosphere created by the Revolution in France, but also by the fact that although evangelicalism had a foothold in the Kirk and among the seceders, the main evangelical excitement lay among people outside the structure of Church and State built up so carefully during the ascendancy of the Moderates. Although the accusations of Jacobinism hurled at the Anti-Slavery Society and the missionary societies were clearly unjustified, what was true was that these movements, despite the patronage of men at the centre of affairs like Wilberforce, did represent an attempt to achieve social and political influence, if not power, by a much wider section of the Scottish population.

The reaction to this was certainly fierce. Professor Robison of Edinburgh University attributed such wild revolutionary, indeed bloodthirsty, words to Robert Haldane that the latter was forced to demand an apology in such terms that Robison thought he was being challenged to a duel.[10] The General Assembly was only marginally less extreme in its utterance than had been the good Professor. At its meeting in 1799, the Assembly passed an Act which closed presentations to benefices to all except those regularly licensed by a Presbytery of the Church of Scotland. This was to block any presentation of an English Dissenter for a living. The same Act also forbade any communion with, or granting of the freedom of the pulpit to, any except those regularly licensed. This closed pulpits to other Scottish

Presbyterian clergy as well as to visiting English preachers whether of the Established Church or Dissenters. This particular clause may have been aimed at the Cambridge don and preacher Charles Simeon and the other regular evangelical Anglican visiting preacher, Rowland Hill.[11]

At the same Assembly a Pastoral letter was approved and ordered to be read in all the parish churches of Scotland. This formal statement of the official position of the Kirk began with a bitter attack on the French Revolution and on any in Britain who wished to change the present constitution of the United Kingdom. It called on the people of Scotland thus:

> Instead of being captivated by that empty sound of liberty, which has proved to be only another name for anarchy or tyranny, let zeal for true religion ever remain in your minds, united with attachment to our happy constitution, and with loyalty to that gracious Sovereign with whom Providence has blessed us.

Remembering the international situation and the recent happenings in France, these opening paragraphs were perhaps understandable. However, the letter went on to reveal that its main target was not any overt Jacobin conspiracy but was the Society for the Propagation of the Gospel at Home.

The Pastoral Letter accused the servants of the Society of being agents of social and political disorder. They had set up their Sunday Schools, preached to open-air gatherings, organised prayer meetings in private homes, all without the authority of 'presbytery, minister or Heritors'. The Pastoral went on to accuse the Society's servants of

> committing in these schools the religious instruction of youth to ignorant persons, altogether unfit for such an important charge who presumed not only to catechise, but also to expound the Scriptures; or to persons notoriously disaffected to the civil constitution of the country; and connecting these schools with certain secret meetings, in which, as we are informed, every person is bound not to spread abroad anything that is said or done at the meeting, to the prejudice of any of the members; into which no one is admitted without the consent of the whole of the members; and which keep correspondence with other societies in the neighbourhood.[13]

Here the Assembly is extending its opposition to include the Foreign Missionary Societies because of their extra-ecclesiastical status. This condemnation of lay preaching and lay Sunday School teaching on the grounds that it had not been authorised by the appropriate authorities (where would this have left Calvin or Knox?) was deliberately linked in the text to political disaffection. This was understandable in the year 1799, when minds were deeply concious of the Presbyterian-led rising of the United Irishmen, among whose leaders who were executed was Henry Joy MacCracken, one of the founders of the Sunday School movement in Belfast. The evangelical movement in the eyes of churchmen of the day appeared to verge on the treasonous. Indeed this view is made explicit in the paragraph which reads,

> Much reason there is to suspect, that those who openly profess their enmity to our ecclesiastical establishment are no friends to our civil construction; and that

the name of liberty is abused by them, as it has been by others, into a cover for secret democracy and anarchy.

Even more extraordinary than this bizarre performance by the Established Church was the alacrity with which its traditional opponents, the various 'Seceder' churches, also condemned lay preaching and the new Sunday Schools. Indeed the General Associate Synod beat the Auld Kirk to the punch and condemned them at their annual meeting in 1798. The fear and suspicions with which the evangelical movement, notably in its anti-slavery and foreign missionary activities was viewed, had been developing for some time. As early as 1796, the Cameronians, the most radical of the old Calvinist anti-establishment groups, had excommunicated some of its members for attending a service where the minister had preached a sermon calling for support on behalf of the newly formed LMS. The antagonism reached its peak with the preparation of a bill to be laid before Parliament in 1800 which would have gravely inhibited the Methodist Church and sunday schools in England. It also would have had the same effect on the work of the Haldanites in Scotland as well as the supporters of the LMS in both countries. However, the influence of Wilberforce on Pitt was sufficient to prevent the Bill reaching the House. It was the threat of this bill that elicited from Robert Haldane his *Address to the Public concerning Political Opinions*.

Opposition to the work of the Haldanes by no means ceased with the lifting of this cloud. Typical of the continuing tension was the action of the Secession Church in deposing its leading minister in the north, George Cowie of Huntly, for allowing James Haldane to preach from his pulpit. This is yet another intersection of the conflicts of these times with the life of John Philip, for Cowie was to become his close friend.

It was during this period of intense opposition that the Haldanes took the first steps which led to the creation of the modern Congregationalist and Baptist denominations in Scotland. The first step was the creation in 1798 of the Circus in Little King Street, Edinburgh. This was a meeting-house modelled on similar centres, usually called 'tabernacles', which had been built in England a generation earlier. Sunday and week-day preaching services were to be maintained in the Circus by a succession of preachers from any denomination so long as they were evangelicals. Anyone and everyone could come to these services and there were no seat rents. The Circus on its own was an interesting evangelistic venture but when the Haldanes subsequently opened similar centres in Glasgow, Huntly, Thurso, Wick and Dundee, a new denomination was well on the way to being formed and when in each of these centres congregations were formed which deliberately adopted a Congregationalist form of policy, then the deed was done.

The new Church was full of vigour and spread rapidly. However, it soon split in two over the issue of infant baptism. It was the ever-seeking, ever-questioning Haldanes who themselves led the Baptist break-away and aligned them with an existing group of churches, 'The Old Baptists of Scotland', to form in 1810 the new Baptist Union of Scotland. The recently formed Congregationalist Church continued to grow despite this drastic amputation. Its leader, who replaced the Haldanes, was Greville Ewing. He had been one of the few ministers of the Kirk who had evinced concern for the new missionary enthusiasm for outreach both at home and abroad. He had preached at the Circus and supported the London Missionary Society and, as a result of the increasing tension at the turn of the century, had resigned his ministry in the Church of Scotland in order to serve the new Congregationalist body.

Evangelicalism or Revival was sweeping the English-speaking world at that time, so it was not surprising that Scotland was no exception. However, despite the theological unity of this movement throughout the English-speaking world, the groups that provided the most positive response to it in any society varied according to the nature of that society. In Scotland, the existence of a newly expanded and prosperous middle class together with a large new literate and prosperous class of skilled artisans provided a receptive audience. Most of those, and they were many, influenced by evangelicalism stayed in the Auld Kirk and made much more powerful an already existing 'popular' party which eventually came to dominate the Assembly and whose attempts to end patronage and regain for congregations their right to call their own ministers eventually led to the Disruption of 1843. Others brought new vigour to the traditional 'secession' kirks which, partly at least, culminated in the creation of the United Presbyterian Church in 1847. They also created two entirely new ecclesiastical bodies in Scotland, the Congregational and Baptist Churches. The membership of these two new bodies was drawn from that stratum of Scottish society where as we have seen it is difficult to decide where the boundary between prosperous working class and lower middle class lay.

John Philip's parents were members of the Auld Kirk.[14] We know very little about them except that his father was a weaver, since there is little material extant for this period of Philip's life. However, as we have seen, the books that were kept in the Philip's home show that his father was not an 'enthusiast'. However, some of Philip's uncles were—indeed they were members of the Glassite Church. The Philip family then conformed to the pattern of the weavers who tended to be either non-religious or 'independents'.

John seems to have finished school at eleven, when he started to learn his father's trade. His standard of education must have been reasonably high, because Macmillan reports that at the age of fifteen he contemplated a West Indian clerkship. However, he went instead to live with one of his Glassite uncles at Leven where presumably he finished his weaving apprenticeship. Then in 1794 he changed the direction of his life by going to Dundee as a clerk in one of the new spinning mills there. Indeed he soon became manager of the mill making the transition from the clearly working class, if prosperous, status of weaver to spinning mill manager.

During all this time, the three main sources we have to his early life all agree that he continued to read avidly and to add to his formal education by attending evening classes at an 'academy'. It also seems that while in Leven, under the influence of the Glassites, the young man seems to have come to hold a deeply serious evangelical faith. The first noteworthy expression of this was his eagerness to enter into a public debate with an 'infidel' shortly after his arrival in Dundee. He was therefore ripe and ready for plucking by the Haldanite revival.

Wardlaw says that the Reverend Thomas Durant was the key influence on Philip in this period, both in terms of helping to form his new beliefs and also in steering him towards the ministry of the Congregational church and going to the college at Hoxton in England for training.[15] This influence may be confirmed by John's naming his third son Thomas Durant Philip. Be that as it may, Macmillan, relying on the biographical fragment composed by Philip's son Thomas Durant and his grandson, Frederick, doesn't mention Durant at all. He says

> John Philip himself came under the influence of the Haldanes, the founders of Scottish Congregationalism; on their advice he betook himself in 1799 to the Hoxton Academy of the English Independents.[16]

There is no necessary contradiction in the two accounts. Durant was an agent of the Haldanes, a local leader of Congregationalism in Dundee, but remained loyal to Congregationalism when the Haldanes went over to Baptism. Wardlaw, a staunch Congregationalist, was probably still remembering with bitterness the Haldanes' actions which led to the creation of a separate Baptist denomination and preferred to ignore their influence.

Whatever significance we attach to the influence of Durant as compared with that of the Haldanes is less important than the fact that this up-and-coming young man decided to enter the Christian ministry. His evangelical faith had already got him into difficulties apparently. Soon after his promotion to be manager of the mill in Dundee he had resigned over his inability to persuade the owners to allow him to pursue the policies he believed to be appropriate. These seem to have been to do with the employment of children in the mill, problems over work conditions for women and over wage rates. This shows that in early life he was already the strong and determined character who would arouse so much trouble in the Cape.

Macmillan says that after his resignation he was soon doing well as 'an independent master'. This is however very misleading, and is indeed a product of Macmillan's misunderstanding of Scotland at the turn of the eighteenth and nineteenth centuries. There was no way in which Philip, fresh from a handloom weaver's home, after only a few months as a power mill manager, could have got together the capital to become the owner of a factory of any kind. The biographical fragment on which Macmillan relied was written by Philip's son and grandson, who had lived almost all their lives in South Africa, and were ignorant of the social and economic conditions of pre-1815 Scotland. When they said their father became an independent master and when this was taken up by Macmillan, the impression is given of middle-class entrepreneurship. This was not a deliberate falsehood but the product of an ignorance which is understandable and excusable. However the phrase could only mean that when Philip resigned he went back to his, and his father's, old trade, weaving. As a handloom weaver, he certainly was independent, and the owner of his loom and almost certainly of the house in which it was and in which he lived, but as such he was a prosperous skilled artisan and not a middle-class entrepreneur like the owner or owners of the mill from whose service he had resigned.

It is true that at this time he seems to have been considering the possibility of becoming a minister, but this is nowhere mentioned as a source of his difficulties with his managerial post. It was another six months after his return to his old trade that he made his decision to become a minister and went off to Hoxton.

Why then did he quit his post in Dundee? Was he dramatically ahead of his time in attitudes to child labour? Was it his vivid new evangelical conviction that drove him to this decision or was it his strong will that drove him to fight to the bitter end if he was opposed in what he considered right? His confidence in the correctness of his convictions and his stubborn will undoubtedly played a part in his resignation but what provoked the crisis?

If it was the employment of children that provoked the conflict, then it must be said that, at that time, very many equally devout evangelicals had no such scruples. Indeed David Dale attempted to maximise the number of women and children who worked in his power mills because of their docility, as well as their cheapness. Admittedly, in Dale's case, although his conditions of employment were, to modern eyes, very far from satisfactory, for the time they were good. Dale was considered by his contemporaries as a philanthropist because of the schooling and the clean accommodation he provided for his workforce. Philip must have known about Dale and similar model factory and village developments of the time with which Dundee compared unfavourably. However, Dundee's somewhat worse conditions were only marginally worse, as we can see from Professor Smout

> . . . all the children, irrespective of whether they were nine years old or sixteen were working a day of inhuman length. Twelve hours was general, fourteen was fairly common in the east of Scotland especially and there were instances in flax mills of even longer hours worked in a trade rush . . . [this was Dundee]. Two breaks in a day were normally allowed to permit the workers to eat [there were, of course, no works canteens, but they brought food with them and were sometimes allowed to eat it on the premises]. A six day week was worked and there were generally two days holiday a year apart from Sundays.[17]

Dundee mills were not the 'models' produced by Dale and by others at the time, and that might account for a desire in the young up-and-coming ex-weaver to make changes. However, would the frustration of these ideas have been enough on their own to account for his resignation so soon after his promotion? As we shall see again in the next chapter, Philip was a devotee of Smithian economics. He was also a perfect example of the enormous possibilities of social as well as financial advancement opened up in this period of industrial development, a perfect example of a Samuel Smiles style advancement through sobriety and hard work. Why then deliberately go back to the clearly artisan role of a handloom weaver?

None of the sources on Philip's early life give any convincing explanation. Indeed they report the fact rather than explain it. One possible explanation which appears when one looks closely at the particular background of the life of the handloom weavers of Scotland at that time, is that the conditions in the mill profoundly shocked the young man. As we have seen, the weaver and his family all worked very hard. However, they controlled the rhythm of their work and the amounts and times of their leisure which distinguished their life style and their culture from that of the mill workers. To the skilled artisans, among whom the weavers were the elite, the pattern of life of the mill was a kind of slavery—it was a humiliation which only severe hardship could drive them to accept. Now when we look at John Philip, a young weaver, still seeking to educate himself, an enthusiastic evangelical involved in the circles that supported the London Missionary Society and the anti-slavery movement, promotion to managership of a mill must have seemed clearly the due reward of sobriety and hard work, but the actual conditions he met in the life of the mill on the other hand could only be abhorrent. It is also possible that his interpretation of the thought of Adam Smith did not square with the economic belief of the owners.

This incident is a comparatively small one in Philip's dramatic life, yet it is of enormous importance because it enables us to gain an insight into what made John Philip who he was, and is of fundamental importance in trying to understand what he was attempting to achieve in South Africa. His understanding of history and society was based on Adam Smith's understanding of the world which was apparently confirmed by the experience of life in Scotland at the time. After all, the new prosperity which extended to most people in Scottish society had come about as a result of the new developments of laissez-faire economics freed from the old feudal restraints. The general good of everyone seemed to be served by all seeking to work hard and follow their economic opportunities. As we have seen, the Scotland of his young manhood was prosperous as she had never been before and a massive new social grouping as yet still not clearly differentiated between skilled artisan and middle-class groups was creating a new Scotland. It all seemed good and confirmed Smith as the prophet of prosperity, peace and social harmony. The mills gave just a hint of what lay just around the corner, when after the development of certain industrial processes, heavy industry, based on massive factories and mills, would come to dominate the Scottish economy, taking away the brief heyday of the burghs, and making Glasgow both the 'second city of the Empire' and the biggest single concentration of social deprivation in Europe. Philip, living as he did in the Cape from 1819 onwards, simply did not see this development, and the hint that the power mills gave him about the future development of life under laissez-faire capitalism was not interpreted by him as such.

For Philip, education, evangelical Christianity and freedom from feudal restraints had created the prosperity of the Scotland of his youth as Smith said it should. The same combination of factors could do the same for all humankind. Slavery was exactly the kind of feudal restraint on economic developments and on individual enterprise and development that had kept Scotland a poverty-stricken province of Europe for so long. When freed from this by agricultural and commercial enterprise, then the Golden Age of the prosperous burghs, of the weavers and shoemakers, as well as the entrepreneurs, and the Golden Age of the Scottish Enlightenment all followed. This was the 'Christianity and civilisation' about which Fowell Buxton later coined the phrase, but which was firmly grasped by Philip from his early manhood, shaped by the ideas of the Scottish Enlightenment which appeared to be confirmed by what was actually happening in the Scotland of the time.

Only six months after his resignation and return to the weaver's trade, Philip went off to Hoxton to train for the ministry of the Congregational Church. At Hoxton, he embarked on a three-year course which was the wont in those days in such 'Independent' establishments.[18] The course contained a great deal of practical work, which, at Hoxton, was done mainly in London Sunday Schools and in neighbouring congregations. At the completion of his seminary course, he was called to be the assistant minister of the congregation at Newbury in Berkshire. He only ministered there for two years before accepting a call to Aberdeen.

The call came from what Wardlaw refers to as 'the Mother Church of the Congregational Union of Scotland'.[19] This phrase of Wardlaw's is a strange one because it was clearly the various 'tabernacles' set up by the Haldanes and Greville Ewing which were the 'mothers' of the Union. Again one suspects Wardlaw's anti-Haldane bias. If the phrase has any meaning, it is that the Aberdeen congregation was the oldest of the congregations which later formed the Union and unlike most of the others had a pedigree independent of the Haldanes.

The congregation was an almost perfect example of the developments in Scottish society in the 1790s we have been discussing. It was created by nine men who no longer felt at home in traditional Scottish Presbyterianism, whether of the Established or Seceder type. They were classically the kind of men who had become prosperous in this period of growth and did not fit into traditional Scottish structures of Church and State. The leader was George Moir, a hosier. Two others were of the new middle class, another hosier and a man simply listed as a 'merchant'. Two were weavers and thus clearly skilled artisan and four others were on the borderline. Without a great deal more detailed information one cannot decide where their placing in the gradations of class should be—again a perfect example of this group, these were a dyer and the three 'shipbuilders' who might have been either entrepreneurs or craftsmen.

They had been convinced that Congregationalism had been the original polity of the primitive Church by reading King's *Inquiry into the Constitution, Discipline, Unity and Worship of the Primitive Church*. They were ready to be so convinced precisely because they were men of some education, wealth and influence as well as real faith, for whom the Scotland of the Moderates simply had no place. Their church was exactly and essentially 'democratical' as the good Professor Robison and the Fathers of the General Assembly feared about this whole tendency, but not in any Jacobin way as these critics asserted about all such religious enterprise. The prosperity of Scottish Lowland society can be seen from the achievements of the group of nine aided by their first followers, for they were able to complete the erection of a meeting house to seat 1,200 people in 1798 and this not much more than a year after the creation of the congregation. Their first minister was an Englishman, William Stephens of Bingley, who served only three years before being called to work with James Haldane at the Circus. In 1804 the congregation called John Philip to be their minister.

Before Philip arrived in Aberdeen some severe strains had developed in the congregation. This was not at all unusual among these groups of articulate, literate and independent people, but the split was not about believers' Baptism, which, under the influence of the Haldanes, was beginning to divide the young Congregationalist movement elsewhere. It is not clear from the scant records what was at issue, but other than believers' Baptism, the other great debating point at the time was the difficulty that many strict Calvinists felt about the implicit, if not explicit, arminianism of the evangelical commitment to mission both at home and, perhaps especially, abroad. Whatever it was originally, the difference came to centre on the call to Philip, which one of the two groups in the congregation refused to accept.

Philip spent the first two years of his ministry in Aberdeen trying to win them over. It is important to note this because those who have written about Philip have all agreed about his 'self-will'. Even Wardlaw, an emotional hagiographer, says of him that he '. . . could seem arbitrary, even self-willed'.[20] This characteristic could just as easily be called tough minded and independent, but whatever we call it, Philip unmistakably had it. However aggressive or tough as he was when he believed himself in the right, Philip still spent nearly two years attempting to win back the recalcitrant faction and to restore unity to the congregation.

At the end of this time, when his attempts at reconciliation had failed, he decided on a course of action which was certainly as controversial and dramatic as his approach to difficulties in South Africa. He decided to dissolve the congregation and to start afresh with those who would accept his ministry. At least that is how his actions are described in Escott's 'official' history.[21] However, in a little history of the Aberdeen congregation[22] the author insists that a perusal of the congregation's minute books presents a somewhat different picture.

> The dissentients exaggerated their own importance by declaring that three fourths of the members were disaffected. In order to test the value of these assertions, Dr. Philip adopted a very drastic course. In May, 1806, he dissolved the church! The doctor, who is admitted by his friends to have been arbitrary and self-willed, has always been credited with the responsibility of this unique proceeding. It was really the result of an agreement with the church. The first minute book entered after the recovery of the Minute Book makes this clear.[23]

Philip's actions then, were characteristically drastic but not without consultation with others. When will one come to the end of the series of writers who feel they have to respect 'arbitrary and self-willed' as a shorthand for Philip's complicated character, simply because some 'friend', almost certainly Wardlaw, once admitted it?

In this case Philip's ploy worked. Of the 277 adult members of the congregation, 247 stayed with Philip to form the new congregation ready to accept Philip as their pastor. He then entered on a ministry of great influence, not only over his congregation, but with effect throughout Aberdeen and the Northeast.

The record of his ministry in Aberdeen is not as detailed as that of his predecessor or his immediate successor, for he insisted that the very detailed minute book of the congregation be not kept during his tenure of the charge. He said that it made the congregation too much like a secular society or a commercial company. However, Bulloch's history plus a memoir, written to mark his death by Robert Philip (no relation) who had been a student at Aberdeen during John's ministry and had remained a life-long friend, do give us important glimpses of this period in Aberdeen. Ralph Wardlaw's official commissioned and published funeral oration is of no use in this, as in so many other regards, largely because Wardlaw gives the impression of not having any first-hand knowledge of, or any real sympathy with, John Philip.

John Philip was a popular preacher at a time when there was a large and growing public in Scotland for evangelical preaching. A measure of the popularity of his preaching beyond his congregation is a story of how, on one particular evening, the sash of the window behind the pulpit had to be removed to allow him into his place at all; this in a meeting house which seated 1,200 and with a congregation that was never made up of more than about 500 adults in his time as minister.

His popularity extended throughout the Northeast, where he preached in many towns and villages, not only as an evangelical attempting to raise the spiritual life of the area but also as a fervent supporter of the London Missionary Society on whose behalf he constantly attempted to raise both money and volunteers for service overseas. It was in these journeys to the Northeast that he became the close friend of George Cowie, the deposed Secession minister.

There are certain parallels between these years and those he was to spend in South Africa. The Northeast was a separate province of Scotland, essentially Lowland in character and in its economy, yet cut off from the mainstream of Lowland life dominated by Edinburgh and Glasgow. During his ministry of the First Congregational Church, he became a leading member of this provincial society, numbering among his friends Professors at the University as well as leading lawyers, magistrates and the principal businessmen. This must have made his transition to the Cape an easy one, going from one small, largely autonomous provincial society, to another. However, in Cape Town he was to run up against aristocratic English representatives of the Imperial government for whom there were no equivalents in the Northeast Scotland of his day.

The very formal and stuffy panegyric by Ralph Wardlaw and the immediate and intensely personal memoir by Robert Philip are agreed on at least one thing about John Philip's ministry in Aberdeen. As Robert Philip puts it, 'his influence was dreaded by the Bigots of all churches'. We have to consider carefully what this means. Classical Scots 'Moderates' of the late eighteenth century would have seen Philip's 'enthusiasm' and evangelical- ism as bigotry as would many proponents of the liberal theology of the end of the nineteenth and beginning of the twentieth century. What 'bigotry' then feared the influence of John Philip in these first decades of the nineteenth century?

The bigotry that feared him was the bigotry that his fellow missionary- orientated evangelicals were opposing throughout the English-speaking world. This was the bigotry of denominational loyalty, the bigotry of confessionalism that prevented men interpreting Scripture except according to definitions laid down in the sixteenth or seventeenth centuries. This was the bigotry of the Secession churches that led them to reject Whitefield after they had invited him to preach in Scotland, when he refused to preach only at gatherings of the 'elect'. This was the bigotry that made the 'auld licht' groups in the various non-established Presbyterian churches in Scotland cling to the letter of the seventeenth-century covenants and the Westminster Confession and the different bigotry that led the General Assembly of the Church of Scotland to reject the very idea of 'foreign missions' in 1796 and to go on opposing the missionary and anti-slavery movements because of their 'democratical' character.

John Philip, like the group of evangelical leaders in the United States gathered around James Finney, was indifferent to the classic 'Covenants' and Confessions of the seventeenth century. His attitude could be summed up in Finney's famous retort to the challenge thrown out to him by the orthodox Calvinist churchmen of Boston as to his fidelity to the Confessions, 'Did we get rid of Popes to replace them by paper popes?'

Evangelicalism did not care about the classical denominational and confessional divides and conflicts. What mattered was personal allegiance to Jesus, reliance on the Bible and commitment to the spread of the Gospel. This was expressed so very clearly in the early days of the Haldane movement in Scotland when John Philip was first brought into the fold. The Haldanes were happy to receive the aid of Anglican preachers like Rowland Hill, Church of Scotland ministers like Greville Ewing as well as employing and training their own evangelists. Indeed it was one of these Anglican evangelicals, Rowland Hill, who summed up the two patterns of 'bigotry' in opposition to Philip and the movement he represented, when in his *Journal* he denounced the clergy of the Established Church in Scotland as sceptical and the Seceders as blindly intolerant.[24]

What were the positive aims of Philip's ministry? As an evangelical preacher he wanted to bring all his hearers into a warm personal faith in Jesus as their Saviour and to commit them to the spread of this good news about redemption from the power of sin and death to all humankind. He supported the work of the London Missionary Society himself and pointed to it as a channel of service which was an appropriate response to the good news of salvation. In order to further his mission Philip deliberately began a campaign to reach young people. After all, since he was spreading a view of, and response to, Christianity which was new for Protestantism, a new start seemed necessary. The later strong commitment of the main Presbyterian churches of Scotland to the missionary outreach of the Gospel must not divert us from seeing how un-missionary classical Scottish Calvinism was in the eighteenth century and how Calvinist dissenters and the Moderates who dominated the Kirk, bitterly opposed on so many issues, were united in their opposition to missions. In many ways the Haldanes' was a new gospel for Scotland and John Philip had become its principal proponent in the Northeast.

Our few sources on John Philip's years in Scotland are all agreed on the tremendous impact Philip made on young people, both men and women. He made his manse a meeting place for these young people, and he organised for them a series of discussion meetings of such a form that today we would probably refer to them as seminars.

> Reading young men found in Dr. Philip a sympathetic friend and a wise director of their studies. Indeed his house became a veritable seminary, and several who ultimately went into the mission field did not hesitate to say that they had *studied* under Dr. Philip.[25]

Robert Philip, while at Aberdeen University, was a regular member of these meetings in the manse and became a close personal friend of the minister. From his memoir, as well as Bulloch's short work, we learn of other departures from the traditional. First of all girls were encouraged to take part in these meetings, but even more striking, the members—boys or girls—were allowed to raise questions and topics themselves, and indeed were encouraged to propound their own ideas to be criticised by the group and its leader. This was a very unusual procedure in a day when professor as well as preacher was used to being the unchallenged solo performer from pulpit or rostrum, from whence they pronounced on all matters with unchallengeable magisterial authority. The unusual approach in Philip's class is described by Bulloch,

> It was customary for members of the class to propound questions, or to state difficulties arising in the course of Bible study. After hearing various opinions expressed by members it was no uncommon thing for Dr. Philip to turn to Miss Paul, before solving the crux himself and ask, 'Well, Margaret, what have you to say to this?'[26]

Many who attended these gatherings became distinguished men and women, both in Scotland and abroad, but we have no written evidence from them about Dr Philip, except the memoir of Robert Philip who remained in touch with his pastor for the rest of his life. This memoir is of great importance because it is one of the few sources left to us which give some insight into the personal opinions, likes, dislikes and prejudices of the Doctor.

However, even Robert's memoir tells us nothing about John's wife Jane

Ross, despite the fact that she was very very close to him, a close confidant and colleague as well as a wife. Jane was the daughter of an Aberdeen architect, whose whole family was converted by John Philip.[27]

They were married in 1809. After their arrival in Cape Town, she soon became deeply involved in mission affairs. Throughout she acted as unofficial treasurer of the London Missionary Society in South Africa and after 1830 until her death in 1847, she was the official 'agent' of the Paris Evangelical Mission there. Indeed Philip simply could not have achieved what he did without her—when he was away on one of his long treks she acted as the official London Missionary Society correspondent between the field and the Directors at home.

However, Robert Philip's testimony does give us one or two important insights that help us to understand Philip's approach to a number of the problems he faced in South Africa. It is from Robert's memoir that we learn that, however much John opposed the Seceders, the spiritual descendants of the Covenanters, for their bigoted confessionalism, he was inspired by the Covenanters themselves.

> He was not exactly an antiquarian: for neither the old abbeys nor the ruined cathedrals of Scotland had any charm for him, if I may judge from the rebukes he gave me for my frequent moonlight visits to them. But let him only reach a hill grave of a Covenanter, or a Glen where the Covenanters had worshipped and communed at midnight, and his spirit was soon entranced with triumph in their memory.[28]

The Covenanters, it is worth recalling, were deeply religious men and women, whose burning loyalty to a particular Christian vision led them into political action and eventually armed rebellion.

Again, from these reminiscences, we learn that John had no great admiration for the medieval Church, not even for the Celtic Church. This is in stark contrast with many Scots Protestants, both then and later, who have tried to distinguish the Celtic from the early medieval Church and see the former as some kind of early 'Protestantism' suppressed by wicked Rome.

What is very important, indeed perhaps so important as to be a key to understanding Philip's overall strategy in South Africa, is his fascination with Classical Rome and Scotland's pre-Christian Celtic past. This fascination had within it a certain ambiguity—Rome was admired for her even-handed justice and her spread of civilisation, yet Philip also had a pride and admiration of those who had resisted her sway. As Robert Philip reports it

> It was, however, among Druidic and Roman antiquities, that he philosophised most freely. Indeed he had studied Druidism, as well as estimated the influence of the Ceasars
>
> > When Rome leant here
> > On her sentinel spear
> > And loud was her Clarion's blast
>
> Accordingly, although he would point in triumph to the northern mountains, whose echoes never answered her Clarion, and whose summits never enthroned

her Eagles, I have always felt that he would not have been sorry had they ruled there as they did in Kent and Yorkshire; so clearly did he see and show what the country owed to Imperial Rome, and how little to Papal Rome.[29]

We can see a straight continuity between his admiration for Roman justice and civilisation and his campaign for equal civil rights for all British subjects within the Cape Colony. *Civis Britannicus sum* and *civis Romanus sum* seemed to have a direct connection with his mind. Rome had created a great multi-national Empire where all who were citizens were equally treated and where at its best there was efficient administration of government and equal justice for all. Could Britain not do as well as Rome had done and indeed did not Christianity reinforce the demand that she should?

Furthermore did not Philip's insistence on the virtues of Khoi society before the destructive impact of unjust White rule, together with his passionate concern to preserve the integrity, if not the independence, of the Xhosa and Sotho peoples, relate as much to his interest in the old Celtic Scotland as to the influence of the 'noble savage' image which was so widespread in the literature of the Enlightenment?

We shall see later how the ambiguity of feeling that is reflected in this quotation from Robert Philip is reflected also in John Philip's whole approach to the problems of the Cape Colony and the peoples on its frontier. If a people were destroyed by unjust foreign rule as the Khoi were, then Christianity had no chance of growing among them. However, a just imperial authority, like that of Rome at its best, could provide the necessary new foundation upon which both Christianity and civilisation might be built up among just such a people.

In Aberdeen, then, John Philip, though a dissenting minister, had built up for himself a position of some prominence in the society of northeast Scotland. He was the principal promoter of the interests of the London Missionary Society throughout the region, in addition to being a popular guest preacher in Huntly, Nairn, Peterhead and his own Aberdeen. His friends in Aberdeen felt that they wanted to make some sort of public mark to recognise this situation. These friends included Professors Tulloch, Dewar and Ewing of Aberdeen University. These men, with the support of several local ministers of the Kirk,[30] initiated procedures for the award of the LLD by Aberdeen University. This was, however, frustrated by opposition within the Senate. This was understandable since Philip was not an uncontroversial figure and tension was still very high in the Church of Scotland between evangelicals and Moderates.[31] They then turned to Glasgow to discover that Glasgow University had recently enacted legislation barring any clergy but those of the Kirk from receiving honorary degrees. Philip's friends persisted and turned to Princeton University which had especially close connection with Scotland. Princeton University then awarded him the honorary degree of Doctor of Divinity in 1820. Meanwhile, however, the Directors of the London Missionary Society had also decided to obtain for Philip some kind of public honour and they approached Columbia University, New York, which awarded him the honorary degree of DD some months before the Princeton award.

This initiative by the Directors of the Society would seem to have been part of their campaign to persuade Philip to leave Aberdeen and help them deal with the crisis that had arisen in South Africa. During 1817, it was borne in on the Directors through the correspondence of their agents in South Africa and by complaints from Governmental sources, that the mission in South Africa was in danger of collapse, and even of possible forcible closure by the authorities in the Colony. Something urgent had to be done to drastically reform the organisation of the Society's work there, as well as to restore the morale and discipline of the staff.

The Directors, as we have seen, decided to send out a commission of two to assess the situation and plan the necessary reforms. One of the Commissioners should stay on as a Resident Director of the Society to represent the Board in the field and to ensure that the necessary reforms were carried out.

It was decided that one member of the two-man commission should be John Campbell who had been a close associate of the Haldanes in their initial campaigns in Scotland. This was, as remarked before, in some ways a strange choice, for although Campbell had a knowledge of the staff and of the country due to his service on the Commission of 1813 which had been charged with reorganising the mission in the difficult period after the death of Dr van der Kemp, it was also clear that the work of the 1813 commission had been a failure.

It was the second member of the commission who was to stay on as resident Director, and the Society initially advertised for volunteers to fill this vital post. However, in the letter sent to John Philip advertising this post, on 10 October 1817, Burder, the Secretary of the London Missionary Society, enclosed a personal note asking Philip to apply. This was followed a month later by a letter signed jointly by Burder and the Society's Treasurer, Hankey. This letter is worth quoting in some detail because it makes clear, first, that they wanted Philip for the job despite the general advertisement and second, because it makes clear once and for all the remit Philip was given. This was to be Resident Director at the Cape and not to be a missionary in the ordinary sense. This gives the lie to those writers since, and to some of Philip's colleagues at the time, who accused him of arrogating to himself episcopal powers.

> Mr. Campbell however intends, after effecting with the brother who shall accompany him whatever is practicable for the Settlement of the Society's affairs, to return to England. But it appears to the Directors necessary that another Brother should accompany Mr. Campbell, to assist him in the arrangement of the affairs that relate to the several stations, and when he has accomplished that work to abide at or near Cape Town, as the Agent, or Superintending Director, on behalf of the Board of Directors at home; to inspect all the affairs and proceedings of the Missionaries; to see that all the Regulations agreed upon are observed; to afford them his advice in cases of difficulty, and to transact any negotiations that may be necessary between the Missionaries, or the Directors, and the Colonial Government at the Cape.

The Directors, Sir, having looked around them among the various ministers of the Gospel in England and Scotland, who evinced their zeal for the cause of Missions, have directed their eyes to you, as being, in every point, in their judgment, a fit and proper person to be their Representative in these momentous concerns; and they have, after solemn prayer and mature consideration, unanimously, and most cordially resolved, and do hereby communicate to you that resolution, that you are earnestly requested to undertake for them, or rather for our dear and common Lord and Master, this labour of love, and go forth in His name, to promote His blessed cause in South Africa.[32]

Philip's immediate reply, to the first enquiry, is, in style, typical of evangelicals of that day. He is quite clear that he and his wife are ready to respond to the Society's request if they can be sure that it is the Lord's will. he wrote on 24 October 1817

I have trembled, and prayed, and con . . . [illegible] with my dear partner over the contents of your last letter, and the result is, if we can be certain it is the will of God, we are both willing to go to South Africa, and to live and die there. We are the Lord's, and we have often said to him that we are his, and that we were willing to serve him in any way or in any place he might prescribe or point out to us, and if it is his will to let us see our way clear, we are ready to leave home and friends, and to go to the utmost ends of the Earth for his name's sake.[22]

However, his congregation in Aberdeen and many of his friends there and in the surrounding area were far from convinced that this was the Lord's will, and their importuning troubled him greatly. On 29 November he wrote to the London Missionary Society officials again, saying that he was greatly concerned about his replacement in Aberdeen. He explained that this was not simply a matter of supplying a pastor for one congregation but someone who was to 'carry on the work of God in the extensive and destitute country which lies between Aberdeen and Inverness'. He was clearly very troubled and was on the verge of asking the Society to look elsewhere for their Resident Director.

At least two well-subscribed petitions were sent by his congregation to the Society asking the Director to desist from their attempts to recruit Philip.

On 5 December, Philip wrote to Burder to inform him that several local ministers of the Kirk had joined together to dissuade him from accepting the Society's offer. Indeed things got to such a pass that on 14 January 1818, the Congregation formally notified the Society that they would withdraw all support from the Society if it succeeded in persuading their minister to go to South Africa.

By this time Philip was so upset by the proceedings that he wrote to Hankey that he could not go against the express wishes of his congregation. He went on to name possible alternative candidates for the post—men, he insisted, who could do the job as well as he, and, in addition, extricate both the Directors and himself from this predicament.

The Directors, however, did not give up, but persevered in pressing both the congregation and Philip to agree to their request. They insisted that they were the vehicle of the true 'call' to Philip.

At last, in July 1818, the congregation gave its assent to their minister's going to South Africa, although it was not until September of that year that they finally accepted that this was a final break and not simply a two-year secondment, indeed as late as February 1819 the deacons were contemplating keeping his church vacant in case Philip might return.

4

John Philip and Civil Rights

> His reorganisation of the mission did not, however, meet with universal approval. Robert Moffat, for example, was strongly opposed to the office of Superintendent and the episcopal powers with which Philip had vested himself. Until 1825 the two got on fairly well but after that Philip's increasing involvement with politics greatly embittered Moffat.[1]

This article on Philip in the *Dictionary of South African Biography* illustrates very clearly how John Philip still provokes strong partisanship more than one hundred years after his death. A little farther on the author of the piece says of Philip's *Researches* that the book's main characteristics are the numerous contradictions and false statements, which have since been conclusively exposed by researchers.

The burden of the writer's intention is unambiguous—Philip was a dishonest commentator on South African affairs and that while holding the office of Superintendent previously held by van der Kemp and Read, he arrogated to himself powers contrary to the policy and tradition of the London Missionary Society; further, his involvement in politics was a deviation from his calling.

The latter charge is one which will underlie most of the chapter about Philip's campaign for the granting of civil rights to all 'free persons of colour'. The other charges can be dealt with immediately.

Let us look first at the accusation of the untrustworthiness of the *Researches*. Despite its title this two-volume work was not an academic book but a piece of propaganda written in the heat of bitter controversy. In it Philip aimed to clear the name of van der Kemp and to persuade the British public that the Imperial government had to reform its administration of the Cape Colony if that Colony was to be governed according to British traditions of justice. In the narrative there are many stories of ill-treatment of the Khoi and San peoples. These Philip gathered from the papers held at Bethelsdorp and from many informants—Khoi, missionary and others. A number of these stories have been challenged by historians and a number may have been inaccurate or at least open to other interpretation. However, the main thrust of the argument of his book has not been gainsaid, that is that the Khoi, San and Bastard populations of the Colony had not got the basic civil rights due to subjects of His Majesty and that they were often badly mistreated. We have already referred to reports by British and Dutch government officials about 'dreadful crimes' committed against the indigenous inhabitants of the Colony.[2] Philip's aim was not to decry the trekboers as essentially evil men. On the contrary his aim was to show that British policy created a situation where, given human nature, injustice flourished.

In contrast with Philip, the author of the article in the *DSAB* was not supposed to be writing a propaganda piece in the midst of bitter political controversy but a sober historical essay. Now, in any such essay there will always be judgements with which other historians will disagree, but this biographical article contains gross errors of fact which are not incidental to the argument, but unlike those he attributes to Philip, they are essential to his argument.

None is more unambiguous than his reference to 'the office of Superintendent and the episcopal powers with which Philip had vested himself'. This statement is central to the picture of Philip that the author is attempting to paint and is totally inaccurate. As we saw in the previous chapter, John Philip was not appointed as a missionary of the London Missionary Society nor was he initially appointed to the office of Superintendent held first by van der Kemp and then by James Read.[3] In 1819 John Philip was appointed a Director of the London Missionary Society and posted by his fellow Directors to be resident at the Cape to supervise the work both within and without the Colony on their behalf. Any 'episcopal' powers that he had he did not acquire for himself but were granted to him before he set foot on South African soil. His later widespread influence with the Rhenish, Paris and American Board Missions came from his appointment by their home authorities as adviser to their respective missions in the South African field.

The *DSAB* article is correct in asserting that Moffat opposed Philip after 1825 and that Moffat talked as if Philip was a power seeker gathering more and more authority into his hands contrary to London Missionary Society practice, but a perusal of the London Missionary Society archives shows Moffat to be wrong. The *DSAB* article repeats as fact Moffat's wholly inaccurate assertions.

It is true that Moffat complained about Philip's politics. Just what these 'politics' were is the central theme of this and the next chapters. In this chapter we will deal with Philip's campaign to change the structure of British rule for the benefit of the colony's indigenous and slave populations; in the next two, his attempts to affect British policy towards the peoples beyond the colonial frontier.

Of course, both Moffat in the past and the author of the *DSAB* article in the present, as well as many in between, seem to have a clear line in their minds between what is political and what is 'religious' or 'missionary' activity. These lines of division are almost always drawn on the basis of presuppositions about the nature of politics and of Christian missions that are as unacceptable to many today as they were to Philip. This kind of categorisation uses the adjectives 'religious', 'spiritual', 'missionary' of activities which do not challenge or disturb the social and political status quo; any action which tries to change the status quo is ipso facto not 'religious' or 'missionary' but political and in the best tradition of *1006 And All That*—'a bad thing'. This attitude was widely held in the nineteenth century and is still held by some in the twentieth. In the nineteenth century it came near to being the orthodoxy of the leadership of mainstream British

Protestantism—witness the official historian of the London Missionary Society writing in the 1890s. Although he backs Philip, the author accepts that missionaries should have nothing to do with politics as a basic and sound principle.

> No aphorism is more common in the press today, and no principle has been more steadily acted upon by the great missionary societies of Europe and America, than that missionaries, as such, have nothing to do with politics. Sound as this maxim may be, it is from the Christian standpoint inevitable that if the Government of a country allies itself with cruelty, social wrongs, and oppression, the Christian missionary, working within the sphere of such a Government, MUST find himself in active opposition to such things.[4]

From Philip's viewpoint almost nothing he did was ever 'political'. At no time in his life did he experience in Britain, or afterwards in South Africa, anything even resembling democratic politics. For him, a man of the eighteenth century, a century which in some senses did not end until 1832, politics meant the factional fighting over patronage within the aristocratic oligarchy who dominated the unreformed House of Commons. Even when he was working closely, first with Wilberforce, and then with Fowell Buxton, the leaders of the Anti-Slavery Society, though he saw their activities as in some sense political, he and they felt them to be clearly above what was ordinarily meant by politics. As he insisted in the preface of his *Researches* in 1828

> No question can be more simple and less incumbered with difficulties than the one before us. We ask for nothing unreasonable, nothing illegal, nothing new. We have nothing to say to politics. The question under discussion here is a mere question of civil rights.[5]

Of course this is somewhat disingenuous, a piece of special pleading in a work aimed at changing the opinions of the small literate public who could influence the Government and the House at that time. However, he is able to say what he does because of the common meaning of politics at the time. In that light the remark was fundamentally true. The politics of the 1820s were still those of faction fights between the Whig and Tory oligarchs and with this kind of politics Philip refused to have anything to do. As Lord Charles Somerset's biographer clearly shows, Brougham led a group of Whigs, supported by *The Times* and *The Morning Chronicle* in a vendetta against the noble Lord. Philip, despite his bitter differences with Somerset, at no point cooperated with them and on his return to the United Kingdom in 1826 he pointedly refused to join in the hue and cry then being raised against Somerset by his enemies.

Philip saw all that he did as being of a piece. He was committed to the Christianising of the non-Christian peoples of South Africa. This task was for him inextricably bound up with 'civilising' these same peoples. He did not agree with so many of the anti-mission majority of Christians in Britain, who, as Principal Hill had declared in the General Assembly in Scotland, believed that no one could be Christianised who had not first been civilised. However, along with the rest of the minority of Christians who did support missions, he saw Christianity and civilisation as inextricably bound together. People who truly became Christian were inevitably civilised in the process. The freeing of people from 'spiritual barbarism' had, as its inevitable concomitant, their social and economic uplift.

This union of ideas stemmed at least in part, as has often been pointed out, from the cultural myopia of most Europeans who believed their civilisation to be the summit of human achievement. However there was another factor, not so often commented upon in the literature, yet profoundly influencing the minds of the missionaries to keep these two ideas of Christianity and civilisation together. This was their own experience of life. Until well into the second half of the nineteenth century, the majority of missionaries were drawn from the artisan class and related groups in the lower middle class. These men and women had 'got on' because of their Christian faith and the dedication to hard work and the virtuous life that accompanied such faith in their milieu. In Africa they believed that in turn, the Khoi, the Griqua, the Xhosa could also 'get on' by following the same path.

Robert Gray's recent study, *The Labour Aristocracy in Victorian Edinburgh*, shows that the social groups from which the missionaries came accepted what came to be seen as the classic Victorian attitude of getting ahead through hard work and frugality, through self-help and maintaining a respectable lifestyle. They did this, however, not in slavish imitation of the upper classes but because these things were essential for their survival. Without them, these men and women feared they would slide back into the poverty and wretchedness that was the lot of most of the labouring poor in Britain in the nineteenth century. They were not then, for the most part, 'Uncle Toms' though some of course were Tory. On the contrary, Gray shows that they followed a pattern of life which was, as Gray asserts, following the communist theoretician Gramsci, the seed-bed from which the radical leadership of the working class sprang.

Philip, like so many of his colleagues, came from this group. They had 'got on' simply by becoming dedicated Christians. They accepted this philosophy with such little critical reflection that it was to them not a theoretical proposition but a basic self-evident fact of life. Philip and his like-minded colleagues were not socialists—most were not even 'radicals'—but their position was radical enough when face to face with the essentially feudal and hierarchic society of the Cape Colony. The British officials there were *ancien régime* Tories with a rigidly defined hierarchic understanding of society; the Boers, whether trekboer or akkerboer, were people who also saw society rigidly demarcated, in their case on the basis of slave and free, and of race, which was so closely associated with slavery. In contrast with this, even the most conservative of the London Missionary Society missionaries saw society as being fluid. Christianity and civilisation gave a human being the chance of advancement so that he or she could gain the position in society that his or her talents and virtues merited. Africans could enter this society and find their appropriate place in it through the inextricably entwined combination of Christianity and civilisation. This attitude made these missionaries unsympathetic observers of traditional African culture, but it made them receptive of Africans, whether Khoi, Xhosa, Tswana or Sotho, as individuals capable of advancement, of getting ahead. Thus the Scottish missionaries on the Tyhume river sent to Scotland in 1846 Tiyo Soga, who went on to graduate in Arts and Divinity at Glasgow University and return as a missionary to his own people and be the beau-ideal of their work. Soga and the Church Missionary Society Bishop, Adjai Crowther, were both products of this evangelical missionary understanding of the nature of conversion and the oneness of humanity. Soga did not live to suffer the indignities that were to be heaped on Crowther, as on many other African converts of the missions, from the men who in the last decades of the century rediscovered African culture with enthusiasm and felt that Africans should stay within it.

This egalitarianism of evangelicalism in the first half of the nineteenth century was based entirely on an individualistic understanding of humanity, and it was also deeply influenced by the thought of Adam Smith. Curtin in his *Image of Africa* has delineated very precisely this 'conversionist' attitude to culture and humankind. Philip and the men of the London Missionary Society shared this 'conversionist' outlook. Too often when this period of the nineteenth century is discussed, it is distorted because the writer looks at the period from the perspective of the late Victorian period or of the early twentieth century. By that time the struggle of the labouring classes had come to be one against the middle classes, who had come to power on the success of free enterprise capitalism and free trade. However, in the first fifty years of the nineteenth century in South Africa that was not the nature of the struggle. In the Cape Colony, the landless Khoi were trapped in a society which was slave orientated in its thinking and structures, ruled by *ancien régime* Tories. In that context, in a society at that stage of development, the ideas of Adam Smith were a progressive and radical force. Philip along with his allies in the mission like Read and Wright had to be involved in politics so long as the structure of Cape Society prevented their converts from having the freedom to pursue the ideology of self-help and hard work, of getting on, which was integral to the Gospel in their view.

The 1820 Settlers

Strangely John Philip's first political clash with the British authorities had nothing to do with the indigenous inhabitants of the Cape or with his missiological theories but stemmed from his relations with a new element in Cape Society, the British 1820 Settlers. It is interesting to note that Moffat did not complain of Philip's actions in this matter.

These settlers were the first major input of British people into the permanent population of southern Africa. There had been a small but steady trickle of British individuals into the Cape, some substantial men like Benjamin Moodie who bought a large Boer ranch at Swellendam, others who were army and navy deserters some of whom drifted north becoming part of the northern frontier 'Bastard' community, though others stayed in the colony. The new settlers used English and are seen as part of what has been deemed Lord Charles Somerset's anglicisation policy. Perhaps it would be more correct to suggest that their arrival made such a policy necessary.

As long ago as Colonel Collins' report on the state of the border country in 1809, the Government had been pondering how to provide the density of White families on the frontier that would be a really effective barrier to Xhosa advance. By a happy coincidence in 1819 emigration was one of the solutions many put forward to deal with the unemployed in Britain whose numbers had grown remarkably after the end of the Napoleonic Wars. In July 1819 the House of Commons voted a large sum of money—£50,000—to finance an emigration scheme to the Cape. To the administration there, in the midst of yet another bitter Xhosa war, the scene seemed set to find the resources for the density of population necessary for establishing a firmly held frontier. This conflict was that initiated by the Xhosa invasion of the Colony and their attack on Grahamstown, a campaign inspired by the prophet Nxele or Makana as he was often called.

As we noted in another context, with the Xhosa finally defeated and Makana exiled to Robben Island, Somerset attempted a final settlement of the frontier question which had dogged administrations at the Cape since van Plettenberg. He informed the defeated Xhosa that the Fish was still the frontier, but all Whites and all Xhosa should stay out of the territory between the Fish and the Keiskamma twenty-five miles to the east. This was to be the 'neutral territory', and on the colonial side of the Fish, Somerset hoped to plant new British settlers. They were to be settled on farms of one hundred acres, small units compared with the 6,000 acre trekboer ranches, thus creating the density of settler population advised by Collins in 1809. An empty buffer zone, backed up by a dense settler population on the lower Fish would at last give the Colony the solid frontier it had always lacked.

The seeds of trouble were sown immediately however. Lord Charles Somerset was an able man despite his irascible temper and his almost neurotic family pride. He was quite clear that his frontier policy would only work if he had an adequate garrison. In particular at least one full regiment of cavalry he held to be essential. He estimated that a force of 4,500 was the basic minimum necessary to look after the Colony in general and bring peace to the eastern frontier in particular. However, at the very time he reported to London his plans for securing peace on the eastern frontier, so Lord Bathurst, the Secretary of State for the Colonies, embarked on what was to be the classic British policy for the Cape over the next fifty years, financial retrenchment. He overrode Somerset's recommendation of a garrison of 4,500 including a cavalry regiment and assigned a force of 2,400 with no cavalry.

> This was a bitter blow, for Lord Charles had regarded the dragoon regiment as the groundwork and mainspring of his system of frontier defence.[6]

Lord Charles himself was also responsible in part for the future difficulties;

for in reporting to London the success of his campaign against the Xhosa and the details of the peace, Somerset referred to the strip between the Keiskamma and the Fish as 'the ceded territory' and most significantly as 'as fine a portion of ground as is to be found, and, together with the still unappropriated lands in the Zuurveld, . . . worthy of consideration with a view to systematic colonisation'. Yet he had insisted to the Xhosa that this was to be an empty 'neutral belt'.

The scheme of settlement of the British settlers contained within it another tragic flaw. The land was not suitable for Collins' idea of close settlement on small farms. Given the agricultural techniques of the time there was no way that European families could make a living on farms the size that were assigned to the settlers. The countryside was cattle country suitable only for ranching. In any case not all that many of the settlers were agriculturally experienced and could not have managed even on better soils with more regular rainfall than available in the eastern Cape. The settlement was never effective in this planned form—indeed it soon appeared to be a disaster. In three successive years, the wheat crop on which the success of the settlement was to depend, failed entirely. Then in October 1823, massive rain storms hit the area, washing away the sod cabins of the settlers as well as the good top soil in certain sections.

By the end of 1823, the vast majority of the British settlers had ceased the attempt to work on the land and had drifted into the townships, first of all Grahamstown but also the new townships of Bathurst and Port Elizabeth. There, many of them, following the trades they had pursued in the United Kingdom, achieved some degree of prosperity. Those who stayed on the land came to be large-scale ranchers, like their trekboer neighbours. The British, however, showed some real initiative and introduced merino sheep for wool raising which, together with ivory trading with the Xhosa, contributed to some prosperity among the British settlers.

Despite a limited prosperity for a few, a Distressed Settlers Fund was set up to deal with the serious difficulties a large number of families underwent. John Philip was asked to preside over the committee controlling the affairs of this Fund and he gladly complied with this request. It was the kind of civic task he had been used to performing during his long ministry in Aberdeen.

In the period 1824 to 1826, the people associated with this Fund were driven to become what amounted to an informal opposition party to the Governor, Lord Charles Somerset, and to his administration. The British settlers pressed for freedom of assembly and for a free press, both of which Somerset opposed. This was perfectly understandable. Somerset represented a ruling élite who, in Britain, had in 1819 passed the Six Acts which profoundly limited the rights of freedom of assembly in the United Kingdom itself.

During this struggle, Philip became friends with two fellow Scots who were to remain both allies and friends throughout all his struggles in South Africa. They were Thomas Pringle, who left South Africa in 1826 to become Secretary of the Anti Slavery Society, and John Fairbairn, who was soon to become Philip's son-in-law. These latter two men were also to be Somerset's main protagonists in the struggle for a free press in South Africa.

Philip also worked closely and amicably, at least at first, with other settler leaders like Duncan Campbell, Donald Moodie and J Centlivre Chase, who later were to be the leaders of White opinion on the eastern frontier bitterly critical of Philip, and the whole enterprise associated with the London Missionary Society and the Scots missionaries at Lovedale in the Tyhumie Valley.

The troubles between the 1820 Settlers and the Governor persuaded the Government in London to set up a Commission of Enquiry into the affairs of the Cape Colony. The arrival of the Commissioners in the Cape did not immediately quieten the settler outrage, rather it provided a focus for it. However, outrage did abate somewhat when Somerset himself paid a visit to the frontier districts in 1825. He decided immediately to transfer the bitterly unpopular landdrost, Rivers, and then brought into play the classic manoeuvre of pre-Reform Bill British politics; the distribution of patronage. 'Places' were given to a number of settler leaders, which was immediately effective in cutting down the liveliness of opposition among the British settlers to his administration. This is exactly what was commonly meant by politics in the eighteenth and early nineteenth centuries. And in this sense Philip could correctly maintain that he neither had nor wished to have anything to do with politics. It is very significant that his erstwhile allies and later critics, Moodie, Campbell and Philipps, all became functionaries of one sort or another at this time.

Be that as it may, for a brief time British settlers were engaged in a bitter and vociferous struggle with the colonial regime. The focus for many of their complaints was two landdrosts, Rivers and Cuyler of Uitenhage, both of whom were of British origin. The latter was the same landdrost against whom the missionaries at Theopolis and Bethelsdorp had long complained.

Thus for a short period, the only time in his career, Philip had significant White support for his 'political meddling'. Most settlers were not in the least interested in the problems besetting the Khoi and other free 'persons of colour', but in campaigning against the pattern of colonial rule that oppressed them both, they helped the Khoi. However, in Pringle and Fairbairn, his two close allies in this campaign, Philip gained two powerful and loyal friends and supporters.

Philip and Lord Charles Somerset

On their arrival in Cape Town early in 1819, John Campbell and Philip's primary task was to survey the work of all the stations of the London Missionary Society and to review the overall organisation and strategy of the Mission. They were then to make such reforms as they deemed necessary. Campbell was then to return to the United Kingdom leaving Philip as a Director of the Society resident in the Colony to represent his fellow Directors and to supervise the mission on their behalf.

His first task then was to restore good relations with the colonial authorities. Since 1817 the ban on missionaries going to work beyond the frontier had been vigorously implemented and the Governor had been threatening to close some if not all the Society's stations.

From the moment of their arrival both deputies had gone out of their way to conciliate the senior officials in Cape Town. As Macmillan writes

> Thanking Somerset for his early help, they wrote assuring him that their instructions from the Society inculcated 'respect' and 'cheerful compliance' with the reasonable demands of the civil authorities'. To Colonel Bird a few weeks later Philip remarked that van der Kemp himself before his death, owned to having 'begun at the wrong end'.[7]

It is quite clear from his correspondence in the London Missionary Society archives that initially Philip was impressed by Lord Charles Somerset and by the Colonial Secretary, Colonel Bird. In 1820 during the rule of Sir Rufane Donkin, Philip seems to have struck up a genuine personal friendship with the Acting Governor, who, on the strength of it, ended the ban on missionaries crossing the frontier. Robert Moffat was then able to go to Lattakoo in 1821 and begin his life's work there, and the Methodists were able to open up work to the north among the Namaqua and to the east among the Xhosa.

During these first two years of his service, Philip was based almost exclusively in Cape Town where his task was to sort out relations with Government, while Campbell toured the stations. Immersed as he was in the White society of the capital, Philip seemed to accept the official line on the recent past. He was also undoubtedly influenced by the papers left in the office by Thom who had been a member of his congregation in Aberdeen. Thom's judgement would probably not have been enough on its own to give shape to Philip's ideas because, before he left the United Kingdom, Philip had expressed doubts about the former's judgement. He wrote in December 1817 from Aberdeen to Burder, a Director of the London Missionary Society,

> I have seen a confidential letter written to his father since his marriage which alarms me a little. I am apprehensive he cannot now be removed, and, it is a question with me how far his continuance there would be compatible with the happiness and usefulness of one above him at the station . . . I dare not question his piety, but there is something in his spirit I could wish to see altered or amended.[8]

However, the minutes of the notorious 'Synod' called by Thom, when added to the reports of the senior British officials, all contributed to the formation of his first judgement of the situation which was that most of the trouble had been the result of the actions and the errors of judgement of missionaries. He even went so far as to roundly condemn James Read, who would soon be his most reliable and lifelong supporter in all that he was to do in South Africa. He wrote of Read at this time to the Directors

> Had Reid [sic] held the confidence of the Directors but four years longer, the whole would have been ruined. After the ruin had become general he would

have come Home—his representations would have been believed—the Government would have got the whole blame—and the defence of the Government would have come out, and disgrace and ruin would have been brought upon the cause of missions over the world. . . . The ungodly world does not cry out against Morrison [sic] and Milne as against Dr van der Kemp and Read. The world are accurate judges of character, and of the civilising effects of missions.[9]

Doctors Morrison and Milne had the good fortune to work in China before there were any significant European interests there, unlike van der Kemp and Read. Philip himself was soon to be vulnerable to the same logic that he applied in the report of 1819 to Read and the saintly old Netherlander. All three worked in an area of White conquest and occupation of the territory of a Black indigenous population. In this context, the White world, which Philip sees as so reliable in its judgements, has always cried out against missionaries who challenged White supremacy on behalf of the indigenous population and has gone on to compare them unfavourably with missionaries who did not; notably in South Africa, the Moravian brethren at Genadendal were consistently praised by the critics of the London Missionary Society. Not only have the partisan founders of South African historiography, Theal and Cory, so condemned Philip, but even modern historians have damned him with faint praise and insisted that he must have been a peculiarly arrogant and difficult character. That he was tough, single-minded and at times arrogant, it would be useless to deny. However, the situation of a landless people without legal or civil rights is a situation that might seem to justify aggressive action. Yet even liberal and humane White writers seem to think it did not demand such extremes or at least try to blunt the thrust of Philip's complaints, by scathingly referring to injustices in Britain about which the same missionaries did not seem so upset. There is an exact parallel to the period before the Civil War, evangelical abolitionists are 'debunked' by writers pointing out that they were not particularly concerned about the increasing injustice of the condition of the new White proletariat of the North. Surely because these groups ignored, or were blind to one set of injustices, does not invalidate their protest about another?

In these first two years then, Philip criticised van der Kemp and Read in terms not dissimilar to those in which he was to be condemned later. This was part and parcel of his initial desire to set things right for the London Missionary Society with the Governor and his officials. In addition, as we have seen, the written evidence he had read in the Cape Town office, combined with his residence in Cape Town which ensured that he heard only one side of the story, convinced him.

Strangely, it was his actions undertaken on behalf of the 1820 settlers that initiated open conflict with the Government, though Philip himself had begun to change his mind about the nature of British rule before the difficulties had gone so far. The two areas of confrontation are so interrelated, both in time and in the central theme, which was the quality of

Government in the Colony, that it is difficult to disentangle them. However it is best if they are looked at separately.

Somerset left for a short stay in Britain shortly before the arrival of the settlers. It was his deputy Sir Rufane Donkin who supervised their initial settling-in period. Somerset came back in 1821 and was deeply upset at what he held to be Donkin's insubordination during his absence. There is no doubt that on his return he appeared irascible in the extreme and soon it appeared that he saw dangerous radicals besetting him round, but it must be acknowledged that Donkin, who was exceedingly rude to him on his return,[10] had been insubordinate in one highly dangerous area. Somerset, having made his agreement with the Xhosa in 1819, did seem to have wanted to try to preserve the neutral belt as a buffer between colonist and Xhosa despite casual remarks about land good for settlement. Donkin had very quickly allowed the Xhosa to cross the neutral territory to a regular fair at Fort Willshire, so that very soon some '1820' men were doing well, but as ivory traders not as farmers. He also, and this was much more ominous, established a settlement of ex-soldiers within the 'neutral' belt; this confirmed in the eyes of many Whites and of the Xhosa that this land was not neutral but had been ceded to the Whites.

Somerset also soon became upset by a series of lawsuits against officers of the Administration, master-minded by an extraordinary, almost maniacal, advocate called William Edwards—lawsuits which were dealt with rather badly by the courts. The judiciary and many officials were of poor quality at this time. However, to Somerset this kind of criticism of the administration or of the courts was treasonous. It was in this situation that Thomas Pringle and John Fairbairn along with another Scot, a printer named George Greig, applied to Somerset to establish a newspaper— The Commercial Advertiser. Their publication was in trouble almost from the beginning. Somerset had already referred to Pringle when reporting the application to London as 'an arrant Dissenter who had scribbled'.[11]

In May of 1824 only five months after its first issue, the Fiscal tried to prevent the paper reporting the latest in the series of scandalous cases, where Edwards, the central legal figure in the cases already referred to, was to be tried for libel of the Governor and other officials. The Commercial Advertiser was forced to suspend publication as was a literary journal founded by Pringle and the Reverend Abraham Faure, a Dutch Reformed Church minister. It was at this critical moment that a placard accusing Somerset of homosexuality appeared nailed to trees and other prominent places in Cape Town. It would appear that this placard originated with Edwards although nothing was proved at the time nor can it be proved now. This provoked a series of house-to-house searches of likely suspects, which seemed to include mostly people who had annoyed the Governor at some time or other. The British settlers around Grahamstown got particularly excited about this. Macmillan in his The Cape Colour Question quotes Campbell and Moodie, both later to serve as government officers, writing of this period as 'a reign of terror'.

It was at this most inopportune time that Philip, who was chairman of the

Distressed Settlers Relief Fund felt that he had to oppose the Governor's wish to appoint Landdrost Rivers to that Committee. Since Fairbairn and Pringle were friends of Philip, since Philip owned one of the machines used by the printer Greig and since Philip had already begun to supply the anti-slavery lobby in the House of Commons with information about the Colony, it seemed to Somerset that he had found his main foe and the source of much of the trouble in the Colony. The measure of the state of mind of the Governor can be judged by the fact that he chose to have published, at Government expense, an obscure pamphlet to do with a church controversy in London in 1815, which accused Philip of lack of integrity and he can also be judged by a somewhat mysterious sentence from a despatch of July 1824 to the Secretary of State quoted in the Cambridge History volume on South Africa.

> I would rejoice in an opportunity to expose Philip and Wright but though I am aware of all they do by secret intelligence upon which I depend, I should, if I were to bring their conduct forward, disclose the only source of intelligence upon which I depend and which I consider of too much importance to the safety of my government to give up.[12]

That Somerset's bitter antagonism to Philip was to a great extent unjustified and a product of his feeling of profound insecurity at the time is conceded by his sympathetic biographer, A K Millar. He makes clear that after a period of friendly relations, Somerset then decided that the Distressed Settlers Fund of which Philip was Chairman was a deliberate slight on his administration and when one of the printing presses impounded when the *Commercial Advertiser* was banned turned out to belong to the London Missionary Society it seemed clear to him that Philip was the key villain in the whole piece.

> In a letter to Mr. Bigge (of the Commission of Enquiry) he commented 'After I left you on Tuesday I received a great deal of intelligence respecting the conduct of the Press and perhaps you will not marvel to learn that Dr. Philip is the Head Huntsman and that Mr. Fairburn [sic] Mr. Pringle and Paddy Wright are the whippers in—that they met at dinner once every week when their paragraphs were concocted. The Doctor gave out when he left town that he went out of his way to avoid the constant solicitations made to him to sign a memorial for a free press and he wished to take no part—those matters were not within his calling! Villain—Hypocrite! When he himself is the primum mobile.'[13]

Somerset's somewhat bizarre behaviour can be understood as being due, at least in part, to the bitter campaign being waged against him in London by Brougham, who had been joined by the recently returned Rufane Donkin. The final provocation was that to a traditional high Tory like him, Philip, Fairbairn and Pringle represented the enemy in the United Kingdom, so why not also in South Africa?

However, by the beginning of 1825 he did calm down somewhat and went to Grahamstown to visit the complaining British settlers. There, as we have seen, he quietened down much of the opposition to him. There were no concessions made to Fairbairn however. He was forced to continue his campaign for a free press in the Colony with little sign of concession from the authorities. In this he was supported by Pringle, who was now settled in London, and by Philip. It was only in 1828 that the Government in London instructed the Cape authorities that press laws in the Colony should not depart from those in the United Kingdom.

The importance of these few years, when Philip, as spokesman for White colonial dissidents, was the subject of persecution by the Governor, was in the status it conferred on him when he began to press home his complaints about the plight of 'free persons of colour' in the Colony. Sir Rufane Donkin, with whom Somerset had clashed so bitterly, remained a supporter of Philip while it seemed that Philip would help in Brougham's campaign, and his support helped Philip's standing with the authorities in London and Cape Town.

Philip and the Khoi

It was during Somerset's leave in England, March 1820–August 1821, that Philip was converted from his original condemnatory attitude towards the activities of van der Kemp and Read, to a new stance: a position which led him to go much further than they had gone in the past, culminating in a thorough condemnation of the form of British rule in the Colony.

In some ways the change was triggered off by a series of casual events. The Acting Governor, Sir Rufane Donkin, and Philip had struck up a friendship on the basis of which, when Donkin was about to go on tour to the eastern frontier areas, he asked Philip if he could do anything for the missions while he was there.

Philip had recently been troubled by letters from James Read, who, although he was still suspended from the ministry, had been placed in charge of Bethelsdorp by Philip. These letters insisted that the local landdrost was persisting in unjust treatment of the Khoi on and around the Bethelsdorp Institution. Philip passed on these letters of complaint about Colonel Cuyler, to Donkin. He did so in response to the latter's request. Philip insisted that he had given them to Donkin in confidence, so that the Acting Governor might be aware of the difficulties and look into them informally.

However, when Donkin read the letters, he felt that they constituted so serious an accusation against an officer of the Crown that he had to do something about it immediately. Without consulting Philip, or warning the missionaries at Bethelsdorp, he initiated a formal enquiry immediately on his arrival there; a procedure which found the missionaries utterly unprepared to make a coherent and well-documented case. As Philip insisted to the Directors in a letter of 12 November 1824, he would not have given these documents to Donkin in order to initiate a formal charge against Cuyler, without first warning Read to get his case ready.[14]

Be that as it may, Donkin found Cuyler innocent of all the charges made against him. It also became clear that Donkin believed that Read, the unpopular 'trouble-maker' of the 1811–12 period, was up to his old tricks again. He wrote to Philip about his findings at the enquiry and went on to rub salt into the wound by commiserating with him about being so badly misled by his fellow missionaries![15]

Philip was desperately upset by this turn of events. He was inclined to accept what Donkin said; as we have seen he had come to accept the general attitude towards Bethelsdorp adopted by the Administration and some of the London Missionary Society staff. However, the public hearing so blackened the Society's name, just at a time when Philip was hopeful of having ended the bad feeling, that he had to do something about it.

He wrote to Donkin expressing his surprise at the latter's use of what had been an informal and unofficial communication between them. Donkin's response was one which appears very unusual to modern eyes. He referred the correspondence to two other gentlemen so that they might decide whether or not he had acted improperly. In this he was not acting as a government official but as a gentleman in dispute with another about the appropriateness of their behaviour one to another. This would certainly indicate that close affection and respect had come to characterise the relationship between the Acting Governor and the Mission Director.

The two gentlemen who were called to act in this affair of honour, were two naval officers, Sir Jahleel Brenton and Captain Vernon (Brenton was an enthusiastic evangelical).

After some discussion and careful perusal of the correspondence between the two parties, Brenton suggested that Donkin had gone further than Philip might have expected, given the nature of Donkin's offer to Philip and the style of Philip's reply. However, Brenton went on to suggest to Philip that it might be best if he went to Bethelsdorp and had a look at things for himself.

Philip decided that this was sensible advice and set off for Bethelsdorp. There, in the office, he found correspondence between Landdrost Cuyler and various missionaries at the station; correspondence which justified most of Read's complaints. This incident appears almost *un coup de théâtre* but the documents exist in the London Missionary Society archives for all to see. This event confirmed for Philip the growing unease which he had felt for some time about the accuracy of his original judgement about members of staff, above all James Read.

Both Macmillan, in his classic *The Cape Colour Question*, and Gailey, in his article in the *Journal of African History* entitled 'John Philip's Role in Emancipation', see the Donkin incident as the key to the change in Philip's attitude to the British Administration in the Colony and towards Read and other members of the London Missionary Society staff. That it was important there is no doubt, but it did not constitute quite so dramatic a turn about as these authors suggest. It is clear from his correspondence that Philip had had growing doubts about the goodwill and integrity of the British administration for some time.

Indeed the most notable example of this suspicion came as early as 1820, when in March of that year he wrote a long report to the London Directors. This was a survey of the whole situation of the mission and of the actions of

Campbell and himself since their arrival. He marked this report in the margin, 'This narrative for private use and not for publication. J P.'[16] After all he was charged with restoring good relations with the administration because these were vital to the effective working of the mission, and he was therefore walking a diplomatic tightrope.

In the report, Philip alludes to the 'Meeting' or 'Synod' organised by Thom, in very critical terms and goes on

> The proceedings of this Meeting were no sooner known to the Colonial Government, than a revolution was produced in the sentiments of the Governor in favour of the protesting Missionaries. The Men who had before complained bitterly of the indignity with which they had been treated in the Colonial Office, had now reason to be satisfied with the favour they experienced, and the system, that had been adopted respecting the Missions beyond the Colony, was so far relaxed, that Moffat and Kitchingman were permitted to proceed to Namacgualand, the stations for which they were originally intended.

He then goes on to complain bitterly about Colonel Bird's refusal to help Philip, as Director of the Society, remove from the Caledon Institution, a missionary called Seidenfaden. This was a man who had turned the Institution into a private farm and who treated the Khoi there as his indentured servants. Here was a man clearly behaving reprehensibly, the sort of man who did fit the Government's previous complaints about 'immoral' missionaries. Yet Bird refused any Government cooperation and the London Missionary Society could hardly physically evict Seidenfaden. Indeed Bird supported Seidenfaden in his control of the Institution and it was not until 1826 that he was got rid of.

Donkin's rushed Enquiry at Bethelsdorp with its unfair exoneration of Cuyler and condemnation of Read added to Philip's doubts rather than creating a totally new set of ideas in his mind. However, the visit to Bethelsdorp did create a dramatic turnabout in his estimation of James Read. He had been inclined to accept the condemnation of Read that was general among Whites. He did know of his good work with a handful of Khoi evangelists in organising the first mission among the Tswana of Mothibi; work, it is worth noting, that Moffat was to inherit and build upon without any acknowledgement by him or his biographers of Read's vital contribution. But this was not enough to prevent his original reaction to Donkin's report of the Bethelsdorp Enquiry to be one of fury against Read for having again brought the Society into disrepute.

When, at Bethelsdorp, he perused the correspondence in the office, he came to the conclusion that Read was a much maligned man. Philip from that moment on saw him in a new light and, more important, there then began the long and increasingly close relationship which lasted both their lives. Philip soon came to see him as a vital ally in all his schemes and came to rely on him, and later on his two sons, as his most reliable assistants among the frontier Khoi and the Xhosa. Indeed together with James Wright, one of the most creative of all the missionaries sent to South Africa by the London Missionary Society, who worked among the Griqua, the Reads were the members of the London Missionary Society staff most closely involved with Philip's schemes and closest to Philip's heart. Chris Saunders' important article in *South African Outlook* (March 1976) entitled 'James Read: Towards a re-assessment' draws attention to this fact, which is there to be seen in the massive files of the South African correspondence of the London Missionary Society in the School of Oriental and African Studies in London. It seems that the many writers on Philip and the London Missionary Society in South Africa simply could not 'see' what was there because of the nature of their preconceptions or the particular views they were trying to oppose or propose.

This would seem to be the explanation of why Macmillan in his two classic studies plays down James Read and his sons. It is difficult to be certain, but perhaps because in confronting the massed anti-Philip ranks of the South African historiography of his day, Macmillan simply could not afford to undertake, in addition, the rehabilitation of someone like Read, who so thoroughly flouted contemporary White South African mores. Indeed Macmillan appears, at least to some extent, to feel that such a defence was not possible for a man who 'had not the personal qualities or mental equipment for a leader'[17] and at best sums him up in a way that confirms, even if in more sympathetic tones, the judgements of Theal and Cory.

> Whilst there is no reason to doubt his sincere honesty, this good natured artisan missionary was rather indiscriminate and even rash in accepting complainants' stories.[18]

Read had married a Khoi wife. He never deviated from being on the side of South African Blacks in every controversy during his lifetime. He took Khoi and slave complaints seriously, because to him human beings were human beings, whatever their colour, culture or education. These characteristics made him an uncomfortable man to be associated with in the South Africa of his day. Clearly he was not an angel and did make mistakes but certainly no more than Governors who believed whatever one of their magistrates told them.

In his article in *South African Outlook* Saunders deprecates the tendency of pro-Philip writers to 'put down' Read as part of their development of Philip's role. This tendency is regrettably true but has nothing to do with Philip. From the period of the Donkin episode onwards, Philip was a loyal friend to Read and then to his sons when they joined the staff. This is perhaps most clearly and pointedly seen in his defence of them to the Directors of the Society against the accusation of Calderwood and others of the London Missionary Society staff serving among the Xhosa in 1846. Calderwood and his colleagues in the Xhosa area of the mission had set up a district missionary committee (a problem in itself for Philip which will be dealt with in a later chapter). This group of men disliked the relationship the Reads had with Coloured people (as both the Khoi and the Bastards were then coming to be called). They were also upset about the attitude of the Reads to their Xhosa contacts, especially their dealings with the chief Maqoma, fearing that this would 'spoil' the Xhosa as the Coloureds had been 'spoiled'. This is the language that is going to dominate the discussion of missionary relations with Africans from this period right on into the middle of the twentieth century over so much of Africa.

The Block Drift group of missionaries, as Philip refers to them, were also angry with certain things the Reads had said or implied in letters and reports to Philip and the London Directors. In addition, they objected, as had British officials twenty years before, to Read accepting the word of a 'Black' as true when it was in conflict with the testimony of a 'White'. An acrimonious correspondence between these men, the Reads and Philip then ensued. Philip enclosed thirteen letters from this correspondence with his long report to the London Directors. It is this report that seems decisive in making clear where Philip stood with regard to the Reads.

> The parties never can be brought to act together and the only thing we can do with them is to keep them from threatening each other and from open war. They are entirely different men and represent two different classes of missionary. What is esteemed and practised as a virtue by one, is viewed as a crime in the eyes of the other. You will find the key to this secret in the following passage in Calderwood's letter of 8 July, No. 9. 'We object to the kind of intercourse which he [James Read] has with the coloured [sic] people as indicated by his letters.' . . Both parties would do the coloured people good but in different ways. In order to raise the people James Read would treat them as brethren and to this Mr. Calderwood says 'We object' and to this object for the sake of the people themselves.
>
> Both systems have been tried and their fruits are before the public. The Hottentots were converted on the principle of love and those that treat them on the other principle cannot have their love and this creates the [illegible] of the complainants against the Hottentots and the jealousy lest the caffres should be spoiled in the same way. Both parties love the people but the one shows it in a way which the people like better than the other and they cannot be blamed for it. A missionary who was afraid of spoiling the people by shaking hands with them said to me the other day 'I never saw the like of these Hottentots, you can do nothing with them by scolding them; you may do anything with them by kindness.' The attitude indicated by James Read's correspondence is indicative of no disgrace to him. If their colour is not taken into the estimate, there are not two more respectable men; whether black or white, in the district. [This refers to two men whose word Read trusted in a dispute to the fury of Calderwood and Co.]
>
> With all the prejudices against the Hottentots, would the change affected be affected by money? The British Government might give millions sterling to see the caffre nations in the condition of the Hottentots. I have shown you the gulf that lies between the parties and keeps them apart.[19]

This letter when taken with his continuous close relations with Read from the time of the Donkin affair onwards is important in making clear the basis of the policy to which Philip adhered after the dust of the incident had settled. His rather less than sympathetic biographer in the *DSAB*, accurately sums up a problem raised by many writers about Philip's attitude to the problem of 'race' and 'colour'.

> But throughout Philip's life he remained slightly uncertain as to what precisely

he envisaged for the Hottentots. On one occasion he wrote about their future role as landowners and artisans while on another he declared they would have to labour on the farms for centuries to come. On the one hand he endeavoured to create separate Hottentot communities, while on the other he strove for the complete amalgamation of whites and non-whites.[20]

In the massive collection of Philip papers there is no sign whatever that Philip held the belief that the whole future for the Khoi was that they should labour on the farms for centuries to come. However, it is true that while he often talks of their role as landowners and artisans, he also works hard for separate Khoi communities around the mission stations and welcomed Stockenstrom's Kat River Settlement. Indeed this latter attitude, when taken together with his policy which will be discussed in the ensuing chapters, for African treaty states beyond the colonial frontier, has led some historians, notably Eric Walker, to see him as an advocate of apartheid. Did he then sway between different ideas as the *DSAB* suggest or can these two attitudes by reconciled?

Philip's letter to Tidman quoted above represents his basic attitude not only towards the Khoi but to all 'persons of colour'. He believed in the fundamental equality of all human beings—all were sinners, all capable of salvation and the various distinctions among them were secondary matters. In order that the full humanity of a socially and politically deprived people might gain full expression, his tactics did differ according to circumstances. At times guaranteed separate settlements like Bethelsdorp and the Kat River were needed but these were never seen by him as a permanent solution. In a properly organised society people would live together whatever their race and would reach the appropriate level in that society according to their abilities.

The pervasiveness of 'scientific racism' and 'social Darwinism' in so much of Western thought from the 1870s until well into the twentieth century put great barriers in the way of writers of that era coming to terms with Philip.[21] Thus it is interesting to note that Macmillan, writing in the 1920s, shies away from Philip's explicit remarks about 'amalgamation' or statements that indicate his belief in the essential equality of Black and White. Macmillan makes no reference anywhere to the long report of 1846 about the Reads, quoted above, nor does he ever dwell on Philip's closeness to Read and Read's sons who were Cape Folk in modern parlance. Indeed in commenting on a long term report from Philip addressed to William Wilberforce in 1824 entitled 'A Defence of the Hottentots', where, interestingly, Philip shows the same understanding of Hottentot humanity as he does in the controversy between the Reads and Calderwood twenty-two years later, Macmillan attempts to dodge the issue. In this letter Philip told Wilberforce that the Khoi were often enslaved by men their moral and intellectual inferiors. Of this Macmillan writes

> This last suggestion, that individual Hottentots might be superior to some colonists, for the time when it was written is a startling hypothesis, and is an instance of Philip's 'extreme' views. It is, however, an isolated statement, and in fact goes no further than to show his profound belief in the potential equality of the races.[22]

Macmillan is trying, at that point, in his book, to defend Philip from the charge of being a dogmatic supporter of an ideology of race equality which Macmillan held to be inappropriate for Philip's era and embarrassing even in his own time. He was, I believe, wrong.

Even if all Philip was doing was insisting on the potential equality of the races, then logically some Hottentots could be the superior morally and intellectually of some colonists. But in any case, Macmillan is wrong because it is not an isolated instance. The whole burden of Philip's campaign for what he called 'equal civil rights' made no sense without the presupposition of equality which the colonists were quite correct in spotting as being Philip's attitude. On a number of occasions when Philip was writing carefully considered reports and not simply one of the many hundreds of letters he wrote dealing with ad hoc problems of many kinds, Philip makes his views on race clear. We have just looked at his letter about the Reads which shows at the end of his life he believed in equality. As he was instructed by the Directors of the Society, after his first two years in South Africa, he reported on his views of the situation in South Africa both within and without the Colony based on the work he and Campbell had undertaken since their arrival in 1819. This was not an idealistic preconception but the judgement of a mature and experienced man after two years of careful investigation. In this report he wrote of Bethelsdorp

> It may seem invidious to compare the Hottentots with the Farmers of South Africa, but without attempting to lessen my Country, I have no hesitation in affirming, that you will find as rational ideas, as large a quantum of intelligence, and as much religion and morality, as much appearance of civilisation as in many villages of the same population in Great Britain.[23]

His book, *Researches in South Africa*, shows this same attitude while again in mid-career in a very carefully prepared report for the American Board of Commissioners for Foreign Missions, he is quite explicit on this issue.

The American Board was the sister society in the United States to the London Missionary Society. They were interested in starting work in South Africa and asked Philip for a report on the possibilities of work as well as a report on South Africa society as a whole. His reply to them was not a casual letter but one of the most important documents produced by Philip. It was read by the whole of the Executive of the American Board and later published *in extenso* in their journal *The Missionary Herald*, the issue for November 1833. This carefully considered statement is certainly 'extreme' in the terms of traditional South African historiography and in Macmillan's terms also.

Natural Capacity of the African Race

So far as my observation extends, it appears to me that the natural capacity of the African is nothing inferior to that of the European. At our schools, the children of Hottentots, of Bushmen, of Caffres, and of the Bechuanas, are in no respect behind the capacity of those of European parents: and the people at our missionary stations are in many instances superior in intelligence to those who look down on them, as belonging to an inferior caste. The natives beyond the colony live in a world of their own, and they know little of our world, but we know less of theirs than they do of ours. In point of abilities and good feelings, I consider the Caffres on the borders of the colony as most decidedly superior to that portion of the refuse of English society that find their way to this country. I have never seen anything in civilised society like the faculty those people have in discerning the spirit and character of men. When Englishmen go among them, they will discover more of their visitors in a few days than some of their own countrymen may have been able to find out about them by an acquaintance of years. We have at this moment a young Caffre chief at one of our missionary stations, who is vindicating the character of his countrymen, and exposing the cruelty and injustice with which they have been treated, in our public journals, with an ability superior to that of any of his numerous and virulent assailants within the colony. Contemplated through the medium of their own superstitions, or that of their general condition, we might hastily pronounce them to be inferior to the white race; but on these points they lose nothing by a comparison with our European ancestors.[24]

The equality of the races seems therefore to have been basic to Philip's view of reality, and whether 'extreme' or not, was consistently expressed in his writings and his actions.

Macmillan was wrong, though understandably so, because his purpose was to try to clear Philip of the charge of being an ideologist within the field of race relations, at a time, the late 1920s, when such an ideological approach was unacceptable even to liberals. Philip did, nonetheless, hold to a consistent philosophy of racial equality throughout his life.

In practice Philip saw two things to be absolutely necessary for the good of all the inhabitants of South Africa— the ending of slavery and the ending of the *de facto* slavery of the Khoi and of the other 'free persons of colour'. He was willing to leave the ending of legal slavery to the work of Wilberforce and the Anti-Slavery Society in Britain, where, at Westminster, it could alone be effectively done. He saw his own particular task to be the ending of the practical servile status of the Khoi and other persons of colour in the Colony.

The future of South Africa was one which Philip saw in class terms, as a problem of economic structures and relations as much as a problem of race. He had resigned his managership in Dundee all those years ago because the owners would not let him end child labour and pay better wages. He had advocated this policy not out of an idealism that took no account of economic theory and economic realities. On the contrary he believed them necessary to an efficient running of the factory and in accordance with the best economic theory. Macmillan was right to defend him against the charge of being an unrealistic idealist, but his policy was ideologically based. He was a firm believer in the theories of his fellow townsman, Adam Smith, that the power of laissez-faire capitalism of the Smithian sort would bring good to the whole community. This was part of his intellectual debt to the Scottish Enlightenment. Indeed, Philip cannot be understood apart from these ideas.

His *Researches* appear, at first reading, a product of the Enlightenment rather than evangelicalism. In fact these two are not necessarily opposed as is so often assumed—they blend to an astonishing degree in the thought of many Scottish evangelicals of the first decades of the nineteenth century, notably Thomas Chalmers.

Philip believed that if the Khoi, and eventually the slaves, were granted equal civil rights with British citizens in the Colony, and if the barriers to their owning land, to their pursuing trades and to receiving education were removed, then not only the Blacks but all would benefit. He saw the Cape as an economically backward society, imprisoned in its backwardness by the slave structure of its economy. Labour was either that of formal slaves, or Khoi and others who were brought to the labour market by force and with no economic or legal autonomy. This structure, he believed, helped no one, not even the masters. If all had the same civil freedom, if all were able to bring their labour to the free market and sell to the highest bidder, if they could own land and engage in trade and pursue trades, the benefit to all would be direct and of significance to the whole economy. Not only would the Black quality of life and standard of living improve, but as more prosperous consumers they would provide a growing market for British and colonial goods.[25] Slavery and forced labour were felt on the other hand by the colonists, Boer and British, to be necessary to any hope of prosperity for them. Philip, however, insisted that, on the contrary, it was the slavery and forced labour that were the essence of the system that held back the prosperity of everyone. The system was not only inimical to a worthwhile life for the Blacks but prevented economic development for the whole community.

This belief did not only stem from Philip's intellectual commitment to the ideas of the Scottish Enlightenment but, as we saw in the last chapter, was as also produced by his own experience of life. He and many of his fellow missionaries believed that in the situation in Britain where they had equality before the law, where they had access to Christianity and were able to pursue the Christian virtues of sobriety and hard work, not only had they 'got on' individually, but more, the prosperity of the whole nation had developed on this foundation. Africans could also 'get on' and the whole society prosper if the same situation was created in the Colony.

Philip, in keeping with this theoretical position concentrated his attention on the Missionary institutions. He hoped that there, virtuous hard-working communities would be free to grow. There was no hope of this so long as the British administration looked on them as a labour reserve for local public works, the local colonists and the Cape Corps. If the institutions could be free to get on with their task, and then be seen to work, it would be possible to persuade the British authorities in Cape Town or, if need be, in London, to legislate for the granting of equal civil rights for all Khoi and other free persons of colour. It was therefore essential that the institutions, especially the much criticised Bethelsdorp be made to work, and be seen to work.

It was thus that in his voluminous correspondence on these issues, he can be found to be calling for civil rights for all, and at other times, insisting on the rights of the separate 'segregated' institutions. This does not represent confusion or contradiction over what were his aims. There were two stages

in his strategy. Unless institutions were made to work, he had not the proof
he needed in his pleas for equal civil rights. Of course, when such freedom
was gained, many Khoi would remain labourers, but others would be free to
achieve what was in them, free to become skilled artisans, small
businessmen, independent farmers and herders and so on.

It is clear that he embarked on this scheme as early as 1821, and notably,
that he chose the much maligned James Read as one of the key men for the
operation.

Closely related to this development policy was a change in the mission's
policy with regard to complaints about specific wrongs done to individual
Khoi and Khoi families. These abuses were, for Philip, signs of the disease
that afflicted the Colony, its whole slave-based hierarchical structure. It was
the entire system that had to be changed if progress was to ensue. This is a
vitally important difference between his understanding of the situation and
that implied by the policy pursued by van der Kemp and Read in the past.
They had attacked specific examples of injustice as if they were aberrations
of an otherwise sound system, or a result of the faults of wicked men in
office. Philip saw the system as being at fault, leading even good men into
bad actions.

However, to return to the policy Philip initiated in 1821. He pointed out
in the preface to his *Researches*, that the poor and squalid conditions of the
Khoi stations in the Colony left the mission and the Khoi open to the
assertion that the kind of development he hoped for was not possible for
such a backward people. The highest priority, then, had to be given to
making the stations models of industry and propriety, models of
Christianity and civilisation. On the basis of this, major steps could then be
taken towards freedom for all the Khoi.

It was in October 1821 that Philip put to the inhabitants of Theopolis and
Bethelsdorp an improvement plan which necessitated the destruction of
most of their old reed and daub houses and the building of stone houses
along a pattern of orderly streets. Philip clearly believed this to be a good
thing in itself, but ever more it was a step towards their proving to the world
their worthiness of the civil rights denied them. Philip makes this point
explicitly in his *Researches*

> I particularly pointed out to them the advantage which an improvement in their
> houses, and in their industry and mode of living, would afford their friends, in
> pleading their cause. I stated to them that it was vain to attempt to plead their
> cause, while their enemies could point to Bethelsdorp in its present state; that
> the world, and the church of Christ, looked for civilisation and industry as
> proofs of their capacity for improvement, and of the utility of our labours; that
> the men of the world had no other criterion by which they could judge the
> beneficial results of missions; that results were to them what the external
> evidences of Christianity are to an unbeliever . . . I added, that they were not to
> consider what I now recommended as carnal things, and, for that reason, of no
> importance; that the words of unerring truth said—'By their fruits ye shall
> know them;' that money was a carnal thing, and yet Paul speaks of the gift he
> had received from the church at Philippi, as 'of a savour of a sweet smell,
> acceptable to God;' that our food and drink were carnal things and that we

could not live without them; that to feed the hungry, to clothe the naked, to give drink to the thirsty, are carnal things, and yet our Lord, in the xxxvth chapter of Matthew, has taught us that the reality of religion in the heart will be decided by these things in the day of judgement. . . . I declared to them publicly, and as in the presence of God that if they would furnish me with the argument I wanted, an argument absolutely necessary to silence their enemies, and essential to the success of any attempts which might be made in their favour, I should first do everything for them, in my power, with the colonial government; and, if my efforts in that quarter should fail, I assured them that I should use my utmost endeavour to influence the Directors of the London Missionary Society, whose favourable regards for them they had experienced, to use their influence with the government at home to redress their grievances. And I solemnly pledged myself (believing, as I did, that their oppressions were illegal, as well as unjust in principle), that, if these resources failed, I should never cease, while the exercise of my reason was continued to me, and while I could use my pen, to employ every lawful means to procure for them their just rights as subjects of the British government.[26]

Both at Theopolis and at Bethelsdorp the people responded enthusiastically to Philip's pledge, and he entrusted Peter Wright at Theopolis and James Read at Bethelsdorp to be the supervisors of the stations under the new plan.

Initially there was a marked measure of success in implementing these plans, not only in terms of new houses built but also through a significant growth in economic activity. Some families had already built up a little wealth through timber cutting, an industry which continued, and some now invested this in waggons and began a lucrative number of transport businesses through hiring out to the colonists and to the government. Aloe juice was collected which was reasonably profitable because of its popularity in the British medical practice of the day. At both stations, apprentices were trained in carpentry and bricklaying, as wheelwrights and masons. It was the needs created by the 1820 settlers that brought this small amount of prosperity to the settlements. This was a practical working out of Philip's insistence on the mutual relations of the races, and that prosperity depended on all being able to take advantage of the opportunities offered.

It was this prosperity that allowed a good deal of the new building Philip had called for, to take place. Indeed the prosperity was such that the people were able to pool financial resources at both stations and buy new farms, two at the mouth of the Gamtoos River, which became Hankey station, where Philip is buried, and one at Bethelsdorp, thus increasing the size of the institution.

However, signs of development did not go unnoticed by the administration and the local colonists, Boer and British. A new wave of criticisms of the institutions began, only now they were not criticised for their backwardness and lack of organisation but for their progress in advancing the Khoi. It was asserted that they were taking the Khoi away from the service of the colonists which was their proper place. Tragically for the inhabitants of the stations, even during the comparative economic boom of 1822 to 1825, a majority of the men at both stations still had to hire themselves out to the local Whites. This entailed all the old difficulties associated with this kind of service. These had been complained of from the time of Read's famous letter of complaint of 1808. They included the attempt by the farmers to keep Khoi in their permanent employ by the withholding of pay and by contracting of the older children near the end of the parent's contract so as to keep the family for a further period, the parent's feeling compelled to sign another contract; and the classic complaint, that any person of colour found on the road without a letter from a white explaining his being there, was liable to arrest by any burgher and then to be allocated for labour by the local veldt-kornet to a local farmer as a vagrant.

There were also new actions which were abuses of justice by any standard. The landdrost, Colonel Cuyler, suddenly denied the right of the Bethelsdorp men to cut timber in the Tsitsikamma forest, a key source of the settlement's wealth, giving it to some British newcomers. Philip brought pressure to bear in Cape Town and this right was restored in 1824. However, it was a blow to the development plan and forced more men and women to go into the service of the farmers in order to obtain income.

Jane Sales quotes another infuriating example

> Bethelsdorp men were required to spend months cleaning the water sluices at Uitenhage for the water-fiscal who was paid for this responsibility, on the basis of a contract he had tendered to the Landdrost. Then he used the landdrost's powers of requisitioning Hottentot labour to have the manual work done free or at very low rates. When the missionaries complained about the long absence of some of the men, they were told that these men would be released when others were sent to replace them. The fury of the missionaries increased further when they were told by the men that they had had to help build the water-fiscal's house and that they had had to work in the private fields of the landdrost.[27]

The importance of the majority of the men being away cannot be exaggerated. Often their children went with them which had drastic results for the school as an institution as well as for the individual children. Again, when in addition the landdrost, as he was by law entitled to do, called on the men of the institution for government road works, carrying the mail and so on, important work on the station had to stop or be drastically curtailed and the growing group of enterprising families at Bethelsdorp suffered grievously. Philip makes the fact of injustice to the Khoi of Bethelsdorp irrefutably clear in a letter to the Directors in January 1821.

> If an Hottentot possessing one wagon by which he is able to earn 76 dollars by one journey to Grahamstown is liable to be dragged from his employment to serve for 4/- a day, the people liable to such exactions, labour under oppression.[28]

Initially, as we have seen in his speeches to the people at Theopolis and Bethelsdorp, Philip had thought that reform could come through pressure on the colonial authorities. He quickly came to the conclusion that only representation to the government in London could effectively bring about the necessary reforms in the Cape.

When in the British Parliament it was mooted, largely on account of the distress of the British settlers in the eastern Cape, that a Commission of Enquiry should be set up to enquire into the affairs of the Colony, Philip used every contact available to him in London to have the problem of the slaves, the Khoi and other free persons of colour made part of the remit of the Commission. It was his old friend, Sir Jahleel Brenton who was instrumental in persuading Wilberforce that the plight of the Khoi was intimately associated with the problem of slavery in the Cape. Once convinced that this was the business of the anti-slavery lobby, Wilberforce pressed this matter in the House and had it accepted.

When the Commission arrived in the Colony, Philip was advised to make particular contact with two members. J T Bigge and Major W M G Cole-brooke. He helped them settle into their houses at Cape Town and acted, on certain occasions, as a guide companion on their tours of inspection. He was someone of whom the Commissioners took notice. This was not simply as a result of Wilberforce's influence, but because, on their arrival at the Cape, the Commission had been deluged by complaints by the 1820 settlers. Philip was Chairman of the Distressed Settlers Fund and appeared to them as a champion of the settlers as well as of the Khoi.

However, Philip began to rapidly lose hope in the Commission as a quick and effective means of remedying the situation of the Khoi. Indeed the Crown Commissioners seemed to be taking an unconscionably long time to report. They began quickly enough, recommending a Council of Advice made up of senior officials which placed a limit on the powers of the Governor. The Council came into being in May 1825, and later that summer it became widely rumoured in the Colony that Somerset's days as Governor would soon be over.

There was, however, no sign of any action on the civil rights front, or of any prospect of submission of a full report to Parliament. So in the summer of 1825, Philip made up his mind that the campaign directed at influencing the Government in London, which he had promised at the Bethelsdorp and Theopolis meetings, would have to be undertaken. Some action with regard to his position with the Government in London was probably necessary, in any case, because the campaign of calumny against him on the part of Somerset was having effect. A long letter from Hankey, the Treasurer of the London Missionary Society, in June 1825 related how Hankey had had to spend a great deal of time clearing up the impact Somerset's charges had made on the minds of officials in the Colonial Office. Hankey went on to raise the possibility of Philip's return to the United Kingdom in order to lobby ministers and MPs now that Somerset's days seemed to be over. He went on to insist that the London Missionary Society, however, must stay out of political matters. By this he meant 'politics' in the contemporary sense—that is, the manoeuvring of factions in the unreformed Parliament to remove Somerset and even impeach him. Hankey went on

> That which seems most to mingle with politics—the state of the native Hottentots, while it may doubtless be handled by political leaders as in their province, it may be pursued by us, distinctly as a great moral and religious topic and be advocated on its proper grounds.[29]

He went on to warn Philip, however, that accusations were still being made against him to the Colonial Office and was clearly nervous that the Society might get into the bad odour with the Government that had obtained between 1817 and 1819.

Philip agreed that it would be politic for him to return to London, both to mend political fences and to further the cause of Khoi civil rights. However, the tone of Hankey's letters seems to have convinced him that the latter campaign would better be carried out in cooperation with the leaders of the Anti-Slavery Society than with his fellow directors of the London Missionary Society. They, as reflected in Hankey's letters, seemed to have too many other concerns and, in addition, they were too apprehensive that his activities might again endanger the future of the Society's work in South Africa.

The Visit to Britain and Ordinance 50

Before returning to Britain to press the case for civil rights for all the King's subjects, Philip spent the last months of 1825 touring all of the London Missionary Society establishments inside the Colony. He reported on each one as he visited it in an individual letter to the Directors. These letters reflect the solid achievement of the previous six years in the reorganisation of the stations and, more important, the restoration both of a high morale and of a sense of purpose among the missionaries and the Khoi.[30] He also visited the Griqua stations beyond the frontier to the northeast, the import of which will be discussed in a later chapter.

The letters helped prepare the London Directors for his return, but the long and exhausting trek was also a form of 'prep' for the rigorous examination he was bound to receive when pressing his case in the United Kingdom.

Philip sailed for London early in 1826, followed by Lord Charles Somerset, who was ordered home, at least temporarily. Somerset's erstwhile Colonial Secretary, Colonel Bird and his Acting Governor, Sir Rufane Donkin, had played a large part in the agitation which forced the Secretary of State, Lord Bathurst, to recall Somerset to face charges of mismanagement of the Colony's affairs. There were many who were out 'to get' Somerset and Philip could have been a most useful ally in this campaign. After all, Somerset had dealt with Philip in a peculiarly venomous manner, not only seeking authority to deport him to the United Kingdom but outrageously using the Government press to publish material calculated to bring Philip's name into disrepute. Philip had been only too well aware of all this and had been desperately upset and angry about it. Indeed in a long essay which he wrote in the mid-1840s for the Buxton family as an aid to a projected life of Sir Fowell Buxton, he reported that various public figures had approached him with offers of help if he was prepared to cooperate in a campaign to impeach Somerset.

It is very important to note his response to these tempting offers—tempting both at the level of personal grievance, and also because they might have been a short cut to gaining his aim of civil rights for all free persons of colour in the Cape. If, as has often been asserted by various historians, Philip was easily bedazzled by association with the rich and powerful; if he was 'harsh, and even venomous, to his opponents', why did he not join in the anti-Somerset campaign? When we consider how Lord Charles had behaved towards him surely it would have been understandable; indeed to the easily flattered and venomous man portrayed in the *Dictionary of South African Biography* and in other sources, it would have been too good an opportunity to miss.

In fact, Philip made it clear from the beginning of his visit that he wanted nothing to do with any personal attack on Somerset; what he wanted was to change the system of government at the Cape. As he said, somewhat ruefully, to Miss Buxton,

> I found many at that time, who for party purposes, were willing to assist me in an impeachment of his Lordship, but, who took no interest in the deliverance of a people from the most cruel slavery, or in the salvation of the Missions.[31]

Philip was single-minded and relentless, but his concern was not personal pride but the future of the missions and that of the indigenous people of South Africa. He had, by this time, become certain that the problems of the Colony were not a matter of individual misuse of power, corruption or wickedness. If there was to be any hope of a true flowering of Christianity and civilisation in South Africa then the system of government had to be changed.

In this concern for changing the system of colonial government, he got little help from the other Directors of the London Missionary Society, which was as he had feared. He was welcomed enthusiastically enough on his return, but when he asked for the Directors' help in pressing the need for reform on Lord Bathurst, the other Directors rebuffed him. They were still trying to recover from the recent clash with the British Government over the Smith incident in Demerara.

In this situation specific complaints about abuse of power was one thing but a campaign to change the nature of colonial rule was another. Indeed, in the memorandum he wrote later in the 1840s for the Buxton family, Philip insisted that his fellow Directors asked him to desist from any such wide-ranging campaign.

This presented Philip with a major problem. Wilberforce was now in retirement and he did not know Fowell Buxton, the new leader of the Anti-Slavery Society. If, in this situation, he could not count on the support of the leadership of the London Missionary Society, he was in a very weak position indeed from which to bring about any reforms to benefit his people. He began by trying to change the minds of the other Directors by means of a long report surveying Government policy towards missions in the Cape. The reaction of his fellows was not very enthusiastic. Indeed the report was not a well-thought-out document. Philip was, at that time, still suffering from the effects of the savage and sudden attack on him by Somerset. This he could only explain by postulating a vendetta by the authorities against the London Missionary Society as such. Although he was beginning to see that these reactions could be explained by Somerset's personality, and even more by the Government's unhappiness about the London Missionary Society's approach to the status of the Khoi and other free persons of colour, whether on or off mission stations, the anti-mission theory is still reflected in the report. In this report he contrasts the Government's patronage of the Moravian Mission at Genadendal with its treatment of the London Missionary Society. The other Directors disliked bringing another Society into the dispute and were not persuaded of the vendetta. They refused to change their minds about acting as a pressure group on Government to bring about fundamental reform at the Cape.

It seems likely that by this time, Philip was not so much attempting to persuade his fellow Directors to be a pressure group, as simply trying to enable them to understand his position. He certainly needed to be sure that they did because he was now coming under attack even from some within that small circle of people in Britain who supported missions.

In January 1827, the Reverend J Ellis, a staunch member of the London Missionary Society, presented a long detailed condemnation of Philip's conduct in South Africa. Notably the Ellis paper attacked Philip's 'political meddling' on behalf of the Khoi. The charges were so carefully prepared and they were from so senior a member of the Society that Burder, the Secretary of the London Missionary Society, felt he had to answer Ellis's letter point by point.

This answer, on behalf of the Board of Directors, is important on two counts; first, because it was a sign that the Directors had decided to support Philip and not his critics; second, because it shows how far they still were from understanding his position. Perhaps the key passage is,

> The Society in reference to the Aborigines of South Africa, seeks the redress of specific grievances, the existence of which the principles of the Government of which they are the subjects do not sanction but condemn—expresses a hope that their relation to the British Government may be more distinctly recognised—their rights, hence resulting, protected—and lay before H.M.'s ministers, for the Colonial department, a document of facts affecting their ill-treatment under the abused sanction of British authority, which has been placed in their hands and which it would be contrary to their duty to withhold from the inspection of Government.[32]

As early as 1822, as we have seen, Philip was beginning to see that the problems of the Cape were more than the rectifying of specific abuses. He was even then rapidly moving towards the conclusion that it was not the abuse of British rule that was wrong but the very nature of British rule. The erratic behaviour and personality of Lord Charles confused his thinking for a time, but only for a time.

However, so long as the London Missionary Society was still sympathetic and he retained his Directorship, that was enough. He had made up his mind, before leaving the Cape, that real help in bringing about change would not come from the London Missionary Society but from the Anti-Slavery Society.

As we have seen Philip did not know the new leader, Fowell Buxton, but he set out to convince him as he previously had convinced Wilberforce that the fate of the free persons of colour was bound up with the fate of the slaves.

Because of his old Clapham Sect connections, Philip was invited to stay with the Buxtons at their house at Cromer in December 1826. This was a fateful visit because it brought Buxton into South African affairs and gained Philip an ally whose support he was able to count on till Buxton's death in 1845.

Philip forcibly pointed out to Buxton that there was little to be gained by all his efforts, if all that freedom was to mean for the slaves, when emancipation came, was that they were placed in the landless, rightless, oppressed state of the Khoi. Buxton was convinced and from then on saw the situation in South Africa as part of the remit of his Society.

Early in 1827, Philip's fellow Directors of the London Missionary Society also decided not simply to defend him but to take a more positive stand in his support. They decided to present a memorial, drawn up by Philip, to Lord Bathurst. The Secretary of State's reply was that nothing could be done about reforming the administration of the Cape until the report of the Commission was received. There was still no sign of that happy event but no matter, this action by the Directors was a confirmation that the attempt to turn the London Missionary Society against Philip had failed.

The Directorate of the London Missionary Society however, was still not an effective tool for political pressure on the Government, which had to be brought through the Anti-Slavery Society and the Evangelical Parliamentary Lobby. Philip threw all his energies into supplying them with information and attempting to turn their strength in the direction of gaining the reform of Cape Government he felt to be so essential. On the advice of Buxton, he decided to write a book, his *Researches in South Africa*. This work had a delayed impact in South Africa which will be considered later. In Britain it gained only a limited readership, almost entirely made up of people already, at least potentially, sympathetic to the cause. However it did bring South Africa to the attention of that active section of the public who had, until then, concentrated their attention on the West Indies and West Africa.

In this work, Philip sought to present a defence of the memory of Johannes van der Kemp and, above all, an exposé of the basic injustice of the structure of the administration of the Cape Colony.

These two volumes are still capable of raising people's blood pressure. W A J de Klerk says of the *Researches*, 'In this the Xhosa and the Hottentots were praised, the colonists and officials generally and heartily damned.'[33] Professor Galbraith sees him as guilty of serious mis-statements in the *Researches*, and in the recent *Dictionary of South African Biography*, we find it said,

> In order to arouse sympathy and concern for the Hottentots Philip wrote, as deliberate propaganda, a book in two parts . . . the contents were concocted from various documents such as travel journals and memoranda drawn up by

Philip in the course of his stay in South Africa. The colonists' dealings with the Hottentots, Bushmen and Griquas were denounced as inhuman, while the indigenous peoples were extolled as blameless, upright people whose moral life was being undermined by the colonists. While the good work of the missions were lauded to the skies, the Cape Government and the colonists were reproached for attempting to impede the extension of missionary activity.

The author of the article goes on to accuse Philip of deliberate distortions, and, much more important, of not really knowing the Colony, or Dutch—the language of the Boers, the slaves, the Khoi and the Griqua.

These accusations can be rebutted but at a number of different levels of seriousness. Initially the recent *DSAB* accusation of Philip's not knowing the Colony and not knowing Dutch can be immediately dismissed. Certainly after his return from this trip to UK, his many many tours made him the single most informed man about the whole Colony. But even before the visit, his tour of inspection of all the stations in and out of the Colony was such an extensive survey of the Colony and beyond as very few had ever undertaken. In addition he was in constant correspondence with missionaries all over the Colony and beyond, in particular, Read and Wright who each had an extensive network among the indigenous people. This correspondence, combined with his own travels, gave him a knowledge of South Africa few could match. Clearly, to many of his White contemporaries, reliance on Read and African sources of information was a confirmation of unreliability rather than of sound knowledge. That is an opinion which is understandable when held by people in his day, hardly so in an historian.

It is quite clear from the records that he knew Dutch, the language of the Cape folk and his beloved Griqua. Indeed as early as October 1820 he had begun to preach in Dutch.[34]

On an apparently more serious level of challenge to Philip's reliability, is the complaint of Galbraith, de Klerk and the writer of the Philip entry in DSAB that the *Researches* was a propaganda piece designed to serve a particular political end.

But Philip never pretended that it was anything else than his placing a case before the British public in order to bring about political change. This surely does not make it, *ipso facto,* unreliable. The despatches of Governors, or those of the Secretary of State are also usually serving some policy end or other. We do not see them as some form of objective truth, but neither do we write them off because of this. Philip's *Researches* must be treated as on a level with them. To attempt to dismiss them as propaganda as if Governor's reports of the same period were qualitatively different in their reliability as a source of information about South Africa, is somewhat *faux naif* on the part of an historian.

Again and again these critics assert that the *Researches* is primarily an attack on the colonial population, particularly the Afrikaners; that it was primarily a vehicle for anti-colonist invective. Certainly the volumes contain individual stories of cruelty, examples of the injustice and at times brutality with which Khoi, San and others were treated. These can be paralleled in the writings even of those who are pro-colonist. However, much more important is Philip's overall intention. These stories, which he relates, are all part of a consistent argument which is not to persuade the British public that all colonists, Boer or British, are evil human beings but, on the contrary, to bring about in the British Parliament a condemnation of the form of British rule in the Colony and effect reform of the colonial administration.

It is wrong to maintain, as many still insist on doing, that Philip was anti-Boer. He was no British 'liberal' equating Britishness with justice and truth. Far from it—the burden of his argument was that the ills of South Africa primarily stemmed from the form and the policy of the British Government at the Cape. Even the vaunted Hottentot Code, the legislation of 1809 and 1812, he regarded as fundamentally bad legislation, enshrining in law what had been regarded as abuses of the old Dutch Company system. From his own observations, from the reports of Read, Wright and other missionaries, of Khoi, slave and Xhosa informants, Philip tried to create a picture of the recent history of the Cape that would force the British Government to change its general policy towards, and the form of its administration of, the Cape Colony. Philip made no attempt to set things down from the perspective of official or colonist. Why on earth should he have? Their points of view dominated both the life of the Colony and the picture of the Colony available to the Government in London; Philip's task was to provide an alternative view of the Cape Colony, an alternative view of South Africa.

Naturally, because of the nature of his sources of information, many individual stories of the actions of commando, of individual landdrosts and individual colonists, can be challenged on the basis of alternative evidence, presented by these people themselves and other Whites. Professor Macmillan in his classic *The Cape Colour Question* answered a large number of these specific complaints about the accuracy of particular stories. He is not finally convincing in all cases—some of the accusations and his defence against them would bring the verdict of 'not proven' in a Scottish Court, rather than 'not guilty' and a complete vindication of Philip in every detail. Most of these differences stem from the differing weight to be put on the evidence of White and Black information.

However, one accusation, which originates in Cory's *The Rise of South Africa*, is made in the *DSAB* article on Philip which is much more important. This accusation is that he deliberately falsified the map of Theopolis station in order to accuse the Government of stealing land from the mission. If this were true, it is a very telling blow against Philip's reliability as a witness to South African affairs and to his integrity as a human being, let alone a Christian missionary.

Professor Macmillan in *The Cape Colour Question*[25] effectively rebuts this most serious charge by Cory. There is no need to repeat this careful and thorough rebuttal here. However, it must be insisted upon, because *forty years* after Macmillan's irrefutable demolition of Cory's accusation, the accusation is repeated in the *DSAB* article. Not only this, but it is repeated in the context of the remark about recent researchers having disproved so many of Philip's accusations; and this without any reference to Macmillan's defence at all.

The most famous example of Philip's inaccuracy or of his gullibility in terms of trusting Black witnesses was his accusations in the *Researches* against William Mackay, landdrost of Somerset East. In July 1830, Philip was tried for libel in Cape Town and found guilty. Given British libel laws, most of the early accusations by Woodward and Bernstein in *The Washington Post* that opened up the whole Watergate scandal would have led to libel cases in which reporters would have been found guilty. Also Philip, given the wave of bitter unpopularity with Whites which he was facing in 1830, had little likelihood of facing any but a bitterly hostile judge and jury.

However, even if he had relied on totally untrustworthy testimony in the case of Mackay and had done so on a number of occasions as suggested by his enemies and later critics, this is all beside the point. No one has been able to challenge the main thesis of *Researches*, which is that the Khoi and other free persons of colour were deprived of the basic civil rights which pertain to British subjects and that Cape Colony legislation and the style of the administration kept them in a state of subjection so as to ensure that they constituted a pool of docile and readily available labour for Whites. Indeed the more some critics dwell on the dubiousness of Philip's evidence for the details of a particular commando raid or abuse of power by a particular landdrost, the more the same critic will avoid any direct discussion of the main thesis of Philip's book.

The system, which was Philip's principal target, was enshrined in the so-called Hottentot Code set by the Ordinances of 1809 and 1812, called by many, without intentional irony, the Magna Carta of the Hottentots. In the *Researches*, Philip showed convincingly that these regulations enshrined in law the abuses of the old Dutch East India Company system, whereby the apprenticing of children was used to hold whole Khoi families in *de facto* servitude. He also exposed the hollowness of the humanitarian language used to justify the legislation.

> The pretext that the law is designed to prevent the children of the Hottentots from being exposed to the dangers of starvation, may have been imposed upon the distinguished individuals under whose authority it was issued; but everyone acquainted with the state of the Colony must be satisfied that this pretext is entirely fallacious.[35]

Not only had British legislation made obligatory the worst issues of the Dutch system but the new British colonists behaved no differently towards the Khoi than did the trekboers. Philip pointed out that in the early 1820s there had been a move to break up the London Missionary Society Institution at Theopolis and distribute the Khoi inhabitants as labourers among the neighbouring British settlers.

Again and again he insisted that the antagonism towards the London Missionary Society settlements was more now, because of their success—the very thing demanded of them by the British authorities in 1819. The

London Missionary Society success in its reorganisation had led to the creation of a class, growing steadily in number, of literate and comparatively prosperous Khoi and other Black families. These carters, carpenters, smiths and so on, were becoming a small but significant element in the economy of the eastern Cape. It was these families, Philip insisted, that were so often picked on by veld-kornets and landdrosts for compulsory labour, thus upsetting their businesses. This was all part of the fundamental approach of the administration that wished a permanently pauperised Khoi community. Of this, Philip wrote

> There is no tyranny so cruel (says Montesquieu) as that which is exercised under the pretext of law, and under the colour of justice; when wretches are, so to speak, drowned on the very plank to which they clung for safety.[13]

This was the main thrust of Philip's book and of his campaign, both in South Africa and the United Kingdom, to give the Khoi and all other free persons of colour, the basic civil rights of all British subjects and to enable them to bring their labour and what little capital they had, to a free market.

In England, the forces of the Anti-Slavery Society were marshalled in support of this end, and, after a good deal of negotiation with the members of the Government in private, Buxton put to the House of Commons on 15 July 1828 the motion:

> This House humbly solicits His Majesty to cause such instructions to be sent to the Colony of the Cape of Good Hope, as shall most effectually secure to all the natives of South Africa, the same freedom and protection as are enjoyed by other free people of that Colony whether English or Dutch.[38]

The Government, as had been privately agreed previously, accepted the motion and it was passed. It was *two days later* that, in the Cape, Acting Governor General Bourke promulgated Ordinance 50. This Ordinance, in its first three clauses, gave in detail the very equality called for in the House of Commons Resolution. The Ordinance had been drafted, after careful advice from Andries Stockenstrom, a landdrost, son of a landdrost, who at various times in 1825 had conferred with John Philip about 'the situation of the aborigines'. The two men, missionary and Afrikaner, had reached some agreement in principle. This is not to claim Stockenstrom as a mouthpiece for Philip—he was always his own man—but it is not surprising because of their agreement in general, that the Ordinance fulfilled many of Philip's hopes.

It is however, important to note that had there been no Ordinance 50 at that time, Bourke, or his successor, would have had to draw one up because of the Resolution of the House of Commons—the Resolution which was a direct product of Philip's campaign.

Following the report of Ordinance 50 arriving in London, there was a good deal of discussion among the Directors of the Society, the evangelical parliamentary lobby and other interested parties as to whether Ordinance 50 adequately fulfilled the intention of the Resolution of the House of 15 July or not. Philip was clear that it did. He was especially pleased by the second clause which not only ended compulsory labour except that for which

Whites were also liable, but, more important, it ended the whole concept of vagrancy, the burden under which the Khoi and other free persons of colour had laboured for so long.

Despite his enthusiasm for what the Ordinance did, Philip was unhappy that the reform was in the form of an Ordinance of the Cape Government only, and did not have formal confirmation by Westminster. Any ordinance could simply be overturned by another subsequent ordinance so that, on its own, Ordinance 50 might have had only very temporary effect. The simple decision of the Governor and Council in the Cape could restore vagrancy or special forced labour regulations applying only to persons of colour. Because of the lack of permanence in the legal situation, Philip insisted that some specific guarantee of the permanence of Ordinance 50 had to be made by the Government in London. He convinced the still active Claphamites—Buxton, Charles Grant (later the Colonial Secretary, Lord Glenelg), Dr Lushington and others—that this was necessary and pressure was brought to bear on the Cabinet. As a result the essential matter of Ordinance 50 was promulgated as an Order-in-Council which gave it a very different legal standing.

This Order-in-Council of January 1829 was the foundation on which Philip, Read and the other LMS radicals believed a new kind of society could be built in the Colony. It was certainly an essential element in the foundation upon which the non-racial Cape constitution of 1853 was developed—a constitution, which, though dented and bruised by many different forces, maintained a non-racial legal structure in the Cape Colony, until that Colony disappeared with the creation of the new Union of South Africa. The non-racial legal principles of the Colony disappeared with it.

In his long report for the Buxton family in 1845, Philip saw his own role as a vital one in this development in the affairs of the Cape. White political opinion at the time and since, both those who applauded and those who deplored these events, has always agreed with Philip's judgement in this matter. However, of this judgement Professor Galbraith in *Reluctant Empire* says,

> This impression of direct influence gave him status at the Cape, but it was almost certainly untrue, for by the testimony of the staff he had only one interview with the Colonial Secretary, and that was at the solicitation of the Directors of the London Missionary Society, whose Secretary was also present on that occasion. Such deviations from facts subject him to the charge of deliberate falsehood. The allegation is unduly harsh, but he possessed a conveniently unreliable memory.[39]

This really is quite extraordinary. Here is a liberal modern historical researcher showing Philip to be a liar in a vital matter, however much Galbraith softens the accusation by his form of words.

It is true that Philip had only that one interview with the Colonial Secretary. However it also is true that he was a key, if not *the* key figure in the campaign that led to the Order-in-Council. As we have seen, Philip had, for two years, been in constant and close contact with Buxton, Lushington, Grant and others of the Clapham Sect. They, in turn, were constant in their lobbying of the leading figures in the Government, notably Murray, the Colonial Secretary. Buxton and the others who pressured Murray, knew nothing of South Africa except for the information Philip fed to them. He did not have to see Murray personally in order to have influence—he secured it through his Claphamite allies. However, even more telling and significant is that Philip had direct and vitally important contact with someone in the Colonial Office who in many ways, was more important than Murray; this was 'Mr Secretary Stephen' himself. In Stephen's papers it is clearly recorded that he was in regular touch with Philip during this period, dining with him on various occasions; most notably it is recorded that he spent a whole evening with Philip discussing the terms of Ordinance 50 and the framing of the Order-in-Council needed to make it permanent.[40]

The Vagrancy Ordinance of 1834

Very pleased at the outcome of his labour Philip returned to South Africa in 1829. His return marks the beginning of that phase of his life which has led some missionary historians to dub him the 'Protestant Pope of South Africa'. This was because there went out with him to South Africa, the first party of the Paris Evangelical Mission (PEM). Their deployment was to be in the hands of Philip, who was to remain as adviser to the mission for the rest of his active career. He was also, at this time, asked by the Rheineschen Missionsgesellschaft to see to the disposition and organisation of their first party of missionaries to serve in South Africa. His formal relationship with this society was neither so close, nor so long as that with the PEM and later the American Board of Commissioners for Foreign Missions, yet contributed to his key role in all areas of Protestant Missionary activity except that of the Methodist Missionary Society.

All of this meant that for the first few months after his return he was overwhelmed with work and responsibility. He had no sooner disposed of the backlog of work waiting for him inside the London Missionary Society and the external tasks given him by the other societies, when the crisis of the Mackay libel case struck.

Philip has been aware as soon as he returned to South Africa that there was a widespread antagonism to him among the White population of the Colony. This stemmed partly from the passing of Ordinance 50 but also from stories coming back to the Colony that he had spent his time in England libelling the White population. His book was seen as an anti-White diatribe. The administration share this antagonism and the Governor, Sir Lowry Cole, refused to grant him an audience on Philip's return to the Colony.

The Mackay libel case resulted in Philip having to pay £200 damages plus £400 in legal costs. This was an overwhelming sum in those days, especially for someone whose salary came from a Missionary Society. Philip was saved from ruin by his evangelical allies in the United Kingdom organising an appeal for assistance which paid off the required sums.

However, what hurt Philip most about the trial was that it brought home to him how unpopular he was among the White population. Some of the most bitter of his opponents were 1820 Settlers who, only recently, had lauded him as their spokesman and protector.

Before this terrible cloud of bitterness had dispersed, Philip was plunged into yet another acrimonious controversy. This was over the exact area of landholding of the Theopolis Institution. Professor Macmillan has most thoroughly dealt with the accusation that Philip deliberately falsified maps and records in order to defend and make good the London Missionary Society's position, but though the outcome at the time was a victory for the London Missionary Society the controversy was exhausting and depressing for Philip.

In 1830 *De Zuid Afrikaan* began to appear in Cape Town and the following year saw the birth of the *Grahamstown Journal*. This created a very different situation from that which Philip had known before his trip to England. Then Whites had generally regarded him as a friend and the only newspaper in the Colony, the *Commercial Advertiser*, edited by Fairbairn, was on his side in most matters. Now the generality of Whites were at best suspicious of him and at worst bitterly hostile, and two newspapers had come into being, dedicated to opposing his belief in a non-racial basis for the economic and political development of the Colony. Their columns were filled with bitter attacks on Philip, letters and articles which questioned his integrity and character, as well as opposing the policies which he supported.

One bright spot in all this for Philip was that, although Sir Lowry Cole would not deal with him, the Governor was open to the advice of Sir Andries Stockenstrom. While Philip was still in the United Kingdom a very important event indeed had taken place at the instigation of Stockenstrom. This was the creation of the Kat River Settlement. Stockenstrom had persuaded Cole to give over land in the Kat River area to be occupied by free persons of colour from all over the Colony. Stockenstrom's intention was partly to provide a strong military buffer against the Xhosa, but he also saw the settlement as a means of providing a place for the Khoi and other free Blacks to develop under the new freedom granted by Ordinance 50.

Though many families were drawn from all over the Colony, in fact a large number of those who chose to go to the settlement were families of some standing, with both a little wealth and some skills, from the various London Missionary Society Institutions. Some of them formed a congregation of the Dutch Reformed Church. However, a majority came together and decided to constitute a congregation of the church, which in true Congregationalist tradition, should call a minister for itself.

Philip was present at the large meeting they held to discuss the call. He was delighted when they unanimously decided to call James Read as their minister.

In a report which appeared in *The Evangelical Magazine*, Philip recorded that, at that same meeting, speaker after speaker had likened their plight to that of the Children of Israel in bondage in Egypt and that a new day had dawned with the coming of Ordinance 50 and the creation of the Kat River Settlement which was their Promised Land.

For the Coloured population, as they were now sometimes beginning to be called, these might have been days of joy, but for many Whites a crisis of enormous and far-reaching importance was now at hand.

This was created by the fact that as the year 1833 went on, it was clear that Buxton was at last going to achieve the freeing of slaves, the end to which Wilberforce had devoted his whole life. When emancipation came, the free persons of colour would outnumber the Whites in the Colony by about two to one.

Most Whites already felt greatly threatened by the liberating of so many Blacks as a result of Ordinance 50. The now 'vagrant' Khoi would soon have many other masterless men added to their numbers. White opinion now rallied around a campaign to introduce a vagrancy act to curb this menace. The agitation had begun almost as soon as Ordinance 50 had been promulgated. The Colony was filled with rumours from all corners of the danger to Whites from these violent vagrants.

During 1830 Philip became increasingly disturbed because of the enormous numbers of these reports reaching Cape Town. Although he felt sure the majority of the free people of colour were not behaving in this aggressive manner, he was afraid the wild actions of some might be endangering his plans for the integration of all into colonial society and the colonial economy.

Accompanied by Fairbairn, he set out on an exhaustive tour of the Colony to find out for himself how things were. He found little evidence at all of the crime wave that was reported as threatening to engulf the White population. A crime wave that is still reported as having occurred by writers like Ransford (*The Great Trek*) and de Klerk (*Puritans in Africa*). Philip wrote a long detailed report to Dr John Fletcher, a personal friend and staunch London Missionary Society supporter in England. In this Philip reports

> You will recollect that I always said that unless the Charter of the Hottentots is sealed by the King in Council it will be worth nothing and everything which has arisen since my arrival here justifies the opinion I then formed. The Charter was no sooner published than letters and petitions and declarations proceeded from every quarter declaring that everything in the colony would be lost if it was carried into effect. When I arrived in the Colony the office of the Commercial Advertiser was filled with communications from the country stations that the Hottentots had left their former masters, that they were living in the bushes in hordes supporting themselves by robbery and stealth. One writer had three thousand sheep destroyed by the freed Hottentots out of a flock of five thousand. Others pretended that they must sell their farms and their stock on account of the robberies committed by the Hottentots and one actually sold his farm making *this* pretence. The editor of the Commercial Advertiser has exposed and confounded many of those accusers; but the assertions were reiterated and he was told that he had never been in the country. . . . It was necessary that something should be done. Mr. Fairbairn has been with me during the journey except when he deviated from the road to obtain a more perfect acquaintance with the actual state of the colony. We now come to the actual result of the journey of nearly 600 miles. We have not met one party of

Hottentots in the Bushes nor with one Hottentot not in service. At Cape Town we were told we should find it at Hottentots Holland, at Hottentots Holland we were told we would find it at Zwellendam, at Zwellendam we were told we should meet with it at George, at George it was at Bethelsdorp, Algoa Bay, Uitenhage. Now we are told it is at Grahamstown and Theopolis and when we get there I hope we shall find it gone to Caffirland.[41]

On their return from the long tour, Philip and Fairbairn tried, through the columns of the *Commercial Advertiser*, to calm things down. They were unsuccessful. Indeed the volume of rumours and fears were greatly increased through the activities of both the *Grahamstown Journal* and *De Zuid Afrikaan*.

The pressure became very intense and Sir Lowry Cole and his Colonial Secretary, Colonel Wade, came to be fully in sympathy with this campaign.

It was the Emancipation Act which finally decided them that they should act. Wade circulated all the 'proprietors' of the Colony in January 1834, assuring them that, before the interim 'apprenticeship' period laid down by the Emancipation Act had expired, legislation would be in being which would not only prevent vagrancy but, and this is the nub, ensure a steady supply of labour. This legislation he insisted would compel

not only the liberated apprentices to earn an honest livelihood, but all others who, being capable of doing so, may be inclined to lead an idle and vagabondizing life.[42]

In May 1834, a draft ordinance along these lines was laid before the Council. However, there was, by that time, a new Governor, Sir Benjamin D'Urban, appointed by a new Government in Westminster, the first of the newly reformed Parliament. When he saw the legislation, D'Urban suggested that it be dropped. However, led by Wade, the Council was adamant and the Ordinance was passed.

This was precisely the situation that Philip had foreseen in 1828 when he pressed for the Order-in-Council to set Ordinance 50 apart from normal ordinances. In terms of that Order-in-Council D'Urban made it clear that the new Ordinance would have to be agreed by the British Government before it could be promulgated and so he referred the matter to London.

Meanwhile, Philip had been bombarding the Governor's office with memoranda composed by himself, some by other missionaries and a large number of petitions from Cape Folk communities. The most important of these latter was one presented to and endorsed by a mass meeting of the various communities of the Kat River Settlement. This meeting was presided over by James Read. These petitions reflected what was reported at the time by most missionaries of the London Missionary Society, even those not particularly alive to the political issues of the day, which was that the whole Cape Folk population was profoundly disturbed by anger and fear. One tangible sign of this was a massive movement of Cape Folk families onto the London Missionary Society properties and into the Kat River Settlement.

Philip kept Buxton abreast of all these developments so that he could approach Lord Aberdeen well armed with information. When the Secretary of State received the draft Ordinance, which was opposed both by his new Governor in the Cape and by the evangelical anti-slavery lobby at home, he had no hesitation in disallowing it.

Consternation was the response of the White population of the Colony to this action by Lord Aberdeen. Their confidence in the complete justice and certainty of their case (after all, the new legislation had been planned by the old Governor, Cole, and the Colonial Secretary, Wade) was such that in many of the eastern and northern districts, veld-cornets had already begun applying the proposed Vagrancy Ordinance.

Philip recorded many examples of people having to obtain the old style passes from veld-cornets or from a 'baas' before being able to go about their legitimate business. Much more depressing were incidents which occurred when these over-confident officials arrested the men of a number of independent Cape Folk families for refusing to work for local farmers. It was no comfort that they were quickly released, once word of Aberdeen's decision was spread throughout the Colony, for, during their period in detention, most of them had lost their cattle, the very basis of their prosperity and independence.

In many works of South African history, the promulgation of Ordinance 50 is referred to as a turning-point in the history of Cape Colony. However, it is arguable that it was the disallowance of the proposed Vagrancy Ordinance of 1834 that was the critical moment for the colonists. It was, at last, borne in on them just what the entrenchment of Ordinance 50 in law meant in a situation where statutory slavery was also ended.

It is a matter of debate whether the Great Trek would have occurred without the additional conflict over British policy towards the defeated Xhosa after the War of 1834–36. What is certain is that some families had decided to trek and others had begun to trek away from the Colony, as soon as it was clear there could be no effective vagrancy legislation. The main thrust of what became known as the Great Trek was certainly after the War but, even so, the disallowing of the Vagrancy Ordinance figures in the records of Voortrekker discussions as of great importance in fact, and as the symbol of all that the trekkers rejected by embarking on the Great Trek.

John Philip was closely associated in the minds of all the colonists with the failure to obtain vagrancy legislation and the hated policy towards the Xhosa. So Philip became a figure representing the enemy in the minds, not only of the Voortrekkers and their sympathisers, but in the minds of British settlers of the eastern Cape also.

However, when Lord Aberdeen's decision came to the Cape, it seemed to Philip that a new day had dawned. The new Governor, D'Urban, was personally sympathetic to him; Buxton appeared to be at the height of his influence in Westminster; the position of all British 'persons of colour' seemed assured; the days of bitter conflict and misunderstanding seemed to be over.

5

John Philip and the Eastern Frontier

Doctor Philip returned to Cape Town in September 1829 to face many difficulties. Some of these were internal to the London Missionary Society in South Africa but most stemmed from the widespread antagonism towards him on the part of many Whites, in the administration and among the population at large, particularly in the eastern frontier districts. The difficulties within the mission will be considered in another chapter—it is sufficient to say that on his return there was a mass of tiresome administrative and personal problems that had to be resolved. These took up a great deal of his time and energy and drained him emotionally at a time when he needed quiet and the support of friends. He needed support because of a trial for libel, the sharpest expression of the antagonism and the distrust so many Whites felt towards him.

The libel case was brought by Mackay, landdrost of Somerset East. As we have seen, this famous case, which Philip lost, has been used again and again to discredit Philip as a reliable witness of events in South Africa, and clearly this was the intention of those who encouraged the bringing of the case by Mackay. In the short term, it also presented enormous financial difficulties to Philip; £200 damages and £400 costs were a major blow to add to the emotional distress the case caused him and his wife, the indefatigable Jane. The evangelical circles in Britain which had hitherto backed Philip, did not fail him at this juncture, and the necessary funds were raised to pay the damages and costs.

There is no doubt, however, that the case left Philip wary and suspicious of possible plots against him. When one remembers the wave of hysterical suspicion that overwhelmed so many otherwise rational men on both sides of the controversies during Somerset's tenure of office at the Cape, it is not surprising that Philip, in letters to the London Missionary Society Directors and to the Buxton family, does from time to time exhibit a tendency to find plots when there are none, or at least none of which we can now find evidence. However, these occasions are few and do not amount to evidence of the persecution complex of which he has been accused by some. On the contrary, one can argue that he ought to have been more suspicious of those in authority. As we shall see in his relations with Sir Benjamin D'Urban, the new Governor appointed in 1834, a little more caution and suspicion might have held Philip back from the ready, indeed enthusiastic, cooperation with that gentleman's policies towards the Xhosa which subsequently left Philip so vulnerable to accusation of double-dealing, indeed of inciting the Xhosa to war.

The Mackay case itself did offer a number of features which tended to confirm Philip's suspicions that Sir Lowry Cole and some of the Governor's entourage were deliberately planning to discredit him.

The *Researches*, were, as Philip again and again made clear, not aimed at presenting individual Whites, be they Afrikaners or Englishmen, officials or ranchers, as evil men, whose wickedness caused all the problems of South Africa. The main thrust of the book, and of Philip's campaign in the United Kingdom, was that the system of government in the Colony was at fault and it was the system which caused so many to behave so badly. The many individual instances of injustice or cruelty were told to illustrate that main point. As we have seen, most of these instances were gathered by Philip from van der Kemp's papers, from James Read and from the many adherents of the London Missionary Society at Theopolis, Bethelsdorp and the missions beyond the Colony. However, of all the possible individual stories that might have been challenged in a libel action only this particular incident relating to the landdrost of Somerset East was. The incident had been related to Philip by Thomas Pringle, who insisted that his principal informants had been Mr Hart, the acting landdrost of the District and Mr Onkruydt, the Secretary of the Heemraden, though there were Khoi witnesses also.

The trial took place after Pringle was back in England and so could not attend, and the majority of the Khoi witnesses simply did not appear at the Court in Cape Town; of the two who did, the evidence of one, favourable to Philip, was disallowed on a legal technicality, the other was made to appear confused and unreliable by the prosecution. Mr Onkruydt simply denied having talked to Pringle about the matter at all. Given the state of the eastern frontier region from which the Khoi witnesses had to come and the vast distances involved, it is easy to understand that all but two of the Khoi witnesses did not reach Cape Town but in the circumstances of the timing of the trial and violently expressed antagonism towards Philip on the part of many Whites including officials, it is also easy to understand why Fairbairn and others associated with Philip, suspected that the witnesses had been prevented from coming.[1] Mackay himself added to these suspicions in the minds of Philip's friends by insisting that he was 'compelled' to bring the action. In the circumstances Philip wrote to his fellow Directors in London

> It is necessary that you should know the fact whatever use you may make of it; that the highest authority in the Colony has had its hand in all the proceedings which have been [illegible] against me. I had scarcely arrived in the Colony when this became apparent. Mr. Mackay has all along declared that he was *compelled* to prosecute me, and his case was selected because they know that it was furnished me by Pringle and it was known that he was out of the Colony. They have not dared prosecute me in any instance I supplied.[2]

Nor indeed did any other prosecution for libel take place. To Philip and Fairbairn this appeared as confirmation of their suspicions.

Whether the Governor, Sir Lowry Cole, had any hand in the raising of the case against Philip it is now impossible to tell. What is clear is that he and succeeding Governors were always wary of Philip. Although, on his appointment as resident Director, one of Philip's primary tasks was to restore good relations between the London Missionary Society and the Cape Administration, he was shrewd enough to see soon that it was more important to have access to and good relations with the Colonial Office in London, where the real power lay. Of course, if good relations with the officials in Cape Town could be maintained, well and good, but Whitehall was more important, as was proved in the campaign for civil rights in the Colony, above all in the matter of Whitehall's endorsement of Ordinance 50 which gave it a different status from other Ordinances of the Cape Administration.

So long as the evangelical lobby was an effective pressure group in London, it gave Philip his most effective tool in his attempt to achieve the political ends he believed vital to the fulfilment of the missionary task in South Africa.

However, this tool also brought with it grave handicaps. The first was that any Governor, however sympathetic, and there is no indication that Cole was ever sympathetic, was uncomfortably aware that in Philip there was a potential critic with direct access, through Buxton, to his superiors in London. It would also be no bad thing in the eyes of the Governor facing the difficulties of the Cape at that time to have such a critic discredited.

The second handicap that access to Government in London brought to Philip, was that it associated him with the policies of the Imperial authorities in the minds of the colonists, Afrikaner and English; to the Afrikaners, the Government in London was not only distant but appeared alien and antagonistic towards them; to the English, the authorities in London were distant and constantly blind to the real difficulties facing the people on the spot.

Despite having some influence in the 1830s Philip, in fact, never again had the same influence in London as he had in the matter of Ordinance 50. This did not deter colonists and officials from seeing the hand of Philip in anything emanating from London which they deemed to be overly pro-native. Philip, in his turn, did little to disabuse them of this, since for the rest of his life, Philip clung to the idea that the Imperial Government in London was the only hope for the just settlement of the various conflicts between colonists and Africans. Only such an externally imposed settlement could create the necessary conditions for the effective spread of Christianity in South Africa.

However, despite the bitterness and distress of the libel case Philip settled down to his tasks, high among which was his continued concern for the 'free people of colour' in the Colony.

As recorded in the last chapter, Philip set out with Fairbairn early in 1830 on a long journey by land to the eastern frontier. This was to visit the various stations of the Society but also to investigate the many rumours of Cape Folk vagrants causing trouble throughout the Colony. He and his companion were able to report that the stories were greatly exaggerated if not entirely groundless.

On this journey, Philip visited the new Kat River Settlement of the Cape Folk. The visit to the Settlement brought together Philip's concern for the Kat River Settlers, his affection and respect for James Read and a new concern for the problems of the relations between the Xhosa and the Colony.

This new venture on the Kat is generally seen as the achievement of Sir Andries Stockenstrom, though there is a case for suggesting that Thomas Pringle thought of it at least as early as did Stockenstrom. In 1823 Pringle wrote a paper 'Hints of a Plan for Defending the Eastern Frontier of the Colony by a Settlement of Hottentots' which outlined a plan for a settlement not too different from that of 1829. Whether Pringle's paper sparked off the idea in Stockenstrom's mind or whether it simply confirmed ideas he already had does not now matter. Pringle and he certainly thought alike in this matter and discussed together the state of the 'free people of colour' on many occasions, as we can see from a memorial Pringle wrote in support of some Bastard tenants and acquaintances of his who sought permission to own land and gain burgher rights in the days before Ordinance 50.

> They are people of colour or Bastaards, according to the phraseology of the Colony. In other respects I consider them as respectable as the generality of burghers in this neighbourhood, more so than many who have lately got grants of land. I have known the Memorialists for several years and am well acquainted with their characters and sentiments, and hesitate not to say that I believe their attachment to the Government and their respect for the constituted authority to be unquestionable. I have spoken respecting the application of these people for land to Mr Mackay, the landdrost of this district. He seems to have doubts on the subject. Indeed, Captain Stockenstrom is the only provincial magistrate I have conversed with who appears to entertain judicious views on such points.[3]

Stockenstrom's 1829 scheme, implemented by Sir Lowry Cole, included the two main ideas of Pringle's 1823 paper, first to give the Cape Folk a chance to show that they could create a prosperous and civilised community and second to use their presence as a buffer between the Xhosa and the rest of the Colony. The 1829 scheme however, included something not in Pringle's original idea and something which he criticised in his book *A Narrative of a Residence in South Africa* published in 1835. This was the planting of the new settlement on the land of Maqoma's Xhosa from which the latter were moved by force. In 1828 Maqoma had raided a number of Thembu villages as a punishment for their misbehaviour and their refusal to accept his authority. The Thembu appealed for help to the colonial authorities. Many settlers had been complaining of cattle thieving by Maqoma's people and this incident gave the Governor ample reason, from his point of view, to expel Maqoma from lands which he held simply by the grace and favour of the Governor, though it was accepted that they were, for all that, the 'homeland' of Maqoma's people. Cole was not particularly sympathetic towards the Cape Folk, but a settlement along the lines suggested by Stockenstrom appeared a far more effective barrier to prevent Maqoma's people creeping back into their old lands than a scattering of White ranches. Some in Government also felt that such a community, free of London Missionary Society influence, would lessen the influence of that Society on the Cape Folk community.

As was anticipated, a large number of the families which came to the new settlements were from the London Missionary Society stations at Theopolis and Bethelsdorp. Indeed many of the mission families which had achieved the greatest degree of financial and educational advance went there—in some ways, the cream of the crop of London Missionary Society achievement. This at first perturbed Philip somewhat. However, the result was something far from that anticipated by the colonial authorities. Although they sent Mr Thomson, Brownlee's successor as a 'government missionary' on the frontier, as the official Dutch Reformed Church minister to the people of the Settlement, only a minority of the Christians accepted him as their pastor. As noted already, the majority got together and petitioned John Philip to allow them to call their own pastor. The man they chose was James Read. If there was one member of the London Missionary Society staff whom Whites, both official and unofficial, distrusted and disliked more than John Philip, it was James Read. However, in the new situation of the Cape Colony, these free people could not be prevented from this action. Philip, after ascertaining that Read was willing to accept the call, agreed to his going.

This decision was important at a number of levels. The first was ecclesiastical. The calling of James Read to the Kat River and his ordination to full ministry of Word and Sacraments, marks the birth of the first real Black congregation of the Christian Church in South Africa. The Kat River situation was not the usual one of a chief allowing a missionary to work and live among his people, nor of a missionary gathering a group of people around him on a mission station where they were entirely dependent on him and the missionary society. Here was a community of Christian people exercising their right under Congregational polity of calling a man to be their minister and, as a result of that call, the man being ordained to the full ministry, again a basic element in both Congregationalist and Presbyterian polity. Kat River was not a mission station but a congregation of the Christian Church in the full legal and ecclesiastical sense of those words. The Christian communities among the Griqua were, at this time, gradually developing in this direction, but Kat River was the first to achieve it.

The second important point, made by Read's calling and ordination, was that the London Missionary Society, at least in the persons of Philip and Read, had still great standing with the Cape people, quite apart from their creation of havens for them on the mission stations.

Thirdly, this call from the people of the Kat River enabled Philip to publicly recognise his friend and confidant in a way that ended the cloud under which he had lived for so long. It was remarked in the last chapter that Philip had entrusted Read with the renewal of Bethelsdorp even though the latter had been suspended from full missionary status as a result of Thom's 'Synod'. Now Read was not only restored to full status as a missionary in the service of the Society, he was ordained to the ministry, a status which he had not held at any time before.

Fourthly, Philip's close involvement with Read and his Kat River people, brought him hard up against the problem of the Xhosa frontier.

As he admitted later, to the Aborigines Committee, Philip had not thought much about the problems of the Xhosa people up until then. It had been the problems of the northern frontier that had most concerned him from almost the beginning of his stay in Africa. The plight of the San, and more particularly, that of the Griqua peoples were of great concern to Philip. It was the situation of the Griqua that first provoked Philip into a consideration of the ways British policy towards people beyond the frontier could aid or hinder the spread of Christianity.

During the 1820s he was not unaware of the problems in the eastern region of the Colony. The missionaries of the Society working with the Xhosa both within and without the Colony, regularly reported on their work. Indeed, on his last long tour of inspecton before going to England, Philip met Dr William Wright, the representative in South Africa of the Society for the Propagation of the Gospel. Wright was returning from a journey through 'Kaffirland', and met Philip at the house of Andries Stockenstrom where Philip was staying with Thomas Pringle. Stockenstrom recorded in his autobiography that

> Wright, having for some time been travelling on the Frontier and through Kaffirland, was literally frantic about the injustices and oppression which he had heard of and witnessed.[4]

There is no record in the massive correspondence of Philip still extant, nor in the notes made by Professor Macmillan of the correspondence, now destroyed, formerly held in South Africa, that this encounter and the routine reports from the east had any significant impact on Philip's thinking or actions at that time. The administration of justice within the Colony was still his main concern. The problem of the frontier was secondary, and within that problem, the Xhosa frontier ranked after the problems of the north in Philip's mind. He returned to England, campaigned for equal civil rights for all free people within the Colony and wrote the *Researches*.

It is clearly from the time of the major trek to the east with Fairbairn and the call from the Kat River to Read that the problems of the eastern frontier began to loom large in Philip's mind. On the eve of his departure he wrote to Mrs Buxton

> Our great people here know that everything is not well on that [eastern] frontier and have some dread of an exposure. My journey, however, is purely missionary, and beyond the duties of a missionary it is not my intention to go.[5]

What Philip was referring to would appear to be the treatment of Maqoma. John Ross of the Glasgow Missionary Society had worked among Maqoma's people at a station called Balfour. When Maqoma had been removed Ross had gone with him and taken up his case. Ross was a close friend of James Read and both had drawn Philip's attention to Maqoma's plight and his bitter sense of having been betrayed by the British.

In this matter of the eastern frontier, Philip has been accused, both by his contemporaries and by writers since, of being unaware of the terrible difficulties faced by the Whites in the area, and indeed of maligning their characters. Yet in this affair, as we shall see, his attitude was the same as it had been in struggle for civil rights within the Colony. Of course there were unscrupulous individuals involved, but the crux of the matter was British policy. It was government policy which created the problem and that was what had to change if unscrupulous men were to be checked and averagely decent men were to be shielded from the pressures that drove them to be ruthless and unscrupulous. This attitude is essentially the same as the classic evangelical critics of slavery in Britain and the USA who held that it was slavery that made men cruel and inhumane, not inhumane men who made slavery bad.

In any case, Philip was quite well aware of the problems faced by the settlers. Had not his own friend and fellow 'agitator', Thomas Pringle, led a commando when his estates were left unprotected from San raids in 1825? In defending himself to Fairbairn and Philip, Pringle encapsulated the frontier problem in a few sentences

> Your damnations against my Bushman commando do not alarm me. There is no 'damned spot' on my hands . . . if attacked, I will resist even to slaying them, approve who may. But in regard to these poor wretches, though many of them are murderous I pity them more than blame them and in letters to the landdrost on the subject have thrown out a warning, almost a threat, about bloodshed. . . .
>
> At present they have scarcely any choice but of predatory warfare and precarious existence, or servitude to the Boers. The only certainty they have is the desert and the best parts even of it are taken from them. Is the vindictive spirit they exhibit in such circumstances to be wondered at? And yet to us who are exposed to their attacks, their hostility is no joke.[6]

So despite his great joy in finding the Cape Folk thriving in freedom on the Kat River and being able to mark so signally with favour his friend James Read, the upshot of this first long trek was a sense of gloom. The situation of the eastern frontier was marked by violence, injustice and insecurity. Rumour and counter rumour ran round both sides of the frontier as to the intention of the rival groups. What was also clear was that the tension was not simply between colonials and Xhosa. The people of the Kat River, despite the fact that a majority of the adult males had served the Colony well both on commando and in the Cape Corps, were objects of suspicion and envy among many Whites. So much so that in November and December of 1831, rumours, apparently emanating from Grahamstown, went round among the trekboers suggesting that the veterans of Kat River were going to rise in rebellion and lead the Xhosa in an invasion of the Colony. The local veld-cornets called out the burghers on commando and they rode out to attack the Settlement. Luckily, the military commander on the frontier, Henry Somerset, had also heard the rumour and rode with a small escort to the Kat in order to investigate. He arrived before the commando on New Year's Day, 1832. He found all at peace, indeed a large majority of the population were attending worship in their various churches. Somerset then rode back to meet the commando and after some discussion persuaded them to stand down and return to their homesteads.[7]

Philip viewed the general situation as being so serious and threatening that he directed the men of the Paris Missionary Society, who had sailed back to South Africa with him, not to attempt to enter upon work in the

Xhosa area. Meanwhile, he watched and waited and planned another journey to the area. However, his view of the frontier was altered from the perspective he had had in the 1820s, for he now had on the frontier a man in close touch with the Xhosa and one whom he trusted, James Read. Read, although deeply involved in church and school in the Kat River Settlement, was also in touch with Xhosa, both directly and through his many Coloured contacts in the army and in various forms of service up and down both sides of the unclear and contested line between Xhosa and White. He now kept Philip informed, indeed it could be suggested that it was Read's presence in the heart of affairs in the east that brought them to such prominence in the activities of Philip.

The Eastern Frontier on the Eve of the Sixth Frontier War

In order to understand Philip's actions from 1830 onwards, it is necessary to briefly review the recent history of Xhosa–colonial relations. As was noted at the end of Chapter 1, by the early 1820s the old pre-1819 situation was gradually returning in the 'ceded' territory, where Xhosa and White groups were again living side by side with their flocks. In addition Whites were again crossing into acknowledged Xhosa territory from time to time in search of good pasture as were non-ceded territory Xhosa doing the same thing in the other direction.

The result of all this was that all the old complaints of Xhosa pressure on water and grass and of their cattle-lifting making life intolerable for the White ranchers, were again rife. For their part, the Xhosa complained bitterly about the way the patrol system was being used indiscriminately to deprive the Xhosa of their cattle. There was one new element however. The Xhosa had in 1819 lost a significant area of land for the first time in their history. This rankled bitterly in their minds and also created there a fear that the Whites intended to take more land. This fear was heightened by the treatment of Maqoma between 1819 and 1833.

Technically it was not the patrols as such, of which the Xhosa were complaining, but the way the 'spoor' law was being operated. Although there were earlier attempts to operate a somewhat similar system, the spoor law that was at the root of so much controversy in the 1820s and 1830s originated with an agreement made between Governor Somerset and Ngqika in 1817. This agreement said that a rancher who had lost stock through theft by Xhosa should complain immediately to the nearest military authority. The rancher would then, accompanied by a military patrol, follow the spoor of his cattle to the village of the thieves when the cattle would be recovered, or an equivalent number of Xhosa cattle be taken in restitution. Just what was an equivalent number left a great deal of room for conflict. This system was not dissimilar to traditional Xhosa practice. However, as it came to be applied, it did not include the element vital in traditional law of gaining the willing cooperation of the chief or chiefs. Even more serious, however, was the development in Colonel Somerset's understanding of spoor law, which was completely outside of traditional procedure. This was that, if the result of following the spoor did not clearly indicate the guilty village, then the patrol could, as a reprisal, take cattle from the village or villages they deemed most likely to be guilty.

Even Cory and Theal, those stalwarts of traditional South African historiography, admit that the system did not always work well. Eric Walker is also critical,

> According to local officials the colonial losses were heavy and, as a rule, recoveries comparatively small; but the later history of the Basuto border suggests, both in the Sovereignty and early Free State days, men who claim compensation always 'stand upon their biggest foot'. . . . Probably the colonists took as many cattle as they lost; it is possible they took more, for they rated colonial cattle higher and higher in terms of Kaffir beasts as the quality of their own improved.[8]

Walker goes on to add that it was the threat to the land that upset the Xhosa. All of this misses part of the point. It was the way the system was operated that the Xhosa detested. They saw it as arbitrary. The innocent were often, to their fury and bewilderment, punished for crimes they had not committed. The Xhosa had a concept of justice and truth, perhaps different from that of the Whites but real nevertheless. Walker is correct to insist that the fear of losing the land was associated with the patrol system. The Xhosa, particularly, in the years immediately before 1834, felt that the system was geared deliberately to deprive them of their cattle and so drive them into war, the outcome of which could be a colonial claim for more land.

No Xhosa spokesman, nor any White sympathiser, denied that there was a problem created by the lifting of cattle by some Xhosa. However, the patrol system clearly did not stop it, and, indeed angered more and more people against the Whites. The practice was open to so many deliberate as well as accidental abuses by both White and Xhosa. Pieres gives two examples of how a shrewd Xhosa headman could turn the patrol system to his advantage. He reports how Ngqika wished to punish the Ntsusa clan

> A military patrol was sent after a group of Xhosa who had stolen some horses. Tyhali, Ngqika's son and right-hand man was called in and traced the spoor till it was lost. He then pointed out the Ntsusa as the culprits, complaining that they were 'the terror of the country' and 'the resort of all the Xhosa who fell under the displeasure of their chiefs'. . . . As a result a commando was sent out against the Ntsusa. The device of accusing his enemies of depredations in order to instigate the Colony to send a commando against them was also tried against Aqeno.[9]

This technique was clearly open to any chief accused by a patrol when they had not clear spoor—he could 'trace' the spoor elsewhere.

However, the most devastating criticism of the whole system is that made by Sir Andries Stockenstrom, a veteran of many a patrol and commando. To the Parliamentary Select Committee on Aborigines he explained the problems of its operation and the devastatingly bad effect it had on White–Xhosa relations.

I had long since made up my mind that the great source of misfortune on the frontier was the system of taking Kaffir cattle under these circumstances by our patrols, and I shall give my reasons; if Kaffirs steal cattle, very seldom the real perpetrators can be found, unless the man losing the cattle has been on his guard and sees the robbery actually perpetrated, so that he can immediately collect a force and pursue the plunderers. If the cattle be once out of sight of the plundered party, there is seldom any getting them again; our patrols are then entirely at the mercy of the statements made by the farmers, and they pretend they are leading them on the trace of stolen cattle which may be the trace of any cattle in the world; on coming up to the first kaffir kraal, the Kaffir knowing the purpose for which the patrol comes immediately drives his cattle out of sight; we then use force and collect his cattle, and take the number said to be stolen or more; this the Kaffirs naturally, and it always appears to me, justly, resist; they have nothing else to live on, and if the cows are taken away the calves perish, and it is a miserable condition in which the Kaffir women and children, and the whole party are left; that resistance is usually construed into guilt and it is almost impossible then to prevent innocent bloodshed; it also often happens that when a patrol is on the spoor of cattle really stolen, they find some individual head of cattle which is knocked up or purposely left behind by the real perpetrators, in a kraal, and that is taken as positive proof of the guilt of that kraal, and leads to the injustice I have previously pointed out.[10]

Further in his evidence to the Committee and in his *Autobiography* Stockenstrom returns again and again to this theme. In the latter work he also quotes a long report from Sir Harry Smith, that other great frontier veteran, which agrees with his criticism of the system in great detail.[11] Both of these men wished to end cattle-lifting by the Xhosa and both showed their firmness in action in support of the trekboer and of the English settlers on many occasions, but they saw the patrol system as no help, indeed they rather saw it as a major hindrance to establishing peace. They both pointed out that far too many colonists left their cattle unattended for days in the bush. Then if some were found to be missing, they called for a patrol to follow some spoor or other and seize cattle from the Xhosa 'thieves'. Yet to quote Stockenstrom

On returning home he has found his cattle in another direction or found them destroyed by wolves, or through his own neglect.[12]

Both Smith and Stockenstrom insisted that the colonists had to herd their cattle properly: the presence of herders then, and only then, gave the system a chance to operate justly. Otherwise they had to agree with the Xhosa that the patrol system appeared as a form of raiding the Xhosa cattle. Read's correspondence with Philip and Fairbairn from 1829 onwards is full of stories describing such incidents, as are some letters still extant from Ross to Philip. These sources of information were and are considered biased by some, but the tenor of their reports is confirmed by Stockenstrom and Smith, who were always sympathetic to the colonial farmers, particularly the trekboer who saw Stockenstrom as one of themselves. The widely known bitter attacks on Stockenstrom by the Grahamstown English should not be allowed to obscure the great affection in which he was held by the frontier Boers. Indeed their warm welcome to him when he returned from

Europe to the frontier in 1836 is in particular contrast to the behaviour of the Grahamstown English towards him.

In the year that Philip returned to South Africa, the situation on the frontier, already violent and confused, was greatly embittered by two events. The first was the expulsion of Maqoma and his people, together with the remnants of Ngqika's people, from their lands; the second was that the rains failed and a terrible drought affected most of the frontier region.

The drought conditions meant that throughout that year, 1829, Xhosa and settler were driving their herds across the countryside in search of adequate pasture. One area, the upper Fish River served by the Kat, Mankanza and other small tributaries, was spared and had good sweet grass. Although much of this area had been nearly empty of people since it had, almost alone of so-called 'neutral territory, been treated as neutral, Xhosa and trekboers poured into it with their herds, in fierce competition for survival. This created a situation ripe for violent clashes even if all the herders involved had been saints, which they were not. Outside this area the suffering was terrible as all the contemporary sources are agreed.

In the midst of all this suffering, the Governor, Sir Lowry Cole, expelled Maqoma and his people from their lands on the Kat, and in their stead created the Kat River Settlement for 'Hottentots and Bastards'. The immediate reason for taking action against Maqoma, an action fully supported by Stockenstrom as Commissioner-General on the eastern frontier which he still defended in his evidence to the Aborigines Committee, was the attack made by Maqoma on the Thembu described previously.[13] In addition, during 1828 a large force of Colonial troops and burgher commando had marched right across Xhosa territory, and, with their aid together with that of the Mpondo, had driven off the Ngwane people of Matiwane who were pressurising the Mpondo and Xhosa peoples as a result of the pressure they, in turn, were suffering from the results of Zulu expansion. As a consequence of this expedition, the rumours that had been rife for a decade of the turmoil among the African peoples to the north and east being caused by Zulu expansionism were confirmed. Now Maqoma seemed to be adding to this turmoil by creating even more refugees, this time seeking refuge in the Colony which wanted the entry of no more Kaffir groups to complicate the already dreadfully confused situation in the eastern region. In the Governor's eyes Maqoma only held his lands by grace of the British authority which was conditional on his good behaviour. He had clearly now forfeited the Governor's favour. So in May 1829, in the midst of a serious drought, Maqoma, his people and the remains of Ngqika's people, were expelled to seek refuge where they could among their fellow Xhosa to the east.

Maqoma was genuinely bewildered at this turn of events as the Glasgow Missionary Society missionary John Ross tried to explain to the authorities. The authorities were unwilling to listen. Indeed Mrs Ross, in a letter to her parents, bitterly complained that her husband had received a rather brusque, if not rude, response to his pleas.[14]

In Maqoma's eyes he had been behaving responsibly, he was being constantly exhorted to maintain order among his people, and, when in his own lands among his own people he did just that, he was told that he had committed such a grave crime as to merit the punishment of being driven from his traditional land.

All the bitter memories of the treatment meted out to his father Ngqika were revived for Maqoma and his folk. As he put it to Fairbairn when the latter interviewed him on his visit to the frontier accompanying Philip the next year

> Though his father Gaika, and his chiefs, had accompanied the Colonial forces against Ndhlambi, after Ndhlambi was defeated they deprived them of their country as if they had been the offenders.[15]

Quite apart from the bitter sense of the injustice of the decision, Maqoma and his people were in an appalling dilemma—where could they go with their herds in this time of drought? Colonel Henry Somerset, the military commander on the frontier, came to their aid and gave them permission to come back across the frontier the next year and settle back on the Kat on land unoccupied by the Coloured settlers of the Kat River Settlement.

Interestingly, these two groups were able to live together amicably. Read and Maqoma struck up an acquaintance, and the two peoples managed the matter of strayed or stolen cattle with a minimum of friction.[16] It would certainly appear that their successful attempt to deal with this problem is *prima facie* evidence to confirm that Stockenstrom was right. If cattle were herded and not left to roam, and if relations of mutual respect, which protected chiefly dignity, were maintained, the cattle-lifting problem could be dealt with in a reasonable manner.

It was, then, a situation of fear, of mistrust, of theft and punitive expedition which Philip found when he came to be concerned with the situation of the eastern frontier. He learned a great deal on his visit during 1830, and continued to become more and more acquainted with eastern affairs through correspondence with James Read and John Ross. The latter, having failed to get anywhere with the authorities themselves, seems to have turned to Philip as a source of possible help in this matter, as a way of getting behind the local authorities to the centre of power, Westminster.

There was certainly plenty for Philip to be informed about since, just as in 1812 and 1819, the clearing of Xhosa from their lands did not decrease, but increased, trouble on the frontier. In particular, cattle-stealing increased, which is not surprising in a period of drought, with people dispossessed of their lands and with many chiefs, not only Maqoma, unhappy about cooperating with the colonial authorities whose actions seemed at times to be so arbitrary. However the British authorities, who did not view their actions as being in any way arbitrary, were increasingly worried and depressed by the continued difficulties. As early as January 1830, Cole was complaining to Whitehall of the increasing cattle-lifting and the consequent increased patrol and punitive commando action. He insisted that in the previous few months, over 5,000 head of cattle had been stolen and only about 1,500 had been recovered.

On May 6 Sir George Murray replied to Cole

> I have received your despatch of 2nd January last, in which you report the
> results of your recent visit to the eastern frontier of the Colony under your
> government, and I am happy to learn that all serious apprehension of an
> invasion from Caffraria has subsided [a product of Grahamstown rumour
> 'factory']. I concur with you however in regretting that a portion of the ceded
> territory continues to be occupied by bodies of Caffres whose numbers I collect,
> from the tenor of your despatch to be considerable. This is undoubtedly a great
> evil; for while on the one hand, it is not to be expected that these people will ever
> voluntarily evacuate the Colonial territory, I am not on the other hand,
> prepared to authorise you to expel them by force of arms from *the land of their
> birth*.[17]

He went on to instruct the Governor to point out the example of the
Government's treatment of Maqoma to the Xhosa chiefs and people within
the colonial boundary. If they did not cooperate with the Governor, his was
to be their fate also.

However, despite the continued welter of cattle-lifting followed by patrol
and commando, only Maqoma and his people were singled out to be ejected
again. In 1833, they were again removed to the east at the point of the
bayonet. Again they were allowed back briefly to be driven out again in
1834. This behaviour may have been the application of a consistent policy
but it certainly bewildered both Xhosa and colonists as to what the British
authorities intended for the region.

In the meanwhile, Philip had again been on the frontier. While staying
with Read on the Kat River, he renewed his acquaintance with Maqoma. He
also had interviews with Tyhali, with Sandile and his mother Sutu, the
widow of Ngqika, as well as with Bhotomane and other chiefs. There is no
doubt that the Xhosa chiefs most closely involved in the area were
beginning to look to Philip as an ally, who might be able to help them
somewhat, even if he could not entirely right their wrongs. As early as his
visit with Fairbairn in 1830, there are signs of this. Fairbairn's notes of his
conversation with Maqoma reflect the chief's determination to put his case
as fully as possible to a European witness. Just how important this new
White contact might be became more clear to the Xhosa through their
contacts with Read, and the Kat River Folk who held Philip to be their
champion. If Philip and his allies had done so much for the Cape Folk
might they also be able to do something for them? Although there is no
documentary evidence of his advising Maqoma in this way, the fact that
Ross, who was his friend and who had taken up the cudgels on his behalf,
saw Philip as an important ally in this matter, could not have escaped
Maqoma, and that they actually discussed Philip seems highly likely.

Although there is no record of Philip communicating his thoughts on the
frontier problem to Cole (unlikely in any case because Cole had made his
distrust of Philip manifest from the moment of the latter's return to the
Colony), or to Whitehall, it is clear that after his first trek to the frontier in
1830, he was laying the ground for some kind of appeal to London about
these affairs. On his return from that trip, he initiated a series of letters to

Buxton, describing frontier affairs and preparing him for action. The first of these letters reveals Philip in the same state of angry indignation as Dr Wright had shown at their meeting four years before in Stockenstrom's house. In this letter, he foresees for the Xhosa the possibility of the same fate that had befallen the Khoi. Just as the Khoi had been, they would be deprived of their lands and thus cease so to be a nation, becoming what might be called in modern terminology, a landless proletariat. He also insisted that there were those on the frontier, officials and British colonists as well as trekboers, who eagerly awaited such a development, such was their hunger for estates. However, even in his rage, he insists that, as in the matter of civil rights for the Cape Folk, the key issue was government policy, not individual wickedness. It was the lack of a consistent, humane and just policy from London, that caused all the difficulties, in Philip's view.

On his 1832 visit to the frontier, Philip carefully and systematically obtained the opinions of the principal Xhosa chiefs on the frontier, and then went north to visit the Society's stations among his beloved Griqua. On his return to the Colony, he found himself in the midst of an uproar. On the eastern frontier, he had been accompanied, for about three weeks, by a visitor to South Africa, the Honourable Alexander Bruce. The latter had been so incensed by what he saw, and, more especially, by what he heard from the Xhosa chiefs, that he published, in Fairbairn's *Advertiser*, a series of criticisms of frontier affairs, and a series of accusations about individuals on the frontier.[18]

The editor of *Grahamstown Journal* rose up to demand that a full enquiry be held into these allegations so that this maligner of these colonists might be exposed. Philip, who was in Grahamstown at this point on his way home to Cape Town from his long trek, agreed with the *Journal* and also asked for a formal enquiry. This was in February 1833. Cole would have none of it, declaring that these were the same old accusations that had been made in the past and had been answered and that in any case, the accusations coming from the source they did need not be taken seriously.[19]

Philip made no further public move on this matter, and there is nothing in his correspondence with the London Missionary Society Directors in London of any consequence about the frontier for some time. However, he made arrangements to discuss frontier matters with Stockenstrom who had just resigned as Commissioner-General of the eastern Cape and was about to go to Europe leaving his homeland, South Africa, for ever as he thought. At this meeting, Philip gave Stockenstrom a bundle of letters for Buxton, as well as a letter of introduction to Buxton which Stockenstrom could make use of if he wished.

Then in June 1833, a fresh element entered the controversy which, to the critics of the patrol system, appeared to be the last straw. This was Cole's 99th Ordinance. The administration had been worried for some time by the inability to raise adequate military force on the northern frontier by means of burgher service commando. In the north the small population of mainly Boer ranchers was very widely scattered indeed and so the burghers were unwilling to leave their families in such isolated circumstances. In addition a number of the families were in the area simply as transients on their way to a new life on the other side of the Orange outside the Colony, so why should they accept the burden of commando duty? Cole therefore issued an ordinance which laid down penalties for refusing this service. What excited the critics was, however, the second element in the Ordinance, which laid down that any official even down to the rank of acting-veld-cornet could now legally call out and lead a commando. Although the Ordinance was drawn up with the northern frontier in mind, it made no reference in its terms about its applying only there. This boded ill for the affairs of the Xhosa frontier. In that area most local officials were themselves ranchers who might lose cattle, or whose close friends or relations might, and they were now to be given the authority to call out a proper legally constituted commando without higher authority. This was exactly opposite to what Stockenstrom believed to be the solution of the problems of law and order on the frontier. Of this situation, Pringle wrote bitterly in his *Narrative of a Residence in South Africa*, published in 1835. He pointed out that some of the veld-cornets and acting veld-cornets in the area of his family estates in Albany who would be given these new powers, were men whom he already named in his book as being guilty of quite atrocious behaviour towards the Xhosa.[20] Stockenstrom, while in exile in Stockholm, wrote lines which summarise his views on the situation and fit well with Philip's that it was the system that was at fault. In this passage he defends the character of the Boer ranchers in general, but insists that there was a small section of the White population who did want to profit from the chaos of the frontier, the 'hangers on' whom he bitterly rails against elsewhere in his memoirs.[21]

> There is but a small section interested in the disturbance on the Frontier, and the acquisition of cattle of the natives, but mismanagement makes the good suffer with the bad, and embitters the feeling of all. A thousand times have such men as Van Wyk, Van der Walt, Pretorious, Oberholzenr, Joubert and others . . . spoken to me with the utmost warmth and sympathy of the danger and injustice of taking the property of the Border tribes, and the dreadful alternative to which our wavering policy occasionally drove us. I have found more humane feeling and good sense in these men and the like, than I am disposed to give some of their defamers credit for; and I have never known an instance when the people from the inner parts have been dragged from their homes and avocations to assist in the protection of the Frontier, that every man who could reason on the subject did not curse the iniquities by which so much inconvenience, loss and suffering were brought on themselves and the country. But how can they help their situation? Then where lies the blame? Is it not your system which compels them to be butchers today, and would have to submit to be butchered without resistance tomorrow? I am sick of the business.[22]

It could be argued that this 'small section', even on the evidence of his own writings, is somewhat bigger than he implies here, although he would distinguish between the Grahamstown 'hangers-on' and the trekboers. His fundamental point is one with which Philip agreed, and which historians such as Galbraith in his study of the eastern frontier *Reluctant Empire*, also agree—that the system of government of the eastern frontier made men butchers one day and the objects of butchery the next.

Pringle published his *Narrative* to coincide with the pressure on Whitehall against the patrol system in general and the 99th Ordinance in particular. Philip produced a long memorandum on the subject for Buxton, to back up the work he had already done to prepare their London spokesman to act on this matter. Their reports were sufficient to influence Lord Stanley to disallow the 99th Ordinance, but this by no means ended the problem of law and order on the frontier. The existing situation was not affected at all by the Secretary of State's decision—it was simply prevented from becoming worse.

Cole's sucessor as Governor, it was hoped, might be prevailed upon to look anew at the situation of the eastern frontier and the patrol system. Philip made an immediate effort to meet with D'Urban as soon as possible after his arrival. His primary purpose was to gain British protection for the Griquas in the north, but he also took time to complain to the Governor about the turmoil in Black–White relations on the eastern frontier. He was well received, as were all helpful visitors, by a Governor who seems to have been ready to learn all he could about his new charge. Philip informed the Directors that he had been asked by the Governor to prepare notes for him on the working of the patrol system.[23] In March, Philip submitted to the Governor what was, in effect, a long memorandum which took up points of criticism of the patrol system that have already been noted and which were also central to Stockenstrom's complaints. Philip argued that the whole difficulty stemmed from the removal of Ngqika's people in 1819, and that a new and better system of frontier government must be developed. Stockenstrom also insisted that the patrol system was the root of the difficulty, and in his memorandum to the Governor, submitted shortly before he resigned as Commissioner-General, he stated that Somerset's removal of the Xhosa from the Zuurveld in 1819 was directly due to the patrol system inaugurated two years before.

> All the disturbances on the frontier of late years, all the acts of severity which consequently became necessary, the backward state of improvement of the Kaffirs, and the necessity of still maintaining a military force against them, can be traced to this prolific source. If the seizure of the enormous mass of Kaffir cattle by Colonel Brereton's commando in 1818, had not taken place, that of Colonel Wiltshire in 1819 would not have been necessary, and no possible ground for the expulsion of the Kaffirs from the ceded territories could have existed. And thus it has been ever since.[24]

In the writing of Stockenstrom and Philip on this matter the agreement that everything stems from the patrol system and the displacement of Xhosa in 1819 would seem to raise the possibility of a solution—that is, the withdrawal of the colonial frontier to that which existed before the occupation of the ceded territories. Indeed when one also considers Stockenstrom's other, often used, argument that all the colony's troubles stem from allowing the White population to wander off leaving colonial authority behind them and thus involving conflict with the tribes, the solution of withdrawal would seem to be all the more attractive. Neither of them suggested withdrawal, although they both insisted on no further expansion of White settlement. This was because withdrawal was, in practical terms, no longer possible, not because of the trekboers, but because of the fateful decision to plant British settlers in 1820 on what the Xhosa claimed as their land. Once the British were there at Government request, the Government in London and the Cape had to protect them. Galbraith makes this point and his logic appears unassailable.

The new Governor then had available to him a large amount of information about the eastern frontier and the patrol system. It was also made clear to him, by many witnesses, that the situation was particularly tense because of the treatment of Maqoma, who felt he was being constantly chased from pillar to post, and because of the series of inadequate rains which had led to drought.

In May, D'Urban appeared to decide to use Philip as a confidant about frontier matters. Thus there was a long exchange of letters and a series of meetings between the two before Philip left for the eastern frontier, in the middle of August 1834.[25] This involvement with Philip was in keeping with his enquiring of many others, whom he hoped might help him understand the situation, and so help him prepare, in detail, for the inauguration of the new frontier system, which the Secretary of State had instructed him to organise. This new policy was, in outline, similar to that later insisted upon by the British Government after the War of Hintsa, and made famous as the Glenelg Dispatch. Treaties were to be made with the Xhosa chiefs, who would receive a government allowance and a 'resident' who would help them in the task of maintaining peace with the colony, and in keeping their people in order. A new, and primarily defensive, form of commando system was also to be organised.

Despite his busy consultations with Philip and others about the frontier, D'Urban seemed in no hurry to go there and see to the organisation of the new system. Galbraith has pointed out that D'Urban had much else to occupy him.[26] This is certainly true. He had to supervise the emancipation of the slaves and the arrangements for compensation, to institute new forms of local government, as well as change the form of central government in the Colony by the inauguration of a Legislative Council. In this regard, he had been instructed by Stanley, on the basis of the Order-in-Council of 1829, not to allow any colonial legislation which imposed on Blacks any disability or restriction that did not apply to Whites. This led him to an immediate confrontation with his Legislative Council, which voted by a majority for a Vagrancy Ordinance which in the eyes of the Cape Folk, and of their friends, Philip and Fairbairn, would have nullified all the gains of 1828. D'Urban's disallowing of the Ordinance was in keeping with Stanley's instructions and brought him the increasingly good opinion of Philip, Read and Fairbairn, who did not know, of course, of Stanley's precise instruction.

All these affairs were important, yet it is difficult to believe, looking at the conflict over Ordinance 99 and at Stockenstrom's correspondence to both Cape Town and London, before he left the Colony, that any Governor could not have escaped feeling a certain urgency about the Xhosa frontier.

D'Urban did act, but only through a proxy. The proxy was John Philip.

Philip went off to the east with the Governor's blessing, and with a promise that D'Urban would meet him at the Kat River Settlement, where the Governor would begin his reforming of the frontier system in accordance with Stanley's instructions. Although Galbraith, in his exhaustive study of the frontier problem, rightly points out that D'Urban consulted quite a few people about the frontier, none of the interviews, he quotes, took place later than April 1834, while Macmillan is able to quote an extensive correspondence between D'Urban and Philip on frontier matters between May and August, when it seems that Philip did enjoy a particularly close relationship with the Governor.[27] What is not at all clear is what status Philip had in the eyes of the Governor when, on his visit to the frontier, he spoke with the Xhosa chiefs.

In his evidence before the Aborigines Committee, Philip denied that he had been a formal agent of the Governor or in any way his emissary to the chiefs. Professor Galbraith insists that this cannot be reconciled with his private correspondence prior to his departure.[28] However, when that correspondence is looked at carefully, a slightly different picture emerges than that which is confidently asserted by Galbraith. Typical of this is a formal letter from Philip to his fellow Directors in London, on the eve of his departure in August.[29] In this letter, Philip says that he is off to the frontier to gain information relative to the situation there, and to help initiate the organisation of a new frontier system. He certainly insists that he has the ear of the Governor and that this fact plus the Governor's plans to start a new system must be kept secret from people in the Colony, but it is the picture of a particular confidant he is portraying, not that of a formal emissary with any kind of official message.

What is still not clear is why D'Urban fatally took so long to go to the frontier. He certainly had pressing matters to attend to, but as has been said, in the light of all he had heard from Stanley and from even a cursory reading of the files of his predecessor, surely the frontier ought to have had a greater priority. Certainly Philip set off thinking that the Governor was soon to follow and that they would meet in a few weeks at the Kat River Settlement. In fact D'Urban had still not left when Philip returned in December and did not leave for the frontier until the opening shots of the War of 1835–36 had been fired.

As has already been pointed out, chiefs like Maqoma, Bhotomane and Tyhali had, in 1832, already begun to see Philip as a potentially useful ally in making their case heard. At the time of his new visit, the people of the Kat River, as well as the other Cape Folk on the frontier, were, more than ever, insistent on his role as their champion, because of the defeat of the proposed Vagrancy Ordinance. Had he not orchestrated their letters and petitions of protest about the matter? Thus, at this time of great tension, Philip's visit assumed in the eyes of the Xhosa chiefs great importance, especially when he promised them a speedy visit from the Governor, whom he was sure would listen to their just complaints. Philip's own careful and thorough study of the Xhosa frontier problems, particularly through the help of Read and John Ross, as well as Stockenstrom, meant that he believed that the chiefs did have many grievances, and, given his character, it would seem inconceivable that his belief was not conveyed to the chiefs, even though there is no indication in any source that he made them any specific promises.

On his return to Cape Town, Philip received, from James Read, an alarming letter written at Philipton on the Kat River on 9 December 1834.

> I have a most unpleasant affair to relate. The latter end of the week before last or the beginning of last Ensign Sparks a Boy from Mr. Innes's School late in service, was sent on a patrol after two horses of a Boer. The Spoor came near where some droves of Eno's Caffres were grazing, and it became difficult to trace them further, the Horses were demanded of the Caffres. They declared they knew nothing of them, but Sparks took fifteen Head of Cattle which exasperated the Caffres. The owners of the Cattle followed them to near Beaufort, at last the Ensign ordered his men to fire. He said he ordered them to fire over their Heads, however the Caffres began to throw their Assagais and one wounded Sparks in the Arm dangerously. At this the Caffres fled and the Cattle were taken to the Post. This affair gave great alarm, Somerset came and collected all the troops and they are now clearing the whole of the Ceded territory from Wilshire to the sea. All Eno's and Conga's people. Here we have the old thing over again, for the act of one man perish hundreds of People, and now again just in the time of harvest while the corn is in the field. Can this be Sir Benjamin's orders? Or would they dare take such a step without order? I am sorry for the case at the present moment as the Chiefs will think we have deceived them, and the Governor will only with difficulty get them to speak.[30]

This was the same Eno whose son had been shot on emerging from his house to find out what was happening when a patrol had raided his village at dawn and without warning; something often done to prevent the supposed stolen cattle being hidden away if warning was given, but something quite contrary to the Xhosa understanding of how 'spoor law' should operate. From the Xhosa point of view, it was these actions which began the Sixth Frontier War and so they saw themselves as acting in retaliation against British attacks. This is contrary to the view taken by most historical writing on the subject which sees the war beginning with Maqoma and Tyhali's invasion of the Colony in mid-December 1834.

During Somerset's clearing of the country, Eno had tried to parley and had given over cattle and horses for any stolen, but Somerset had continued his sweeping up operations. During these operations, two things happened—a chief's cattle were taken, which was one way the Xhosa understood of formally declaring war, and in the operations, XoXo, a senior chief, was wounded. A great deal was made in the aftermath of the War, and, by some historians since, that XoXo's wound was only a graze caused by a musket-ball, not a severe wound. However, the matter was deadly serious in such a strained situation. As Philip pointed out later, in his evidence to the Aborigines Committee, among the Xhosa, the person of a chief was always respected in a conflict. The wound itself was slight, but the intention had clearly been to kill, and this was an action intolerable in Xhosa eyes. Jan Tsatsu, in his evidence to the Aborigines Committee was most insistent that the wounding of XoXo would only be taken as a declaration of war by the Xhosa.

Maqoma and Tyhali did, after these events, proceed to organise the attack on the colony with care. They even took the unprecedented step of sending across the Kei to Hintsa, senior chief of the Gcaleka Xhosa, to gain his approval of their plans, which approval they obtained. Thus, although the war was produced by a combination of a series of years of drought, and, in Xhosa eyes, the arbitrary and unjust actions of patrols and reprisal commandos, the war came, not simply as blind instinctive striking back, but as a planned campaign with specific war aims. These were spelt out in a document sent to the colonial authorities by Tyhali. It contained fourteen demands but the essence of the demands of the Xhosa people was the restoration to them of their lands east of the Fish.[31] Their subsidiary aims could be summarised as first, bringing to an end, once and for all, the gradual eating away of Xhosa territory; second, strangely the same aim as that avowed by the Colonial Office, the marking of a definitive and permanent boundary between the Colony and the lands of the Xhosa people.

To most Whites at the time, however, the war was seen in terms of the unpredictable savagery of a primitive people. Their view is summed up in Godlonton's famous *The Irruption of the Savage Kaffir Hordes.* Godlonton was editor of the *Grahamstown Journal* and one of the chief spokesmen for the British settlers in the eastern Cape.

The course of the War can be dealt with briefly. After an initial wave of destruction of White farms and the driving off of thousands of cattle, Sir Harry Smith soon reorganised the regular and burgher forces so as to take the offensive. Maqoma and Tyhali retreated, with their people and cattle, into the Amatola mountains, where Smith knew he could only deal with them with very great difficulty indeed. So he turned to punish Hintsa for his complicity in the affair. D'Urban himself was on the frontier and agreed with this plan. Indeed the Governor had begun to see Hintsa as instigator of the whole thing. The British marched their main force across the Kei. This led to two events of great importance in the history of the frontier; the death of Hintsa and the declaration of the Mfengu as British subjects.

The Mfengu were a collection of Nguni groups who had come among the Xhosa in flight from the appalling destructive events of the Mfecane.[32] They were received by the Xhosa chiefs and would, in other circumstances, have gradually been absorbed, as many groups had been before, into Xhosa society as Xhosa. However, the process had barely begun when D'Urban and Smith arrived with their massive army in the trans-Kei lands. The Mfengu, as comparatively new and under-privileged members of the Xhosa society, though they were in no way slaves as Whites at the time described them, saw the opportunity of bettering themselves quickly. They appealed to D'Urban to be allowed to become British subjects and be given land within the Colony. D'Urban saw them as a possible ally. They could be used to fill up frontier lands, and as the people of the Kat River Settlement already were, become a helpful barrier to stand between the Xhosa and the White settler herds and farms. About 17,000 Mfengu were then accepted as British subjects and along with the cattle with which they had been entrusted by their Xhosa patrons, began to make their way back to the Colony where they were to occupy Ngqikaland round Alice and Fort Peddie. This was on 24 April 1835. At the beginning of May, Hintsa came into D'Urban's camp to negotiate peace. On 10 May a formal ceremony marked peace with Hintsa on the basis of very punitive terms. All Xhosa were to be forever expelled to the country east of the Kei. This was quite extraordinary since Maqoma and Tyhali and their people were still undefeated in the Amatola mountains and were raiding widely over colonial territory. Hintsa was supposed to make Maqoma and Tyhali withdraw, which was both physically and constitutionally out of the question. In addition, Hintsa was to pay to the Governor, as compensation for the damage done to the Colony, 50,000 head of cattle and 1,000 horses, not including the Xhosa stock already removed by the Mfengu.

Hintsa agreed and went with the troops to begin the collection of the cattle. He attempted to escape and was shot and then his body was mutilated—his ears being cut off. This incident had a long-term effect on the Xhosa people, breeding a distrust of the personal integrity of British officers which, on the whole, had not existed until then. The mutilation also deeply shocked Xhosa susceptibilities, especially because it was the mutilation of the body of a great chief. To the Xhosa, from then on, the war became the War of Hintsa, though his actual part in the Xhosa attack had been but one of giving approval and offering his land as refuge in the exigencies of war.

D'Urban's newly acquired territory was named Queen Adelaide Province and the publication of the acquisition of this massive new addition to the Colony aroused a storm of protest among those people sympathetic to the Xhosa cause. The most ridiculous aspect of D'Urban's proclamation was not a feature that was fastened on by critics at the time. This was that the Xhosa of Maqoma and Tyhali had not yet been cleared from the vast stretch of land from the Keiskamma to the Kei. They still held out in the Amatola mountains from which they were still raiding. However, D'Urban went ahead and planted the new Mfengu subjects of the King on the old Ngqika lands around Alice and Fort Peddie. The rest of the new Province the Governor promised to apportion among the White population of the Colony. How was he to proceed with this when the forces at his command were simply incapable of removing the Xhosa from the Amatolas?

In May, D'Urban had thought it was a matter of weeks before he did clear the province of a few stragglers but by July, the enormity of the situation was borne in on him, when, as Galbraith describes it

> The British army and its auxiliaries . . . were reduced to protecting its posts in the 'conquered territory' and maintaining its lines of communication to the rear.[33]

In September D'Urban made peace with the Xhosa forces still undefeated within the new Province. This peace amounted to an admission that the war was ending with victory for no one, but a compromise to resolve the military stalemate. Maqoma's and Tyhali's people and the people of the other chiefs who had fought with them were given reserves *within* the new Province. They were however now to come under colonial law and receive a colonial Agent in every chieftaincy. The rest of he old 'ceded' territory was to be apportioned to European settlers, except for the lands of the Ghunukwebe who had taken no part in the War and the Kat River Settlement. In addition a large area of the new Province, not assigned as reserve, was to be also available for European settlement.

The contradiction between what D'Urban was doing in South Africa at this time and what the Colonial Secretary in London wanted done, plus the lack of any effective communication between the two for a period of about eighteen months, is one of the most extraordinary episodes of British colonial history. In October of 1835, the new Colonial Secretary, Lord Glenelg, warned D'Urban not to give away land or build forts because the reported conquests might have to be abandoned. D'Urban then proceeded with his peace treaty with the chiefs while for several months not informing the Colonial Secretary about anything at all to do with the eastern frontier situation. Meanwhile, having heard nothing in any formal communication from D'Urban, Glenelg sent his famous dispatch of December 1835. In this document Glenelg ordered D'Urban to prepare for the abandonment of the Province, pointing out that he believed, from the information he had received from sources other than the Governor, that the Xhosa had been goaded into the war by past mistreatment. However, the King, as Galbraith has conclusively shown,[34] had forced such a modification of the dispatch, that D'Urban thought he still had a chance to make good his policy. What the King had insisted upon was that Glenelg should offer to change his policy if D'Urban could produce evidence which contradicted that which the Colonial Secretary had received from his unofficial sources. It would appear however that his amendment was only to placate the King—the Cabinet had discussed the dispatch and wished it to be implemented.[35] D'Urban was simply being allowed the courtesy of some sort of explanation before this was done. However, D'Urban did not send any direct reply to this dispatch until December 1836. What was Whitehall to do, but proceed as best they could in formulating a policy without benefit of advice from the Governor of the Colony involved?

What was Philip doing throughout this period? His first response to the news of the Xhosa attacks was to issue a circular letter to all missionaries among the Coloured people instructing them to urge their people to stay loyal and be willing to serve in the colonial forces. This the people did, and the effectiveness of both the Cape Corp and the commando raised from the Cape Folk in the guerilla war, which soon became the pattern of fighting after the initial invasion, has been testified to by many officers.[36] Although, as we shall see, the Governor soon saw the hand of Philip and the 'Philip party' in every criticism of his conduct, and as lying behind Glenelg's dispatch, Philip was, initially, still hopeful that D'Urban, despite the outbreak of war, would eventually create a new and more just frontier system. In January 1834 he had written to the Directors, with great enthusiasm, about the treaty D'Urban had concluded with Waterboer, and the impact the latter had had on Cape Town society, showing how able, cultured and articulate a Coloured man could be. He went on

> When I left Cape Town I expected to have had the pleasure of seeing the Governor enter into treaties of the same nature as that entered into with the Griqua chief, with the Caffre chiefs but from the necessity which prevented the Governor from leaving Cape Town at the time proposed in this I have been disappointed. From a copy of the 'Advertiser' I sent you to-day you will perceive how our hopes of a peaceable arrangement with the Caffre chiefs have, for the present, been blasted.[37]

Philip went on to say how the Colonial Government and the colonists had been warned again and again that a continuation of the old frontier system was bound to end thus, but clearly he still had hope in D'Urban. This was still apparent in his letters during the next two months. He continued supporting D'Urban, and saw him still as an ally in his campaign for a new frontier system. This campaign began with his conferences with D'Urban at Cape Town, and then became a matter of pressing information onto Buxton, so that the latter became aware of the Cape eastern frontier as a crisis point in the Imperial treatment of native peoples. Thus Philip was pleased to hear that Buxton had, in May, got the House of Commons to agree to the appointment of a Select Committee to investigate the treatment of Aboriginal peoples in the British colonies.[38]

It was the Governor's May Proclamation, and the news of the Governor's publicly declared attitude towards the Xhosa, that changed Philip from an ally into a deeply committed antagonist. Had not he and Stockenstrom often pointed out that the war was provoked by the old frontier system, which, in turn, was a product of the expulsion of Ngqika's people from the ceded territories? Indeed, in February in a letter to Buxton when he was still defending the Governor, he had reminded Buxton that the British had taken more territory from 'the natives' in thirty years than the Dutch had taken in 150 years.[39] Now the Governor was proposing another massive piece of 'extermination', that is, in Philip's parlance, the depriving of people of their land.

What was equally bad was that the Governor had fallen into an attitude towards them, typical of the worst of the Grahamstown 'hangers on'. He called them, in an official document, the General Orders, 11 May 1835, 'treacherous and irreclaimable savages'. This has been seen by historians, even by Macmillan, as an unfortunate slip of the pen. However, Philip had every reason to believe it represented the Governor's considered judgement, and that D'Urban had swallowed whole the worst views of the easterners.

John Ross, who was in Grahamstown among the refugee Whites, and in contact with the Governor and his staff, wrote to Philip insisting that this was the case. Indeed, he and others of his society, the Glasgow Missionary Society, had approached the Governor with a petition on behalf of some of the chiefs. The Governor's reported kindness to Sutu, the widow of Ngqika, encouraged them to do so.

> Alas! our views were very different for the only and best and repeated likeness

he could find for the Caffres was that of Wolves. They were more like wolves than men—they were wolves he said, still there were some good ones but chiefly females of whom he thought much. I expressed a wish that he had seen Makoma—friendly as he was. This was not well received. Who? he asked. I answered Makoma. Mr. Laing added and Botman. Poor human nature!! Caffres are wolves, yet some are good.[40]

Philip's worst fears of what might happen in the days of Cole and Wade were now being implemented by the Governor on whom he had pinned so much hope. The final straw came when the Governor officially declared the war to have seen an unprovoked aggression on the part of the Xhosa, just as the *Grahamstown Journal* and *De Zuid Afrikaan* had been insisting from the beginning.

Philip now began to bombard Buxton and Ellis, Secretary of the London Missionary Society, with letters from both London Missionary Society and Glasgow Missionary Society missionaries, all insisting on the fact that the war, far from being unprovoked, was the result of long-standing unfair treatment of the Xhosa. This was not a new gambit to embarrass D'Urban. From his return in 1829, as we have seen, Philip had been feeding information to Buxton about the threat the Xhosa people faced of going the way of the Khoi. He had welcomed D'Urban's appointment as a chance for a new frontier policy to be brought into action. He had warned the Governor that widespread disaster would inevitably result on the frontier unless the policy was changed. In this situation, D'Urban found some support in the correspondence of the Methodist Missionary Society staff in South Africa who, on the whole, supported the stand he took that the attack by the Xhosa had been unprovoked. To the leaders of the Grahamstown settlers, as well as to the Governor, this was as manna in the desert and a grave embarrassment to the London Missionary Society and Glasgow Missionary Society staff. Ross, in his letters to Philip, complained bitterly about public disagreement between himself and Methodists in Grahamstown on this issue.[41]

The information Philip sent to Buxton, drawn from his own visits, but more important, drawn from the witness of men working among the Xhosa, notably Brownlee and Read of his own staff and Ross and Laing of the Glasgow Society, as well as from letters received by Fairbairn at the office of the *Advertiser*, all reached Glenelg who was close to Buxton. This closeness stemmed from their evangelical association but also as a result of Buxton's appointment to the Parliamentary Select Committee. However, it must be insisted that the Glenelg dispatch was not the product of a temporary take-over by the evangelical humanitarians of the Colonial Office. Buxton's information certainly helped confirm that Office's view of the origins of the war, and perhaps more important the evidence of the 'Boer', Stockenstrom, in the first session of the Aborigines Committee did the same. However, the main substance of the dispatch was little different in outline from the general instructions with which D'Urban had been despatched to the Colony in the first place. Galbraith's masterly analysis of the genesis of this dispatch has made this clear.[42] The frontier was to return

to where it had been in 1834, a series of treaties were to be entered into with
the Xhosa chiefs to try to ensure law and order on the frontier and the
reprisal form of the patrol system was to cease. One additional factor was
that a Lieutenant Governor was to be appointed for the frontier area, to try
to ensure the system worked. In January, 1836, Glenelg appointed Andries
Stockenstrom to that post.

Although, as Macmillan notes, D'Urban annotated his copy of Glenelg's
dispatch with marginal comments such as 'This is all Philip',[43] Philip had
little to do with the Glenelg dispatch, and, more important, he disagreed
with it on a number of vital matters. First of all, he was very unhappy about
the appointment of a Lieutenant Governor for the eastern Cape. He saw the
Grahamstown English, his allies of a decade before, as the centre of both
anti-Cape folk and anti-Xhosa feeling. They had been complaining, for
some years, about the distance from Cape Town to the frontier as a factor
in the apparent inability of Government to understand their point of view.
Any form of eastern autonomy was something of which, to say the least, he
was suspicious.[44] The appointment of Andries Stockenstrom to the post
moderated his suspicion of such an arrangement, but did not allay it. There
is nothing in his extant correspondence that shows his conversion to such an
understanding of the administration of the Colony.

More important, and in some ways, more startling, was his total
disagreement with Glenelg's instruction to withdraw the colonial boundary
to the old 1834 position. From his point of view, the situation was such that
the boundary had either to go back to the old line of 1819, or, if that was
now impossible because of the 1820 settlers, then withdrawal from the Kei
to the unsatisfactory line of 1834 was a mistake.

At the time, most people ignored this idea of his, even his friends and
allies in London. Historians have also paid it little attention, yet it was a
most important issue for Philip.[45] Macmillan alone has taken notice of his
attitude, rightly seeing it as part of his general understanding of a policy for
the future of South Africa.

In his letters to Buxton and to Ellis in 1834 and 1835, as well as in his
evidence before the Aborigines Committee in 1836, Philip insisted that the
extension of British authority to the Kei was something he welcomed.
Indeed it is quite clear that he would have welcomed an even greater
extension of Imperial Authority. As in his dealings with the issue of civil
rights in the 1820s, Philip had a Roman ideal in mind. As Rome had
brought justice and peace and prosperity to all within her boundaries
regardless of race, so too could and should Britian. His campaign had been
to make this effective for South Africa and, in a way, he had suceeded with
Ordinance 50, its endorsement by the House of Commons and the proof of
the effectiveness of this in the rejection of Cole's Vagrancy Ordinance. The
solution for the problem of White–Xhosa relations was the extension of
British Imperial authority to the Xhosa.

The key difference between his hopes and the planned action of D'Urban
was that in his plan, the Xhosa would be allowed to keep their land and no
Whites would be allowed to own land among them. Whites could live

among them as traders, missionaries and similar capacities but there would be no taking of the land. In addition, it must be noted the Xhosa would be British subjects, guaranteed their civil rights, as were the Cape Folk and the Mfengu. His position was the product of long thought, the experience of the Cape Folk and the development of the Griqua people. As he wrote to James Read Junior, in October 1835,

> On the subject of it being desirable that the Caffres should be retained as British subjects, I have long made up my mind. The question is not with me what might be, had we such Governors as William Penn, but what kind of Government we have to expect in the ordinary course of things, and as the affairs of our Colony will be managed for a long time to come. The Caffres cannot be otherwise saved from annihilation. Were the Colony surrounded by belts of Native Tribes under the British Government, nations would get time to form beyond us, but no Tribe will be allowed time to rise into civilisation and independence on our borders, if they are in immediate contact with our colonists. We never could have done anything with the Griquas, if it had not been that our work had arrived at a certain point before the Colony was extended to the Great River, and even not withstanding their distance from us, nothing but a peculiar combination of circumstances could have saved, or can even now save them.[46]

He made this judgement clear to Ellis of the London Missionary Society, in a number of letters during 1835.[46] Again in 1836 in his evidence to the Aborigines Committee he reiterated these views. Therein he insisted on three things; first, the strict prevention by the Imperial authorities of any expansion of the colonists beyond the frontiers; second, a band of treaty states, based on traditional chieftaincies bound in a formal relationship with the Imperial Government, ultimately under British authority but without any loss of their land; thirdly, the tribes beyond the treaty states would be contacted by, and have relations with, the Colony primarily through the protected peoples.

It is at this point that we can see the gulf between John Philip and Buxton and his circle, as well as between Philip and the Directors of the London Missionary Society at that time led by William Ellis. Ellis and Buxton worked together during 1835 and 1836, trying to influence British policy towards the Cape, independently that is, of the hearings of the Aborigines Committee. They were most insistent that the frontier system had driven the Xhosa to war and they wished them to have their lands restored and the patrol system to end. In the latter two aims they were supported by both the Methodist Society and the Methodist missionaries at the Cape. The latter would not accept that the Xhosa were driven to war, but they insisted that depriving them of their lands was wrong, and that there were faults in the patrol system.[48]

None of Philip's correspondents heeded his ideas on the extension of effective British imperial authority. Galbraith points out that throughout the first five decades of the century, British governments were constantly striving for economy. Again and again we see Governors at the Cape complaining that they do not have enough of a military establishment to carry out existing policies. Would any government of the time have been willing to expend the necessary resources needed to make such a policy work? However, Philip's ideas are never at this time specifically rejected by Glenelg or the permanent officials like Stephen. Ellis and Buxton who were the channels of communication simply did not transmit them. In the main evidence given to the Aborigines Committee, this point of Philip's was lost.

Despite the total lack of response by his friends in London to his ideas for peace on the frontier, and the complete absence of any reflection of them all in the famous December dispatch, Philip, along with evangelical circles in Britain, and sympathisers in the colony, welcomed the dispatch. Clearly to Philip, its great gain was that there would be no mass removal of Xhosa nor any occupation of their vacant lands by settlers.

The response to the Glenelg dispatch among eastern province Whites in South Africa was very different indeed. Although, as we have already noted, the implementation of the Glenelg dispatch was delayed for a time, the threat it imposed aroused a passionate burst of protest, channelled through the *Grahamstown Journal* in particular. These complaints became even more angry, if that is possible, when the intentions of the dispatch were finally put into effect. One of the main themes in the protest was the influence of Philip and the humanitarian evangelical lobby in England on Glenelg. They were the villains responsible for the tragedy. It became an article of faith that the Xhosa had been effectively defeated and D'Urban had solved the frontier problem at last, only to have success torn from his grasp by Glenelg, acting on the information of Philip and Fairbairn.

That D'Urban's September treaties were forced on him by the fact that Maqoma, Tyhali and their people were still undefeated and still inside the new 'Province' was simply ignored.

Part of the explanation of this fury being turned on Philip and his associates is that D'Urban, from quite early in the war, began to see Philip as an enemy. This stemmed from articles which appeared as early as January in the *Advertiser*, critical of the conduct of the war, bitingly scathing about the cattle reiving by redcoats that was called warfare and the inability of the forces to deal with the Xhosa guerilla tactics. When, in 1836, Philip went to London and gave his evidence to the Aborigines Committee along with his party made up of the Christian Xhosa chief Tsatsu, James Read Senior and James Reaid Junior and a Coloured leader from the Kat River, Andries Stoffels, their censures on the patrol system and on the conduct of the war seemed confirmation of Philip's treachery and the nature of his influence.

The last straw for the British settlers was the appointment, by Glenelg, of Andries Stockenstrom as the new Lieutenant Governor. He had been among the first witnesses heard by the obnoxious committee in London and the reports of his evidence, which so thoroughly condemned the patrol system and highlighted some truly bitter injustices done to the Xhosa, were soon known on the frontier. How could this man dare come among them as their new master?

The story of what occurred on the frontier during 1836 and 1838 has to be reviewed, but John Philip took little active part in affairs, since, for most of that time, he was in the United Kingdom giving evidence to the Select Committee and carrying out the usual speaking engagements of a missionary visiting the homebase of his Society.

On the basis of the September treaties, Sir Harry Smith, the military commander on the frontier, brought peace and some form of law and order to the region. This was mainly through the use of the African troops, both Mfengu levies and the Cape Mounted Rifles. However, he was able to do this by dint of martial law being imposed on the region. He and his local staff, including men like Major Maclean and Captain C L Stretch who were later, as Government Agents among the Xhosa, to gain that people's respect and affection, soon saw that the initial areas assigned to the Xhosa were inadequate and a massive increase in its extent was recommended by Smith and confirmed by D'Urban. So in fact D'Urban himself, without any instructions from Glenelg had already removed most land from being available to Whites, because the war had in effect ended in stalemate.

Then in July 1836, Stockenstrom came as Lieutenant Governor for the frontier area. He knew that Glenelg intended for Adelaide Province to be given up, but he had no specific orders on this and D'Urban seemed still to hope for a change of heart on the part of Glenelg. So Stockenstrom continued to work the existing system, though he did begin to concentrate the British regulars on the old 1829 frontier on which he knew Glenelg intended to settle. However, suddenly everything changed. D'Urban, who had still not provided Glenelg with the counter-arguments he had asked for, received a further dispatch from Whitehall showing Glenelg's intentions remained the same, though it did not contain firm instructions, since the Colonial Secretary still awaited a reply to his dispatch of nine months before. On receipt of it, however, D'Urban, in late October, without any prior warning to Stockenstrom, ordered the evacuation of Queen Adelaide Province.

Stockenstrom reorganised the frontier in a way that possibly went farther than Glenelg had intended. He made the Fish River the effective boundary, where the main troop deployment would be. The old ceded territories were still held to be under British authority, but were 'leased' to the Xhosa and their chiefs, while some White settlers and the Kat River Settlement also remained. Beyond the 1829 frontier, that is beyond the old ceded territories, the Xhosa were left free, except that the Ciskeian chiefs had to receive British diplomatic agents to live with them, as did the chiefs within the old 'ceded' lands. The Mfengu locations were a new element in the situation—they had to receive an agent also and the Xhosa chiefs had to agree to acknowledge Mfengu ownership of the lands given them and their independence there. The old patrol system was to cease.

Just as D'Urban's September arrangements hardly had time to be seen to work or not to work, the new Stockenstrom arrangement was barely given enough time to prove itself. It was, in addition, gravely handicapped from the start. D'Urban was still Governor and remained so until the new Governor, Sir George Napier, arrived in January 1838. The Government in Whitehall quite extraordinarily postponed making a decision about naming a successor until October 1837. This seems almost inexplicable, given the utterly unacceptable rudeness of D'Urban's very belated reply to Glenelg that was sent on 8 June 1836.[49] Even his friends in London wrote to the Governor expressing astonishment at the tone he had taken in writing to the Secretary of State. Galbraith refers to letters from D'Urban to Smith at this time which showed that D'Urban expected to be instantly recalled because of this dispatch.[50] He was not, and stayed on to make the difficult task lying before Stockenstrom even more difficult.

D'Urban, correctly understanding Stockenstrom's role as one of reversing totally his policies, obstructed him in every way possible, at times delaying Stockenstrom's dispatches to London for weeks at time.[51] In addition, the British community around Grahamstown and its mouthpiece the *Journal*, were bitterly opposed to him and harassed him in every way possible, beginning with delivering to him a memorial demanding he apologise for his 'maligning' of them before Buxton's committee. There was also some lack of enthusiasm about their new 'Boer' leader on the part of the British regular officers on the frontier. Although this was the period of the major thrust of the Great Trek of Boers out of the Colony, it is worth noting that, despite the Aborigines Committee and the revoking of the Queen Adelaide Province, which so infuriated the British settlers, the *Grahamstown Journal* and *De Zuid Afrikaan*, the actual frontier trekboers, after the briefest of hesitation, accepted Stockenstrom again, and certainly saw him as one of themselves, an Afrikaner. In his *History of Southern Africa*, Walker seems to think this rather eccentric of them. It was in fact logical—Stockenstrom was a Dutch-speaking frontier farmer born in South Africa, not an Englishman, therefore an Afrikaner. After all, despite the references to the Afrikaner people as Dutch by the British for nearly 150 years, the ancestry of the Afrikaner people was very mixed, as we have seen.

In September 1838, Stockenstrom gave up and resigned, returning to England briefly, before taking up the life again of a Cape Boer. During his years as Lieutenant Governor, despite all the difficulties, he did keep peace on the Xhosa frontier and gained more cooperation from Maqoma, Tyhali and the others than any previous British official.[52]

It was at this time that Philip returned to South Africa. He had, in many ways, wasted his time in Britain. Ellis and Buxton had simply not understood his ideas on the expansion of British authority and his fellow directors of the LMS had ceased to trust him politically, perhaps in other ways also.[58] They had forbidden him to talk directly to Glenelg, though he was someone whom Philip had spoken to on a number of occasions on his previous visit to the UK. He had to communicate with the Secretary of State through Buxton or Ellis which was, in effect, placing a filter between him and Glenelg.

In addition, he had hoped of great things from Buxton's Committee, but little did emerge that directly affected policy, in the short run. It is in fact doubtful if the Committee's evidence had any influence on Government policy at all. Its massive findings have remained as an extremely useful quarry for historians seeking first-hand accounts of affairs in South Africa, New Zealand and Australia.

Back in Cape Town, Philip was still faced by what he considered the major problem besetting the creation of harmonious relations between the peoples of South Africa, and the possibility of the peaceful development he felt essential to the spread of the Gospel. That was the continued expansion of White settlers beyond the colonial frontier and out of the effective authority of the British Government. However, in 1838 it was taking place on a scale unheard of before.

Between 1834 and 1838, the Great Trek had got underway. What was the British Government going to do about it? What did it mean for the christianising and civilising of the peoples of South Africa?

6

The Great Trek

Amidst all the controversies that divide historians of southern Africa, the fundamental importance of the Great Trek is possibly the one thing upon which they are agreed. There are still many divergent opinions about its causes and their relative significance, as well as about its essential nature. Was the Great Trek a singularly large episode in the historic expansion of the trekboers, or was it a self-conscious rebellion by emigration? Recently some historians have begun to insist that it can only be understood properly if it is seen more firmly in its 'African' setting. These writers point out that the Trek could not have broken out of the Colony in the way that it did but for the impact of the Mfecane. It should be understood, they insist, therefore as the last great tribal migration of the many provoked by that disastrous event.

There is no need to work through these and other historical problems associated with the Trek in order to come to an appreciation of the role of John Philip in South African society. However, it is necessary to summarise the main events of this exodus and its immediate aftermath because they are fundamental to the stage 'set', as well as to the plot of the drama in which he played his role.

As early as 1832 some trekboer groups began to discuss the possibility of an organised migration away from the Colony in order to create a new society free from British political control. It would perhaps be more accurate to say that they wished to recreate the old society of the frontier trekboer before the coming of the British.

The stubborn resistance of the Xhosa had checked the expansion eastward, while to the north the lands were unattractive, except those on the far bank of the Orange already occupied by the Griqua allies of the British. The people had to look farther afield if they were to find a new home out of reach of the British. The reports of Afrikaner adventurers who had wandered far beyond the confines of the Colony, beyond the lands of the Griqua and the Xhosa, gave them hope that such a place could be found. However, something more than wanderers' tales was necessary before sober men would sell up their places and move with their families, servants and herds, out into the wilderness. So in 1834, three major reconnaissance parties (kommissietreks) were organised and despatched to find the promised land.

On their return, one of the kommissietreks could give only disappointing news but the other two had news of lands that were rich with grass and water, and equally important, they reported them free from any large African population.

The disappointing news came from the trek that had gone northwards through modern Botswana and on into Namibia. The second party had returned with enthusiastic reports of the well-watered grasslands of the High Veld across the Orange and beyond the Griqua, in what is now the Free State and the Transvaal. It was the third party, however—that which had been led by Piet Uys—which brought home to the Cape the most glowing reports. Uys had led his trek peacefully through the lands of the Xhosa and the Mpondo into what is now Natal. There he had found land that was beautiful as well as fertile, and, in addition, almost empty of inhabitants. Admittedly, just beyond it lay the powerful kingdom of the Zulu, but to Uys this seemed less important than that he had found the most fertile and beautiful land yet seen by Afrikaners in Africa and it was empty.

The route that Uys had followed was not one open to a large migration but the new land could be reached by going first northwards onto the High Veld and then turning south across the Drakensberg thus satisfactorily circumventing the implacable resistance of the Xhosa.

To the discontented and unhappy folk waiting in the Cape for these reports, the good news seemed almost a sign of divine blessing, perhaps it was even divine guidance.

The outbreak of the War of Hintsa delayed the departure of the majority of intending trekkers. However, two groups did set out as early as 1835. One group was led by Louis Trighardt and the other by Janse van Rensburg. These two parties moved steadily northwards across the Orange and then the Vaal. Van Rensburg and his people broke away from the Trighardt trek and apparently made for the Portuguese post at Inhambane and were wiped out by the warriors of the Tsonga people. Trighardt's people, gravely weakened by, what was to them, the new disease of malaria, and their cattle decimated by the tsetse fly, sought help from the Portuguese. Trighardt himself died at Delagoa Bay from whence most of his people were brought by ship to Port Natal in the autumn of 1838.

The main groups, who are deemed to constitute the Great Trek proper, did not begin to leave the Colony until the early months of 1836. The War of Hintsa had given them additional grievances against the British and their rule in the Colony. They were infuriated by what they held to be their ill-treatment during the War at the hands of the colonial authorities. They were angry with the missionaries, particularly John Philip, for having sided with the Xhosa, as they saw it. Finally, they were appalled by what they heard that Philip and others had said about them in their evidence to the Aborigines Committee.

The four principal parties which were the core of the Great Trek were led by Andries Hendrik Potgieter, Sarel Cilliers, Gert Maritz and Piet Retief. Potgieter's and Cilliers' parties left together in the first months of 1836. Maritz's party was a particularly large one which even included an old cannon in its equipment. Although hundreds of family groups were to go on joining the voortrekkers in the territories beyond the Colonial boundary, the last party of the Great Trek was that led out by Piet Retief in February 1837.

Once Potgieter's and Cilliers's parties were clear of the Griqua lands beyond the Orange they had to decide whether to settle on the High Veld or to cross the Drakensberg into Natal about which Piet Uys had enthused so much.

However, before any decision could be reached, indeed even before the arrival of Maritz or Retief, the Voortrekkers met their first serious challenge.

As they had been led to expect, the lands of the High Veld appeared relatively empty of African inhabitants. However, the kommissietrek had failed to make contact with the new Zulu kingdom of Mzilikazi beyond the Vaal. Indeed they seem to have been unaware of the extent of Mzilikazi's authority. This kingdom of the Amandebele under Mzilikazi had been formed when the latter, having broken with Chaka, had marched north to find a new home well away from Chaka's impi. It was a Zulu military society centred on the Marico valley with Mzilikazi's 'Great Place' at Mosega.

The Voortrekkers became aware of this threat to their future plans when some of Cilliers's and Potgieter's people, who had settled on the south bank of the Vaal, sent parties across the river who clashed with the routine patrols of Mzilikazi's kingdom. These incidents alerted the King to what appeared as a threat to his security. He acted promptly and prepared a massive assault on the White intruders.

By the time the Amandebele impi crossed the river in force, Cilliers, Potgieter and their followers had formed a strong laager at Vegkop. The firepower of the Afrikaners from behind their almost impenetrable barrier of circled wagons reinforced with thorn scrub, drove off the Amandebele with enormous loss of life. Although the Voortrekkers suffered very few casualties themselves, they did lose all their herds, so their capability of survival was seriously threatened.

The arrival of Maritz's very large column in the south was what saved them from disaster. Maritz had made an alliance with a small group of Tswana under Moroka, who were struggling to survive in the aftermath of the Mfecane. From this chief Maritz obtained enough cattle to support the beleaguered folk of Cilliers and Potgieter. A commando of his people, with cattle and herders granted by Moroka, brought the 'victors' of Vegkop safely back south to his headquarters at Blesberg.

The united Voortrekkers now formed themselves into an organised community with a formally elected leadership and a structure of government. The simple constitution, adopted by a general meeting of all the trekkers on 2 December 1836, has been described succinctly by E A Walker with a shrewd eye to the future of the trekker republics.

> Potgieter was unanimously elected commandant of the combined treks and chairman of the Krygsraad (Council of War). Maritz was chosen voorsitter (president) of the Volksraad and landdrost of the Court. Volksraad and Court were one and the same body of seven elected persons sitting in different capacities, to make laws and administer justice under those laws. Here was Leviathan in miniature. But it was a limited Leviathan. For though 'the Generality of Men, composing Het Volk', swore to obey these judges, the seven

were themselves bound to adhere strictly to such laws and regulations as might be passed at a general meeting. Thus from the start there was doubt whether the last word lay with the Volksraad or with the Sovereign People. It was a question that was to vex the future Transvaal to the end of its days as a republic.[1]

What was not in question was the intention of the Voortrekkers to create for themselves a sovereign republic outwith any form of British authority. This was also unambiguously asserted by Piet Retief in his famous 'Manifesto', delivered to the *Grahamstown Journal* on the eve of the departure of the last of the primary constituent parties of the Great Trek, 2 February 1837. Whatever else it may have been, the Great Trek was a casting off of British authority.

That for many years Voortrekker independence was not formally recognised by the British authorities is understandable—they were not willing to accept defeat. However, what is more difficult to understand is why the British authorities in the Cape went on behaving for over a decade, as if the Voortrekkers were not self-conscious, deliberate rebels, but as if they were a largish bunch of traditional trekboers, who had gone rather far in seeking pasture. This, as we shall see, had a serious effect on British attitudes and policy, when these same Voortrekkers came into conflict with the Griqua and Sotho states, which were loyal allies of the Crown.

This newly formed miniature 'state' was in a very precarious situation, as it was without recognised territory, without any legal recognition under international law and was also still threatened by the unbroken power of Mzilikazi. Potgieter quickly decided that the latter problem was one which had to be solved forthwith. The herds lost at Vegkop had to be recovered, and the Amandebele were taught a lesson that would keep them out of the way of the Volk.

It is interesting to note, in the light of the simplistic understanding of Voortrekker attitudes that later both liberal and some Afrikaner nationalist historians attempt to put on this period, that Potgieter sought help from the Griqua in this venture and the Griquas responded by sending a mounted commando to his aid. So early in 1837 Potgieter led northwards a commando of one hundred Voortrekkers and forty Griqua. They drove straight for the centre of Amandebele power, Mzilikazi's 'Great Place' at Mosega. There they inflicted heavy losses on the impis of Mzilikazi who chose to fight in the traditonal closely packed Zulu military formation on open ground against mobile and well-organised firepower. They thus created an ideal situation for Potgieter, a situation where even poor markmanship is rendered effective. The commando returned in triumph driving 7,000 head of cattle before them.

It seems appropriate at this point to suggest that traditional Zulu discipline and tactics, so effective against African traditional armies, simply invited slaughter when used against either mobile or strongly entrenched firepower. Had the Amandebele, or later the Zulu, learned to fight the patient guerilla war of attrition fought by the Xhosa with such stubborn courage, the history of southern Africa would have been somewhat different. Although in British, as well as Afrikaner, tradition, it is the

Ndebele and Zulu who are remembered as the great threats to White military dominance, in fact they were always easily defeated by well-organised firepower. Isandlwana was the exception that proves the rule. It was the Xhosa and, to a lesser extent, the Sotho of Moshweshwe, who were able to fight White armies effectively and achieve stalemate at least, over a whole campaign.

After the victory at Mosega, the newly achieved unity of the Volk was gravely threatened by the mutual hostility and temperamental incompatibility of Potgieter and Maritz. However, the arrival of Retief and his trek appeared to solve the problem of authority. Everyone readily agreed that he should become sole leader of the Maatschappij.[2] The people appeared to feel that he could lead them effectively into the promised land wherein their 'new Eden' (a name formally proposed by some for their new state) would be set up.

This happy unity of feeling, however, did not last long with regard to the decision, taken at the same time, that Maritz should be landdrost and voorsitter of the Volksraad. Potgieter and his followers soon began to make their unhappiness felt about this arrangement.

Meanwhile, almost daily, small parties of Afrikaners from the Colony were arriving to add themselves to the new society. A decision had to be made, and made quickly, as to the final destination of the trek. The veld, where they were, was incapable of supporting such a large number of families with their herds—the majority would have to move on, either to the Transvaal, or to Natal. Retief, with the support of Maritz, was for Natal, while Potgieter was for crossing the Vaal.

The increasing tension and division among the trekkers was exacerbated by the arrival from the Cape of a somewhat larger than usual party. This group was led, nominally, by Jacobus Uys, but real authority lay with his flamboyant son Piet, the leader of the Natal kommissietrek. Piet Uys immediately caused difficulties, because he bitterly resented having no alternative but to accept the Nine Articles of Confederation with which the Maatschappij had bound itself together in June, on the eve of his arrival. He and his party, all bound to him by ties of blood, were in the classic trekboer mould of individualistic independence, and were irked at being controlled by a system about which they had had no say.

The 'Nine Articles' read as much like the rule book of a Protestant Church as they did rules for a political association. The nearest parallel one can think of are the constitutions of the early New England colonies, where the rules defining church membership also defined citizenship, a situation common enough in the early seventeenth century, but somewhat unusual in the nineteenth. The 'Nine Articles' drew very firm lines as to who could be accepted as members of the Volk and also the forms of behaviour that would lead to exclusion from it.

The very first article set this ecclesiastical tone of the whole, by insisting that all must publicly repudiate connection with any of the 'missionary societies of England'. This article seems to have been designed as a symbolic rejection of the 'Philip party' but was also aimed at ending the influence of the Methodist missionary, James Archbell, who had accompanied the trek thus far. His role within the Maatschappij was now at an end.[3]

It is more than a little ironic that the newly appointed predikant of the Volk, and victor over Archbell, was Erasmus Smit who had been, from 1804 until 1822, a lay missionary in the service of the London Missionary Society.

It is perhaps the bitter sense of being left out of the new structure that accounts for the apparent contradiction of Uys now throwing his weight behind Potgieter, and insisting that it was in the North that the future lay. How else can such support be explained, coming from the man who had returned to the Colony only two years before on fire with enthusiasm for Natal?

Officially the Maatschappij was committed to going to Natal, which was certainly Retief's firm intention. However, Potgieter and Uys succeeded in causing so much doubt that no one was enthusiastic about making a move. However, move they must, since the eastern Free State simply could not support them.

Both Natal and the Transvaal were suitable in every way, with plenty of space for the families to find farms for themselves suitable for their style of ranching. However, each area also carried with it a threat to the security of the Volk. In the north, this was posed by the Amandebele; in the south by the Zulu of Dingane. However, Potgieter and many others were sure that, as a result of Vegkop and the Mosega commando, the Amandebele threat could be dealt with without too much difficulty. Could the same be said of Dingane?

Constantly arguing and quarrelling, the Voortrekkers with their mass of wagons and herds slowly edged their way towards the Drakensberg. It was abundantly clear to Retief that unity must be preserved, almost at any cost. The new state had to be one and not degenerate into a mass of petty chieftaincies. Only a well-organised state containing the majority of the Voortrekkers could achieve the three basic things necessary for success. The first was defence against any Zulu threat. The second was the need to convince the British that the new state was viable, politically and militarily, and so give it a chance to obtain at least *de facto* recognition. Thirdly, only such a state could cope with the continuing steady flow of families from the Colony, without continual social and political disturbance.

In September of 1837, a decisive meeting was held of all the leaders at Tafelkop. The meeting was to decide once and for all the destination of the trek. In fact no agreement was reached. On the contrary the community was unambiguously split in two. Though with a great deal of hesitation, the majority of the Maatschappij decided to follow Retief. However, many opted for the north with Potgieter and Uys.

Yet this is rather too precise. Those who said they would follow Retief still hung back from actually moving down the Drakensberg passes to Natal. They still hung back waiting, but waiting for what?

Retief now showed his qualities of leadership. He alone could end this indecision and he decided to do so by boldly entering Natal with whoever would follow, even if only a few, and establish his claim to the new lands.

Meanwhile in the North, Potgieter and Uys also displayed bold decisiveness. They planned and executed a brilliant campaign at the head of 400 horsemen against the Amandebele. In the Marico valley, through nine days of running fights, they defeated Mzilikazi's army. By late November, 1837, the Amandebele had had enough, and the king led his people across the Limpopo making his new 'great place' at Bulawayo. The Voortrekkers were now undisputed masters of the High Veld. Retief aimed to achieve the same in Natal which would also give the Maatschappij access to the sea.

Only a few people did follow Retief—the authorities vary as to the number, anything from twenty to fifty wagons are asserted to have followed him by different writers. Just about the time Mzilikazi was deciding to cross the Limpopo, Retief visited the British settlement at Port Natal. This community of adventurers had had long and reasonably cordial relations with the Zulu, so they could provide him with advice and interpreters. In any case, he had to approach Dingane from their direction, since he knew that to approach directly from the direction of Mzilikazi's lands would be interpreted as a hostile act.

The motley crew who inhabited Port Natal welcomed him because they had just heard that Captain Allan Gardiner, a lone and somewhat eccentric missionary of the Church Missionary Society, had persuaded Dingane to accept a missionary at his 'great place' and cede southern Natal, including the Port, to Her Majesty's Government. It is doubtful if the British Government would have done anything to make this cession effective, but the Port Natalians so abhorred any such idea, that absorption into a Voortrekker republic seemed a preferable alternative.

Thus Retief was welcomed, given advice on how to deal with Dingane and sent on his way with an interpreter to help him.

Dingane received his visitors cordially enough. He was well used to European visitors whom he had often been able to turn into clients of the Zulu kingdom as were the British in Port Natal. He promised Retief, many of whose people were now moving down into Natal, that he and his followers could settle there. Retief appeared to be willing to accept this on the King's terms. The possibility of a client relationship with the Zulu King seemed to be one he was willing to accept when he undertook Dingane's commission to recover Zulu cattle recently stolen by Sekonyela.[4] Retief and his men set off and accomplished their task quickly and efficiently.

On their triumphal return from Sekonyela's, the nduna, who had accompanied them, informed Dingane of the prowess of Retief and his men, as well as the things he had been told about the Voortrekker exploits against Mzilikazi. Dingane immediately decided that, far from being useful clients of the Zulu royal house, these people were a threat to its security. As such they had to be dealt with. At a feast in their honour, Retief and his unsuspecting followers were massacred. The impi then marched out to destroy the various Voortrekker groups already in Natal. The situation became so threatening to Whites, that the British at Port Natal took to the ships for safety.

However, Dingane then made a fatal error—he did not press home his advantage. Largely through arrogant self-confidence, the Zulu allowed the remaining Voortrekker groups to concentrate their strength in a traditional laager. These survivors were soon reinforced and reorganised by Andries Pretorius with his men from beyond the Drakensberg.

Pretorius then took the offensive and at Blood River on 16 December 1838, scored a decisive victory over the Zulu army. Like their Amandebele cousins, the impi were broken by well-managed fire-power, the decisive factor in any formal battle.

A new trekker Republic was proclaimed in Natal despite the presence of redcoats under Major Chambers, newly arrived at Port Natal, who vainly reminded Pretorius and his people that they were still the subjects of the Queen. The British were unable to do much because the Government in London wanted no extension of British authority in southern Africa. Indeed they were pressing the Governor in Cape Town to withdraw his small garrison at Port Natal. He kept them there as long as he could, while he attempted to persuade the burghers to accept British authority, and also to persuade London to declare Natal annexed to the Crown. He failed on both counts, and in December 1839, the garrison at Port Natal was withdrawn.

The Voortrekkers promptly raised their flag over the port and then, in alliance with Dingane's half-brother Mpande, they overthrew the Zulu King. Mpande now ruled the Zulu as a client of the Natal volksraad, which, in addition, exercised a loose sovereignty over the scattered Voortrekker communities beyond the Drakensberg. Dingane had envisaged a White client community settling in Natal to bolster the Zulu kingdom but the exact opposite had come to pass. There now existed an independent Voortrekker republic with access to the sea, something which Retief at least had wanted from the beginning of the trek. The question was, however, could the new leader Pretorius get the British to accept the independence of this fledgling state and so gain for it recognition in international law? To this end, Pretorius, in 1840 and again in 1841, sent a delegation to the Governor in Cape Town to discuss such recognition. In 1840, they took with them a formal document addressed to the Governor,[5] asking for the Voortrekkers to be recognised as a free people. Some months later in 1841, the volksraad sent a draft treaty of alliance between their republic and 'the Government of Her Majesty the Queen of England'.[6]

Although Lord John Russell, the Colonial Secretary, was inclined towards a re-occupation of Port Natal at least, Napier, the Governor, was inclined to let things be—his attitude indeed to most things. Eric Walker is inclined to think that Napier was even willing to negotiate with Pretorius on his requests of September 1840 and January 1841. There are documents in Bird's *Annals of Natal* which indicate that Walker is correct and that Russell even considered granting the Voortrekkers some sort of autonomy under a very vague British suzerainty. Whether Pretorius and the volksraad would have accepted such an arrangement is another matter.[7]

However, the possibility of a total acceptance of the situation by the Government of Great Britain ended abruptly when Pretorius led a raid against a southern neighbour, the Baca people, whom he accused of cattle-reiving. He returned from this punitive expedition, not only with cattle but also with some dozen or so African teenage 'apprentices'. Here was the re-introduction of slavery which the 'Philip' lobby had insisted would happen if the Voortrekkers were not kept under British authority. When, in addition, the senior Mpondo chief, with the aid of his resident Methodist missionary, appealed for British help, because he now felt threatened by the Republic, both the Governor and Whitehall had reluctantly to agree to a fresh review of the situation. Their initial decision was to intervene to protect British interests, while stopping short of annexation. A garrison of redcoats was sent to protect Faku and his Mpondo. However, at this juncture, Pretorius and the volksraad sealed their own fate by expelling southwards from Natal all Africans surplus to their economic requirements.

This was the kind of behaviour that seemed to confirm all the warnings of Philip and the humanitarian lobby. What was more important, in government eyes, was that it put pressure on the Mpondo and Xhosa, and so threatened yet again the peace and security of the Colony's sorely tried eastern frontier. As a result, Napier, without waiting for approval from London, sent a force to take and garrison Port Natal. This they rapidly achieved, and were then promptly besieged there by Voortrekkers in May 1842.

Napier had barely despatched Colonel Josias Cloete with a force sufficient to raise the siege, when the new Colonial Secretary, Lord Stanley, instructed him to abandon Port Natal again. Whitehall was alarmed that Napier's actions could very well pull Britain into an open-ended commitment to control the Voortrekkers wherever they went. The very policy being pressed by the 'Philip party' as a second best to the British stopping the Voortrekkers from going anywhere at all. Despite their constant verbal assertion of the continued authority of British law over the Voortrekkers, the British Government did not want to be drawn any further into Africa—the plight of inland Africans was simply of no concern to them, so long as Imperial interests in the Cape itself were protected, and the strictest possible economy of expenditure maintained.

Fortunately, from the Philip viewpoint, Napier delayed implementing Stanley's instructions. The latter changed his mind and got Cabinet agreement on the annexation of Natal. Over a year of negotiations followed this decision before Natal was finally effectively annexed to the Crown as a district of the Cape Colony in August 1845.

By that time, many of the Voortrekkers had streamed back across the Drakensberg to rejoin their fellows on the High Veld, and away from the hated British authority. The Government was happy to see them go—-control of the Voortrekkers was not the aim of British policy, despite the plea of Philip and his friends. The annexation of Natal was to ensure that no other power could gain a possible naval base on the southern African coast and to protect the eastern frontier of the colony from the kind of pressure that would come, through the difficulties a Voortrekker Republic in Natal would have caused the Xhosa and Mpondo peoples.

The complicated story of the development of two Voortrekker states on the High Veld, that is the Orange Free State and South African Republic, is not central to the concerns of this study of John Philip. They did impinge on the development of the Griqua and Sotho chieftaincies, and this is dealt with in the next chapter. However, what is of central importance to any study of South African history, is that the Republics constituted an abrupt and profound change in the general situation of southern Africa.

First of all, there were now powerful White communities outside even the token control of the Governor at Cape Town. Communities that would remain so, unless the British made an equally decisive change in their traditional policies in southern Africa, and invested money and troops on a large scale, in order to bring the Voortrekker communities, and the lands that they occupied on the High Veld, under British rule. Secondly, the scale of Black–White contact was profoundly changed.

> In 1835, the division of fertile South Africa between Bantu-speakers and white colonisers from Europe still held. Only in the frontier area adjacent to the Fish River was there contact and intermingling on any scale. Elsewhere—as at Port Natal, where English traders and hunters were established, southern Transorangia where graziers from the Cape depastured their stock—the white presence was on too small a scale to be of demographic significance. Five years later, however, by 1840, the frontiers of contact had been extended in vast convoluting lines from the Keiskamma in the South, northwards over the Orange and the Vaal, and across the Drakensberg into Natal.[8]

As early as 1832, Philip and Stockenstrom were aware that there was widespread uneasiness among the trekboer population of the eastern and northern frontier regions. There were even hints of permanent emigration beyond the reach of the British colonial authorities. As early as June 1834, D'Urban's attention was drawn to this unrest by one of his officers, Duncan Campbell, Civil Commissioner of Somerset. He reported that many families were no longer crossing the Orange to seek temporary pasturing for their herds but were going off apparently on a permanent basis.

> The present emigration, however, appears of a different character to those to which I have alluded [the seasonal seeking of pasture]. The Border farmers set themselves down on the nearest part of the adjoining territory where the objects of their search could be procured, and they nearly all returned to their farms but far the greater proportion of those who have gone on the Key and to the northwards of Philippolis, are from the border districts, and many of them, I have no doubt, have gone there for the purpose of farming permanent establishments, but whether that object be mixed up with a desire to elude the [illegible] of the Bill for the abolition of slavery, I have not been able to gain any satisfactory information, nor have I been able to ascertain the probable number of slaves, nor of farmers, who have gone there. The number of the latter gone from Somerset and Albany do not exceed half a dozen, one of them, Lewis Trichard has five slaves and another L. van Dyk, has two the others none.[9]

Two years before, Stockenstrom, who had the advantage of being an Afrikaner, had noted the phenomenon, and had come to a clearer understanding of it. His findings do not seem to have reached D'Urban's eyes, or, if they did, they did not gain his attention.

As Civil Commissioner for the frontier area, he had crossed the Orange to investigate complaints from Philip about trekboer interference with the Griqua communities. Of this visit, during which he persuaded most of the families he met to return within the Colony, he wrote

> During my intercourse with the Boers on the above expedition the bad effects, which I had expected from the destruction of the link which had long existed between the Government and the governed, became to me very glaring. The most thinking and sensible of the old inhabitants, in their accustomed familiar intercourse with me, lamented despondingly the loss of these 'Voorstanders van t'Volk' (leaders and defenders of the people) who always knew at least something of the views of the Rulers, and to whom the most ignorant of the people could apply for information or advice as to a Father, Brother, Uncle or other friend—at least as to an equal. 'Now', said one of the old leaders 'we have a Civil Commissioner to receive our money for the Government and for land surveyors, a Magistrate to punish us, a clerk of the Peace to prosecute us, and to get us into the Tronk, but no Heemrad to tell us whether things are right or wrong, when we can make neither head nor tail of them, for our oldest and wisest men know as little of the Government as we do. The fact is that many of us begin to think that the old Dutch Boer is no longer fit for this country. The Englishman is very learned and we are very stupid. They and the Hottentots will squeeze us all out by degrees. We return now to the Colony because you desire it, but many will not stay long.'[10]

Already in 1832, here were people deeply upset by the new situation of life under British rule in the Cape Colony. They lived far from the Xhosa frontier and were ready to trek long before the War of Hintsa, which had no direct bearing on them anyway. It was the new status of the people who were to become the Cape Folk that distressed them, together with the alien system of local government, brought into being by the colonial authorities in December 1827.

Very soon after his arrival in Cape Town to take up office, D'Urban was warned by Philip of the dangerous mood of many of the trekboer population. Philip, from personal observation and the reports of his colleagues, appears to have understood this mood as stemming from the threat to the abolition of slavery, and Campbell's report appears to indicate that some of the administration shared this view. Philip was very apprehensive that this restlessness among the trekboers would lead to their crossing the Orange in strength, and overthrowing the Griqua states there. D'Urban was ready to be sympathetic towards the Griqua at this time, and in response to Philip's requests concluded a treaty of friendship and protection with the Griqua of Waterboer.

He planned a similar treaty to be concluded for Kok's people but the outbreak of the War of Hintsa prevented its being signed at that time.

Although Philip and his circle, as well as the British authorities, were aware of widespread unhappiness among the trekboer population and of a general movement of families out beyond the frontier, neither the organised nature of the Voortrek nor its specific intentions were known until the publication of Retief's Manifesto. Even after this it was very difficult for Philip or the authorities to know exactly what was going on outside the Colony.

What added to the confusion was that there was another movement going on at the same time. This was the continuation of the traditional slow expansion of trekboer families across the Orange; a continuation of their traditional way of life. Of these families Walker says

> The pre-Trek Boers and some of the scattered groups which drifted out of the Colony alongside the Trek parties meant to take the Colony with them as their fathers had done before them. Not so the Trekkers of the Trek. Many of them were the sons or grandsons of the men of Graaff-Reinet in whom republican ideas had stirred in 1795, and all had grievances.[11]

That there was a profound gulf between those whom Walker refers to as 'the pre-Trek Boers' who continued the old trekboer ways, and the Voortrekkers is undoubtedly true. However, Stockenstrom's report gives us leave to doubt if the trekboers intended to bring the Colony with them as their forebears had done. They also clearly had such grievances that they did not want to take the Colony with them. However, they did differ from the Voortrekkers in the haphazardness of their movement. One could say that, like the Voortrekkers, they wished to live outwith colonial laws, but they had no clearly worked-out and generally accepted picture of what they wanted in its place—the Voortrekkers certainly did. The behaviour of the trekboer community in the area of Adam Kok's Griqua in the 1840s, under their leader Michiel Oberholster, is a classic example of their inability to decide whether to finally break with the Colony or not.[12]

It is not simply that modern historians have drawn a clear distinction between the Voortrekkers and the trekboers beyond the Orange—they saw themselves as being different communities.

The Great Trek was a planned, self-conscious withdrawal from British rule. D W Kruger has summed up their position well, although he attributes it to all Afrikaners, which was manifestly not so.

> Most Afrikaners were convinced that the British Government was more interested in the welfare of the Hottentots and ex-slaves than in that of the respectable Colonists. They considered themselves step-children of the government. Their resentment was increased by the vacillating policy of successive Governments towards the marauding Bantu tribes on the Eastern border. The vast and empty plains across the Orange River boundary of the Colony beckoned them. The Great Trek, unlike the expansionist movement of the eighteenth century, was undertaken in order to put a distance between the emigrants and the Colonial authorities, and to found a new state where no equality between whites and coloureds should be preached and practised. This meant the throwing off of British authority altogether.[13]

Many, probably most, Afrikaners did feel themselves to be unjustly treated by the British authorities. However, many, like Oberholster's people who left the Colony, did not share all the beliefs of the Voortrekkers. It is significant, with regard to Kruger's assertion, that a majority of Afrikaners did, in fact, remain within the Colony; also that their beloved 'Boer Kerk' condemned the Trek. If it is insisted that this was because of the large number of Scottish ministers recently come to serve in the Kerk, no such 'get out' is available to explain away the opposition of the militantly pro-trekboer *Zuid Afrikaan* to the ideals of the Voortrekkers.[14]

For John Philip the Great Trek threatened to destroy much that he hoped for. His favourite example of what Christianity and civilisation could do for an African people were the Griqua communities. How would they fare now? What of the Sotho and Tswana beyond the Orange—were they to go the way of the Khoi in the old Cape? Only the exertion of British power could avert what was for him a tragedy. Philip was slow to move on this issue, however, because he was in the United Kingdom from the spring of 1836 until the spring of 1838. The visit had been deemed important because of the high hopes he had of the Aborigines Committee. Whether two years away from where the action was, and where his ultimate concerns lay, was worth it, is very doubtful considering how little effect the Aborigines Committee had on British policy in South Africa.

7

Philip and the North

Moshesh the king of the Basutos, of whom James Backhouse and George Washington Walker give some account, is one of the most extraordinary men I ever met with, and I had almost said a miracle of a man, when his circumstances in Africa are taken into consideration, and the French mission among his people, present one of the loveliest pictures under heaven. . . . Have I been permitted to visit that country, and to see the heavenly vision I have seen, merely to witness it and then be obliged to say—it has fled for ever![1]

These words from a letter to Fowell Buxton written at the end of his trek through the lands north of the Orange, are vital to an understanding of Philip's actions and concerns during the 1840s. They reflect his view, formed in the 1820s, that African peoples stimulated by a missionary presence could grow both in Christianity and civilisation, if the process was not interfered with. If, however, Whites seeking land (it was irrelevant whether these be English or Afrikaner) were allowed to invade their territory, then all was lost.

It was the early development of civilisation and of an indigenous and flourishing Church among the Griquas that had first convinced him of this. Now, on the long trek, he had seen among the Sotho developments that appeared to him confirmation of his thesis. All the more exciting since the Sotho had been a hitherto untouched people, unlike the Griqua who had roots that were to some extent Christian and civilised in the old Colony. Yet, at this moment of joyous excitement, the whole thing was in danger because of the Great Trek.

The poignancy of his words to Buxton is made sharper by their anticipatory echo of the words of Martin Luther King on the eve of his assassination. King assured his audience that he was not afraid, because he had seen the promised land to which his people were going—not even his death could remove his joy, because their entry to it was assured. Unlike Martin Luther King, however, John Philip was afraid. He was afraid that unless the British Government took decisive action to prevent it, the Great Trek would result in a 'Bondage in Egypt' rather than a 'Promised Land' for the African peoples beyond the frontier. They would come to suffer the fate of the Khoi in the old unreformed Colony.

When, in 1838, Philip returned to the Cape from London, having presented his evidence before the Aborigines Committee, he found awaiting him a large number of difficulties within the London Missionary Society missions in Southern Africa, as well as a very unhappy situation in the Union Congregation in Cape Town of which he was the pastor. These difficulties took up a great deal of his time and energy in the next three years. Indeed, in a letter to Tidman in 1842, Philip deplored his long delay in coming to grips with the problems beyond the northern frontier. He explicitly stated that it was the troubles in the Cape Town congregation which had distracted him unduly. This letter, it must be noted, was written when he was in a state of anguish over the Voortrekker threat to the Griqua and Sotho, and his hopes for their advance in Christian civilisation. When all the correspondence for the period 1838 to 1842 is examined, a somewhat different picture emerges. Certainly the problems of the Union Congregation and among the mission staff did absorb a great deal of his time and energy, but he was not totally immersed in those problems to the exclusion of all else. The continuing difficulties faced by the Cape Folk also took up much of his time and energy—rightly so, because of the central place they had taken in all that he had done since coming to the Cape.

On his return to the Cape in 1838 he found that the status of the Cape Folk in the Colony was still in need of active defence. He was immediately plunged into orchestrating the alliance of missionaries and the Folk, particularly those of the Kat River communities, to defend their rights.

Because of the stereotype of Philip as someone who was obsessively anti-Afrikaner, it is worth noting that this campaign was rendered necessary by the pressure, not of the Afrikaner community, but of the eastern province English, particularly the Grahamstown community. Philip was well aware of this and often complained of the antagonism shown to him, and the Cape Folk, by the English settler community, an antagonism which saddened and disappointed him. In his journal of the northern trek he makes a good many mentions of visits with both trekboer and Voortrekker families. Indeed he specifically contrasts the friendly reception he received in one trekboer home, where he had been invited to lead Sunday service, with the attitude of the Grahamstown community.

> My own countrymen who were born in a land of liberty I have invariably found to be more virulent in their prejudice against me for my exertions in favour of the coloured population of this country.[2]

Andre du Toit and Herman Giliomee seem to think that the lack of Afrikaner criticism in the eastern province was because so many had trekked. However it is worth pointing out that Stockenstrom also points to the virulence of the Grahamstown folk in 1836 and contrasts it with the kindness and loyalty shown him by the Afrikaner community there.[3] In both the War of the Axe and the War of 1851, there were still plenty of Afrikaners in the eastern province, enough to form strong burgher forces.

It was the Kat River people who seemed particularly to arouse the antagonism of the Grahamstown community. A classic example of this was the incident of the commando raised among the frontier farmers to attack the Kat River people, so fortunately turned back by Colonel Somerset—a commando raised on the strength of a barrage of rumours emanating from Grahamstown that the Kat River people were about to rise in rebellion.[4]

During these first three years Philip may have failed to concentrate on the north as much as he ought to have done, but it was not because he was totally involved in petty domestic squabbles as he, in his anger and guilt, suggests to Tidman.

The time and energy he continued to devote to the cause of the Cape Folk during this period can be seen in the frequency with which their problems and situation within the Colony appear in his letters between 1838 and 1841. In 1840, for example, he organised the compilation of a massive report on the conditions of the Cape Folk in the Colony. This report was not merely a series of anecdotes, a style of communciation often referred to as a 'report' in this period. On the contrary, his was a careful study of wages, work conditions and the cost of staples for the Cape Folk, across the whole Colony. Philip produced this paper for transmission to the United Kingdom, by collating reports from the missionaries in every district of the Colony. The district summaries, which are all in the London Missionary Society records, covered the same issues in the same order and so appear to be answers to a questionnaire, though no such set of questions is to be found in the London Missionary Society Archives.

This extract from the Swellendam district illustrates the range of Philip's enquiry.

> It now seldom happens that either man or woman hire themselves to farmers for a longer time than one month. I know only one man who is at present engaged for one year and the wages he received is 18 Rd. Formerly they received their payment chiefly in goods, but during the three last years in which we have had drought and scarcity of provisions they were generally paid in money. The monthly wages which they received are from 4 to 7 Rd. On journeys they receive from 6-10 Rd. per month. For a journey to Cape Town the leader gets from 6-8 Rd. per month, the Drivers from 8-12 Rd. and their food. . . . Harvest work used to be 4 sch., now 1 Rd. per day, sheep shearing used to be 4 sch. now 1 Rd. per day. The price of wheat used to be from 5-8 Rd. per Muide. It was last year from 21-28 Rd. and in the present it is 19-23 Rd. The price of barley was formerly from 2-3 Rd. per muide, last year it was from 7-10 Rd. and is at present 6 Rd. A slaughtered sheep was from 3-3½ Rd. at present from 6-10 Rd.[5]

As early as the 1820s Philip had seen the future of the Griqua and of the Cape Folk as linked together. His pressure on D'Urban to sign treaties of protection with Kok and Waterboer was integrally linked to his campaign, at the same time, to prevent the U-turn in British policy towards the Cape Folk that the proposed Vagrancy legislation of the time represented.

In the earlier period, he was attempting to protect the Griqua from the pressures applied to their autonomy by the creeping encroachment on their lands by trekboer pursuing their traditional way of life. In 1838, that trekboer community was still there, north of the Orange, and by this time it was a reasonably well-organised community led by Michiel Oberholster. From his return Philip became increasingly aware that this old threat, serious though it was, paled into insignificance before that posed by the Voortrekkers.

However, in 1838, Philip was in the same situation as were most people in the Colony, including the Governor. No one seemed to know, for sure, where the Voortrekkers were exactly, or what were their intentions. On receipt of the news of their actions in Natal, Philip began a campaign, aided, and at times, spurred on, by his old ally and friend, Fairbairn of the *Advertiser*. Their campaign aimed at stirring the British Government into re-asserting British authority over these rebels by annexing Natal. During these months, as the news of what was going on to the east filtered through to the Cape, Philip unequivocally exposed the depth and bitterness of his feelings about the threat that the Great Trek posed to all his hopes for the future. In a letter to Ellis, sent off on hearing the news of the death of Retief and his followers at the hands of Dingane, he referred to the event, one of such symbolic and emotional importance to modern Afrikanerdom, as 'God's just retribution'![6]

This bitterness stemmed from his understanding of the situation, which was so much more wide ranging than that of most of his contemporaries. Even as he campaigned for the British occupation of Natal, his thoughts were with the peoples north of the Great River and the Drakensberg. His informants there assured him that all the Voortrekkers were not in Natal. What if the rebels' aims involved a Republic, not only of Natal, but extending to the High Veld as well? Even if that were not so, if and when the British did act in Natal, unless they stopped the Voortrekkers, as they had signally failed to do in the Cape, the Afrikaner response would be again to flee British authority and return to the High Veld. What then lay in store for the Griqua and the Sotho?

The British administration showed little concern for these problems, indeed little awareness of them. Meanwhile, Philip's fears increased when his contacts in the north informed him that there were indeed moves among the Voortrekkers to form a Republic stretching far beyond Natal. He received this news long before the officials in Cape Town had any notice of it. Philip's sources now covered a larger area than in the 1820s—they were not only his staff among the Griqua and Tswana and their many contacts among these peoples, but also the staff of the Paris Evangelical Mission serving among the Sotho of Moshweshwe. The origins of this mission go back to Philip's first visit to the United Kingdom 1826–29. After he had completed his *Researches*, he travelled in both France and Germany to encourage the Protestant Societies there to take an interest in southern Africa. Two missionary societies responded to his pleas—the Rhenish Mission Society and the Paris Evangelical Missionary Society (PEMS). Both of these societies agreed to begin work in southern Africa and instructed the staff of the new missions to treat Dr Philip as their adviser and also to use him as their agent in negotiations with British authorities in the Cape and, if necessary, in London. In 1829 the first missionaries of the PEMS travelled out to the Cape with him, and the first four men of the Rhenish Society, at whose ordination at Barmen Philip had been present, followed soon after.

The first Paris Society party went north to work among the baHurutse peoples beyond the Vaal. In 1833, Casalis, Arbousset and Gosselin, who made up the second party of Frenchmen, were staying with Dr Philip in Cape Town when he told them of the appeal he had received, while at Philippolis, from Moshweshwe. Neither he nor they were sure how serious the appeal was. However, on arriving at Philippolis on their way north, Casalis and his companions were convinced by Adam Krotz, the Cape Coloured Christian who had previously met with Moshweshwe and had talked to him of missionaries, that his call was seriously meant and worth pursuing. Since the country to the north was greatly disturbed by the activities of Mzilikazi, the trio decided to accept Moshweshwe's invitation and the long and close relationship between the Sotho and the Paris Mission began.

This widespread network of informants in the North gave Philip an advantage over the Governor, who was not in a position to receive reports about affairs beyond the Colony and the area of struggle in Natal.

During the last months of 1840, and the early months of the new year, the information coming back to Philip about the activities of the trekboer community north of the Orange, as well as those of the Voortrekkers, alarmed him exceedingly. If the activities of these two allied, but by no means yet united, groups were not checked, then the threat to the independence and future development of Griqua and the Sotho was grave indeed.

He forthwith began what appears to have been a concerted barrage of letters to the Governor, appealing for British intervention in the North in order to complete the work began in Natal. After all, the Great Trek was a rebellion quite deliberately and self-consciously undertaken. Philip insisted on this understanding of the Trek. As he explained to Buxton,[7] he did not see the Voortrekkers as a number of colonial families who had happened to stray beyond the colonial frontiers. There were many such, but the Voortrekkers were not simple trekboers—they were rebels, deliberately trying to create a new nation opposed to Britain. One of the problems he faced during these years was that British officialdom long continued the pretence that Voortrekkers were simply large parties of trekboers.

In June 1841, Philip addressed a long letter to Governor Napier in which he urged Sir George to build upon the policy initiated by Sir Benjamin D'Urban in his treaty of protection and alliance with Waterboer. Surely it was appropriate for the Governor at this time of crisis beyond the Great River to make the treaty with Kok, planned by D'Urban but so long delayed, and also to extend British influence in what the Governor must see was a key area for the safety of the Colony by making a similar treaty with Moshweshwe and his Sotho? If not, then the activities of the Afrikaners, of both communities, would create a situation of such turmoil on the northern frontier that it would become yet another area of expensive conflict for the British.

Six days later, on 18 June, Philip was gratified to receive a letter from Eugene Casalis, the leader of the Sotho Mission and already a close confidant of Moshweshwe, asking him to inform the Governor that Moshweshwe was interested in gaining British protection in the face of threats to the security of his kingdom posed by the activities of the Voortrekkers. Philip passed this letter on to His Excellency, along with a letter which arrived the same week from Adam Kok, asking for the friendship of Great Britain along the lines of the treaty discussed in 1834 but never signed.[8]

However, it was difficult for Philip to press too hard on this matter as yet, since at that time he had no first-hand knowledge of the situation in the north, and the Governor had no knowledge of it at all, other than that supplied by Philip's missionaries and their Griqua and Sotho allies.

As with every major problem he had faced in the past, Philip decided to go and see, for himself, before proceeding further. Long treks all over South Africa were a consistent feature of Philip's life, whether they were undertaken for purely administrative reasons, or to see for himself a situation about which the people were complaining. These treks, conducted at the slow pace of the ox waggon, during which he often spent weeks in one district, gave Philip a knowledge of southern Africa very few of his contemporaries could match, certainly which no British contemporary could. Although he never learned to speak any Bantu language beyond polite greetings, he did speak and write Dutch, the language of the Cape Folk as well as of the Griqua and the Afrikaner.

The long trek, upon which he now embarked, lasted from September 1841 until July 1842. This trek was particularly important because on his return he was able to give first-hand accounts of people and events in the north to the Governor, who was so desperately short of information.

Philip travelled first across the Colony to the eastern frontier, in order to meet up with James Read Senior, who was to be his companion on the trek until he returned to Grahamstown in June 1842.[9]

The two companions headed northwards. They visited the London Missionary Society stations among the Griqua, among the Tswana, and also, the French stations among the Sotho. Philip and Read conducted a very great deal of mission business, but an equally important object of the journey was to assess the political situation in the area, and gain the opinion of African leaders upon it. The two men spent a great deal of time talking with chiefs of many ranks, from village headmen to 'Kaptyns' like Waterboer and Kok. Perhaps most important of all, they had a series of meetings with the great man himself, Moshweshwe. It is also important to notice that the two missionaries had a number of meetings and discussions with Afrikaners—some of the old trekboer variety, who held to Michiel Oberholster as their leader, but also, with some of the 'rebel' Voortrekkers.

It was after this long, exhausting, but also exhilarating, journey that Philip wrote of seeing the heavenly vision that he feared was about to disappear. He was now firmly convinced that it was British intervention alone that could save the day. If the British did intervene, he insisted that Oberholster's people would accept British authority and settle down to a life that did not fundamentally threaten the Griqua and Sotho. If the British did not intervene, then the trekboer community would be drawn inevitably into union with the more powerful and numerous Voortrekkers, and a new state under Pretorius would emerge. This state would recreate in the north, a society like that of the old unreformed Colony, with the Griqua and Sotho playing the roles of the Khoi and the slaves.

As Philip reached Grahamstown on the return leg of his long trek and wrote his initial letters on this matter to Hare and Napier, the British were moving into their final and decisive intervention in Natal. By the time he was safely back in Cape Town, Philip was comforted and encouraged by the fact that Natal was to be a British possession. Little was he to know that this same Natal would not develop along the lines of the Cape Colony.

Philip was then ready and well equipped to begin in earnest his campaign for British intervention beyond the Orange. He was encouraged initially by the warm response evinced by both Napier and the Lt Governor, Hare, to his original letters on the topic. Their actions in Natal gave him confidence that Britain could be persuaded to act in the north also, so long as it was clearly to the advantage of the Colony and did not cost too much.

The safety of the Colony and expense were the two factors fundamental to British policy makers. He had to keep them in mind and they shaped all that he wrote to the authorities in his campaign to prod them into action.

His confidence in the possibility of British action may seem, in retrospect, ill-founded, but in his eyes he had ample encouragement from the history of the previous twenty years. Ordinance 50, its special status granted by Parliament, the defeat of the projected Vagrancy Ordinance, the frustration of Governor D'Urban's plans to grant Xhosa lands to White settlers, followed by the action in Natal together formed a substantial foundation for such confidence.

Philip was not, as is sometimes suggested, foolish enough to believe that all these gains were the result of his personal influence. In 1842 he was quite clear that his personal influence was limited, particularly since the aftermath of the War of Hintsa. After all, he remembered only too bitterly how humanitarian circles in Britain, including his fellow Directors of the London Missionary Society, had paid no attention to his pleas for the Ciskei Xhosa to be incorporated into the Colony while retaining all their lands. Indeed they had appeared not to understand him, let alone support him. No, the history of the previous twenty years did not make him overestimate his own influence, but it did appear a sound basis for confidence in the belief that the British could be persuaded to create a situation in South Africa where all could obtain peace and justice so long as it did not cost too much.

Above all, he tried to hammer home the logical necessity of what he suggested, if Britain's actions in Natal were to make any sense. The threat of which he complained in the north was the same threat to the stability of African peoples on the frontier of the Colony created by these same rebels in Natal. Surely he could persuade the Governor and his staff to see that exerting British authority over Natal was the job only half done. To complete the task of protecting the interests of the Colony, Britain had also to become the responsible authority in the Griqua and Sotho areas.

On 25 August 1842,[10] Philip sent to Napier a long carefully worked out report on what he believed was the situation north of the Great River, and suggesting ways of dealing with it, to the best advantage of the Colony, and the tribes beyond the frontier. This plan, he insisted, was all the more necessary because, as he had suggested to the Governor the previous year, the occcupation of Natal, without British authority being exerted north of the Orange made things there even worse. He insisted that the majority of the Voortrekkers in Natal would soon inspan again and continue their rebellion by trek. When they rejoined their fellows on the High Veld then an even greater threat would hang over the Colony as well as over the Griqua and Sotho. His forecast of Voortrekker actions was soon only too clearly fulfilled.

In his letter, he pointed out to Napier that he had been advocating this approach to the British authorities for some time. He summarised at great length his approach in the past to both Cole and D'Urban. He now insisted, as he had done to them, that the terrible confusion and suffering, and perhaps most important to Whitehall at least, expense of the eastern frontier would soon be repeated in the north, unless action was taken to forestall such a calamity. In the north he asserted that the Griqua, who were well on the way to becoming a Christian and civilised nation, had ensured

> that during that period and along the line of the frontier it had not been necessary to erect one military post or to employ British Soldiers and that on all occasions when the Government had required their services to assist in suppressing banditti who might have committed injuries upon the Boers and their families, they had always showed the greatest readiness to comply with its wishes.
>
> That I knew nothing in connection with the Colony more devoutly to be wished than to see the Caffres in the circumstances of the Griqua; sensible of the blessings that would accrue to them from living under the law and protection of the Colonial Government and on such a supposition I stated that I felt that His Excellency would be the first man in the Colony to forward them with all his influence any plan that might have for its object their incorporation in the Colony.[11]

Since he had written this, the Great Trek had happened and Natal had been annexed. Surely it was all the more imperative that the Griquas at least should be admitted into the Colony.

> Government guaranteeing and legalising to them according to Colonial usages, their rights to their lands and all the privileges of British subjects.[12]

In this letter, and in one couched in very similar terms to Lt Governor Hare, Philip was still singing his same old song. However, Napier and Hare were more likely to listen than the Governors of the past, because it was Philip who brought them information on what was going on in the north. He had been there and talked with so many of the principal people while they were in Cape Town or Grahamstown, prey to rumours, but with little solid information. Philip played on their apparent receptiveness for all he was worth. His hopes were for the incorporation of the Griqua into the Colony with full rights as British subjects and a treaty of protection and alliance with Moshweshwe. If incorporation was not possible, then he pleaded for treaties with Kok and Moshweshwe similar to that which D'Urban had concluded with Waterboer.

Of such a treaty with Kok he said

> It might be useful to him among his own people and teach the Boers to respect his authority, and, situated as he is upon the borders of the Colony, make them fear to make any hostile attack upon himself and his people. It would be a demonstration on the part of the Government in favour of the Coloured people that would relieve their fears and in the meantime prevent any aggression being made upon them by the farmers [13]

This sentence brings us firmly up against his belief in the essential link between the fate of the Griqua and that of the Cape Folk. Before considering the response of Napier and of Whitehall to Philip's pleas, it is worth looking at what his correspondence at this time reveals about his deepest and most firmly held beliefs about the future of South Africa.

The series of important letters he wrote to Napier and Hare in 1841 and 1842 and to Buxton during the same period must be read in conjunction with what he wrote in the Journal of his Trek of 1841–42.[14] In the letters to officials, and even at times to Buxton, he wrote, just as he did in his *Researches*, in terms that would appeal to his readers. We must therefore distinguish between that which he advocates, because it will appeal to British official and politicians, whose support was vital to him, and those things which are fundamental to his most central convictions.

During this lobbying campaign, his letters are full of how much his suggestions as to British policy would benefit the Colony. He believed that to be true, but the primacy he gave to it in this correspondence is a product of political good sense, and not a reflection of the order of priority in his own mind. This order can be seen in his personal letter to Buxton with which this chapter begins, and in the journal of his trek.

In that journal he reveals his thoughts in a way that he rarely did in these latter years in correspondence with anyone, in Britain, except the Buxton family. After all, his last visit to the United Kingdom had convinced him of the lack of understanding there of his position, even among the Directors of the London Missionary Society. In the entry for 28 March 1842, he wrote

> The great bane of Africa is the minute fractions into which its tribes have been broken up by the Slave Trade: we have here materials for a noble building but nothing can be done towards it till the fragments are joined together. The Gospel is the only instrument by which this object can be accomplished. To employ this instrument with effect, men of enlarged vision as well as fervent piety are called for and in the Griqua Mission we have the men and the materials and providence has furnished us in this instance with a site on which we may erect a Temple to God from which may issue forth the Law of the Lord in the power of the Spirit of [illegible] turning the hearts of the Fathers to the children and the hearts of the Children to the Fathers.[15]

When this journal entry is taken with his words to Buxton about his glimpse of God's promise among the Sotho, we have the key which enables us to understand a great deal that has puzzled historians about Philip.[16] The puzzling matters are two: first Philip's consistent exaggeration of the role of the two Griqua captaincies, as defenders and protectors of the Tswana people; and second his equally consistent advocacy of the widest possible claims as to the extent of territory over which Moshweshwe had sovereignty.

If we consider the Griqua first, it is true that in 1824, mounted Griqua riflemen had saved the Tswana groups huddled for protection around Robert Moffat's mission from destruction by raiders during the aftermath of the Mfecane. Indeed, in a Moffat source, in no way sympathetic to either Philip or the Griqua, much was made of the key role played by the Griqua in preserving the southern Tswana during the Mfecane.[17] However, it cannot be asserted today by a historian that the Griqua, in general, acted as protectors of the Tswana peoples during this period. Indeed, on a number of occasions in his own correspondence, Philip complained of Griqua raids on Tswana groups, though he always added that these actions were those of dissident groups, hankering after their old Bergenaar ways.

The evidence of this kind of action, of which there is more than Philip ever indicated, has forced many commentators to see his claims for the Griqua captains as another example of his unreliability, a confirmation of his being a man whose geese were always swans. At the time, Moffat, Calderwood and their allies among the London Missionary Society staff, interpreted his pro-Griqua stance as a simple desire on Philip's part to bolster the importance of his 'own men' over Moffat and his friends; some modern commentators have adopted this explanation of Philip's attitude.

However, when his trek journal is read along with his letter to Buxton, we can begin to see a different explanation for this discrepancy. The Griqua captaincies had to be built up, and their existence guaranteed by the British because theirs was the only authority that gave hope for the creation of the kind of sociopolitical base he believed necessary for the development of Christianity and civilisation. The multiplicity of small fissiporous chieftaincies among the Tswana of the area, particularly when brought under pressure from the Voortrekkers or Amandebele, could not possibly provide such a base or any secure future for their people.

It is this same belief that leads him into being such an ardent advocate of Moshweshe's authority. In this area at least, Philip was nearer the truth than most of his contemporary critics. In terms of African traditional practices, the chieftaincies, which the Methodist missionaries in November 1843, declared to be independent of Moshweshwe, had all, at one time or another, acknowledged Moshweshwe's sovereignty.[18] The large Sotho state that Moshweshwe claimed as his, appeared to Philip as a Godsend, even more than the Griqua captaincies. Here was the viable African political unit he believed to be essential for a Christian and civilised future. Neither Methodist missionaries nor Voortrekkers must be allowed to weaken it.

Initially it was the threat the Voortrekkers posed to the Sotho kingdom which agitated Philip. It upset him more deeply than anything else had done since the conflict over the civil rights of the Cape Folk in the 1820s. The British were the only source of strength powerful enough to outweigh that of the Voortrekkers, so they had to be brought in.

In stark contrast with his lobbying in the 1820s and 1830s, Philip, in this campaign, concentrated on influencing the British officials in South Africa, those at the local level as well as the Governor and his staff. He was encouraged in this approach by the sympathetic ear he had been granted by both Napier and Hare. He was also bitterly aware that, in the 1820s, his direct access to London over the heads of the local administration had not helped at all to get a sympathetic hearing for the cause in South Africa itself. As he informed the Directors in London, he had done his best on the trek to the eastern and northern frontiers, to influence and inform as many local Government officers as he met on his travels. He hoped, in this way, to further influence the information and opinions reaching Cape Town. This method of conveying his interpretation of events, inside and outside the Colony, was 'a way that will be less offensive and more influential than if it were coming directly from myself'.[19]

From the point of view of the Governor and his staff, the most important information gained by Philip was of the intentions of the Voortrekkers. He insisted that they intended to create a Republic which would take in all the country outside the Colony including that of the Griqua and the Sotho. Philip had spoken with numerous Afrikaners on his trek, both trekboer and Voortrekkers. It had become clear to him from these conversations that there was a united movement among the trekkers from Natal (where they still were in numbers at that time) to beyond the Vaal. Philip informed Hare of this in his first report to the British authorities, written before he had got back to Cape Town. This was the first hard information the Governor and his staff had received about the Voortrekkers on the High Veld and the scope of their ambitions.

> You must be aware that a political organisation has already been formed among bodies of them reaching from the Orange River lands to Natal, by Pretorius, that they have taken oaths of allegiance to him, as president of that Republic; and I am credibly informed that they make it their boast that they will soon have back by their arms, the farms they sold to the English.[20]

His last remarks in this extract were clearly the result of taking boasts too seriously, boasts almost certainly made to alarm the 'Kaffir boetie'. However, his basic information about the extent and the unity of the network of Voortrekker communities was only too accurate, as the British were to find out.

This new campaign was perhaps the best orchestrated of any by Philip. When Napier and Hare received his long reports, containing both important information and his suggestions as to how the British could cope with the situation by a process of treaty making, they also received letters from his African and missionary associates in the north. Moshweshwe wrote again asking for a treaty of friendship and protection and along with this missive came one from the French missionaries, pleading the same case. In addition, Adam Kok, and his resident missionary, also wrote letters in the same vein, warning particularly of the threat that lay over them of absorption into a Voortrekker state.[21]

Philip's letters to the Governor and Lt Governor were very long. They contained a careful analysis of what he believed to be the situation beyond the Colony, and a number of carefully worked alternative lines of policy with which to deal with it.

To Napier and Hare, he insisted that it was directly in the interest of the Imperial Government to maintain the political and territorial integrity of the Griqua and Sotho states. Supporting these three chieftaincies was a far more economical way of preserving peace on the northern frontier of the Colony than allowing Voortrekker expansion to create the kind of vastly expensive border conflicts that the Colony had so often endured on its eastern frontier.

Philip insisted that since the British were now taking action in Natal, it was only logical to act in the north otherwise the expenditure in Natal could turn out to be a waste of resources.

> The unparalleled and most critical state of this colony at the present moment requires that immediate attention be directed to this subject but the country of Moshesh borders on one part of the Colony only, and to protect Moshesh and his people against annihilation and to secure us against the dangers to which we must become [indecipherable] should such a catastrophe occur, it will be necessary on the part of the Government to extend its protection to the nations along the northern banks of the Cradock after its junction with the Vaal river from the western limits of the territory of Moshesh to the termination of the territories of the Griquas to the West; altogether an extent of frontier of upwards of three hundred (300) miles in length.[22]

He went on to point out that, had the Great Trek not happened, the Government would never have needed 'any other warden' on the northern frontier than the Griqua captains. Indeed, he reminded the Governor and Lt Governor, that in the past the British had never needed to raise military posts in the north, thanks to these men. The fact of never needing posts in the north was true, though the accuracy of his insistence on the Griquas as the great peacemakers and protectors of the Tswana is, as we have seen, another matter. However, he went on, the Great Trek had occurred and everything was now different. Only Moshweshwe, Kok and Waterboer stood between the Voortrekkers and the creation of a new state on the northern frontier inimical to the Colony. Matters were coming to a head, he insisted. Moshweshwe and Kok, because they were not protected by a treaty, were already suffering seriously from the infiltration of Voortrekker groups onto their land.

In Kok's area, there were also traditional trekboer groups, who accepted Michiel Oberholster as their leader, and those people, he believed, were open to persuasion to accept British authority and live amicably with the Griqua, something they had done, to some extent, until the arrival of Voortrekker troublemakers. However, he insisted that they were too weak, on their own, to resist Voortrekker pressure upon them, unless specifically detached from it by a British initiative.

He capped all of these arguments by insisting on the economy of these measures. If such an initiative was not taken, the consequences would be far more expensive to the British Treasury in the long run,

... while to aggravate the bitterness of disappointment it will be known that all these evils were foretold and might have been prevented with little trouble and at trifling expense.[23]

In his letter to Napier, he reminded the Governor of the suggestions he had made to Sir Lowry Cole ten years before, which was that the Griqua captaincies be incorporated into the Colony. He insisted that this scheme was only acceptable if it led to the Griquas being guaranteed their existing lands and their full rights as subjects of the Crown. Had this happened as he suggested, it is worth noting that the Griquas would have gained the same rights as the Cape Folk and although Philip could not know it, many would have gained the right to vote, when the franchise was granted in 1853.

Philip went on to indicate that he felt that Moshweshwe and his people should not, at this time, be offered incorporation within the Colony, but the Sotho chief should be given a solemn treaty of alliance and protection, which defined the limits of his territory. He also advised that a diplomatic agent should be stationed at his capital. Philip admitted that the extension of the frontiers of the Colony he envisaged might not be acceptable to Whitehall, so, as an alternative, but clearly a second best, he suggested treaties with Kok and Moshweshwe similar to that concluded with Waterboer. However, there should be an additional element—Waterboer, as well as the other two chiefs, should have a British Resident with him, and each chief should receive a small subsidy from the British Government.

Initially things appeared to go Philip's way. Napier took Philip's reports very seriously and sent them together with the letters from the chiefs and their missionaries to Whitehall. In his own accompanying despatch, he took up Philip's suggestion of the incorporation of the Griqua territories within the Colony, only to reject it, however. Instead, he pressed very firmly for Philip's alternative strategy of treaties of friendship and protection for all three chiefs.[24]

He also issued stern warnings to all British subjects beyond the colonial frontiers, not to infringe upon the sovereignty of native chiefs. These were pointless, however, since there is no indication that he was willing to send troops to enforce the warning. In addition, since the Voortrekkers had explicitly denied that they were British subjects, it was fundamental to their position to deny that this warning had any bearing on their actions. Again we see how out of touch the British authorities were with the feelings of the Voortrekkers.

Before the Colonial Office had time to decide on any policy at all for the area, events occurred which seemed to confirm all Philip's warnings and forebodings. Jan Mocke, the leader of the Voortrekkers in Kok's area, returned from helping his compatriots in Natal. He put his people into a laager immediately, because he insisted, the missionaries were exciting the 'natives' to attack him. He marched with a commando to Alleman's Drift on the Orange, a main frontier crossing from the Colony. There he proclaimed the lands north of the river to be a republic.

Adam Kok got wind early of Mocke's intentions. He immediately wrote to the nearest colonial official, who was Rawsthorne, the Civil Commissioner at Colesberg, and made sure, through Peter Wright, 'his' missionary, that Philip was informed, and received a copy of his appeal to Rawsthorne for help.[25] Kok also protested in the strongest terms to Mocke about the latter's bringing a commando onto *his* land, again making sure that Philip got a copy. After dispatching these letters, Kok, with a number of his elders including Wright, rode to Colesberg to consult Rawsthorne.

When the Griqua party arrived at Colesberg, they found Judge Menzies there, performing his circuit duties. The good judge, after consultation with Kok and his advisers, issued, in the name of the Queen, a proclamation on 22 October 1842, taking possession of all lands up to Latitude 25°N, and east of Longitude 22°, except for those territories recognised as being under the Portuguese Crown. He, together with Rawsthorne, then met with Jan Mocke for a long and conclusive colloquy. The Governor on hearing of this proclamation immediately disavowed it—he could have done no other.

In the months that followed, none of the parties involved were at all clear as to what was going to happen. The poor trekboer community of Michiel Oberholster was particularly bewildered, being quite unable to decide what was best for them. Meanwhile Kok's people went into laager as had Mocke's Voortrekkers already. However, what became increasingly a concern to the colonial officials and seemed to confirm Philip's warnings, was that the colonial Afrikaners close to the frontier became more and more explicit in their sympathy for Mocke. Philip had insisted to the Governor that if a Voortrekker Republic was created on the northern frontier, massive problems would ensue with regard to the loyalties of the colonial Afrikaners adjacent to it. When the local Afrikaner community went so far as to send messages to Mocke, offering to come to his aid if he were attacked by the Griqua, Philip's prophecy seemed only too likely to be fulfilled with a vengeance.

Rawsthorne was now placed in an intolerable position. As Philip had been at pains to point out, there were, traditionally, neither redcoats nor Cape Corps stationed on the northern frontier. Thus Rawsthorne's only force with which to maintain order was the burgher commando, made up of the very men who had offered their help to Mocke!

The hard pressed Civil Commissioner appealed to the Lt Governor, pointing out the gravity of the situation and his helplessness in the face of it. Hare responded promptly, proceeding north to Coleberg with a force of British regulars together with a unit of the Cape Mounted Rifles. There, during the last days of December 1842, he began a series of meetings with Griqua leaders and with Oberholster who, helped by the presence of red-coats, had decided his loyalties lay with the Colony.

As Peter Wright reported to Philip, the meetings, which lasted into the first week of 1843, were dominated by the senior of Kok's elders, Hendrick Hendricks. Of his opening speech to the conference, Wright enthused to Philip in his report of the 6 January.[26] It was the best speech he had ever heard from a 'native', and he insisted that it had deeply moved both Rawsthorne and Hare. Wright did not report this speech in great detail, nor the other later speeches made by Hendricks, which he also admired. This was a pity, for that would appear to have been the only source which would have let Philip learn of Hendricks' words in detail. It would have delighted Philip, if he had heard them, for Hendricks worked Philip's 'line' for all it was worth.

According to Robert Ross, in his most thorough and exciting study, *Adam Kok's Griqua*, Hendricks was the outstanding political figure in Kok's captaincy. It is quite clear he was no mere mouthpiece for Wright or any other missionary. He chose the line of argument that he did for a variety of motives as do most politicians; partly because he believed some of it, partly because he felt it would appeal to the British and partly because it appeared to be the best way out of the immediate difficulties. What is very interesting is how close his line of argument was to that which Philip had been pressing on the British authorities. Indeed, he expressed Philip's arguments more pithily and forcefully than Philip did in any of the four long letters to the Governor and Lt Governor of 1841 and 1842. This extract from Hendricks' opening speech could not have put Philip's beliefs more clearly.

> It was the English who made the Hottentots free. It was not until England put her hand on the land, was there any resting place for the Griqua—and never never will there be security for the Griquas and the Black nations of Africa until England continues to hold her hand over the country.[27]

It is evident from Ross' study that Hendricks was a shrewd and intelligent politician. He obviously made use of his friendship with Peter Wright to gain as much knowledge of the British as possible. Ross emphasises Wright's importance as one of the few missionaries that the Griquas trusted absolutely. What he does not note (it was after all not within his area of concern) was that along with the Reads, Wright was one of Philip's closest allies. Indeed, as we shall see in the next chapter, he was one of the few missionaries that Philip trusted completely. Wright, the Reads and Philip worked closely together—they were a team, and even if Philip was leader, the others were not simply his mouthpieces. So in Hendricks' performance we get an interesting insight into the chain of communication of ideas. It clearly was not one where Wright and the Griqua produced raw data, as it were, for Philip to process, but a complicated two-way interaction. This mutual exchange of information and ideas led both ends of the chain to press the British for the same kind of protection from Voortrekker ambition.

Hendricks, like Philip, insisted that the British must treat Kok, Waterboer and Moshweshwe in the same way and on the same footing. Only British power could save them from incorporation into a planned new Voortrekker Republic.[28] Philip and Hendricks were correct in their analysis of the problem and of the necessary solution—that only British imperial power could control the actions of the Voortrekkers. Where they both were wrong, was in their belief that the British Government could be persuaded, at that time, to use its power in that way. However, the Khoi and the slaves had been freed, the Vagrancy Ordinance had been rejected, D'Urban's plans had been frustrated and the Kat River Settlement flourished—was not all this enough to give both men confidence that Britain could be spurred or persuaded into action?

Without any very clear decisions emerging from the conference, the presence of Hare and his troops was enough to persuade Mocke and his people to disperse and to keep the loyalty of Oberholster and his folk. So the immediate crisis passed.

However, with the ever-welcome aid of Fairbairn and the *Advertiser*, Philip pressed on with his campaign to achieve security for the peoples beyond the northern frontier; a security which was still seriously in doubt, despite Hare's decision that it was safe to withdraw the troops. The main overt opposition to these proposed treaties came again, not from the Cape Afrikaners, but from the Grahamstown English. The *Grahamstown Journal* which regularly criticised Philip and denigrated the Cape Folk, in particular those of the Kat River, now added the Griqua to its list of targets. It ran a series of articles and editorials at this time scornful of the Griqua and their leaders. The Griqua were unworthy of a formal alliance with the British Crown. Indeed the *Journal* asserted that they were morally incapable of honouring a treaty.[29] Just as Philip held that the future of the Griqua was linked to the prospects for the Cape Folk, so, apparently did the *Journal*.

In this critical situation, Kok's Griqua suffered a massive blow with the tragic death of Peter Wright on 15 April 1843. This was also a severe blow to John Philip. He lost one of the tight little group who shared his religious and political attitudes and aims. Robert Ross notes that this death was a blow to the Griqua[30] but his concentration on the Griqua end of affairs prevents him appreciating what a loss Wright's death was to Philip. W Y Thomson, whom Philip sent to replace Wright, was a good man, although he never achieved the identity with the Griqua that Wright had done, nor was he one of the close circle around Philip.

Of Wright's death and the gap it caused in the Griqua communications with the colonial authorities, Ross writes, 'John Philip was, however, ready as ever to profer his advice'. This is said as if Philip was an external interferer in Griqua affairs. However, as we have seen, Philip was no casual meddler—he had for years held the Griqua cause as central to the cause of the Mission, indeed his difficulties with Moffat stemmed largely from the latter's annoyance at the way Philip held up the Griqua as the showpiece of the Mission. Wright's role among the Griqua cannot be separated from Philip, not that Wright was simply the latter's agent but that both worked intimately together for the same ends. It is worth noting something not recorded in Robert Ross's study, that Mrs Wright, when she had recovered sufficiently from her grief, went back to stay with the Griqua. In 1848, Wright's son, with Philip's encouragement, joined his mother there, as a member of W Y Thompson's staff.[31]

Despite the gap caused by Wright's tragic loss, the campaign for treaties continued, with Fairbairn's *Advertiser* consistently supporting the cause. By the end of 1843 success seemed on the point of being achieved. Napier had taken all their lobbying very seriously, and now sent two Cape Afrikaners, Veld-Kornet G D Joubert and Commandant H T van der Walt, into trans-Orangia to investigate matters on his behalf. Their reports agreed with Lt Governor Hare's advice, that the British interests demanded peace in the area, and that the Philip line on treaty making seemed the obvious and cheapest way of achieving this end.

So to Philip's delight, on 29 November 1843, a treaty was signed with Adam Kok, along the same lines as that which had been signed with Waterboer back in 1834; then on 13 December, a similar treaty was signed with Moshweshwe. A period of comparative peace followed in trans-Orangia. In retrospect, we can now see that this calm stemmed, not so much from the effect of the treaties, as from the disarray among, and the bitter disputes between, the various Voortrekker communities, scattered from Natal to the low veld near the Limpopo. It was these disputes about leadership, organisation and future aims, that absorbed Jan Mocke and his people, thus giving the Griqua and Sotho some respite.

However, all was not entirely peaceful, and a dramatic conflict, with great long-term significance, broke out over the Moshweshwe treaty. This trouble came from what was, at first sight a surprising source, the Methodist Mission in South Africa.

The problem stemmed from the fact that, unlike the two treaties with the Griqua captains, Moshweshwe's treaty defined precisely the geographical boundaries of his sovereignty. The Chief had complained, at the time, and in some subsequent letters, about this definition. The boundaries needed to be re-drawn even further out, in his view, since, in the text of the treaty, some of the territory of Moroka's Rolong and Gert Taaibosch's Kora had been left out. As chiefs owing him allegiance, all of their territory should have been included, but he did not press the issue too hard since things had gone his way in general.

Be that as it may, only two days after the signing of the treaty, William Shaw, the head of the Methodist Mission in southern Africa, wrote to the Governor complaining of the treaty in quite different terms. Methodist missionaries had, for some time, been settled with chiefs in the Caledon valley. As far as Moshweshwe, Cassalis and Philip were concerned, these chiefs were all vassals of Moshweshwe, and their territories were rightly included in the treaty definition of the kingdom of Moshweshwe. Shaw viewed the situation quite differently and insisted on the independence of the 'Methodist' chiefs over Moshweshwe, and complained of the injustice the treaty did them.

Thompson, in his *Survival in Two Worlds*, asserts that Philip actually drafted the territorial definitions on the treaty. The present writer has not found any unambiguous confirmation of this in the London Missionary Society archives nor in those of the Colonial Office. What is clear, however, is that the provisions in the treaty follow, almost to the letter, Philip's definition of Moshweshwe's kingdom in each of his long letters to Napier and Hare. In the minds of colonial Whites, these treaties were associated with Philip and with his close allies, the French missionaries.

All of this added extra vigour to the Methodist complaints, for relations between them and Philip had been bad for some time. The main conflict had originated in a conflict over the meaning of the War of Hintsa. Although Shaw had not wanted the Xhosa expelled from their lands, he and his fellow Methodist missionaries (all of whom were from 1820 settler families) vehemently insisted that no blame for the war could be attached to the White settlers. They had joined in the Grahamstown denunciation of Philip, Stockenstrom and company. The letters John Ross sent from Grahamstown to Philip at the time reflected the bitter division between the Methodist missionaries and the other missionaries.[32]

The Methodist missionaries were all members of 1820 Settler families, including William Shaw their leader. The only major Protestant group which had not been encouraged to come to South Africa by Philip, they had initially polite but distant relations with him. However, as soon as he became involved with Xhosa affairs, their attitude towards him had become very critical. Although most were ready to complain to the authorities about acts of gross injustice, their inextricable involvement with the English settlers (many of their congregations were White settler congregations) meant that they tended to have a very different view of frontier affairs from that of the LMS and Glasgow Mission men in the area. From the time of the War of Hintsa, relations between them and the LMS grew progressively worse. However, in Philip's latter years, Shaw did come to have more sympathy with him and even joined with him in his apprehension about the attitude of influential figures in Grahamstown towards the Xhosa and their future.[33]

In Philip's view, it was essential for the future of Christianity and civilisation among the peoples beyond the Orange, that Moshweshwe's power should be as extensive as possible. The division of the trans-Orange region into a series of petty chieftaincies was something to be avoided, almost at any cost. However, he had not drawn the boundaries of Moshweshwe's kingdom in the way he did, either on the basis of ignorance of the position of the number of the petty chieftains or in deliberate defiance of their rights. Nor was he scheming to undermine the work of the Methodists in any way. He presumed he was simply defining the political situation within which they were working already, and would continue to work. He drew up the definition of the boundaries, which he sent to the Governor, on the basis of the information given to him by Moshweshwe and Casalis. As we have seen, the two most recent biographers of Moshweshwe, Thompson and Sanders, are agreed that all of the petty chiefs included in Moshweshwe's domains by Philip had, at one time or another, carried out some action which according to African traditional practice was a recognition of Moshweshwe's sovereignty over them.[24]

In balancing the respective merits of Moshweshwe's claims with those made by Shaw, it is vital to take account of the profoundly different role played by the French missionaries among the Sotho, with that of the Methodists in the smaller chieftaincies. The French, particularly Casalis, were close allies of Moshweshwe—indeed they saw themselves as, in some ways, his subjects, and Casalis was literally a King's counsellor. On the other side, as Thompson points out, the Methodists did not play this kind of role, and tended to see the chiefs as dependent on them. In fact it was they, the missionaries, who took the initiative, both in complaining about the terms and in maintaining the dispute, not the chiefs themselves.[35]

Moshweshwe agreed with Philip as to definition of his territorial sovereignty, somewhat expanded in the way he suggested at the time of signing. For the rest of his life he held it to be the true definition of Lesotho. His delight in the treaty had been transmitted to Philip by the French Mission.[36]

However, the long drawn out dispute, initiated by the Methodist missionaries on behalf of their charges, irritated the British officials immensely and dimmed their enthusiasm for the treaty somewhat. They misunderstood what was going on, and their misunderstanding is repeated, over a hundred years on, by Galbraith, when he says

> The treaty with Moshwesh instead of being a means to order had thus become a source of conflict and the rivalry of missionary societies had encouraged divisions among tribes that it was imperative to unite.[37]

Philip's belief was equal to Galbraith's—that it was imperative to unite those tribes, as we have seen. It was the Methodists who interpreted the whole matter in terms of petty mission rivalry. At no point in all the corresponding on this matter, is there even a hint that Philip saw his backing of the authority of Moshweshwe as a means of putting down the Methodists and aiding 'his' missionaries.

With Philip as their spokesman in the Colony, Moshweshwe and his aide, Casalis, waged a campaign not only to have the British hold to the terms of the treaty, as far as territorial definition was concerned, but also to expand the area recognised as Moshweshwe's to take in all the lands of the Kora and of Moroka.

Initially, things seemed to go fairly well. Even in the Griqua area, where the most intense pressure had been exerted by the migrant Afrikaners, there was a period of about eighteen months of peace following the signing of the treaties. The situation was, in fact, very fragile and Philip was aware of this. Philip, W Y Thompson and Casalis all hoped that the treaties would not prove empty gestures and that the British would hold to them, and enforce them, if necessary. However, they were aware that there were specific problems that remained unresolved. What would the British do if there was a major threat to the authority of Moshweshwe or either of the Griqua captains by the Voortrekkers? Would the treaties prove to be as of little value as the Cape of Good Hope Punishment Act because the British were unwilling to bear the cost of any military action beyond the colonial frontier? What would happen if the Voortrekkers, having absorbed the results of their rebuff in Natal, got themselves together again and took the political initiative in trans-Orangia? Would those emigrant families, who had leased land from Kok, move away on the expiry of their leases, as laid down by the treaties? How far did Kok's authority extend over the trekker community in reality, as opposed to the letter of the treaty? The unresolved questions seemed almost endless.

However, during this period of calm, John Philip appeared to be in a comparatively optimistic frame of mind about the future. Macmillan in *Bantu, Boer and Briton*[38] quotes from a series of private letters from Philip to a number of individuals in the United Kingdom which, he felt, showed Philip to be in a most buoyantly optimistic mood indeed. However, there are no copies of these letters in the archives of the London Missionary Society.

The letters in the archives, while not indicative of despair, are not such that they could be cited as evidence of confidence in a favourable future. Perhaps this is because the letters rarely mention the northern frontier but concentrate on the critical state of Philip's relations with many of the London Missionary Society staff, those associated with Moffat and Calderwood, and on his relations with his fellow Directors in London. Although this crisis will be dealt with fully in a subsequent chapter, its effect on Philip were such that it is necessary to outline the problem here.

The London Directors had at this time acceded to the pressure from Moffat and Calderwood and ordered that the work of the Society in Africa should be organised on the basis of local missionary committees. Philip had opposed this idea from its inception and their decision, when viewed in the light of their lack of sympathy with or interest in his political concerns, drove Philip into a mood of deep disillusionment with the Society; so much so that he offered his resignation. Peter Wright (before his death), Thompson, Atkinson, the Reads and all the other staff who could be called pro-African, rallied to support Philip and wrote to the Directors begging them not to accept the Doctor's resignation.

The Directors agreed to refuse to accept Philip's resignation, and they persuaded him to work on, despite the institution of the committee system. Philip accepted this with reluctance. He was now even more convinced than before that the Directors of the Society were of no use to him in any attempt to campaign in Britain about his concerns over British policy in South Africa. What was worse, the failure of Buxton's Aborigines Committee to have any impact on British policy, Buxton's failing health and the lack of an obvious successor, all pointed to the fact that the humanitarian lobby was no longer the power it had been.

It may be that this optimism about British intentions in South Africa, which Macmillan found in Philip's personal letters no longer available to us, was an exaggeration due to Philip's need to feel that something was going well. In the London Missionary Society archives, the letters reflect a deep sense of disillusionment with the London Missionary Society, with his fellow Directors in London, as well as with many of the staff in South Africa.

John Philip was, in this period, feeling increasingly alone, aged and tired. By this time his handwriting is almost illegible, so much so that the overwhelming majority of the letters he sent, were written by a different hand, and only the signature is his. He was soon to be struck a terrible emotional blow when in July 1845, his son William and his grandson, John Fairbairn, were drowned in a tragic accident. This was an emotional blow from which the seventy-year-old man never fully recovered.

The arrival of the new Governor, Sir Peregrine Maitland, in March 1844, appeared to be a significant event for the humanitarian cause in the Colony and on its borders. Maitland was, in stark contrast with his predecessors, a pious, evangelically inclined Christian.[39]

However, Philip was soon rudely shaken out of this sense of confidence. Many of the questions posed by the settlement in the areas north of the Orange were now put sharply and the answers were not to the liking of Philip nor his Griqua and Sotho allies. As Philip had suggested long before, the intransigent Voortrekkers had withdrawn from Natal to the High Veld and, after a period of confusion, they, and those who had never gone to Natal in the first place, were able to reorganise themselves into an effective political force.

At Potchefstroom in April 1844, Voortrekker leaders had come to an agreement and passed the famous Thirty-three Articles constituting a new Voortrekker State.[40] The state constituted in these Articles paid no attention at all to the Napier treaties with the Griqua and Sotho states. The leaders were, however, well aware of them, and entered into negotiation with Kok to persuade him to abrogate the Napier treaty and enter into a formal relationship with them. These negotiations had been entered into only after Jan Mocke, that perennial gadfly of the Griqua, had almost provoked an open conflict between Griqua and Voortrekker commandos. Potgieter, the Commandant of the Voortrekkers, intervened and attempted to woo Kok from his British alliance.

Kok refused these blandishments, and made sure, through the agency of Thompson, that Philip was kept in detailed touch with all that was going on. As Kok expected, Philip passed all this information over to the Governor. Thompson reported to Philip[41] that Kok had maintained, in reply to Potgieter, the same views on the situation so eloquently expressed by Hendricks two years before. He insisted that the only hope for Griqua survival was a strong British alliance.

Having made sure the British were aware of what was going on, Kok then decided to put the worth of the treaty to the test. In March 1845, acting on the authority which he believed it had given him, Kok tried to arrest Jan Krynauw, a Voortrekker. Kok failed to get his man but, in response to his actions, the local Voortrekker community went into laager and, significantly, were joined in their defensive position by the trekboers of Oberholster. Yet again Oberholster, in a crisis, went back on his much-repeated oath of loyalty to the Crown. Kok's people also went into laager and were reinforced by a mounted commando of Waterboer's people. How far the Griquas were deliberately testing out the effectiveness of the treaties cannot now, at this distance, be confirmed, but the actions were carefully planned. Robert Ross notes that it was only after the harvest was safely gathered in that Kok made his move.[42]

Thompson kept Philip fully informed of all these events and he, in turn, informed Maitland. From the point of view of the Griqua and Philip, all appeared to go well at first.

In April, Rawsthorne, as Civil Commissioner of Colesberg, crossed the Orange and met with the Voortrekker leaders at Allewyn's Kop, close to Kok's capital, Philippolis. Rawsthorne's attitude was entirely consistent with the Napier treaties. He informed the Voortrekkers that they were still British subjects. They were to return all the Griqua horses and cattle they had lifted so far in the campaign, and, much more important, all wrongdoers were to be surrendered to him, to be tried, within the Colony by the colonial courts. He pointed out that British troops were on their way from the Cape and that they would enforce his ruling and the authority of Adam Kok.

The stunned Voortrekkers were willing to return the beasts, but would accept nothing else until it had been discussed by the Raad set up by the Thirty-three Articles. They were clearly insisting that they were not British subjects and owed allegiance to another state. They then proceeded to withdraw some forty miles and set up a new laager at Zwartkoppies.

The redcoats and Cape Corps then arrived, and briskly dispersed the laager with little loss. Oberholster's people changed sides, yet again, and took the oath of allegiance to the Queen. The Voortrekkers however remained defiant and withdrew across the Modder River, beyond the Griqua captain's area of authority.

Philip was overjoyed at this active vindication of his policy, which, he felt, must surely convince Waterboer, Kok and Moshweshwe of the usefulness of their policy of alliance with Britain. However, Maitland now decided to go north himself and settle the problems beyond the Orange once and for all. It was at this point that things started to go wrong, and from Philip's point of view, they continued to go wrong until his death.

When in September 1844 Maitland had visited Colesberg, Thompson had gone down to the Government post to consult with him. He had suggested to the Governor a possible long-term solution to the Griqua–Afrikaner tension in Kok's area.[42] He reported to Philip, subsequently, that the Governor had seemed impressed with his suggestion that Kok should give up all claims to the land north of the Riet River and that, in return, all emigrant farmers should move out of lands south of the same river. The lands to the south of the river would then be unambiguously Griqua.

However impressed Maitland had been by Thompson's suggestions the year before, he did not follow them in his negotiations in 1845. The negotiations were conducted at Touwfontein, and there the Governor's decisions were clearly weighted in favour of the emigrant Whites and to the disadvantage of the Griqua. Thompson, who played a major, but fruitless, role as one of Kok's counsellors during these negotiations, sent a careful report on them to Philip which included copies of the letters and notes exchanged by the two sides.[44]

One feature that runs through these notes is that all the negotiations seem to have been conducted by the Reverend B Maitland, the Governor's chaplain and secretary. Since Galbraith suggests[45] that most of the

Governor's despatches to London were the work of John Montague, the Colonial Secretary, one begins to wonder what role, if any, Maitland himself played in the affairs of the Colony?

At Touwfontein, the British imposed on Kok a division of his territory into two, but unlike Thompson's suggestion of the year before, the inalienable part left to the Griqua was small, leaving the larger part of their land open to occupation by the emigrant Afrikaners. It was no consolation to Kok and his allies that the chief's sovereignty was recognised by the British as applying to the whole.

Thompson, with the support of Philip, put to the Governor two strong reasons why this proposed situation was unacceptable to the Griqua. First, the division gave away much too much land as alienable, particularly since there was no provision in the proposals for the removal of those settlers already occupying farms in the inalienable area. Second, what did Kok's sovereignty amount to when the proposals insisted that cases of law-breaking involving Whites had to be tried by the British Resident who was to represent the Governor in the area?

Chaplain Maitland was adamant in his reply on behalf of the Governor that no changes could be made in the agreement as he had laid it down. This fundamentally anti-Griqua posture on the part of the colonial administration was confirmed in the following months by its refusal to expel any emigrants whatsoever from the inalienable lands, though many of them had been leaders in the 'rebellion' which had not only challenged Kok's authority, but Britain's also.

This complaisance towards the rebellious Whites still occupying inalienable land was particularly galling to Philip. He had, through Thompson, insisted to Maitland that the Afrikaner actions had been undertaken corporately, therefore the whole community involved in the taking up of arms had to be treated as one and expelled. Maitland, when this was put to him, had replied that this was an understanding of the situation which he could not accept. He further rubbed salt in the wounds of the missionaries and the Griqua by asserting that the Griquas had provoked the whole affair by their rash and provocative action in attempting to arrest Krynauw! As regards any future action by Kok to implement the division of the land as laid down by the treaty, Maitland said

> His Excellency would not authoritatively intervene to prevent Captain Adam Kok from practically applying the law but he would not in any case the party sought to be deprived of property resisted expulsion, march British troops for the purpose of carrying the law into effect.[46]

Further, in the same letter, Maitland made it quite clear that he had set his face against Philip's other ploy to provoke him into decisive action against the Voortrekkers. This was Philip's insistence that the Voortrekkers had set up a state, whose authority was the only authority they recognised. Thus they were rebels against the Queen, whether or not their actions against Kok had constituted rebellion.

Despite what Retief had said in his 'Manifesto', despite the unambiguous creation of an independent state in Natal, despite the recent creation of a volksraad at Winburg, Maitland insisted that the Voortrekkers were simply individual British farmers who had crossed the border of the Colony. He said

> It will be obvious to Captain Kok that the Emigrant British Subjects resident in his Territory are not to be dealt with by him as if they professed an independent Government. Such an Independent Government Her Majesty the Queen, whose ally he is, has declared she will not permit her Emigrant Subjects to establish legally in any quarter, and much less, of course, in the territory of an independent Chief. Under these circumstances it is clear that no general measure of ejection, applicable indiscriminately to all emigrants, would be regular or proper.[47]

The Governor was not going to do anything at all about the Voortrekkers, and Thompson communicated to Philip, his and the Griquas, bitter disappointment. However they felt they had no alternative but to sign the treaty. Where the Governor's sympathies lay was quite clear now to all the parties to the Touwfontein agreement.

Philip was very disheartened by all this. His fear that the exciting possibilities for the development of Christianity and civilisation among the Griqua and the Sotho, about which he had so enthused in 1842, might disappear before his very eyes was then heightened when Maitland now turned to negotiate with Moshweshwe. The Governor, to Philip's horror, suggested that he would negotiate separately with all the 'Methodist' chiefs and only then with Moshweshwe. However, after some deliberation with his officials, he resiled from this idea and decided to negotiate with Moshweshwe alone.

The Governor offered a similar arrangement to the Chief of the Sotho as he had to Adam Kok. The Sotho lands were to be divided into an alienable and an inalienable area, on the same terms as with the Griqua. One key difference appeared in the offer to the Sotho from that made to the Griqua. Moshweshwe was requested to define for himself the alienable part of his territory. This was a difference of major importance and it is not clear from the correspondence in the Colonial Office archives why Moshweshwe was treated so differently at this point, especially when, initially, Maitland had adopted the most unfriendly of attitudes in contemplating recognition of the autonomy of the 'Methodist' chiefs.

Moshweshwe, for his part, grabbed at the offer and defined as the alienable area a small wedge of land lying in a triangle formed by the confluence of the Orange and the Caledon Rivers and a line drawn between the two from Commissie Drift to Buffelsvlei Drift.[48] Given all that had gone before it seems extraordinary to record that Maitland accepted this little more than token gesture of compliance from Moshweshwe, but he did. He only waited until he had sent a representative to check on the actual location of the Voortrekker families in the area. His representative was Gideon Joubert, the veld-kornet whom Napier had sent into the Sotho lands in 1843. Despite the fact that Joubert reported on Moshweshwe in very unfavourable terms, and also that the majority of White families were

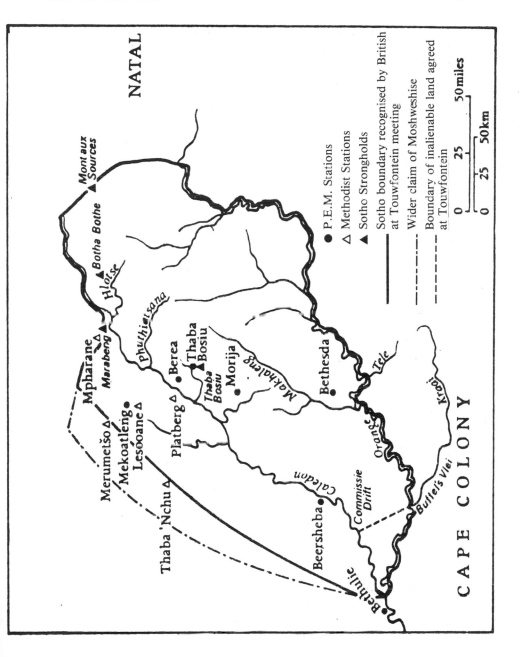

NATAL

Mont aux
Sources ▲

▲ Botha Bothe

Hlotse

Phuthietsana

Mpharane
△ Maraberg ▲

Merumetšo △

Mekoatleng ●
Lesooane △

Platberg △

Berea ●

● Thaba
Bosiu ▲

Thaba
Bosiu

● Morija

Mokhalong

● Bethesda

Tele

Thaba 'Nchu △

Caledon

Commissie
Drift

Orange

Kraai

Buffel's Vlei

Beersheba ●

Bethulie

CAPE COLONY

● P.E.M. Stations
△ Methodist Stations
▲ Sotho Strongholds
──── Sotho boundary recognised by British
       at Touwfontein meeting
─ ─ ─ Wider claim of Moshweshise
- - - - Boundary of inalienable land agreed
        at Touwfontein

0   25   50 miles

0   25   50 km

concentrated in areas other than the suggested inalienable area, Maitland accepted Moshweshwe's proposal.

Maitland returned south before the formal signing of the treaty. This was done by Major Warden, who took up his post as British Resident for the lands beyond the Orange. This appointment was very different from Philip's suggestion in the past, that Waterboer, Kok and Moshweshwe should each have a British Resident with them to help them to uphold the law and enforce the treaties. Warden was meant to maintain order among all the various groups and to do so without effective force to back him up.

The whole episode would almost lead one to believe that Maitland was in the business of making treaties which were bound to fail to bring about an effective settlement, defining the terms so as to silence temporarily the pro-African lobbyists like Philip, while leaving the Voortrekkers with a free hand. However, there is nothing in his correspondence with the Colonial Office which indicates any such Machiavellian sophistication on his part. His own inadequacies, his desire to do something to solve the problem, while doing nothing to upset the Treasury with its implacable insistence on colonial retrenchment, go a long way to explain his strategy.

One thing became obvious to Moshweshwe and his allies, almost immediately after Warden's arrival. This was that Maitland had so readily accepted Moshweshwe's definition of inalienable land because, as Warden soon made clear, the British were not going to lift a finger to remove any Voortrekkers from the land so designated by the treaty.

In addition to all this, Moshweshwe and Philip knew nothing of the contents of Joubert's report. It did not appear to worry them since he had been friendly and sympathetic on his last trek north of the Orange. His new report went into the files in Cape Town and became the most up-to-date official appreciation of the situation beyond the Orange River. The report was decidedly anti-Moshweshwe. At one point Joubert even refers to the King as 'schepsel'. In his translation for *The Basutoland Records*, Theal renders this as 'troublesome person' which greatly softens the Dutch expression, literally 'creature'. Joubert also asserts that the Methodist claims with regard to the independence from Moshweshwe of Moroka, Taaibosh, Davids and Baatje, are justified. He goes further and asserts that beside them, Moshweshwe is unreliable, nor has he real power.[49] The military defeats at the hands of Moshweshwe's Sotho were, in the not too distant future, to prove to the British authorities how misleading that judgement was.

Thus, even as the ring of treaties which Philip had advocated for so long was completed, their ineffectiveness was made painfully clear to the Griqua leaders, to Moshweshwe and to Philip. Worse was to come—Maitland came southwards from the Orange to deal with the Eastern frontier and the Xhosa. At this point Philip reported to his friends in the United Kingdom his deep uneasiness about affairs in the North, about future relations with the Xhosa and perhaps most heartbreaking of all to him, the fact that every effort was being made by many Whites to depress the economic and social status of the Cape Folk.

8

The Last Years

The last six years of John Philip's life constituted a terrible period of distress and disappointment for him. This distress was at the most intimate level as well as in his public life. In July 1845, his son William, pastor at Hankey, together with his grandson, Johnny Fairbairn, were drowned. Then in October 1847, his beloved Jane, who had not only been his wife but his colleague and administrator, died. Many of his friends thought that this was a blow from which he never fully recovered. To add to his misery, that same month another grandchild, the daughter of his elder daughter, Mary and the Reverend George Christie, was killed in a tragic accident.

In the wider world of his public life, all seemed equally dark. The agreements with Kok, Waterboer and Moshweshwe at Touwfontein appeared to complete his idea of circling the Colony with a ring of allied African states but he was aware how little weight could be put on them. Touwfontein was a defeat not a victory.

It was not only beyond the Orange that all he hoped for appeared in danger; the position of the Cape Folk within the Colony and the relations of the Colony with the Xhosa also seemed to be heading for disaster. In March, 1845 he wrote to Tidman

> The Governor is in a painful situation, he knows the danger and that should the flames of war break out between the Boers and the Griquas it will end in the destruction of the Native tribes and that of the missionaries beyond the Northern boundary of the Colony but he shrinks from the responsibility of adopting vigorous methods. . . .
>
> Whilst our missions and the Natives are exposed to imminent danger beyond the boundaries of the Colony; the enemies of the coloured people within the Colony are using all the means in their power to enslave them. Having failed in all their other attempts to bring 80,000 people under the most cruel bondage by Vagrancy Acts, the Municipalities have by surreptitious means got hold of a power from the Government by which they hope to prevent them residing at the villages or grazing their cattle on the common lands and so oblige them to reside on the lands of the farmers. Should their plan be successful the coloured people will not have a hut in the Colony, not the property of their oppressors nor a spot where they can breathe the air of freedom except at our mission institutions.
>
> . . . You must know that the Caffreland missionaries have lost the confidence of the chiefs. . . . This is a lamentable state of things and one that cannot be defended. The Reads form the only party among our missionaries in whom the chiefs have confidence and this is one cause of the hostile feelings manifested against the Reads and the reason why they find it necessary to give up holding intercourse with the chiefs. This alienation of the chiefs from our missionaries has been growing for years past. It may be traced to various sources and late events in connection with the Governor's recent visit to the Eastern Frontier

have brought it into public notice. The chiefs blame the missionaries for the active part they took in recommending to the Governor (which they did as a body) alterations in the amended treaties which the chiefs consider adverse to their views and interests and (as coming from missionaries) in some cases insulting to them.[1]

If we look first at the situation of the Cape Folk within the Colony, we find that they were in a situation which du Toit and Giliomee have categorised as being 'trapped in a limbo between abject poverty and political equality'.[2] They specifically name the Khoikhoi as trapped in this way, but by the 1840s, Khoikhoi, people of mixed race and the freed slaves were becoming one people—the Cape Folk, who were beginning to be referred to in that period as the Coloureds.

What du Toit and Giliomee appear to ignore is that among the Cape Folk, there were groups on the mission stations and at Kat River who were not in the limbo to which they refer. These folk were prosperous to a degree, owning cattle and other property, some using their skill at a trade to build up a little wealth and security. And it was precisely these people who seemed to be the particular object of the bitter antagonism of many Whites in the eastern frontier area, particularly the Grahamstown community. This despite all the outcry about the fear of the danger caused by 'vagrants'.

It was this situation of the Cape Folk that particularly depressed John Philip. The struggle to make effective their equality with other subjects of the Queen seemed unending for the Cape Folk and their friends. All over the Colony they were under pressure which was aimed at reducing them to the status of a labour force for White enterprise. The harassment took many forms. The LMS staff reported that in many districts, the new municipalities were attempting to withdraw from the Cape Folk the right to herd their stock on the municipal commonage. In addition, many missionaries reported that things were being made so difficult for both parents and children that the Cape Folk were withdrawing their children from the municipal schools.[3] One of the most detailed and explicit reports on these difficulties came from Elliot at Uitenhage, a man who often differed with Philip over the Cape Folk and their future. Soon after Philip's complaint to Tidman, Elliot also wrote to the Secretary of the Society. In this letter he detailed the pressures being exerted upon his people in Uitenhage to prevent their enjoying their full rights as subjects of the Queen.[4]

As has already been noted, what saddened Philip in particular, was that the English community of the eastern Cape were taking the lead in what could be called the anti-philanthropic cause during this period. They mounted the waves of criticism of the missionaries, particularly those of the LMS and the Scottish mission, for their uncritical sympathy for both the Cape Folk and the Xhosa. They also maintained pressure on the colonial authorities to get tough with 'vagrants' as well as with the Xhosa 'marauders'.

In their study of Afrikaner political thought, du Toit and Giliomee take note of this, and seem to feel that it can be explained by the removal from the area of so many Afrikaner families as a result of the Great Trek. This is not an entirely satisfactory explanation. English antagonism towards the Cape Folk had been complained of by Philip before the Great Trek. Perhaps more important is the fact that, despite the Voortrek, which also drew from areas other than the eastern border districts, there were still many Afrikaner families remaining. After all, Andries Stockenstrom had still enough Afrikaners around him to form a substantial burgher force in the War of the Axe. In this connection it is not relevant to remember that, in the furore over Stockenstrom's appointment as Lt Governor after the War of Hintsa, it was the English of Grahamstown who bitterly attacked him throughout the period of his appointment. In contrast, as he notes in his autobiography, the Afrikaner community, after only a little hesitation, rallied round him with loyalty and affection.[5]

It may be that the Great Trek took away from the eastern districts of the Colony the most radical and articulate of the Afrikaner community, but there were still many Afrikaners there, and they did not play a leading part in the anti-missionary, anti-Cape Folk agitation of the period.

The Grahamstown Journal led this agitation. Interestingly, as we have seen, the *Journal* linked the Griqua with Cape Folk, just as John Philip did. At the time of the negotiations north of the Orange, the *Journal* published a series of pieces denigrating the Griqua. It insisted that the Griqua had neither the moral nor social qualities necessary to allow them to be partners in a treaty with Her Majesty's Government. These weaknesses were linked to the inadequacies that the *Journal* perceived to be the characteristics of the Cape Folk.[6]

There are two other important sources of insight into the attitudes of the English community of the eastern Cape at this time. The first is a song, partly in Afrikaans, perhaps more accurately, in Cape Dutch. The authorship is attributed, by many authorities, to Andrew Geddes Bain. In the late 1830s and throughout the 1840s this song was often sung with short dialogue sketches performed between each verse, by the various amateur dramatic groups in the Colony. The original sketches pour a great deal of derision on John Philip and Fairbairn together with Jan Tsatsu and Andries Stoffels, the Xhosa and Kat River leaders who accompanied Philip to give evidence to the Aborigines Committee. These clearly reflect the feelings of the frontier Whites in 1838 when the song and sketches were written. However, the song itself went on being used throughout the 1840s and significantly it is reprinted during this period again and again in the English language newspapers in the east.[7] I have found no reference to its having been published in the *Zuid Afrikaan* or any other periodical catering to the Afrikaner population. This may be partly due to the fact that the song is deriding die Taal, the incipient Afrikaans language, as well as the Cape Folk.

> My name is Kaatje Kekkelbek
>   I kom van Kat Rivier
> Dere is van water geen gebrek
>   Maar scarce van wyn en beer.

Myn a.b.c. at Philip's school
    I learnt ein kleine bietjie
And left, with wisdom just as full
    as gekke tante Meitjie
With my tol de rol, etc.

But A.B. ab. or I.N. ine
    ik dogt, met uncle Plaatje
'Snt half so good as Brandywyn
    or vette Karbonaatje.
So off we set, ein heele boel
    Stole a fat cow and sacked it
Then to an Engels settler fool
    We had ourselves contracted.

His va'islands sheeps was plenty vet
    Zyn Brandywyn was sterk ook
Maar we hombogged hom out of bot'
    For very little work ook.
And wat he voud not give, one took
    For Hottentot is vryman
We killed his fattest ox and ook
    Ons drained his vatjes dry man.

We next took to the Kowie bos,
    Found sheeps that was not lost aye
Maar de schelme boer het ons gevang
    And brought ons voor McRosty
Daar was Saartje Zeekoegat en ik
    En ou'Dirk Dondewetter
Klass Klauterberg en Deidrik Dik
    All sent to de tronk toget'er.

Drte maants ons daar got byaar Kos'
    For killing os en hamel
Ik said should I again get los
    I'll call again on Campbell
De Jud came round—his sentence such
    As we dogt just and even
Six months hard work'dat means in Dutch
    'ses maanden lekker leven.

Die Tronk het is een lekker plek
    As twere not juist so dry sir
Maar now dat ik is los again
    At Todd's I'll wet my eye sir.
At Vice's home in Market Square,
    I'll drown my melancholies
And at Barrack Hill, dere's Schotsmen daar
    Will treat me well at Jolly's.

Next morn day put me in de black hole
  For een rixdoaldon stealing
And knocking down een vrouw that had
  Met my sweetheart some dealing
Maar I'll go to the Govurnor self
  Dats groot onregt by jingo
I've as much right to steal or fight
  As kafir has or Fingo.

The second important source lies in the speeches and letters of John Mitford Bowker. The well-documented popularity of Kaatje Kekkelbek is a useful check on popular attitudes to set alongside the calculated speeches and memoranda of one of the most active leaders of the English settlers. Before a historian too quickly comes to a conclusion about popular attributes from the speeches of a leading politician, it is important to have some genuinely popular source as a check. Kaatje Kekkelbek and the attitudes of Bowker dovetail into one another beautifully.

In Bowker's speeches and letters,[8] he is bitterly critical of British policy towards the tribes beyond the northern and eastern frontiers, and he links this mistaken policy to a fundamentally wrong attitude to the indigenous population in general, including the Cape Folk. In this, at least, he is in full agreement with John Phillip—that is, in linking the two areas of 'native' policy in this way.

One of the most famous, and often quoted, speeches was delivered to a meeting of settlers in August 1844. In this speech he made his notorious 'springbok' analogy with regard to the fate of the Xhosa people before the onward march of civilisation. As the great herds of springbok that had once covered the land had disappeared before the onward march of progress so should the Xhosa. The difference would be that there would be no sense of regret that all must feel at the passing of the beautiful antelopes. He went on

> My feelings towards the Kafir are not of that stamp. I know he has disregarded the zealous missionary for years. I know he has once over-run and destroyed these districts, and I fear him, knowing him to be ready and willing to do it again. I know him to be the great bar to all improvements amongst us, I know that rapine and murder are in all his thoughts, and I have seen them in his looks and hate him accordingly . . . and begin to think that he too, as well as the springbok, must give place, and why not? Is it just that a few thousands of ruthless, worthless savages are to sit like a nightmare upon a land that would support millions of civilised men happily? Nay; Heaven forbids it; and those dreamers who have been legislating for the protection of the aborigines have been unwittingly aiding in their downfall.[9]

As in a number of his speeches and letters, assertions like that above, which appear to demand literal genocide, are softened by remarks that the 'kaffirs' can stay. They can stay, but only under the new colonial dispensation desired and hoped for by Bowker and his hearers. In this new era, all missionaries would appear to be removed from the Colony, and under the strict and just tutelage of the colonists, the Xhosa might begin slowly to develop in both Christianity and civilisation.

   This is a theme which he took up again and again, and its popularity
among English settlers can be gauged from the repetition of many of his key
phrases in the petitions from the eastern Cape in the years 1844–46.
   A clear summary of his ideas on Christianity and civilisation can be seen
in the letter that he wrote to Montague, Maitland's Colonial Secretary on
25 November 1844.

> The cant of the present day is leading well-intentioned people far astray from
> the promotion of true civilisation in Africa. Niger Expeditions, Aborigines
> Protection societies, Anti-Slavery societies, Mission Institutions, as at present
> conducted, are things of naught. Savage nations must be taught to fear and
> respect, to stand in awe of a nation whose manners and customs, whose religion
> it is beneficial and desirable for them to adopt. Mankind are [sic] ever prone to
> imitate the manners of their superiors all over the world; and we must prove to
> these people that we are their superiors before we can ever hope for much good
> to be done among them, by conquering them if no milder means are effectual.
> Their haughty arrogant spirit, buoyed up by pride and ignorance, must be
> brought low. . . . But I maintain that many missionaries have done much to
> continue them as a nation of thieves, by holding up all attempts of the colony
> and its Government to repress their thievish disposition, and recover stolen
> colonial property as cruel aggression and bloody commandoes, whilst they
> continue fruitlessly to preach christianity to a nation of thieves. Roman
> manners and customs were rapidly adopted by conquered Britons in the time of
> Agricola, but I am not aware that Agricola ever became patron to an Ancient
> Briton Civilisation Society! . . . colonisation has been fettered with the wild
> theories of pseudo-philanthropists, whose cant and folly has been foisted into
> the very laws of the colonies; and turn which way you will, you meet it in some
> shape, and its oddsprings are—slave piracy—Kaffir depredations—Hottentot
> Vagrancy—a dead weight thrown on all colonial improvements with their horrid
> and inevitable consequences.[10]

In the same letter he refers to the Cape Folk thus

> A vagrant law is much wanted in this colony. . . . The present system which has
> induced the monthly hirings and knockabout lives of the Hottentots, alike
> interferes with their health, morals and civil improvements. The here-today-
> and-gone-tomorrow system of Hottentot service, begets a carelessness of the
> master's property on the one part, and a carelessness of the health, morals and
> comfort of the servant on the other. Can nothing be done to induce a more
> permanent system of labour?[11]

   The Machiavellian villains of the piece, in Bowker's mind, were the
missionaries and their supporters in Britain. Their 'mania' was held by him
as *the* great barrier to development and, indeed, the cause of much
unnecessary suffering on the part of the aboriginal peoples whom 'Exeter
Hall' was so keen to serve. He must have been very pleased that some
missionaries even agreed with him. W B Boyce of the Methodist mission
had in his *Notes on South Africa Affairs* published in 1839, been critical of
what he called the 'prejudice' of some philanthropists, who had harmed the
development of the Xhosa people. He was referring to cancellation of
D'Urban's settlement of the frontier at the end of Hintsa's War. He had
already gained some notoriety during the war because of his constant advice

to D'Urban to be firm with the Xhosa. Macmillan quotes Harry Smith as saying of him, at that time, that he was 'more full of dragooning our new subjects than a hundred soldiers'.[12]

Bowker was so deeply committed to the idea that evangelical philanthropy and the missionary movement always hurt those whom they aimed to protect, that he even went so far as to blame them for the sufferings of the 'middle passage' of the Atlantic slave trade. It was evangelical pressure that led to the British Government attempting to stop the trade by the patrols of the Royal Navy. But for this

> he [the slaver] would carry the slaves to market in healthy, comfortable vessels, and he could then carry food and water sufficient for them, and only half the number would be torn from their homes.[13]

Bowker's line of argument was not an isolated South African phenomenon. He was the most articulate representative, in South Africa, of a growing wave of criticism in the English-speaking world of the more radical forms of evangelical philanthropy. In the United States and in England there was a widespread movement of thought appearing in essays, books and speeches, attacking the movement in the same terms as did Bowker. He was clearly aware of this, quoting, as he did, one of its leaders in Britain—Carlyle—in his 'springbok' speech. He also, again and again, repeats the criticism of the evangelical philanthropists that they cared about the distant 'savage' while being uncaring about the myriads of suffering poor in the slums of industrial England. This is exactly the same as the line found in a vast array of Southern apologists during the 1840s and 1850s, in their attacks on the Northern abolitionists in the United States.[14] The Southern apologists never made clear what they suggested should be done for the industrial proletariat (enslave them?) but Bowker had a solution for the British urban poor, whom Carlyle characterised as 'the pale yellow coloureds' in *Past and Present*.

Colonise Kafirland, and the whole of the fertile

> depopulated tracts between here and Natal; millions of the 'pale yellow coloured' could find food and home there.[15]

Here again we find that Bowker is not a strange eccentric voice but representative of a strong movement, though his reference to emigration is one restricted to the United Kingdom. It is worth asking, in passing, what were the implications of his ideas for the future of the Afrikaner people?

Various historians have pointed out that the period between 1840 and 1870 was not the anti-colonialist, anti-expansionist era that it had been depicted previously in British historical studies.[16] In particular, these writers point to a widespread unanimity of feeling, reaching across from Tories to the so-called anti-Imperialist Radicals, about the need for a dramatic expansion of White emigration from Great Britain and Ireland to the colonies. The Radicals gave the idea their particular slant by advocating a rapid handing over of autonomy in these colonies to local elected legislatures. Semmel goes further than most commentators when he says

The parliamentary campaign of Molesworth and Buller and the other 'colonial reformers' in the forties against the interference of the Colonial Office and its permanent Under-Secretary, James Stephen (Mr. Mother-Country) in the affairs of overseas colonies was not simply an early step towards the Statute of Westminster, as it is usually regarded by historians, but a protest against the efforts of the Colonial Office and the missionary bodies to halt the policy of land-grabbing and the local wars of extermination which the New Zealand colonists were waging against the Maori.[17]

Even without going all the way with Semmel, the consensus of recent historical writing on the subject of British attitudes to the colonies after 1840, is that White immigration into the colonies, where the immigrants were to receive land, and the insistence on the desirability of handing over local autonomy to colonial legislatures, were the dominant themes. There is also agreement that although all politicians of the period used the rhetoric of 'Christianity and civilisation', the days of the influence of the old evangelical/philanthropic lobby were over.

There was the development of another powerful family of ideas at this time in Britain not usually mentioned in the general histories nor in the authorities already referred to. This is the development of a full-blown racist ideology. This is fully discussed in Curtin's *The Image of Africa* and by T. F. Gosset in *Race, the History of an Idea in America*. This ideology was developed, initially, in British intellectual circles, though it quickly spread to the United States and other English-speaking areas of the world. It took the form of seeing the key to all history and all culture as lying in a hierarchy of utterly distinct racial groups—distinct intellectually, morally and physically. It was also linked with the idea of more or less inevitable 'progress' as a law of nature. This group of ideas only gained predominance in the English-speaking world in the later decades of the nineteenth century, after receiving its apparently irrefutable 'scientific' endorsement from distinguished men like T F Huxley and the Social Darwinists. However, it was already a growing force in the 1840s through the influence of men like Knox and de Gobineau. One of its early 'insights' was the inevitable disappearance of inferior peoples before the advance of civilisation and the superior races. Nothing could have suited Bowker and the Grahamstown propagandists better.

John Philip seemed well aware of the growth among politicians and other leaders of opinion in Britain, of the belief in the necessity of massive White emigration from Britain to the colonies, and of the implications of this for the indigenous inhabitants of the colonies.

> . . . you must take a rapid view of the History of our colonies and the spirit of Colonisation now manifesting itself in Great Britain and the rank and station of the men who are its chief promoters. You are not ignorant that there is a strong growing party at home who look upon colonisation as the panacea for all the evils of the new and old world with Earl Grey at its head. This party embraces much talent, has much influence and is supported by a great portion of the Public Press, and they have found that missionaries stand in the way of their places and they do not wish to see the Aborigines of barbarous countries

converted to the Christian faith, but they wish to see these countries we are now evangelising emptied of their inhabitants and in the possession of white men. Should not something be done to enlighten the eyes of the world and of the church on this subject?[18]

Philip shows nowhere any indication that he has become aware of the development of a race ideology. However one very percipient observer in South Africa did catch the development in Britain of a racist ideology, claiming the authority of the laws of nature. This was William Porter, the brilliant Irish Presbyterian who was Attorney General of the Cape Colony. Throughout his long service in the Cape, he kept in close touch with his father and brother, both radical Presbyterian ministers, who moved, during this period, into the leadership of Irish Unitarianism.

In writing about the appearance of this ideology of race and progress, which he finds manifested in the agitation of the English settlers of the eastern Cape, he wrote

> This profound contempt of colour, and lofty pride of caste contains within it the concentrated essence and odious principle of all the tyranny and oppression which white has exercised over black. But the Cape-frontier Englishman is not alone. A member of the British House of Commons, in one of the New Zealand debates, has lately said, that the brown man is destined everywhere to disappear before the white man, and *such is the law of nature*.[19]

Porter saw that Bowker and his ideas were not simply a Cape phenomenon but part of a general movement in the English-speaking world.

While he does not discuss the development of this new ideology in the English-speaking world, Galbraith cites two very explicit examples of it. The first is from *The Times* of 21 June 1851. The paper insisted that there was no alternative policy towards the Xhosa other than extermination or complete subjugation—what was meant by the latter phrase is not entirely clear. The paper went on to draw a significant parallel with the United States where there was no Indian problem because the whites were unrestrained by philanthropic pressure groups backed by the Imperial government. Philip would have wholeheartedly agreed had he read the piece.[20] Perhaps even more significant is the quotation from a letter of William S Hogge, one of the two Assistant Commissioners sent out by the Secretary of State to help Sir Harry Smith sort out the Xhosa war and the troubles in the Orange River sovereignty. This letter was a private one, sent to Grey and to be found in the Grey Papers only. Hogge says

> The history of the Cape is already written in that of America, and the gradual increase of the white race must eventually though slowly ensure the disappearance of the Black. Providence vindicates this its unalterable law by rendering all the philanthropic efforts that have been made to avert such destiny subservient to its fulfilment.[21]

Walker, de Kiewiet, van Jaarsveld, Davenport, de Klerk and so many writers on South African history have made it so clear that the Afrikaner was cut off from the changing current of European thought. In this they were usually referring to various forms of what might be called 'liberalism', for example de Kiewiet's famous phrase 'the impact of city-bred liberalism upon Cape rural conservatism was severe'.[22]

We can agree that nineteenth-century Europe, Britain particularly, did import new ideas into South Africa but they were not all related to urban liberalism. The powerful new ideology of race as the key to history and progress was also imported into South Africa from Europe and had nothing to do with Afrikanerdom. This may help explain the silence of the Afrikaner community throughout the 1840s in this quarrel. They may have sensed that the vision of the future held by men like Bowker left little room for them and their lifestyle. Already this ideology placed great emphasis on the 'Anglo-Saxon'. Did this include them or not?

The influence of this racist philosophy in Britain was already so strong by 1850, that J J Freeman could not control his bitterness towards it in his *Tour of South Africa*. This was a published version of his report to the LMS of his visit to South Africa to survey the work of the Society and plan its leadership on the retiral of John Philip. Of Britain's assumption of the Orange River sovereignty, he wrote

> And after all, let it be remembered, these are *only coloured races*, and semi-civilised tribes, who ought to be put on proof that they have a right to occupy any nook in this fair globe of ours—a globe, evidently destined for the Anglo-Saxon race! The least they can do is to beg pardon, as Robert Hall said in another case, of every man they meet, for having ventured to come into the world.[23]

However much colour played a part in the Voortrekker's ideal society with its proper relations between master and servant, the Voortrekkers had no ideology of race—no vision of progress with the 'savage' disappearing before the advance of civilisation as part of 'the immutable law of nature'.

Maitland, the Xhosa and the Beginning of the End

Sir Peregrine Maitland had been instructed before leaving the United Kingdom that the unsatisfactory state of the eastern frontier of the Cape Colony was the most immediate task he faced on taking up his post. The Colonial Office had, however, given him no indication of the line he should pursue in order to improve matters. From March to September 1844, Maitland waited in Cape Town and tried to build up an appreciation of the frontier situation before taking action. Just what sources he relied on for the information needed for such an appreciation is not clear. He did not consult Philip or Stockenstrom on this matter, though Philip did ply him with information on the difficulties beyond the Orange. C L Stretch, the Commissioner with Ngqika's people, and the official best liked by the Xhosa, was not consulted either. The Governor was certainly well aware however, of the 'Grahamstown' view of frontier problems, not only from the '*Journal*' but also from the many petitions that had been pouring in from the settlers and accumulating in the files.

These petitions pictured the frontier area as being in total disarray, with the Xhosa 'savages' raiding and robbing at will and going unpunished. These views were so well known that as early as 1843, Stretch, Stockenstrom and even Boyce, the usually pro-settler Methodist missionary, agreed that for some *English* in the east, only war to drive the Xhosa beyond the Kei, would suffice.[24]

That there was disorder on the eastern frontier cannot be denied. However, it stemmed not from the deliberate aggression of the Xhosa people led by their chiefs, but from the inadequacy of the British administration. Too few officials, with inadequate police resources, when combined with Xhosa chiefs beyond the frontier losing their traditional authority because of the profound changes happening within their society, was the primary cause of the situation. Walker insists, and no one has refuted his arguments, that it was marginal men who caused most of the robberies and assaults: white gun runners and horse thieves, Mfengu who had left their reserves to work as individuals among the White farmers, and Xhosa who had been entering the colony in large numbers, not sent by their chiefs as raiding parties, but individuals and small groups going as migrants, seeking work with the encouragement of the settlers and the colonial authorities. These Xhosa were people over whom chiefs had no control whatsoever.[25]

Settler society, in so far as its views are expressed by the *Grahamstown Journal*, Bowker and his allies, did not perceive the situation in this way but understood the disorder as stemming from the inability of 'savages' to keep a treaty.

In an extraordinary way, the propaganda mounted in the eastern districts for a change in colonial policy on the frontier, was believed only too well by the settlers themselves. The constant reiteration of stories of disorder aroused a great deal of fear and anger, which in turn led to encounters between settler and Xhosa that need not have led to difficulties but for the anger and fear the campaign had aroused. A prime example of this was the regular publication of the 'non-reclaimable' list of 'stolen' cattle. This was a list of stock unable to be accounted for, and presumed stolen, because of the turbulent situation and yet not technically reclaimable under the terms of the treaties. These lists were always treated by the settlers as an accurate reflection of the level of stock thefts which in turn encouraged them to assume that any missing stock must be stolen. Of the system Stretch says

> The establishment of the Not Reclaimable List was the heaviest blow ever struck at the Treaties. It was arranged and carried into effect about the beginning of 1839. It was the fountain of the system under cover of the Treaties, the most pernicious, which it undeniably subverted and it was the commencement of the debt against Caffreland, which increased according to the inclination of reporters for the Press. It was worse than the patrol system, for in that the chief could form some estimate of our procedure, but this 'Not Reclaimable List' was stabbing them in the dark. . . . Every hoof missing from a farm, whether lost or strayed was sure to figure in this list.[26]

Thus on the colonial side of the frontier, the threat to law and order was massively exaggerated, while on the Xhosa side, the constant tirade of anti-treaty, anti-Xhosa rhetoric, the unsympathetic attitude of Hare, the continual blaming of the chiefs for everything that went wrong, all contributed to the widespread belief among the Xhosa that a major move against them was in preparation. As Philip warned, in his gloomy letter to Tidman, things were made worse because the missionaries among the Xhosa were unpopular, and simply could not do for them what the London Missionary Society and Parish Mission staff did for the Griqua and Sotho—that is, act both as a buffer and an effective means of communication between the White authorities and the chiefs and their people. The Read family were trusted as were Niven and Ross of the Glasgow Society, but very few others.

The situation was certainly unsatisfactory, with settlers and Xhosa growing more and more antagonistic, each increasingly distrustful of the other. However, Walker points out that by 1845 the value of property in the eastern Cape had quadrupled since 1837.[27] This was largely due to the boom in the newly established wool trade which was a new factor on the frontier, but it was the kind of development which could not have happened if law and order had broken down to the extent described by the Grahamstown propagandists of the period.

It is fruitless to speculate how things might have gone had the new Governor decided to try to make the existing treaty system work more effectively for when Maitland went to the frontier it was with the firm intention of changing the situation. The changes he made provoked a crisis, not only in British–Xhosa relations but also in the fortunes of the Cape Folk. He arrived on the frontier in September 1844, and imposed new 'treaties' on all the Xhosa groups, including those like the Gqunukhwebe, who had been consistently cooperative with the British.

At first sight, the new agreement seemed to differ very little from the old 'Stockenstrom' treaties. There were, however, three important differences. The first was that the old regulation forbidding the 'patrol system' was omitted from the new agreements. The second was a point that particularly troubled Ngqika's people,—the new clauses attacked traditional customs like witch finding and lobola (bride-price) and also seemed to put Christian Xhosa outwith the jurisdiction of their chiefs. The third difference was by far the most important and fundamental. Although the new agreements were described as treaties, they were not so. The new agreements were dictated to the various Xhosa groups by the Governor and assented to by the chiefs, usually in the face of a deliberately calculated show of British military power.

Although most missionaries appear to have approved of the 'religious' elements in the new agreements, John Philip did not; he saw their imposition as key to the deplorable breakdown in Xhosa–missionary relations of which he complained to Tidman in March 1844.

Whether or not Maitland's new treaties were such a decisive change in British policy as I have suggested is almost irrelevant for, on both sides of the frontier, it was seen as just such a change. Calderwood, the leading LMS man most actively sympathetic towards the Government, soon to serve as a Government agent amongst the Xhosa, insisted that the imposition of these new agreements upon the chiefs was an act of war against the Xhosa, and would be seen as such by them.

He was proved correct. The Xhosa, well aware of the campaigns by Bowker and the *Grahamstown Journal* against them, were astonished by Maitland's actions, and observed the reaction of the frontier Whites to the Governor's new initiative towards them with apprehension verging upon panic. Stretch, in his famous Memorandum describes a frontier scene typical of the time.

> About seven days elapsed when the arrival of the Governor at Fort Beaufort was announced to me, I went there and was present at the rejoicing and effigy burning—it was a novel sight to Tsatsoe and some influential Caffres who were with me in the shade on one side of the scene of riot and drunkenness; whilst his Excellency, Sir P. Maitland and his son Capt. Maitland viewed it from the other. The natives, Hottentots and Caffres for many of both classes beheld it, at once perceived that the clamour was triumphant.[28]

Walker, Galbraith and other historians believe that two years of drought also helped to ready the Xhosa for war. However, J B Pieres in his more recent study of the period disagrees. He insists that the drought was effectively ended before war preparation began, and that an epidemic of smallpox which had also distressed the Xhosa, was also over.[29] Far from preparing them for war, these events had confirmed the chiefs in their intention to try to keep the peace, by making the Stockenstrom treaties work, and so protect their people after these crises. It was Maitland's initiative that drove them to despair and into preparation for war. They became convinced that they were about to be forced down the road which the Khoi had already gone—they were to lose all their land.

They began to prepare for war, and did so in such a public and open manner that official, settler and missionary circles all appeared well aware of it. Many missionary and trading families moved out of Xhosa territory and when the Xhosa warriors did invade the Colony, many Whites had already gathered round military posts and other strong points.

The war finally broke out, after months of increasing tension, when a party of Cape Corps were ambushed by Xhosa who rescued one of their people being taken for trial within the Colony for the theft of an axe from a European's store. The Khoi prisoner, to whom the accused had been shackled, was killed. Hare, the Lt Governor, decided that Chief Tola's refusal to give up the members of this raiding party was an act of war by the Xhosa nation against the Colony. He promptly invaded the Xhosa lands in strength. However, the Xhosa were ready for war, and his column was defeated at Burnshill losing most of its baggage train. While the troops made their way back, Xhosa warriors flooded into the Colony, attacking Kat River as well as the White settlements. The massive attacks on Kat River upset the Reads, but they really could have expected little else, because of the prominent part in the colonial forces Cape Folk played in this, as in previous wars. Indeed, at Burnshill, it was the Kat River contingent under

Andries Botha that distinguished itself by saving the ammunition waggons, when the rest of the train was being captured, and by their skilful covering of the retreat of the rest of the army.

Despite the fact that so many people—Philip, Stretch, Fairbairn, Calderwood and even Boyce—had warned in the previous months that Maitland's actions were bound to be seen as aggression in Xhosa eyes, no one spoke up on their behalf when fighting broke out. Even Jan Tsatsu who is quoted by Galbraith as being alone in raising his voice in their support seems to have made his public statement before the outbreak just as the others had done.[30] Clearly, he did side with his people when the war broke out, unlike his attitude at the time of the War of Hintsa.

What was much more unusual was that Fairbairn explicitly supported Maitland and Hare in the columns of the *Advertiser*, something that certainly raised eyebrows among his Philip in-laws.[31] Galbraith and others seem to assume that Philip was in agreement with his son-in-law in this, as he so often was in their close relationship over so many years.[32] However, there is nothing in the mass of extant correspondence to confirm this. Certainly, as in the War of Hintsa, Philip called on the Cape Folk and all other dwellers in mission institutions to support the Colony. This was consistent with his firm belief that only British power, channelled through a sensible policy, could bring both peace as well as justice to South Africa. This being so, in a frontier war while the fighting was actually going on, the Government had to be supported. His comments to Tidman, on reporting the outbreak of the War, have also been interpreted as support for Maitland's policy. He said to Tidman that if, as he had suggested at the time of the War of Hintsa, the Xhosa had been made British subjects, this war would not have happened. However, his demand in 1836 was for the Xhosa to be made British subjects, but with full possession of their land—none of their territory was to be given to White settlers. That was a view that could hardly be seen as in accord with views of Maitland or the eastern province settlers in 1846. Certainly, at the outbreak of the War, Philip said nothing in support of the Xhosa, though he had been warning repeatedly in the months before, that they were being pushed almost beyond endurance.

After the initial success, the Xhosa were driven back onto the defensive. There then followed the same ghastly programme of British columns of redcoats, Cape Corps, Mfengu and Coloured levies, criss-crossing the Xhosa lands, chasing small independent guerilla groups, while burning villages, crops and foodstores, driving the Xhosa herds before them. This dragged on and on. In January 1847, Maitland was replaced by Sir Henry Pottinger who was astonished to discover that fighting was still going on. In December of the same year, Sir Harry Smith returned to the Cape as Governor of the Colony and High Commissioner for South Africa. He brought the fighting to an end. He imposed a settlement on the Xhosa chiefs—the days of treaties were over—the old ceded territories were incorporated into the Colony, and the old Queen Adelaide Province was made into an Imperial territory, directly under the authority of the High Commissioner, British Kaffraria.

Smith then dashed off to deal with the Voortrekkers, the Griqua and the Sotho. When he declared the lands between the Orange and the Vaal to be British, he appeared to be fulfilling the demands which John Philip had pressed for so long with regard to the north. However, this was not so. Smith had no such long-term aims of 'equal rights for all Her Majesty's subjects' in the new sovereignty—he aimed simply at ending disorder. To achieve it he was ruthless and arrogant with the Griqua,[33] and although he initially appeared understanding in his dealing with Moshweshwe, he left Warden at Bloemfontein. Warden was anti-Sotho and pursued an anti-Moshweshwe policy.[34] In 1849 he imposed on Moshweshwe a new boundary based on the claims of both the Voortrekkers and the 'Methodist' chiefs. The new 'Warden Line' took from the Sotho the fine corn lands west of the Caledon River. Because of the continuing unrest, Smith felt a decisive course of action had to be followed, and ordered Warden to remove Moshweshwe and install one of the other chiefs, amenable to Warden, as the new Sotho leader. Warden's attempt to do this by force of arms was decisively repulsed by the Sotho in June 1851. The chaos into which the sovereignty then fell played a fundamental part in the later decision of the Imperial Government to give up all claims beyond the Orange in February 1854. That decision marked an end to British attempts to control affairs in the north and left the Sotho, Griqua, trekboers and Voortrekkers to their own devices.

Disaster for the Cape Folk

John Philip was depressed and apprehensive about the situation of the Cape Folk before the outbreak of the war. The war and its aftermath appeared to confirm all his worst fears.

In 1846, as in the War of Hintsa, the Cape Folk rallied to the British cause, making the point of their loyalty very clearly through the distinguished conduct of Botha and his Kat River men at Burnshill. An outstanding example of this enthusiasm was the initiative taken by Joseph Read. He was commissioned and led a special corps of Cape Folk, San and Mfengu, from Kat River outstations, an action which he knew would prevent his hoped-for ordination to the ministry. Philip, while encouraging support for the Colony, felt that no one could be a minister to Cape Folk and Xhosa if he had taken part as a combatant in these frontier conflicts. In the face of the appeals of Joseph's father and brother, Philip was adamant on this, despite great personal respect and affection for Joseph.[35] A total of six or seven Cape Folk were given Colonial Army commissions, and their troops played a vital part in Stockenstrom's clearing of the Amatola Mountains. This was a Xhosa stronghold which the British had failed completely to clear of Xhosa warriors in the War of Hintsa. The commitment of the Cape Folk from the Kat River and the missionary institutions was an essential part of the British war effort. Galbraith quotes Sir George Berkeley, the British Commander, as saying that the 'Hottentot' troops were the most effective that he commanded in the guerilla campaigns which characterised this war.[35]

Despite all of this admirable effort on behalf of the British authorities, the War of the Axe began a period of major crisis for the Cape Folk.

They had for some time past been well aware of the attitude of the English settlers of Grahamstown and the eastern Cape towards them—after all they could read! However, they clung on to their belief that, whatever was said in Grahamstown, the Government of the colony supported them. Their history since Ordinance 50 and everything that John Philip and the Reads told them confirmed this. Surely their total commitment to the Colony's defence in this bitter conflict would establish, once and for all, their status as free British subjects?

To their horror, and to the distress of John Philip and their other friends, it soon began to appear that a revision of policy towards them, as radical as that in the area of relations with the Xhosa, appeared to be taking place. Despite their outstanding service and the appalling suffering which they underwent, they seemed to get no sympathy or understanding, let alone justice or support from the colonial authorities. Had there been explicit recognition of their services and support for their families, they could have shrugged off the attacks on them and their loyalty, which continued to be published in the columns of the White presss. Attacks which were all the more infuriating when they occurred at a time when, as Cory, an unambig-uously pro-settler historian, points out, 90 per cent of the Kat River men were serving in the forces of the Crown while the White civilian community, English and Afrikaners, furnished only 3 per cent of their available manpower.[97]

When the war was but a few weeks old, John Philip was already alarmed about their situation. He wrote to Tidman

> On the people of our Missionary Institutions the burden of war will fall with a peculiar and destructive weight . . . the levies from the white colonists are as yet confined to young and unmarried men: and a proportion of these only are taken, but the married and all that are capable of bearing arms at our Missionary Institutions are liable to be called out. The harmful effects of this measure cannot at present be calculated. It is for one thing the ploughing season and their families will be in an awful state for the want of a harvest.[38]

Soon after, early in June, he complained in a further letter that the institutions and Kat River had by this time been stripped of all their fit menfolk from the ages of sixteen to sixty.[39] James Read added to the tale of woe when he pointed out that the waggon oxen at Kat River had been reduced from 1,500 to a mere 'thirty or forty span fit to drag a waggon'.[40]

What is often overlooked in considering the service of the Cape Folk in the Xhosa wars is that, apart from the comparatively small number serving as 'regulars' in the Cape Corps, the overwhelming majority who served as burghers or in levies, did so without pay. They were given rations and ammunition only. Their families had been given some rations rather fitfully in the War of Hintsa, but in the War of the Axe, only while Stockenstrom was in command were some rations and seed sent to the families and that only to Kat River.

To suffer such appalling hardship while being maligned by the *Grahamstown Journal* and others was bad enough, but worse was to follow. The appointment of Sir Henry Pottinger as Governor of the Cape with the new title and authority as High Commissioner for South Africa brought about a rapid deterioration in the situation.

As we have remarked already, Pottinger thought he was coming to South Africa to organise a post-war settlement. He was astonished to find that he had, in fact, to continue to organise the suppression of continued Xhosa guerilla activity, though this was diminishing slowly as various chiefs came in with their warriors to surrender. He was further incensed when he discovered how little response there had been to calls for service made to the White civilian population. In casting around to strengthen the forces for what he hoped were to be the last efforts to end the fighting, he demanded 400 armed men for immediate service from the Kat River, whose occupants, he believed, held their land by military tenure. He exploded with rage when his emissary got no response at Kat River from what bewildered male inhabitants that were there. Although it was almost immediately explained to him that he had been mistaken over the matter of tenure, this appeared not to assuage his anger with the Kat River people and, indeed, with the Cape Folk in general.[41] He came to a firm conclusion that the Cape Folk in general held an unjustifiably privileged position in Cape Colony. Perhaps his long experience of India was a handicap to his understanding Cape society. What is also puzzling is how his staff allowed him to make the demand at all, military tenure or no military tenure, since they must have known of the service already rendered in the war by the Kat River and other Cape Folk contingents?

When Pottinger, instead of demanding, asked for support, he got it. Despite the fact that the war had left them with almost no herds and few waggons, deprived them of two harvests, Andries Botha raised a new force from men only recently stood down from service, on the receipt of rations and a blanket each. So it was that Berkeley, Pottinger's commander at the front, could write to him in March 1847 pointing out that 900 of the 1,000 male adults of the Settlement were again on military service with the Crown.[42] At the end of their service, Botha's contingent received no pay, bounty or booty—indeed their army blankets had to be returned to store.

Up to this point much of Pottinger's behaviour towards the Cape Folk could be put down to the anger of a man caught up in a difficult and unexpected situation not of his choosing. However, his continued actions with regard to the Cape Folk would seem to indicate deliberate policy.

As more and more Xhosa chiefs surrendered, the men of the Kat River and the missionary institutions were stood down and returned to try to pick up the pieces. In the midst of these difficulties, Pottinger appointed, as magistrate for Kat River, a notoriously anti-Cape Folk, English settler, Biddulph. John Philip and the Reads saw this appointment as an attack on Kat River in particular and the Cape Folk in general. They wrote, on his appointment in May 1847, complaining of his unsuitability for the post because of his known views.[43] Their fears were confirmed when Biddulph wrote a long report on the Kat River Settlement, surveying it from its inception. The report was, in style and content, another version of the 'Grahamstown' denigration of the Cape Folk and the Kat River experiment in particular. Stockenstrom referred to it as 'a string of defamatory libels'.[44] If it had gone no further than the Governor's desk it would have been bad, but Pottinger gave it far more prominence than most reports from magistrates received. He sent it on to London with his endorsement, and also published it with the same endorsement in the Government *Gazette*.

The Cape Folk were used to these accusations of their inferiority as a people, of the 'stupidity' and 'credulity' of their friends, Stockenstrom, Philip and so on, when they came from the eastern province Whites. They did not matter too much, in their view, as long as they could rely on the support of the Imperial authorities. Philip had always urged this. They, in turn, believed it—after all that was why they served with such distinction in two costly wars. What was shattering to their morale and self-confidence was that these traditional attacks upon them now had the endorsement of the senior Imperial officer in South Africa.

To many of them, Pottinger's next action was confirmation of a revolution in government policy toward them.

In an effort to get the settlement on its feet again, the Kat River people began a massive lumber operation—after all there was a ready market for lumber with the re-building necessary after such a destructive war. Pottinger now placed a tax on six shillings per load of lumber cut. Stockenstrom bitterly complained

> . . . But the Governor, no doubt by the way of stimulus to this industry, ordered that a tax of six shillings should be paid for each waggon-load of timber that should be cut by the very men who had so lately been denuded, on account of the Queen, of the Queen's blankets, under which they had fought for that Queen! . . . and in no part of the Colony had, in the most prosperous time, so high a tax been imposed as here fell upon the Hottentots in their misery![45]

Philip was depressed by this return of events. His forebodings in his letter of March 1845 had been fulfilled, but that could only be a cause of pain to the lonely old man. The missions in the lands of the Xhosa were destroyed, but they could be rebuilt. What was far more depressing was that what appeared to be happening to the Cape Folk. The Kat River community and the missionary institutions had been reduced to dire economic straits because of the war. Despite the sterling service given to the colony by their inhabitants, the Cape Folk appeared to be not only losing the support of the Imperial authorities, but also to be becoming the object of their antagonism and suspicion. There was even talk of a new Vagrancy Ordinance—exactly what was always being asked for by some White group or other in the eastern Cape. Now it was being discussed by officials around Pottinger, whose antagonism towards the Cape Folk was unmistakable.

The arrival of Sir Harry Smith to replace Pottinger in December 1847, gave a little hope, at first, that things might change. However, even in the early days after his arrival, there were doubts in Philip's circle. At first these centred on Smith's extraordinary treatment of the Xhosa chiefs, but in Cape Folk circles there were doubts also. James Read Jun wrote to the Directors

> When Sir Harry Smith came to the country, the inhabitants of Kat River sent him a memorial requesting that inquiry be instituted with regard to defamatory charges which had been published against the Settlement by his predecessor. In his reply Sir Harry was kind, condescending and conciliatory—but evasive.[46]

After some time, Smith did remove Biddulph, but the Governor replaced him with another English settler, Thomas Bowker, the brother of the settlers' leading spokesman of 'springbok' speech fame and advocate of Vagrancy legislation. It was a measure of the intolerable nature of Biddulph's period of office that the Kat River people welcomed the change at first. Not for long—soon letters of complaint about Bowker and one of his assistant, Cobb, the superintendent at Blinkwater, began to flood across Philip's desk for transmission to London and to the Governor. The people were particularly upset when Andries Botha was removed as veld-kornet and even more so when it was decreed that law and order was to be maintained by a body of 'Kaffir' police, recruited from the very Xhosa groups whom the Cape Folk had fought in two recent wars.

By March 1850, things were so bad that James Read Jun sent a memorandum nineteen pages long for Philip to read and then pass to the Governor.[47] The pages are a catalogue of misdeeds by the officials and acts of injustice and insult towards the Cape Folk. Read insisted that Bowker was deliberately trying to destroy the Settlement. Philip agreed with them. It now appeared that the campaign to reverse the gains made by the Cape Folk towards recognition as equal citizens, conducted for so long by Bowker, Godlonton and their supporters, had gained the support of the colonial authorities. This was a massive blow to one of the main pillars of Philip's work in South Africa. He had always insisted to himself and others that the Imperial authorities could be relied on for justice. Of course they had to be lobbied constantly to keep them up to the mark, but ultimately the British Government and Parliament could be relied on. More than that, Philip believed that they constituted the only force that could make sure of justice in South Africa. If that was to be doubted then where did he stand? John Philip, old and tired, longing to hand over authority to a suitable successor, never quite faced up to this, even though in his situation this failure was understandable.

What left the old man even more bitter and unhappy was that in the midst of all these difficulties for the Cape Folk, one of his own staff appeared to go over to the enemy in a very public manner.

In February 1848, when he was working as Philip's assistant both at the Union Chapel and in the work of Resident Director, William Elliot, formerly of Uitenhage, wrote a long letter to the Directors outlining a possible new policy for the missionary institutions.[48] In his work in Cape Town, Elliot had become well aware of the drastic and long-term fall in the income of the London Missionary Society and of the constant demands from London for retrenchment which Philip had been receiving. The old man had for some time been trying to avoid doing anything about them, pleading the desperate needs of the institutions due to the wars. Elliot's scheme was, he believed, a clear way of saving money, as well as aiding the Cape Folk to 'stand on their own feet'. He wrote

> The crowding together of large masses of persons, all of one class, and that a pauper class, in limited locations, almost without means of bettering their condition and without adequate motives for industry, can only be justified by that necessity which once existed but which is altogether precluded by the altered state of the colonial law, which now extends protection to the black man as well as to the white. It strikes me that our Missionary Institutions might be converted into flourishing villages; but to effect this, the people must have a bona fide interest in the soil, with the uncontrolled power of transferring their property. Were this effected, wealth would soon be accumulated, a superior class of men would be introduced to our Mission villages and the Society would soon be relieved from the burden of a system which cannot but work badly in as much as it is by no means in keeping with the spirit or the circumstances of the times.

Macmillan in *The Cape Colour Question* and Elliot's biographer in the *Dictionary of South African Biography* both agree on Elliot's good intentions. Certainly, if one considers his suggestions *in vacuo* they appear as a reasonable, possible alternative policy. With some modification, such as an insistence that no villager could sell his land to a stranger without the assent of the local community and some kind of London Missionary Society trustee, they might have been workable. It was an opportune time, in some ways, to raise the matter and other issues of fundamental policy, since the London Directors were sending out J J Freeman to review the South African situation in order to make recommendations about future policy as well as about the role to be played by Philip's replacement.

In every other respect, Elliot could not have chosen a more inopportune moment. His confident assertion that, unlike the past, the law 'extends protection to the black man as well as the the white' would have appeared as shameless cynicism to the people of Bethelsdorp, Blinkwater, Kat River or for that matter, Elliot's own old parishioners at Uitenhage, whose freedom Elliot himself had warned was in danger even before the war had begun. His assertion that the people were all of the pauper class may have been almost true because of the losses and devastation of war, but he must have known that before the war there had been a real if small measure of prosperity and accumulation of capital for at least some in institutions, and for many at Kat River. Of course he did not write of Kat River, but the use made of his arguments in the colonial press was against Kat River as well as the institutions. When the 'paupers' of Bethelsdorp read his report in the *Zuid Afrikaan* or in the *Journal*, they must have been furious, since they were awaiting compensation from the Government for their waggons taken into the commissariat and destroyed in the fighting. As late as March 1850 they were still waiting. Elliot's case hung on their being paupers—since when were people who owned wagons and the oxen to draw them classified as paupers?[49]

It was the publication of Elliot's report in the colonial press which changed the matter from being a difference over policy, internal to the mission, into an apparent endorsement of the views of the Cape Folk held by Godlonton, Bowker and company. Elliot in order to bring pressure on Philip, had sent copies of his report to various Directors of the London Missionary Society in London. One of them, from motives which we can no longer probe, had it published in an evangelical magazine, *Evangelical Christendom*. It was there gleefully seized upon by a reader or readers in South Africa and republished in *De Zuid Afrikaan*, the *Grahamstown Journal* and other organs of the White press. Here was a leading experienced missionary exposing the institutions to be what the settlers of the eastern province had always asserted, havens for indigent paupers who would be better elsewhere. These journalists went much further than Elliot, and used his arguments in ways he did not intend, yet he could hardly be blameless. Was he really not aware of the critical situation of the Cape Folk at that time?

Macmillan rather plays down the seriousness of the situation when he says

> One reason for Dr. Philip's curtness was at this time public criticisms of the stations by a missionary which was ardently welcomed by less friendly and sympathetic critics. There seems to have been talk once more of 'breaking up the institutions' and even of a Vagrancy Act.[50]

It is a little odd to describe the organisers of a vigorous campaign against the London Missionary Society and the Cape Folk as 'less friendly and sympathetic critics' and the campaign itself as 'some talk'. In any case, John Philip saw it as a disastrous move in a situation of crisis. He pointed this out to the Directors. Elliot meanwhile held to his views and continued to press them. This forced the old man to turn the tables on Elliot with the use of Elliot's own considered judgement. He sent to the Directors a copy of Elliot's own letter of January 1845, where he, even before the war, insisted that the law was being misused against free persons of colour who lived outside the institutions or Kat River, contradicting another key point in his proposals. Elliot had written from Uitenhage where he ministered to a congregation of Cape Folk and others who lived in and around the township

> From what I have seen of the transactions of the municipality of Uitenhage, I am prepared to receive without any surprise reports of municipal proceedings of the most enormous injustice and absurdity. If I must form any judgment of our village municipalities in general from what I have observed at Uitenhage I must observe that they are nothing but legalised institutions of oppression, by the establishment of which persons of colour have been withdrawn from the protection of the colonial government and left to the cruel mercies of that class

of society which imagines that its interests can only be served or advanced by the oppression of its inferiors. Slavery is ended too recently, its spirit is not extinct.[51]

Elliot persisted in pressing his case and went to London to more effectively present it to the Directors. In February before he left the Cape, he adopted a new line of argument. He insisted that his views were those of

the clergy, magistrates and gentry in the neighbourhood of our Missionary Institutions. They cannot be unacquainted with the real state of things.[52]

Here was another verse of the old song, well known in the Cape, which was to go on being sung well into the twentieth century by critics of John Philip. As Elliot goes on to say, these leading Whites are honourable men and their evidence and judgement must be accepted as definitive. If it is said that they might be biased somewhat, through antagonism to the Society, who is to blame for that but the Doctor?

So by 1849 the chorus of criticism of current policy towards the Cape Folk had added to it the voice of a leading member of Dr Philip's staff. In such a crisis, this was a bitter blow both to Dr Philip and to the people of the institutions and the Kat River.

Although many historians pass this situation by with low-key comments, it was a situation of crisis for the Cape people. Typical of the style of comment of many historians, are explanations of the 'Hottentots' Rebellion' of 1851 as resulting from the 'Hottentots' being upset 'at what they felt had been unjust treatment after the War of the Axe', or again, as in the articles on James Read and James Read Jun in *The Dictionary of South African Biography*, in which father and son are each criticised for being over zealous in pointing out to the people 'some unfortunate government shortcomings'.

Both sides in the disagreement in the Cape in the 1840s were quite clear that it was not a minor matter but an essential one. John Philip, as we have seen, was clear, from at least 1844, that a serious effort was being made to reverse the progress made by the Cape Folk. In December 1847, he was talking of a concerted campaign mounted against the Cape Folk and the Xhosa. He quotes William Shaw of the Methodist Society, given their past bitter disagreements over Hintsa's War and over Moshweshwe and the 'Methodist' chiefs, hardly a friend, let alone an ally, as supporting this view. He quotes Shaw as urging him to have a number of articles written by Fairbairn for the *Advertiser* bound together as a pamphlet and sent to Members of Parliament to counteract 'the growing party who would have all South Africa cleared of Aborigines to make way for white settlement'.[53]

On the other side, the *Grahamstown Journal*, still edited by Godlonton, was equally clear that a battle was being fought, and that a critical point in the struggle had been reached. Commenting on Elliot's report—a bitter pill for the Doctor—the editorial said

On the eastern frontier a contest between stern justice and mistaken philanthropy has been raging upwards of thirty years. Were it competent to decide the issue on the spot, this could not endure. Unfortunately the case had to be referred to the Home Government, and to the British people, who, influenced by certain powerful, presumably religious associations, have given their voices against their fellow-countrymen. There has, however, never been so important a crisis as now at hand, and each party, finding it bears very much the aspect of a death struggle, is preparing its weapons accordingly. The voice of every colonist must be loud in demanding, that every Institution, where a number of the coloured races are, or can be drawn together, shall be broken up and restricted from re-assembling. If we destroy, or prevent the building of the nest, we shall not be liable to the incursion of the brood.[53]

The *Journal* was quite correct—a contest had been being waged for upwards of thirty years. The important difference was that the Imperial authorities now appeared to have changed sides. In the last months before the renewal of fighting between the Colony and the Xhosa, deeply distressing reports of injustice towards the Cape Folk poured into the London Missionary Society office in Cape Town for transmission to London and sometimes for transmission to the Governor.

On the eve of Philip's retirement, his son-in-law, George Christie, went on a tour of the stations within the Colony, leaving his wife, Mary, with her father to care for him. He wrote to the Directors a long report on his tour in which he said that the treatment of the Cape Folk by the government in the last few years

had left on the minds of the coloured people a deep and painful impression that the Government had no disposition to consider their claims and do them justice or even preserve their liberty.[55]

This is a sobering account of the state of mind of a community that only three years before had committed ninety per cent of its fit menfolk to the service of that same Government in a bitter war.

Arie van Rooyen, the first man of the Cape Folk to be ordained to the Christian ministry, other than James Read Jun who was a special case, wrote to the London Missionary Society deputy, Freeman, in similar terms, about the Kat River people.

If things go on, the inhabitants find it impossible to remain any longer. There is nothing but violent oppression.[56]

By July 1850 it was becoming clear that the Cape Folk were in a state of despair which made the rebellion of a minority among them, when the Xhosa war broke out again, unsurprising. Indeed, consideration of how they were treated in these years between 1845 and 1850 makes it surprising that so few did rebel. Their extraordinary situation is revealed dramatically in a letter that their distinguished leader in the previous wars, Andries Botha, wrote to the Governor on 27 June 1850, with a copy to his old friend, John Philip.[57] This is on the eve of the 'rebellion'. Perhaps because he knew how little influence Philip now had with the colonial authorities and even with the London Missionary Society Directors in London, Botha went to plead his case personally, with Sir Andries Stockenstrom, his old Commanding Officer. Sir Andries wrote immediately following their interview to Montagu, the Colonial Secretary, giving a translation of what Botha had told him.

I know that your usual answer will be that we are mad in coming to you with our grievances, as you are nothing more than a Boer in the land; but unless you die or fly the country, you shall have to hear the groans of every oppressed class in South Africa; and such is the state of excitement in the Kat River at present, that without some assistance or advice, I do not know how to prevent serious consequences. You must remember the immigration of some families of the Gonaqua Hottentots into the Kat River Settlement, some twenty years ago, many of whom obtained erfs, and others promises of similar grants. They are, and consider themselves as much Her Majesty's subjects as I am, and as such did burgher duty and fought bravely for the British Crown during both the Kaffir wars. They paid taxes to the Colonial Government as long as they were exacted; were a tower of strength to the rear districts, and there never was a complaint against them. Some time since a number of Kaffirs came and squatted down in the Settlement;—the inhabitants requested that they might be removed. Accordingly, this was done under the direction of the Civil Commissioner of Fort Beaufort, but immediately after this proceeding, the Kat River Magistrate, heading a body of Kaffir Police, caused to be burnt out, not only those who had come in since the war, but the Gonaquas to the last, who had been twenty years in the Settlement, with all the Fingo servants. Not a moment's warning was given. I remonstrated,—the Hottentots entreated for their friends in vain; nothing availed, neither the cries of the children nor the tears of the mothers, some of whom were in child-bed, with babes of three or four days old, on one of the coldest days of this inclement season and that on a Sunday (the day of peace, rest, and prayer), when, even if the act had been lawful, there was not the remotest pretext for haste. The Kaffir Police held the firebrands ready to ignite the huts, while the inmates and property were being bundled out of them; the Kaffir Police exultingly shouting: 'Today we burn Botha out of the Blinkwater as he burnt us out of the Amatola last war.' The Police took possession of all the cattle, some of which has been lost. Thus, about fifty families have been burnt out, who were our friends, protectors, and defenders in two wars and driven like felons and outlaws, among the very enemies against whom they fought, and at whose mercy they will be. The Magistrate has dismissed me, why, I cannot tell. Is it possible that British subjects have to submit to such treatment?[58]

So it was that when Sir Harry Smith first deposed Sandile of the Nqgika and then outlawed him, the Xhosa attacked the troops sent to find the chief and, in a sense, the War of the Axe was resumed. The difference was that some of the Cape Folk changed sides. This is sometimes referred to as the 'Hottentot Rebellion' and, at others, as the 'Kat River Rebellion'. Neither reference is in any way correct, since the majority of the Cape Folk remained loyal and, in particular, the majority of the Kat River people not only remained loyal, but served yet again in the colonial forces.[59]

Despite the 'rebellion' being an act of a minority, the impact was disastrous. All that the old man, dying at Hankey, had feared was apparently coming to pass. White society in general believed that the Cape Folk had gone over to the Xhosa. To many, this was welcome proof of their long-asserted insistence on the unreliability of people of colour, but it was also believed by others who were not so committed. Indeed, the inaccurate picture of mass rebellion has been repeated into the second half of the twentieth century even in work of scholars who are fundamentally sympathetic to the Cape Folk.[60]

John Philip died in the midst of the Cape Folk community at Hankey on 27 August 1851, at two o'clock in the afternoon. He was carried to his grave by the men of Hankey, followed by a cortege made up of his close family and the local Cape Folk. Sadly, death prevented him from knowing that, in the midst of these dark and terrible days for the Cape Folk and the Xhosa, for all that he had worked for and prayed for, there would be one major victory for his ideals. Strangely, this came about through the British decision to grant the Cape Colony an elected legislature, something that Philip had always opposed because he saw it as inevitably leading to further injustice towards 'people of colour'. It was an extraordinary episode in Cape history that, when the ideology of race was appearing among British officials as well as settlers, this legislature was constituted on the basis of a low qualification and a colour-blind franchise.

The Cape Franchise

In the first years of his life in South Africa, John Philip clashed with Somerset the Governor about the autocratic style of his rule. Philip became one of the leaders of White, mainly English, opposition to the Governor, together with Fairbairn and Pringle. He was even popular with the English settlers for a time. Philip was clear however, that the problem was not Somerset's personality, but the nature of British rule in the Colony. He was concerned about 'the free persons of colour' and the slaves, but the nature of British colonial rule was a problem for Afrikaner farmers and English settlers also. British rule was essentially autocratic—the Governor of the colony, always a military man, ruled alone with no formal check on his authority within the Colony itself.

The storm that Somerset's behaviour which was, at times, eccentric to say the least, caused the British Government to give the Governor of Cape Colony a Council of Advice. This body, set up in 1825, was made up of six officials appointed by the Secretary of State. The Governor was normally to act after consulting them. However, he still had enormous authority, for the Council could only debate those matters he brought before it, and they had no authority to initiate business. The only effective check on his authority was still external to the Colony in that he had to explain to the Secretary of State any action that he might take contrary to advice given him by the Council.

The post-Reform Act Parliament in Britain initiated changes in the structure of government of the Cape Colony. An Executive Council was set up consisting of the Governor and his four principal officials. The Governor was, from that time, no longer a one man executive. In addition, a Legislative Council was also created which consisted of the Executive Council members plus the Attorney General and five to seven members nominated by the Governor, who were not to be officials. The 'unofficial' members never reached the maximum figure during the existence of this body and were often fewer than the suggested minimum. More importantly, the unofficials were at no time an effective check on the Executive Council and, as the years went by, they appeared to the colonists to be less and less representative of them.

The demand by the colonists for some representative element in the Legislature of the Colony began in the 1820s and continued up to the creation of the 1853 constitution. In 1826, Fairbairn had begun this agitation when he issued a call, through the medium of the *Commercial Advertiser*, for colonists to unite in support of agitation for some form of representative government and 1,600 of them signed that year a petition for representative government of the colony.

Although Trapido says that John Philip supported him in this, I have seen nothing in the Philip correspondence to confirm or to deny this.[61] Fairbairn was certainly a zealous advocate of representative government at the Cape and was active in supporting it until 1834. His change of heart then when he decided to hold back was ostensibly because of Philip's and Cape Folk leaders' fears for the consequences of such a reform. However, it could be suggested that the decision seemed to stem, not so much from a change of mind, as from personal hurt. Macmillan reports that Fairbairn was rejected by a public meeting in 1834 of colonists in Cape Town as a committee member of an association for the furtherance of representative government.[62] This seems hardly surprising at this time, given Fairbairn's activities in the matter of Khoi emancipation, the slavery issue and the then current agitation for a Vagrancy Act. After his rejection, he contacted Philip and asked him to tell Andries Stoffels, a Cape Folk leader

> that he is quite of his opinion now about a Legislative Assembly, and that he will not advocate the measure any more till the Hottentots and people of colour are fit to take their place in it along with the white population. But he wishes them to make haste, as he is still anxious that such an Assembly should be introduced.[63]

The line that Stoffels had been pressing on Fairbairn was one that Philip held to until his death. He felt strongly that any transfer of power from London to a colonial Assembly spelt doom for the Cape Folk and for the tribes beyond the frontier, unless people of colour were an essential part of the new governmental structure. There is no sign in all his massive extant correspondence that he saw this as a likely possible development. In the last decade of his life, despite real advances in political and legal freedom, the prevailing bitter antagonism of the English settlers together with the clear change in British Governmental attitudes, made the whole situation appear to him in a particularly gloomy light.

The initial response of the British Government to these early demands from the Cape for representative government, took a line of which Stoffels and Philip would have approved. Even the pre-Reform Tory administrations did so. When Lord Milton introduced to the House of Commons the petition from British settlers at the Cape for 'representative government', Sir George Murray, the Secretary of State, opposed the crave of the petition for, among other reasons, the reason that a large slave population and an equally large population of free Blacks not yet ready to play a part in the new arrangements made the demand 'inopportune'.[64]

Pressure continued to come from the colony for such a reform and this was supported by Afrikaner as well as British colonists. London, however, consistently refused to entertain any serious negotiation on the matter until the coming of Earl Grey to the Colonial Office in 1846. This appointment signalled a change in Whitehall attitudes towards the development of elected colonial legislatures and, significantly, towards White emigration from Britain to the colonies. Grey instructed Pottinger, his appointee to the Cape Colony, that the Government was strongly in favour of granting some degree of representative self-government to the colonies despite the difficulties and risks which this might entail.

This change in policy came at an opportune time for the Cape Colony. By 1846, the Legislative Council was seen by most people as serving no useful function on behalf of the colonists. Even the Cape Folk, who until this time had shown deep suspicion of any move towards an elected legislatures, were hardly enthusiastic about the existing Legislative Council as such.[65] So the supporters of an elected assembly were heartened and the subject was opened up again with some hope of progress.

Grey now put a cat among the pigeons by deciding to send to the colony a shipload of ticket-of-leave Irish convicts who were to be settled in the colony. The reaction in the colony was immediate, and it was fiercely antagonistic to this plan. The anti-convict agitation which arose was an extraordinary phenomenon, because it united, in political action, individuals and groups which were usually separate and, indeed at times, deeply antagonistic towards each other. Working together for the movement were Afrikaners, akkerboer and trekboer, the English settlers of all opinions, ranging from a Scots radical like Fairbairn to Godlonton and the Grahamstown merchants, the Cape Folk at Kat River and the institutions, together with the missionaries led by the old Doctor himself.

Grey's action united the Colony in a way that nothing else did at any time in the nineteenth century. Some historians like Davenport in his chapter in volume 1 of the Oxford History see this movement as holding up the establishment of an elected Assembly, but others hold the belief that this extraordinary unity and its power, which almost made the Colony ungovernable was what made Whitehall see that an elected legislature was essential to the future of the colony.

During the furore when the 'ultra' group among the anti-convict leaders organised boycotts and even the mobbing of their opponents, the unofficial members of the Legislative Council all resigned but one. Sir Harry Smith, in order to calm matters down and restore some sort of internal tranquillity to the discussion of the colony's future organised an unofficial election to help him nominate a new group of 'unofficials' for the Council. The electoral lists that were used were the non-racial lists already existing for the election of municipal authorities and Roads Boards. The four who led in the poll were Christoffel Brand, Andries Stockenstrom, F W Reitz and John Fairbairn. Smith nominated them to the Council and added as a makeweight, Godlonton of Grahamstown, who had not come fifth in the poll but lower down. Davenport says of this choice that it equalised east and west as well as Dutch and English in the new Council.[66] What exactly he means by Dutch and English is not clear but the move did not balance Afrikaners and British in any way. I agree with du Toit and Giliommee, who are clear in their book *Afrikaner Political Thought*, that Brand, Reitz and that doughty leader of burgher troops in war, Andries Stockenstrom, were all Afrikaners. Although Fairbairn and Godlonton both spoke versions of the English language they held little else, if anything in common. The four who headed the poll soon made it clear that they formed no sort of balance with Godlonton by not taking their seats, but forming, with the Cape Town municipality, a pressure group for the immediate creation of an elected legislature.

The negotiations which then proceeded are well documented in many works and need no further exposition here.[67] What of Dr Philip in all this? Although there is a significant amount of correspondence about the anti-convict agitation in Philip's files, there is almost nothing on the possible elected legislature. Back in 1830 he had written that the British Government must not

> entrust the white inhabitants with the exercise of an undue power over a people against whom they have manifested such an implacable hatred.[68]

In Dr Philip's judgement, in 1850, the implacable hatred was there, more clearly expressed than ever, on the part of the English colonists. What was much worse, both in the judgement of Philip and the Cape Folk, was that the British authorities now seemed to share this antagonism towards them which, in 1830, they believed had not been the case. Although Philip wrote nothing of any significance in these last months of his life, we can only presume he was still opposed to the idea of an elected body having power in the colony. James Read Jun did write to him in May 1850 asking the Doctor what he thought of the 'new constitution' and saying

> If the justice is done them and if all who have property to the amount of £50 be for electors then will nearly 7 to 800 persons have the right of electing as nearly all are valued by the Road Board at £50–£70.[69]

Clearly the younger Read was wondering whether the proposals, so long as they were firmly based on a low franchise qualification, might be worth supporting. John Philip did not reply, at least there is no reply in the archives.

However, as Trapido rightly points out, what petitions there are from Cape Folk and what reports there are of meetings they held on the issue, all point to their wishing to maintain the status quo.[70] As we have pointed out this was understandable and the more so after the wave of White antagonism that erupted over the so-called 'rebellion of 1851'. On the other hand, what could be worse for them than their situation during the period when Pottinger and Smith were able Governors of the Colony? When it was clear that a new constitution was coming, they threw what little weight they had behind Stockenstrom and Fairbairn, men whom they trusted.

These events which began to unfold in the last months of John Philip's life were events in which he played no part. Yet they led to a franchise which could not have but pleased him, since a significant number of Cape Folk got the vote, which also over the years was extended to not insignificant numbers of Mfengu and Xhosa.

From 1850 onwards, if not before, the British Government was determined to give the Cape Colony some sort of elected legislature which would relieve them of economic burdens and force the colonists to take more responsibility both economically and militarily for the Colony.

As Stanley Trapido rightly says, the conflict from 1850 to 1853 was not about whether there would be an elected legislature but who would be on the voters' roll. The struggle was between, as he says

> the high-franchise party of the English merchants of Cape Town and Grahamstown, led by Robert Godlonton, with the decisive support of Sir Harry Smith, the Governor, and Montagu, his Colonial Secretary, opposing the supporters of the low franchise, the Dutch-speaking farmers led by Reitz and Brand, who had the support of the radical Cape Town editors, Fairbairn and Buchanan and their Coloured followers, all of whom accepted the leadership of Sir Andries Stockenstrom.[71]

This group under the leadership of Stockenstrom was a disparate one, made up of people who had often opposed each other in the past, but were now united by their shared bitter antagonism towards the rich English merchant class and towards being ruled by officials. The Afrikaners were explicit in their willingness to accept the Cape Folk and other 'people of colour' being able to qualify for the franchise in order to defeat the common enemy. It was, as Philip had been asserting for years, the rich English colonists, now joined by officials like Pottinger and Smith, who were the Cape Folk's opponents and the opponents of the Afrikaner Folk.

One official stands out in all this. Attorney General Porter who, long before, as we have seen, had become aware of the new racism coming into South Africa from Britain. His skilful advocacy of the low franchise qualification was a vital factor in its success, though, it must be said, this was achieved as much by the removal of Smith and Montagu, as by the fact that the acting Governor Darling, used Porter as his primary adviser in the matter, at a decisive moment when the British cabinet was making its final decision.

So the Cape Colony in 1853 came to have an elected legislature, whose lower house was elected on the basis of a low qualification and colour-free franchise. In so many ways this was the consummation of much that John Philip had hoped, prayed and worked for. In a vital area of political life, his call of 1828 for 'equal rights for His Majesty's subjects' was made effective. The tragedy was that so many fewer Cape Folk qualified for the vote in 1853 compared with those that could have qualified in 1845. Where were James Read's 700 to 800 at the Kat River in 1853? The terrible destruction of livestock and property in the two wars together with the break up of the Kat River Settlement and Theopolis Institution because of the so-called 'Hottentot Rebellion' was a dreadful blow to the economic situation of the Cape Folk and drastically reduced their potential power under the new constitution. For all that, the new constitution was a posthumous victory for John Philip and his beliefs, when so much else for which he had strived, appeared to have failed completely.

9

Who was John Philip?

Perhaps the greatest difficulty in the way of understanding who John Philip was and those things for which he strove, is what has been written about him since his death. This is true, not only of what was written by the older South African historians, Theal and Cory, who did not really try to understand him, but also by more recent writers, including those who were and are sympathetic towards him. The difficulty arises from the fact that these writers have tended to use their study of Philip as a means towards an end other than presenting Philip to the reader. They have been attempting to influence the political and social attitudes of the South Africa of their day.

Macmillan, whose two major works, *The Cape Colour Question* and *Bantu, Boer and Briton* were based on the collection of Philip papers now lost to us, was quite explicit about this in both books. His avowed aim was to bring about change in the social attitudes and political policies of the South Africa of his day. A worthy aim, no doubt, but one which forces him to highlight some aspects of Philip's life and thought, while playing down others less relevant to his purpose. Thus his working criterion was not Philip but the South Africa of the inter-war years.

Since Macmillan there has not been a major study of John Philip. There have been a number of important articles on him in recent years, however. Again, these articles, in the majority of cases, have been focused on using Philip's life and work as a way in which to form a critique of some aspect of South African life in the 1960s and 1970s. The most important are, perhaps, those by Julius Lewin and Andrew Nash.[1] Lewin's piece, while dealing briefly, but accurately, with the Doctor, is primarily concerned with the role of 'liberalism' in the South Africa of 1960. So with Andrew Nash's article. Despite the fact that Nash is closer to understanding Philip than any other writer, including Macmillan, in this writer's judgement, Nash still does not look at Philip for his own sake or for the sake of understanding the worldwide struggle over the relationship between civilisation and 'aboriginal' peoples of Philip's day. This perceptive article relegates the analysis of Philip's life and times to being simply a vehicle for a critique of the weaknesses of South African 'liberalism' in the twentieth century.

This study has a different aim which is to attempt to understand Philip in the context of his own day. It attempts to see his work within the setting of a particular struggle going on within evangelical Christianity as to the nature of the role of the Gospel in the world and in a conflict throughout the English-speaking world about race and 'civilisation'.

John Philip was a product of the Evangelical Revival which from 1750 onwards had such a profound effect on Protestantism in the English-speaking world. The abolition of slavery came to be a key concern for many evangelicals, particularly their leaders, William Wilberforce and the 'Saints' in Britain as well as of James Finney and the young men and women of the radical abolitionist movement in the United States. For evangelicals of this persuasion, the individual was bound to spread the good news of salvation to be found in Jesus, but was also bound to try to bring about change in society, not only change that might facilitate the conversion of the yet indifferent, but also change to bring society more into line with the mind of the Lord. What could there be in a society that was more abhorrent to the Lord than that some of his children be held in slavery by others? This commitment was often simply to end slavery and in the United States it went together initially with plans for returning the freed slaves to Africa. Concern for the full recognition of Black humanity was not always tied to an anti-slavery stance. However, both in Britain and the United States for a growing group of radical anti-slavery evangelicals, the abolition of slavery became the first step in the process of achieving full human dignity for Black people.

There has been a tendency in American historiography to portray the evangelical abolitionists as not fundamentally interested in Black people; but Sorin's work on the New York abolitionists, together with the work of Dubermen, T L Smith, R H Abzug and others has shown that there was a powerful commitment to the advancement of Black Americans in this group.[2] John Philip has to be seen as one of the British evangelicals who adopted this same stance towards Black people. For those who find his attitudes extreme, it would be salutary to read the words of Theodore Weld, of Gerrit Smith who advocated Christian support for and encouragement of slave uprisings, of Beriah Green who insisted that 'it is wicked and sinful to make a distinction because of colour in any of the social relations of life.'[3] Among the men produced by the Finney revivals and who followed Weld into the radical abolitionist cause, Philip would have been at home, though certainly unhappy about the pro-rebellion stance of some of them.

There was one element in the social reform wing of American evangelicalism which marks it out from the same wing of the British movement—that was the strong millenarian element in American Revivalism. Since the End was close, the work of saving American society from divine retribution was a frantic race against time. This 'race against time' millenarian tinge was present in British evangelicalism primarily among those who felt this same pressure to have all the world hear the good news of the Gospel before the coming judgement. It did not affect the concern for reform in the same way as in the United States. Though Philip did not share the millenarian spur that his American brethren felt, he shared their belief in the implication of the Gospel message for slavery and the relations of Black and White people. If we compare Weld and Philip we find differences in their style and differences that are incidental to one working in the United States of America and the other in South Africa but their fundamental understanding of the role of Christianity was the same.

After a series of famous debates on slavery and the humanity of the Black person, 'the Lane Debates', Weld took the dominant role in writing the constitution of the Lane Anti-Slavery Society. The aims of the Society are summarised by Abzug

> The society's object? 'Immediate emancipation of the whole coloured race, within the United States'—slaves from master and 'free coloured man from the oppression of public sentiment'—'and the elevation of both to an intellectual, moral and political equality with the whites.' Why? because the black man was created by God as 'a moral agent, the keeper of his own happiness, the executive of his own power, the accountable arbiter of his own choice.' Slavery denied this basic principle, 'stifled the moral affections, repressed the innate longings of the spirit, paralysed conscience, turned hope to despair, and killed the soul.' . . . Furthermore, it 'crippled the energies of the whole nation, entailed poverty and decay upon the states that upheld it, fomented division and alienation in our public councils, and put in jeopardy the existence of the union.' Finally, it paralysed 'all missionary effort' and 'exposed the nation to the judgment of God.'[4]

In effect, Weld and the Lane 'rebels' were calling for Black people to participate fully in American civilisation. Christianity and civilisation were the key themes of all Philip's service. In 1833, the year before the Lane debates, Philip had written a long report to the American Board of Commissioners for Foreign Missions about South Africa. This was one of the most carefully prepared statements made by Philip. He wrote

> The desert is unfavourable to the fruits of Christianity and after repeated trials we have found that they can never be brought to perfection, or cultivated to any extent, unless they are literally planted by rivers of water, where they may rise into families and tribes. The ark of the Lord was carried in the wilderness: but it would not have remained long with Israel if the people had been allowed to choose the wilderness for their final abode.
>
> The civilisation of the people among whom we labour in Africa is not our highest object; but that object never can be secured and rendered permanent among them without their civilisation. Civilisation is to the Christian religion what the body is to the soul; and the body must be prepared and cared for, if the spirit is to be retained upon earth. The blessings of civilisation are a few of the blessings which the Christian religion scatters in her progress to immortality; but they are to be cherished for their own sake as well as for ours, as they are necessary to perpetuate her reign and extend her conquests.
>
> Because multitudes in England and America have lost their religion, to which they are indebted for their civilisation, many pious people make light of civilisation as connected with the labour of missionaries: but it should never be lost sight of that if men may retain their civilisation after they have lost their religion, that there can be no religion in such a country as this without civilisation; and that it can have no permanent abode among us, if that civilisation does not shoot up into regular and good government.[5]

Thus Philip's aims for the 'free persons of colour' within the Colony were the same as the radical abolitionists had for their fellow Black Americans. Philip, however, faced a problem that they did not—that of the tribes beyond the frontier.

Philip had two different strategies for dealing with those peoples, to be applied as alternatives according to the situation. If the people were free from any major pressure from White settlers seeking either to displace them or subdue them, then his first strategy was in order. In that situation, he believed that if the African community would receive missionaries and honest traders, then the presence would trigger off a spontaneous development of Christianity and civilisation. The work of Anderson and Wright among the Griqua was his immediate model for this pattern of development. This understanding of how Christianity and civilisation could grow was widespread among missionary leaders in the first decades of the nineteenth century. Henry Venn, the General Secretary of the Church Missionary Society, was one of its most vigorous proponents and it was the philosophy that lay behind the ill-fated Niger Expedition of 1841. In southern Africa, David Livingstone was perhaps its most famous exponent, as well as being its last. He shared Philip's fear that White settlers endangered any such development. It was this that drove him northwards to find an area of Africa where untouched African societies would be transformed by 'Christianity and commerce', his short-hand for these views.

On his long trek of 1842, Philip believed that he had seen this very development beginning to bud, if not flower, among the Sotho of Moshweshwe. However, on that same trek, he became aware of the extent and power of Voortrekker ambitions. So he campaigned hard to gain Imperial protection for the Griqua and the Sotho from this threat to their future. He realistically assessed that for the peoples further to the north and east, he could do nothing. There was no alternative but to leave their future to the mercy of the Voortrekkers and the Ndebele.

In the situation that the Griqua and Sotho were in after the Great Trek, his second strategy came into play. The solution for both the small Griqua states and for the Sotho then became the same solution that he had suggested, fruitlessly, for the cisKeian Xhosa in 1836—incorporation within the Colony. There, with their basic rights and their land guaranteed by the Imperial authorities, they could play their part alongside the Cape Folk in the upbuilding of Christianity and civilisation which would finally 'shoot up into regular and good government'.[6]

Why did so many of his colleagues in the London Missionary Society in South Africa not support him in all this? After all, Ross, Niven and Govan of the Glasgow Mission at Lovedale were closer to him in their understanding of mission and civilisation than were Moffat, Calderwood and possibly the majority of the LMS staff. There is no doubt that some differed from him because of a clash of personality, others over matters of administration and mission policy. The main reason for division, however, was a different understanding of evangelical religion. Robert Moffat and many others of the staff belong to that form of evangelicalism which was much more pietistic in its understanding of the Gospel than was Philip's. For them, individuals were to be converted—converted individuals, in so far as they had political power, would then begin to use it better, but it was not the primary task of the Christian to work for a more just society. Even when put as delicately as Wilberforce did by calling this zeal, the zeal for the 'reform of manners', Moffat's brand of evangelical did not accept it as a primary task, except in areas like the clothing converts ought to wear and the sexual mores of African Christians. Neither Philip nor Weld nor any other leader of their wing of evangelicalism ever demoted the preaching of the Gospel from the position of number one priority, but they insisted that the development of civilisation and good government were inextricably involved in the attempt to live out the dictates of the Gospel. As for Moffat, that form of belief, he felt, led to political involvement which in turn led to the distraction of time and effort into the spiritually and morally ambiguous sphere of political controversy, exactly what he constantly criticised Philip for doing.

Robert Moffat, who was in the United Kingdom between 1840 and 1843 won over the London Directors of the Society to his understanding of the Christian task in South Africa, leaving their fellow Director in the field, John Philip, completely isolated. It was only the support of key members of the staff in South Africa, and the appeals of the French missionaries among the Sotho, that prevented a very dispirited Philip from resigning, as we have seen.

This division within the London Missionary Society staff in South Africa was primarily a matter of the difference over the understanding of the demands of the Gospel—one group with a pietistic interpretation, the other with a deep belief in its direct social implications. Was this the only difference? When the correspondence between Philip and the group of missionaries associated with Calderwood on the eastern frontier is studied, another difference becomes clear. This is a deep disagreement over the estimation of the humanity of the Black person, whether Cape Folk or Xhosa. This difference is highlighted in the conflict between Calderwood and some fellow missionaries with the Reads, father and son. The conflict was about a letter James Read senior had written to a Dr Struthers in Britain. At the centre of the affair was the fact that the Reads accepted the word of two Cape Folk elders over that of a missionary. Calderwood and his friends objected to the contents of the letter and to Reads' decision about whom to trust. The conflict had blown up in 1845 and had caused Philip much bother in terms of awkward interviews and a great deal of correspondence. The Directors in London had promised to deal with the matter but after six months had said nothing. Tired of the whole affair Philip, on 31 March 1846, sent them copies of all the correspondence, thirteen letters in all, and in his accompanying letter said that they should now deem the matter closed. From the point of view of trying to understand this split in missionary attitudes, Philip's accompanying letter is vital. In it he says

> The parties never can be brought to act together and the only thing we can do with them is to keep them from threatening each other and from open war. They are entirely different men and represent two different classes of missionary. What is esteemed and practised as a virtue by the one is viewed as a crime in the eyes of the other. You will find the key to this secret in the following

passage in Calderwood's letter, 8 July, No. 9 'We object to the kind of intercourse which [James Read] has with the coloured people as indicated by his letters'—Both parties would do the coloured people good but in different ways. In order to raise the people James Read would treat them as brethren and to this Mr. Calderwood says 'We object.'

Both systems have been tried and their fruits are before the public. The Hottentots were converted on the principle of love and those that treat them on the other principle cannot have their love and their [two illegible word] of the complaints against the Hottentots and jealousy lest the Caffres should be spoiled in the same way.[7]

It must be remembered that despite all the accusations of dictatorial episcopacy that have been directed at Philip, he had no authority to hire or fire staff. There is no doubt that had he had such powers he would have been tempted to use them against Calderwood. To Philip's relief that gentleman avoided any further conflict within the mission by accepting employment under the Government as one of the Commissioners among the Xhosa.

The division over how the human relations between White and Black were to be conducted, with one side using the idea of 'spoiling' people, language which resonates with the notes of racism, is not an issue in addition to the difference over the nature of the Gospel's demands; it is part of it.

Again we have an exact parallel in the United States. Weld and other Lane Seminary students who broke away from the Seminary and went on to found Oberlin College, the heart of radical evangelical abolitionism, came into conflict with the Trustees of Lane Seminary over the same issue that divided Read from Calderwood and his friends. At weekends, the Lane students had begun the practice of not only doing humanitarian and evangelistic work among the large free Black population of Cincinnati, but also of living with Black families and sharing their lives, even if only at weekends. The trustees led by their president, the famous preacher, Lyman Beecher, wanted them to desist from this practice and also to cease their campaign of public criticism of those evangelical Christians who did not include the achievement of Black equality as part of their anti-slavery stance. Beecher and his fellow trustees were from the same mould of evangelical as were Calderwood, Moffat and the other LMS critics of Philip—good was to be done to and for Blacks, but this had nothing to do with brotherhood or human equality.[8]

This radical egalitarianism in the radical wing of Protestant evangelicalism has not been thoroughly discussed by historians, other than those writing of the American abolitionist movement. One outstanding study of the phenomenon in African history however, is Philip Curtin's *The Image of Africa*. In this work, Curtin characterises the attitude of Philip and Weld as 'conversionism' as distinct from the attitude that came to dominate the second half of the nineteenth century. In this latter period, Curtin calls it the era of 'trusteeship', even Africanophiles saw Blacks as inferior, not to be exploited or treated unjustly certainly, but needing always 'to be looked after'.

The intellectual roots of 'conversionism' have been traced to the thought of the Enlightenment. Certainly Philip was deeply influenced by the Scottish Enlightenment as his *Researches* show. It is also clear that evangelicalism owed more to Enlightenment thought than later evangelicals have been willing to admit, but this is not where the roots of conversionism lie. It seems much more likely that the tap-root of conversionism lies in the evangelical belief that as all humans are equal in sin and guilt before God, the redeemed are also made equal in the eyes of God by their conversion.

Dr van der Kemp's marriage to an African girl, Read's marriage, the Scots Lovedale Mission sending Tiyo Soga to Scotland to train as a minister and their welcoming him back with his Scottish wife, were all practical outworkings of this faith. It was basic to John Philip's insistence that when the autonomy of an African community beyond the frontier was threatened, they should be incorporated within the Colony. There they could follow the path laid down for the Cape Folk, participating along with the Whites in the development of Christianity and civilisation. This was only possible if the British authorities maintained an even-handed 'Roman' approach to the administration of the colony. This was Philip's great weak spot.

From his days as a minister in Aberdeen he had been almost obsessed with the creative virtues of Roman government at its best which in his view had welded many races and peoples together in the one civilised culture. He believed that Britain could and would do the same in this new era. If Britain could not be counted on to do that, what then of all his plans?

Philip had no answer to give to that question, and he was acutely aware of this from 1846 onwards. It is of this period that Macmillan complains, insisting that Moshweshwe could have got a much better deal in the late 1840s if only Philip had remained politically active.[9] In this, Macmillan was mistaken. Philip was still active politically during those years, but only in matters where he felt he could achieve something. There he still acted with vigour, as in the controversy with Elliot over the mission institutions and also in backing the Cape Folk in the institutions and Kat River in their complaints about their treatment during and after the War of the Axe.

However, on larger issues like Moshweshwe's difficulties with Warden and with Smith, though well informed about what was going on he did little. He believed that it was pointless for him to take any action because he adjudged that the Imperial authorities had changed decisively and because he had no more allies in the UK. Even if Buxton had lived longer it would have made no difference because his influence was gone, and there were no other important political figures in Britain sympathetic to Philip's viewpoint. Exeter Hall went on as a place for missionary and humanitarian meetings and rallies, but 'Exeter Hall' as an effective lobby with influence on Government was a thing of the past. His fellow Directors of the LMS were frightened of being 'political', so to whom was he supposed to turn to get help in presenting Moshweshwe's case?

Lord Grey's coming to the Colonial Office marks the new era in which Philip is rendered politically helpless. Grey was an enthusiast for White emigration to the colonies including South Africa. The Governors of this period, Maitland, Pottinger and Smith, were all men whose perception of the humanity of Africans was at profound variance with that of Philip. When a senior British official, like Hogge, could frame a report on the future of the Sotho in terms of the new philosophy of de Gobineau and Knox; when, in other words, Government shared the philosophy of Bowker with its faith in the inevitable and irresistible law of nature leading inferior peoples to give way before the advance of the White man and his civilisation, then John Philip feared that his day was over. This explains his inactivity, not lassitude or misjudgement.

Before this philosophy developed into Social Darwinism and achieved its later dominance in the British intellectual world, the Cape Colony was granted an elected legislature. This turned out to be a somewhat surprise victory for John Philip's ideal, though he did not live to see it. The vote was given on a colour-blind basis, some Whites did not qualify for the vote and some Blacks did. Something of his ideals was built into the life of the Cape Colony, ideals which saw some Mfengu and Xhosa come to gain the vote along with the Cape Folk. The new constitution came into being just in time. It was the result of the somewhat strange alliance, noted in the last chapter, of Afrikaners, English-speaking radicals, the leaders of the Cape Folk, with Attorney-General Porter, who earlier had noted with distaste the emergence of this new philosophy of race and progress.

This alliance had been possible only because, as yet, Afrikaners, in their intellectual isolation, had not got a philosophy of race. As has been said already, they had views on the proper relations of masters and servants, but belief in the inevitable sweeping aside of the inferior races before the advance of civilisation was not part of their thinking. Just how different they were in thought and belief from someone like Hogge or Bowker can be seen in the fact that even the Voortrekker leaders were still capable of considering the use of African allies against other Whites, as had the Bezuidenhouts and other rebels in the early days of the British occupation of the Cape.[10]

John Philip ended his service with the London Missionary Society feeling both helpless and defeated. The helplessness and the defeat stemmed primarily from this profound change in the intellectual climate in the English-speaking world, a change carefully documented by Philip Curtin in *Images of Africa* and Gosset in *Race, The History of an Idea in America*. Once civilisation and progress were associated with one racial group and the Black people seen as essentially external to both, then Philip and his friends were talking a language that appeared to be nonsense. In the United States the same reversal occurred. During the Civil War, the Constitution was amended to give Black Americans their full civil rights, but even during the period of the so-called Reconstruction, a massive effort was begun to prevent their actually enjoying these rights. This process rapidly accelerated so that by the end of the century, the United States was a segregated society in a way that it had not been before the War—Blacks had their civil rights effectively denied them and talk of Black equality was the preserve of a minority of eccentrics.[11] The decade after the end of the Civil War also marked the end of any effective concern within Protestant evangelicalism for the increasingly grim plight of Black Americans. This, despite the fact that the Black American community was one of the liveliest centres of evangelical Protestant Christianity in the world. Nothing, it seemed, could stand against the triumph of the philosophy that said Black inferiority was a law of nature confirmed by modern science.

It is in the light of this worldwide development that we must consider Andrew Nash's most telling criticism of John Philip. He points out that Philip's position is vulnerable at a fundamental level because its success is always dependent upon authority external to South Africa, namely the Government of the United Kingdom.[12]

There are two comments to be made upon this thrust—not to contradict it because Nash's point is incontrovertible, but in modification of its impact. The first is that the 1853 Constitution of the Cape Colony did establish in law something of Philip's vision of equal rights within a non-racial context. This was thereafter something integral to the life of the Cape Colony for sixty years, and not something entirely dependent upon external authority. The second point is that one of the key factors in frustrating the rooting of Philip's ideas into South African life was not the resistance of people in South Africa to his ideas as alien but the capture of the minds of many whites in South Africa by a philosophy of race which was rooted and based elsewhere.

This philosophy of race associated civilisation and inevitable progress with a hierarchic division of humankind on the basis of race. This family of ideas grew up in the United Kingdom and the United States quite independently of affairs in South Africa. It appeared for the first time in South Africa when it was used to bolster the arguments of the leaders of the English settlers in the eastern Cape in their criticism of the missions and of government policy towards the Cape Folk and the Xhosa. For John Philip and those who agreed with him, the decisive change occurred when this philosophy appeared in the thinking of the representatives of Whitehall. When senior British politicians and officials began to consider South African problems within a framework of ideas created by this philosophy, then a new era had begun. This philosophy and the changes it brought about were as alien to the Afrikaner people, Cape Boer or Voortrekker, as was the philosophy of 'urban philanthropy' whose impact on South Africa has concerned so many historians.

The impact of the philosophy of race and progress, particularly in the later form of Social Darwinism, was a major factor in shaping British thinking about Empire for the rest of the century. In one way this confirms Nash's point about Philip's vulnerability, yet it must be added that Nash sees Philip's cause going down to defeat because he did not ensure its grafting into South African life. True enough, but the resistance of White South Africans to his ideas was less of a factor in this defeat than the impact on South Africa of the philosophy of race whose origins were in America and Britain.

What of John Philip as a missionary leader? In many ways he was a success. The collapse of a great deal of the work of the LMS in southern Africa, after his death, was due to forces totally outwith his control. The collapse was the result of the dramatic falling off in support for the Society in the United Kingdom. This had begun in the 1830s and had prevented a number of developments dear to Philip's heart, such as an Institution of Higher Education like that of the Scottish missionaries at Lovedale. He staved off the regular demands for retrenchment for as long as he was able, but after his death, they took effect with a vengeance. Parallel to the falling off of financial support for the LMS there had also been a falling off of missionary personnel. It was an ageing staff that Philip handed over to his successor in 1850, and many of the younger men were sons of existing or deceased members of the LMS South African establishment. The old man himself had given three sons to the mission.

During his time as Resident Director of the Society in South Africa, he expanded the work of the Society, extended its school system and greatly encouraged what was then called 'native agency', that is, the reliance on indigenous evangelists for the expansion of the proclaiming of the Gospel.

It was his influence and contacts abroad that brought the French Mission to South Africa and ultimately to Moshweshwe. In the same way he influenced the Rhenish Missionary Society, the Berlin Missionary Society and the American Board all to begin work in South Africa. To the very end, even when he had lost the confidence of his fellow Directors in London, he still had the admiration and trust of the French, German and American societies.[13]

His belief in 'native agency' was all of a piece with his belief in the nature of the conversion of Africans. It was never developed to the extent it might have been because he was unable to develop the educational structure of the mission as he would have liked. He was also frustrated by the attitudes of Moffat and Calderwood. The long-term differences with them over many so-called political issues was only one facet of their fundamental disagreement over the nature of humanity and the nature of the Gospel. Moffat and Calderwood and their allies in the mission so often complained of Philip's preferment of the Griqua churches and the Cape Folk congregations under the care of the Reads. They did not trust the evangelists produced by them, indeed they constantly complained about them. Although paying lip-service to 'native agency' they never pursued this policy with real vigour. Their whole approach was characterised by Moffat's behaviour, when in 1822 he began what was to be his life work among the Tswana. He arrived among a people who had already been evangelised extensively by a party of evangelists from Bethelsdorp, led and organised by James Read. As soon as Moffat took over, he set about getting rid of them all, on one pretext or another. The story of one of the most outstanding of them, 'Brother Cupido', has been told by V C Malherbe in the *Journal of African History*.[14]

In all his extensive writing about his life and work, Moffat never gave any credit whatsoever to the Christian foundations laid by James Read and the Cape Folk evangelists, upon which he built.

Philip had one major flaw in his missionary thinking. He took the success of the mission in stimulating the growth of strong Christian communities among the Griqua and the Cape Folk as models of what would happen among the other African peoples of southern Africa, if the correct opportunity arose. He was so excited when in 1842 he thought he saw this process beginning among the Sotho of Moshweshwe. In the right circumstances the same would happen with the Xhosa. He was wrong—he gravely underestimated the power of African traditional beliefs and the spiritual validity of African traditional life. The Cape Folk were a people drawn from many ethnic groups whose traditional pattern of life had been destroyed, as with the Griqua. They turned readily to Christianity because it gave them material and social benefits but, just as important, Christianity gave them self-respect and a structure to reality which, deprived of traditional African interpretations of reality, they needed. The success of the missions among the Mfengu can also be partly explained in these terms.

The Sotho and the Xhosa, African peoples with a still functioning set of beliefs and practices, two peoples who were fighting for their independence which included these practices and beliefs, were a very different matter.

Although he so badly underestimated the validity and liveliness of African traditional belief and practices, he never fell into the trap of seeing them as social evils to be removed by the force of European authority and law. When the British attempted this from the mid-1840s onwards, encouraged by many missionaries, he disapproved and pointed out how this policy weakened, perhaps fatally, the position of the mission with the Xhosa chiefs and elders. He went on to bitterly criticise the missionaries who had encouraged this approach by the colonial authorities.[15]

John Philip's understanding of the one humanity shared equally by all persons of whatever race or ethnic origin was a fundamental part of his evangelical faith. It was basic to his perceptions about the nature of the church but also of society. This faith, when informed by the philosophy of the Scottish Enlightenment, particularly the writings of Adam Smith, produced Philip's understanding of what would be best for Cape society. Government had first of all to cut away the chains of slavery and feudal-type economic and social relationships. Then the missions could effectively evangelise and educate, for him two sides of the one process. If this situation could be achieved then prosperity would follow, a prosperity that would benefit all. Again and again he tried to point out that prosperity for employers did not come from impoverishment of employees. As in the Scotland of his youth and young manhood, undergoing the first wave of the Industrial Revolution, prosperity of a kind never known before was shared, to some extent, by all—so, it would be in the Cape Colony. It was a brave vision, but the British Government never quite played its part and the Cape Folk were not allowed to play the part of the 'upwardly mobile' working-class Scots that Philip desired for them.

The criticism of John Philp, so often made in his day and continued up to the present, that he was gullible, spoiling his case by relying on unworthy informants, is hardly worth taking up again at this stage. In controversies about issues as deeply felt and of such life and death importance as those in which he was involved, the calm detachment of the neutral observer will not be found. One thing he did do, which does make him stand out from most of those whose books, pamphlets, letters and so on have come down to us from that period, was that he accepted the word of those Africans and Cape Folk whom he believed to be honest and worthy men, even when it clashed with assertions being made by Whites. Those who judge that attitude, *ipso facto*, to be a fault, tell us more about themselves than about John Philip. This was the 'gullibleness' so often complained of, and it was an attitude entirely consistent with Philip's view of humanity and the enlivening power of the Gospel.

In the last quarter of the twentieth century, many Afrikaners and others still believe that Philip was the bitter enemy of the Afrikaner people. He was not. In his *Missionary Researches* and in his reports, there are many exposures of cruel and unjust actions by Afrikaners, but his aim was always to show that it was the system of government that created the situation that led to these excesses. At no time did Philip assert that it was the Afrikaners, *qua* Afrikaner, that were the root of injustice in South Africa.

Certainly he bitterly opposed the Great Trek and condemned and opposed the aims of the Voortrekker leaders. So did many Cape Afrikaners—the Afrikaners' own Church did the same. Are they to be labelled enemies of the Volk? Philip opposed the Voortrek because he believed that this kind of incursion by White settlers into Africa would prevent the development of 'Christianity and civilisation' as he understood them. He would have opposed, just as rigorously, a similar move had it been made by British settlers. Indeed, in his latter years, as we have seen, Philip insisted that the main opponents in South Africa of all his hopes and dreams were the British settlers, or rather their leaders. From the War of Hintsa, they were his most vociferous critics. They, not the Cape Afrikaners, campaigned against the new status of the Cape Folk and maintained a bitter campaign of calumny against the Kat River people. It was their leaders who propagated the new philosophy of progress and civilisation belonging only to the White race and before which the Brown and Black people must giveway as a law of nature, a philosophy as alien to the Afrikaner people as Philip's radical evangelicalism.

John Philip was buried by a congregation of his beloved Cape Folk in the midst of the Cape Folk settlement of Hankey. He died a tired and sad man, burdened with a sense of defeat. Would that he could have known that his old friend Stockenstrom together with his son-in-law, Fairbairn, were to triumph in their campaign of the low franchise option for the common voters roll in the new Constitution. Within the Cape Colony, at least, something of his vision was established in law, and independent of London.

However, Stockenstrom, and even Fairbairn, were getting on in years. Where were the new men who could follow them as leaders, who could consolidate and develop this approach to life and to 'politics' in the widest and deepest sense? There seemed to be no one.

Yet, with hindsight, one can recognise that there was a potential leader available, a man with the ability to communicate his ideas and with the charisma that the leader of a cause needs. That man was David Livingstone. What if Livingstone had not gone north to find somewhere free from the impact of land-hungry settlers, where 'commerce and Christianity' could really do their work?

He was already beginning to be well known in Britain as well as South Africa; he had courage, an astonishing ability to learn African languages, he had toughness and stubborness, the qualities vital to maintaining a cause through thick and thin. This possibility of Livingstone succeeding Philip as a key figure in South African affairs has been ignored by his biographers, who tend to treat his South African years as a mere prelude to his work in Central Africa. They have also failed to notice his closeness to Philip in their shared sympathy for the Cape Folk and the Xhosa.

In 1852, on the eve of his departure to the north, never to return to South Africa, Livingstone expressed his admiration for the 'rebels' of the Kat River. He insisted, contrary to the settler press, that the rebellion was a confirmation of their true humanity rather than proof of their unreliability and untrustworthiness.[16] He bitterly condemned Calderwood, Philip's old adversary within the mission, for his service with the Government, which he characterised, unkindly, as that of a police informer.[17] At the same time, he made attempts to have the Xhosa case, and that of the Cape Folk, brought to the attention of evangelical circles in the UK and the US. Indeed, in the same letter as that in which he condemned Calderwood, he showed that he had gone on to a stage of radicalism beyond Philip's, much closer to some of the extreme evangelicals in the United States: He wrote

> By the same post I send a letter to my brother containing Sandillah's speech to Renton, to be printed in America. All we learn of the Caffres here is one sided. We must hear both sides. It is well Sandillah speaks out so nobly.
>
> Bringing out converts to assist the English is infamous. We must preach passive resistance or fighting for one's own countrymen.[18]

In a letter, later this month, he also said

> Everywhere there is a strong feeling of independence springing up. . . . The destruction of my property is a fortunate thing for me. There is not a native in the country but knows now for certain whose side I am on.[19]

What Livingstone might have done raises interesting possibilities, but it is vain to speculate since he went north for good. With his departure there was no one to take up Philip's mantle. There were men who held on to the understanding of Christianity that had fired Philip, but none that could develop it in the new era and bring it to bear effectively on the life of the Colony. In their articles, Lewin and Nash both leave the impression that this was, in some way, Philip's fault. Was it? Was it Livingstone's fault? Was his career later an escape from the problems of southern Africa?

Neither accusation can be sustained if the world wide situation is considered. In the United States, after its triumph in the passing of the Civil Rights amendments to the Constitution during the Civil War, the radical evangelical movement disappeared from view. It was another forty years before it re-emerged in a new form in the Social Gospel Movement. From the middle of the nineteenth century, the philosophy which tied civilisation and progress to race, increasingly dominated the thought of the English-speaking world. By the last decades of the century, when in the form of Social Darwinism, it appeared to have the endorsement of modern science, it relegated the understanding of humanity and civilisation which Philip, Weld and the others believed in so passionately, to the margins of Protestant Christianity and of European thought in general. Whether Livingstone had stayed or not, he could have made little difference in the new situation. Thus the weakness that Nash lays at Philip's door, that he did not build a movement to continue the struggle for his ideals, was the result of a massive intellectual shift in the English-speaking world, rather than misjudgement on Philip's part.

What then is there left to say about John Philip? Was all failure? By no means—his re-organisation of the work of the LMS in southern Africa, his recruiting of the Paris, Rhenish and American Board missions to work in South Africa, his constant support for men like Casalis among the Sotho and Ross and Niven of the Glasgow Society among the Xhosa, made a formidable impact on the history of Christianity in southern Africa.

The various political developments that John Philip deemed necessary for the spread of the Gospel and the upbuilding of a Christian civilisation, developments for which he worked with a total commitment to the point of exhaustion, were frustrated in the main. The partial, but very important, exception to this was that the legal and constitutional developments in the Cape Colony, until it was absorbed in the Union of 1910, were based on no distinction between British subjects on the basis of race. This owed not a little to John Philip's utter dedication to his vision of a Christian civilisation.

In the last analysis, it must be said that no one can write the history of South Africa, nor the history of Christianity in southern Africa, without him. Even when he is set up a 'bogey man', he remains still a challenge to the reader, reminding him or her of a special understanding of the Christian Gospel and of an alternative South Africa.

Notes

1 Livingstone's support for the so-called Hottentot Rebellion of 1851 and his insistence of the right of Africans to take up arms against White encroachment on their lands, British as well as Voortrekker encroachment, have been omitted from all his biographies.

2 C W de Kiewiet, *A History of South Africa*, p 43.

3 Quoted in D Eltis and J Walvin (eds), *The Abolition of the Atlantic Slave Trade*, p 42.

4 A London Missionary Society missionary in Demerara (now Guiana) who was arrested by the British authorities in 1823 and charged with inciting a slave rebellion. He was found guilty in very dubious circumstances and sentenced to death. He was already in bad health and died in prison, where he had been kept in appalling conditions, on 6 February 1824.

5 e.g. Bruce Catton, *The American Civil War*, pp 9–10.

6 J C Brauer, *Protestantism in America*, p 176.

7 Quoted in R H Abzug, *Passionate Liberator: Theodore Dwight Weld and the Dilemma of Reform*, p 95.

8 'The Battle Hymn of the Republic', written by Julia Ward Howe. In modern hymnals, the sixth line of this verse is significantly altered to read 'Let us live to make men free'.

9 During this same period, the Reverend Henry Williams of the Church Missionary Society was waging a campaign to protect the Maori people from the encroachment of White settlers upon their land. See his biography, L M Rogers, *Te Wiremu*.

10 J S Galbraith, *Reluctant Empire*, p 82.

11 Robert Philip, *The Elijah of South Africa*.

12 The Foulgers were a prosperous evangelical family associated with the London Missionary Society. When Dr and Mrs Philip went first to South Africa they left Mary and Eliza in the Foulgers' care until the girls finished their education. They were hosts to the Philip family during their visits to the UK and acted as the boys' guardians when they were being educated in Britain.

13 William Philip to John Foulger, undated, A.633, Fa 4, in Cullen Library MSS Collection.

14 Biographical sketch of William by his brother Durant in the collection of Philip Family Letters, recently deposited in Jagger Library of the Univeristy of Cape Town.

15 Peter Philip, *A Fifeshire Family: The descendants of John and Thomas Philip*, p 13.

16 'The Select Committee on Aborigines (British Settlements)', which met to take evidence and report to the House of Commons, 1836–37.

17 William Alors Hankey. Prominent businessman who succeeded his business partner, Hardcastle, as Treasurer of the London Missionary Society in 1816,

although in 1832 he continued as an influential figure in the Society. The LMS settlement where Philip died and was buried was named after Hankey.

18   John Joseph Freeman. A Congregationalist minister who served the LMS in Madagascar from 1827 to 1835. In 1830-31 he spent several months in Mauritius and the Cape. After his return to the UK he was closely involved in the running of the Society and served as its Home Secretary, 1846-51. He visited South Africa for several months to review the situation of the Society's work there on the eve of Philip's retirement. On his return to London he published, in 1851, *The Kaffir War* and *A Tour to South Africa*, in both of which works—the first a pamphlet, the second, a substantial book—he sided with much of Philip's criticism of British policy in South Africa.

19   Mary to Eliza, 15 March 1837, A633, Cc 4, in the Cullen Library Collection.

20   Mary Anne Foulger to John Philip, 11 February 1830, A633, Fa 5, Cullen Library.

21   James Backhouse was a wealthy Quaker, influential in evangelical and humanitarian circles, who travelled widely in the support of the missionary movement. After a lengthy visit to Madagascar and South Africa, he published a very detailed study entitled *Narrative of a Visit to Madagascar and South Africa*, in 1841.

22   Eugene Casalis, *My Life in Basutoland*, p 66.

23   Livingstone to Prentice, 3 Aug 1841, Letter 7 in D Chamberlin (ed), *Some Letters of Livingstone*. Earlier that same year Livingstone wrote to his sisters, Janet and Agnes, expressing similar feelings about John Philip. Livingstone to his sisters, 30 March 1841, I Schapera (ed), *David Livingstone, Family Letters*.

CHAPTER 1
pp 11 to 32

1   S Daniel Neumark, *The South African Frontier*, p 74.

2   *See* G Harinck, 'Interaction between Xhosa and Khoi' in *African Societies in Southern Africa*, L Thompson (ed). Also H Giliomee, 'The Eastern Frontier, 1770-1812' in R Elphick and H Giliomee (eds), *The Shaping of South African Society*, 1652-1820.

3   G M Theal, who worked on South African history from 1880s until the First World War, was the father of South African historiography. He edited two massive editions of European records both in the Cape Colony and beyond. He wrote a number of historical works, the most important being his 11-volume *History of South Africa*. G M Cory did not produce on the same massive scale, but his five-volume, *The Rise of South Africa*, added strength to the foundations laid by Theal.

4   J S Galbraith, *Reluctant Empire*, p 45.

5   *See* Monica Wilson, 'The Nguni' in *The Oxford History of South Africa*, Vol 1 for a succinct summing up of the work of many scholars in this field.

6   Oliver Ransford, *The Great Trek*, p 13.

7   *The Great Trek*, p 23.

8   *Reluctant Empire*, p 31.

9   *The South African Frontier*, Chapter 6, *passim*.

10 W A de Klerk, *The Puritans in Africa*, p 12.

11 His failure to give any notice to this and other fundamental distincitons between New England and the Cape Colony, calls into question the basic assumption of de Klerk's *The Puritans in Africa*.

12   In 1984 two distinguished Afrikaner scholars had begun this vital task, Professor David Bosch of the University of South Africa and Professor Andre du Toit of Stellenbosch.

13   *The Cambridge History of the British Empire*, Vol VIII, p 205.

14   D Moodie, *The Record*, Extracts from the Militia Court, Swellendam, 25 October 1780.

15   *The Record*, p 99.

16   *The Record*, p 93.

17   J B Pieres, *The House of Phalo*, pp 53–4.

18   C W de Kiewiet, *A History of South Africa, Social and Economic*, p 31.

19   *A History of South Africa, Social and Economic*, p 46.

20   *The Record*, Part V, p 17.

21   *The Record*, p 18.

22   *The House of Phalo*, pp 65–9 for an account of the campaign's impact on the Xhosa.

23   *The House of Phalo* Chapter 5 for a perceptive discussion of Nxele and Ntsikana.

24   T. Pringle, *Narrative of a Residence in South Africa*, p 427.

25   *Narrative of a Residence in South Africa*, p 427.

26   *Narrative of a Residence in South Africa*, p 436.

27   *Narrative of a Residence in South Africa*, p 439.

28   In R Elphick and H Giliomee (eds), *The Shaping of South African Society*, pp 291 326.

CHAPTER 2
pp 33 to 51

1   W de Klerk, *The Puritans in Africa*, p 28.

2   Richard Lovett, *The History of the London Missionary Society, 1795–1895*, Vol I, p 50.

3   A D Martin, *Doctor Vanderkemp*, p 146.

4   London Missionary Society, Annual Report for 1804.

5   Throughout its existence, the regiment recruited from among the Cape Folk, had its name changed on a number of occasions. To avoid confusion, it will be referred to as the Cape Corps, or by its later name, the Cape Mounted Rifles.

6   C W de Kiewiet, *A History of South Africa*, p 46.

7   *Doctor Vanderkemp*, p 181.

8   D Moodie, *The Record*, p 26. The underlining is the present writer's.

9   Quoted in Jane Sales, *Mission Stations and the Coloured Communities of the Eastern Cape, 1800–1852*, pp 22–3.

10   J S Moffat, *The Lives of Robert and Mary Moffat*, p 62.

CHAPTER 3
pp 52 to 76

1   T C Smout, *A History of the Scottish People*, p 282.

2   *A History of the Scottish People*, pp 291–3.

3   *A History of the Scottish People*, pp 338–9.

4   W M MacMillan, *The Cape Colour Question*, p 97.

5   A L Drummond and J Bulloch, *The Scottish Church*, 1688–1843, p 143.

6   *A History of the Scottish People*, p 476.

7   Robert Haldane, *Address to the Public concerning Political Opinions*, p 4.
8   *Address to the Public concerning Political Opinions*, p 6.
9   The same Campbell who was to become an important figure in the London Missionary Society and Philip's colleague in South Africa, 1819–20.
10 *Address to the Public concerning Political Opinions*. Appendix entitled, 'Correspondence with Professor Robison'.
11 This Act soon ceased to be observed in practice but it was not formally rescinded until 1863.
12 'Pastoral Letter of the General Assembly to all the people under their charge', 23 May 1799.
13 'Pastoral Letter of the General Assembly', 23 May 1799.
14 The 'Philip' article in the *Dictionary of South African Biography*, says that they were members of the Church of England! This error presumably stems from Macmillan's reference to them as members of the 'Established Church'. The author of the article was apparently unaware that in Scotland, the Established Church was, and is, the Church of Scotland, a Presbyterian organisation.
15 Ralph Wardlaw, 'What is death?' A sermon delivered in Poultny Chapel London, on the occasion of the recent death of the Reverend Dr John Philip, DD. Pamphlet published 1852. p 77.
16 *The Cape Colour Question*, p 98.
17 *A History of the Scottish People*, pp 389–90.
18 This is in contrast with the traditional training for the Church of Scotland and other Scottish Presbyterian bodies which insisted on a four-year Arts course at the University preceding the three-year Divinity course.
19 'What is death?', p 27.
20 'What is death?', p 33.
21 H Escott, *History of Scottish Congregationalism*, p 255.
22 John Bulloch, *Centenary Memorials of the First Congregational Church in Aberdeen*.
23 *Centenary Memorials*, p 55.
24 H W Meikle, *Scotland and the French Revolution*, p 208.
25 *Centenary Memorials*, p 59.
26 *Centenary Memorials*, p 59.
27 Correspondence and Notes of Dr Philip, 1830–1847, Rhodes House Library, Oxford, 'Memoir of his Mother by Durant Philip', MS No. 54. See also '?
28 Robert Philip, *The Elijah of South Africa*, p 41.
29 *The Elijah of South Africa*, pp 43–4.
30 Their support was of vital importance at that time when the Church of Scotland controlled all appointments to and much else in the Scottish Universities.
31 Professor Dewar to Burder, 9 January 1819, SA Incoming Letters, Box 1, Folder 2.
32 Hankey and Burder to John Philip, November 1817, SA Incoming Letters, Box 1, Folder 1.
33 Philip to Burder, 24 October 1817, SA Incoming Letters, Box 1, Folder 1.

CHAPTER 4
pp 77 to 115

1   Entry on John Philip in *Dictionary of South African Biography* (*DSAB*).
2   *DSAB* Chapter 2.
3   *DSAB* Chapter 2.

4 R Lovett, *The History of the London Missionary Society*, Vol I, p
5 J Philip, *Researches in South Africa*, p xxxvi.
6 A K Millar, *Plantagenet in South Africa*, p 102.
7 W M Macmillan, *The Cape Colour Question*, p 123.
8 Philip to Directors, 24 December 1817, SA Incoming Letters, Box 1, Folder 1.
9 Confidential Report to the Society, 20 December 1819, Quoted by Macmillan, *The Cape Colour Question*, p 106.
10 *Plantaganet in South Africa*, pp 135–41.
11 *The Cambridge History of the British Empire*, Vol VIII, p 252.
12 *The Cambridge History of the British Empire*, p 255.
13 *Plantaganet in South Africa*, p 196.
14 Philip to Burden, SA Incoming Letters, Box 1, Folder 4.
15 Philip to Burden, SA Incoming Letters, Box 1, Folder 4.
16 Philip to Directors, March 1820, SA Incoming Letters, Box 1, Folder 1.
17 *The Cape Colour Question*, p 92.
18 *The Cape Colour Question*, p 92.
19 Philip to Tidman, 31 March 1846, SA Incoming Letters, Box 22, Folder 1.
20 'John Philip' in *DSAB*.
21 P Curtin, *The Image of Africa*, Chapters 15, 16 and 17, also T F Gosset, *Race: The History of an Idea in America*, Chapters 7 and 13.
22 *The Cape Colour Question*, p 173.
23 Philip to Directors, undated, marked 'Not for Publication', SA Incoming Letters, Box 1, Folder 1.
24 *Missionary Herald*, Vol XXIX, 1833, p 414.
25 *Researches in South Africa*, Introduction.
26 *Researches in South Africa*, Vol I, p 213.
27 Jane Sales, *Mission Stations and the Coloured Communities of the Eastern Cape*, p 89.
28 Philip to Directors, 20 January 1820, Miscellaneous Africa File 216, No. 131.
29 Hankey to Philip, 17 June 1825, Southern Outgoing Letters, Box 1, Folder 1.
30 These letters are in South African Incoming Letters, Box 2, Folder 2.
31 Quoted in *The Cape Colour Question*, p 215.
32 Notes appended to Mr Ellis's letter of 3 January 1827, SA Incoming Letters, Box 2, Folder 3.
33 W A de Klerk, *The Puritans in Africa*, p 30.
34 Philip to Burden, 1 October 1820, Misc. African Letters, File 215, Letter 125.
35 *The Cape Colour Question*, pp 226–9.
36 *Researches in South Africa*, Vol 1, p 177.
37 *Researches in South Africa*, p 339.
38 Hansard, N S Vol XIX, Cols 1693–4.
39 *Reluctant Empire*, p 84.
40 I owe this information to Dr T Barron of the Department of History of the University of Edinburgh, whose Doctoral dissertation was a study of Stephen.
41 Philip to Dr Joseph Fletcher, 22 February 1830, Africa Odds, Box 2, Folder 4.
42 Quoted in *The Cape Colour Question*, p 234.

CHAPTER 5
pp 116 to 145

1 Anti-Slavery Pamphlets, No. 12, p 7.
2 Philip to Directors, 25 December 1830, SA Incoming Letters, Box 12, Folder 1.

3   Quoted in J Meiring, *Thomas Pringle, His Life and Times*, p 121.
4   C W Hutton (ed), *The Autobiography of the Late Sir Andries Stockenstrom, Bart*, Vol I, p 151.
5   Quoted in MacMillan, *Bantu, Boer and Briton*, p 98.
6   Quoted in *Thomas Pringle, His Life and Times*, pp 115–16.
7   T Pringle, *Narrative of a Residence in South Africa*, Chapter 6 *passim*.
8   E A Walker, *A History of Southern Africa*, pp 180–1.
9   J B Pieres, *The House of Phalo*, p 81.
10 BPP 538 of 1836, answer to Question 969.
11 *The Autobiography of the Late Sir Andries Stockenstrom*, Vol. 2, pp 46–7.
12 BPP 538 of 1836, answer to Question 970.
13 See Chapter 4, p
14 Mrs John Ross to her parents, in U Long, *An Index to Authors of Unofficial privately-owned Manuscripts relating to the History of South Africa*, pp 231–2.
15 Macmillan's notes on the Philip Papers, later destroyed, in Rhodes House Library, Oxford.
16 Read to Directors, 4 July 1834, SA Incoming Letters, Box 14, Folder 3.
17 Murray to Cole, 6 May 1830, CO 48/144. The underlining and the bracketed comment are the present author's.
18 Philip's comments on the Bruce episode can be found in Philip to Ellis, 1 May 1835, SA Incoming Letters, Box 14, Folder 3.
19 *Bantu, Boer and Briton*, p 102.
20 *Narrative of a Residence in South Africa*, Chapter XIII, *passim*.
21 *The Autobiography of the Late Sir Andries Stockenstrom, Bart*, Vol I, p 430.
22 *The Autobiography of the Late Sir Andries Stockenstrom, Bart*, Vol II, p 12.
23 Philip to Directors, 17 February 1834, SA Incoming Letters, Box 13, Folder 5.
24 *The Autobiography of the Late Sir Andries Stockenstrom, Bart*, Vol I, p 348.
25 *Bantu, Boer and Briton*, p 109.
26 J S Galbraith, *Reluctant Empire*, pp 100 ff.
27 *Bantu, Boer and Briton*, pp 107–13.
28 *Reluctant Empire*, p 110.
29 Philip to Directors, August 1834, SA Incoming Letters, Box 14, Folder 2.
30 Read to Philip, 8 December 1834, SA Incoming Letters, Box 14, Folder 2.
31 *The House of Phalo*, p 146.
32 Difaqane/Mfecane. There are two names for the same phenomenon of fundamental importance in the history of southern Africa, indeed its effect reached as far north as the southern districts of Tanzania.

The rise of the Sparta-like Zulu kingdom under Chaka, who built on the foundations laid by Dingiswayo, caused a series of forced migrations of peoples and remnants of peoples, both Nguni and Sotho, across the High Veld and in some instances, across the Limpopo and the Zambesi. This movement caused years of bitter warfare and chaos, with land untilled and herds destroyed. In the area of the present Transvaal and Orange Free State, the old Sotho polities were destroyed, Moshweshwe came to prominence by building a new Sotho polity out of the ruins. Other new African polities were brought into being further north, after much turmoil—the Ndebele state of Mzilikazi, the Kololo kingdom of Sebituane in Zambia, the Gaza kingdom of Soshangane in Mozambique and the Ngoni polities in Malawi and Zambia. This was the Difaqane.

The most important aspect of the Difaqane, for this study, is that it resulted in the High Veld appearing devoid of any major African society to the Voortrekkers, when they arrived there just as the turmoil was ending.

33 *Reluctant Empire*, pp 115–16.
34 *Reluctant Empire*, pp 129–31.
35 *Reluctant Empire*, pp 129–31.
36 Galbraith and Pieres both quote many tributes to them from British officers.
37 Philip to Ellis, 2 January 1835, SA Incoming Letters, Box 14, Folder 3.
38 From hereon this Committee will be referred to as the Aborigines Committee.
39 *Bantu, Boer and Briton*, p 141.
40 Ross to Philip, 5 June 1835, SA Incoming Letters, Box 14, Folder 4.
41 Ross to Philip, 5 June 1835.
42 *Reluctant Empire*, Chapter 6, *passim*.
43 *Bantu, Boer and Briton*, pp 160–1.
44 Philip to Ellis, 19 December 1835, SA Incoming Letters, Box 14, Folder 5.
45 Quoted in *Bantu, Boer and Briton*, p 165.
46 These letters are in SA Incoming Letters, Box 14, Folders 4 and 5.
47 BPP 538 of 1836, pp 625–9.
48 BPP 538 of 1836, evidence given by W Shaw and W B Boyce.
49 D'Urban to Glenelg, 8 June 1836, CO 48/167.
50 *Reluctant Empire*, p 137.
51 *The Autobiography of the late Sir Andries Stockenstrom, Bart*, Vol II, pp 22–4.
52 *Reluctant Empire*, pp 139–41. The weekly reports, published by Fairbairn in the *Advertiser*, reflect very clearly the effectiveness of the work of the Lt Governor on the frontier.
53 *See* 'Introduction'.

CHAPTER 6
pp 146 to 158

1   E A Walker, *The Great Trek*, pp 126–7.
2   The Dutch word from the original records is used since there is no exact English equivalent for a community that is, in one sense, a state, yet has neither fixed territory nor international recognition.
3   James Archbell was a Methodist missionary who offered to accompany the voortrekkers. Since their own Church had condemned the whole venture and forbidden any minister of the Reformed Church to accompany the trekkers, Archbell's offer was accepted.
4   Sekonyela was chief of a Sotho fragment, rendered dangerously effective as raiders by their new-found skill with gun and horse.
5   G W Eybers, *Select Constitutional Documents*, pp 158–9.
6   *Select Constitutional Documents*, pp 159–62.
7   J Bird (ed), *The Annals of Natal: 1495–1845*, Vol 1, Nos 618 and 621.
8   C de B Web, '*The extended Black–White frontier*' in *Perspectives on the South African Past*, p 145.
9   Campbell to the Governor, included in Philip to the Directors, 19 June 1834, SA Incoming Letters, Box 14, Folder 4.
10 C W Hutton (ed), *The Autobiography of the late Sir Andries Stockenstrom, Bart*, Vol 1, pp 390–91.
11 E A Walker, *A History of Southern Africa*, p 197.
12 *See* Chapter 7, *passim*.
13 D W Kruger, *The Making of a Nation*, pp 6–7.
14 *See* A du Toit and H Giliomee (eds), *Afrikaner Political Thought*, p 17.

CHAPTER 7
pp 159 to 184

1   Philip to Buxton, 22 November 1842, SA Odds, Box 3, Folder 5.
2   Journal of 1841–1842 Trek, entry for 1 June 1842, SA Journals, Box 4.
3   C W Hutton (ed), *The Autobiography of the late Sir Andries Stockenstrom, Bart*, Vol II, Chapter XXI, *passim*.
4   *See* p 122.
5   Philip to Ellis, 26 March 1840, SA Incoming Letters, Box 17, Folder 1.
6   Philip to Ellis, 1 June 1838, SA Incoming Letters, Box 16, Folder 1.
7   Philip to Buxton, 25 November 1842, SA Incoming Letters, Box 18, Folder 4.
8   Although neither in the London Missionary Society archives nor in the notes left by Professor Macmillan in Rhodes House of the Philip papers destroyed in the 'Wits' fire, has the present writer been able to find any record of Philip requesting that these letters be sent—their timely arrival appears to be mere coincidence. All three letters are in SA Incoming Letters, Box 18, Folder 1.
9   This is yet another example of Philip's close relationship with, one might almost say dependence upon James Read. A relationship, which, despite their great qualities, Professor Macmillan's two studies ignores.
10 Philip to Napier, 25 August 1842, SA Incoming Letters, Box 18, Folder 3.
11 Philip to Napier, 25 August 1842.
12 Philip to Napier, 25 August 1842.
13 Philip to Napier, 25 August 1842.
14 South African Journals, Box 4.
15 Philip's Journal for 1841–42 Trek, loc. cit.
16 These passages also illustrate his fundamental understanding of the nature of the Christian mission referred to in the Introduction.
17 John S Moffat, *The Lives of Robert and Mary Moffat*, Chapter XII, *passim*.
18 P B Sanders, *Moshoeshoe*, Chapter VI, *passim* and L M Thompson, *Survival in Two Worlds*, pp 126–32.
19 Philip to Directors, 11 June 1842, SA Incoming Letters, Box 18, Folder 3.
20 Philip to Hare, 12 July 1842, SA Incoming Letters, Box 18, Folder 1.
21 Copies of all these letters are in SA Incoming Letters, Box 18, Folder 4.
22 Philip to Napier, 25 August 1842.
23 Philip to Napier, 25 August 1842.
24 Napier to Stanley, 15 September 1842, CO 1450.
25 Wright to Philip, 27 October 1842. SA Incoming Letters, Box 19, Folder 1.
26 Wright to Philip, 6 January 1843, SA Incoming Letters, Box 19, Folder 1.
27 Minutes of the Colesberg Meetings in the Cape Archives, quoted in R Ross, *Adam Kok's Griquas*, p 52.
28 *Adam Kok's Griquas*.
29 Cuttings from the 'Journal' for 1842 and 1843, included in many of Philip's letters to London in SA Incoming Letters, Boxes 19 and 20. Also a selection of such cuttings sent to London by Philip, to be found in Africa Odds, Box 2.
30 *Adam Kok's Griquas*, pp 53–4.
31 Philip to Directors, 18 July 1848, SA Incoming Letters, Box 23, Folder 6. Strangely, this appointment is not noted in Lovett's *History*, Vol I, Appendix 1, Staff Lists.
32 In particular, J Ross to Philip, 5 June 1835, SA Incoming Letters, Box 14, Folder 4. *See* Chapter 5.
33 *See* Chapter 8.
34 *See* footnote 18.

35   *Survival in Two Worlds*, pp 127–33.
36   Dyke to Philip, 13 December 1843, SA Incoming Letters, Box 19, Folder 4.
37   J S Galbraith, *Reluctant Empire*, p 205.
38   W M Macmillan, *Bantu, Boer and Briton*, pp 240–2.
39   Philip to Directors, 24 June 1844, SA Incoming Letters, Box 20, Folder 2.
40   G W Eybers (ed), *Select Constitutional Documents illustrating South African History*, pp 349–56.
41   Thompson to Philip, 25 December 1844, SA Incoming Letters, Box 22, Folder 2.
42   *Adam Kok's Griquas*, p 57.
43   Thompson to Philip, 17 October 1844, SA Incoming Letters, Box 21, Folder 2.
44   These notes and letters are included in Philip to Tidman, 10 February 1845, SA Incoming Letters, Box 21, Folder 2.
45   *Reluctant Empire*, pp 164–5.
46   B Maitland to Kok and Thompson, 27 June 1845, included with all the correspondence and notes of the Conference, sent by Thompson to Philip, in Philip to Tidman, 10 July 1845, SA Incoming Letters, Box 21, Folder 2.
47   Thompson to Philip, 3 July 1845, loc. cit.
48   *See* map on p
49   G M Theal, *Basutoland Records*, Vol 1, pp 103–11.

CHAPTER 8
pp 185 to 214

1   Philip to Tidman, 11 March 1845, SA Incoming Letters, Box 21, Folder 2.
2   A du Toit and H Giliomee, *Afrikaner Political Thought*, p 16.
3   Atkinson to Philip, 24, 27 and 31 January 1843, Africa Odds, Box 6, Folder 6.
4   Elliot to Tidman, 13 June 1845, SA Incoming Letters, Box 21, Folder 3.
5   C W Hutton, *The Autobiography of the Late Sir Andries Stockenstrom, Bart*, Vol II, pp 50–64.
6   *See* Chapter 7 footnote 29.
7   Notes by the editor of *The Journal of Andrew Geddes Bain*, pp 192–202.
8   J M Bowker, *Speeches, Letters and Selections*.
9   *Speeches, Letters and Selections*. The whole speech is found on pp 116–25.
10   *Speeches, Letters and Selections*, pp 131–2.
11   *Speeches, Letters and Selections*, p 129.
12   W M Macmillan, *Bantu, Boer and Briton*, p 151.
13   *Speeches, Letters and Selections*, p 123.
14   L H Fishel and B Quarles, *The Black American*, pp 90–100.
15   *Speeches, Letters and Selections*, p 125.
16   R Robinson and J Gallacher, *Africa and the Victorians*, Also E R Kittrell and B Semmel in their essays in A G L Shaw (ed), *Great Britain and the Colonies, 1815–1865*.
17   B Semmel, 'The Philosphic Radicals' in *Great Britain and the Colonies, 1815–1865*.
18   Philip to Directors, Africa Odds, Box 7, Folder 4.
19   Quoted in J J Freeman, *A Tour of South Africa*, pp 212–13.
20   J S Galbraith, *Reluctant Empire*, pp 248–9.
21   Quoted in *Reluctant Empire*, pp 257–8.
22   C W de Kiewiet, A History of South Africa, p 43. The chapter is headed 'New

Ideas for Old' but he does not mention the spread of new illiberal ideas from Europe which were equally new to the Afrikaner people.

23   J J Freeman, *A Tour in South Africa*, p 303.
24   *Bantu, Boer and Briton*, p 278.
25   E A Walker, *A History of Southern Africa*, p 225.
26   C L Stretch, 'Memorandum on the Stockenstrom Treaties', Africa Odds, Box 2, Folder 6.
27   *A History of Southern Africa*, p 226.
28   Memorandum on the Stockenstrom Treaties.
29   J B Pieres, *The House of Phalo*, pp 132–3.
30   *Reluctant Empire*, p 175.
31   *Bantu, Boer and Briton*, pp 200–1.
32   *Reluctant Empire*, p 174.
33   R Ross, *Adam Kok's Griqua*, pp 63–4.
34   L Thompson, *Survival in Two Worlds*, pp 148–51.
35   Correspondence related to this problem is in SA Incoming Letters, Box 23, Folders 1 and 2.
36   *Reluctant Empire*, p 218.
37   G E Cory, *The Rise of South Africa*, Vol 5, p 14.
38   Philip to Tidman, 15 May 1846, SA Incoming Letters, Box 23, Folder 1.
39   Philip to Tidman, 3 June 1846, SA Incoming Letters, Box 23, Folder 1.
40   Read to Tidman, 31 August 1846, SA Incoming Letters, Box 23, Folder 2.
41   *Bantu, Boer and Briton*, pp 376–7.
42   Berkeley to Pottinger, 23 March 1847. Quoted in full in *The Autobiography of the late Sir Andries Stockenstrom*, Vol II, pp 376–7.
43   Their letters are in SA Incoming Letters, Box 23, Folders 1 and 2.
44   *The Autobiography of the late Sir Andries Stockenstrom*, p 378.
45   *The Autobiography of the late Sir Andries Stockenstrom*.
46   James Read, Jun to Directors, 4 February 1848, SA Incoming Letters, Box 23, Folder 5.
47   James Read Jun to Philip, 25 April 1850, SA Incoming Letters, Box 25, Folder 3.
48   Elliot to Directors, 2 February 1848, SA Incoming Letters, Box 23, Folder 5.
49   Christie to Tidman, 20 March 1850, SA Incoming Letters, Box 25, Folder 1.
50   W M Macmillan, *The Cape Colour Question*, p 276.
51   This letter is included in Philip to Tidman, 11 January 1849, SA Incoming Letters, Box 24, Folder 1.
52   Elliot to Tidman, 2 February 1849, SA Incoming Letters, Box 24, Folder 1.
53   Philip to Tidman, 22 December 1847, SA Incoming Letters, Box 23, Folder 3.
54   *Grahamstown Journal* of 16 March 1850, quoted in *A Tour of South Africa*, p 144. *Note*: Again the Afrikaner is ignored in this as in much of the *Journals*, pleading that it is their fellow-countrymen that the British authorities betray.
55   Christie to Directors, 20 March 1850, SA Incoming Letters, Box 25, Folder 1.
56   Quoted in *A Tour of South Africa*, p 187.
57   Botha to Philip, 27 June 1850, SA Incoming Letters, Box 25, Folder 1.
58   *An Autobiography of the late Sir Andries Stockenstrom*, pp 427–9.
59   Footnote on p 280 of Macmillan, *The Cape Colour Question*, cites a report from the DRC minister of Kat River which lists 818 of the menfolk as loyal and 266 as rebels.
60   e.g. T R H Davenport, *South Africa: A Modern History* refers to the episode thus, 'The Kat River Khoikhoi also came out in rebellion in February, 1851', p 100.

61 S Trapido, 'Cape Franchise Qualificatin of 1853', *The Journal of African History*, Vol V, No. 1, 1964.
62 *The Cape Colour Question*, p 249.
63 *The Cape Colour Question.*
64. G W Eybers, *Select Constitutional Documents*, pp 30–2.
65 *The Journal of African History*, pp 41–2.
66 *The Oxford History of South Africa*, Vol I, p 322.
67 *The Oxford History of South Africa*, pp 322–4 and *The Journal of African History*, passim.
68 Philip to Hankey, 18 August 1830, Africa Odds, Box 7 Folder 4.
69 Read to Philip, 23 May 1850, SA Incoming Letters, Box 25, Folder 3.
70 *The Journal of African History.*
71 *The Journal of African History*, p 51.

CHAPTER 9
pp 215 to 228

1 Julius Lewin, 'Dr Philip and Liberalism', *Race Relations*, April-June 1960. Andrew Nash, 'Dr Philip, the Spread of Civilisation and Liberalism in South Africa', *Proceedings of the Conference on Opposition in South Africa* (Jo'burg 1978).
2 G Sorin, *The New York Abolitinists*; T I Smith, *Revivalism and Social Reform in Mid-nineteenth Century America*; M Duberman (ed), *The Anti-Slavery Vanguard*; R H Abzug, *The Passionate Liberator, Theodore Weld and the Dilemma of Reform.*
3 Quoted in *The New York Abolitionists*, p 115.
4 *The Passionate Liberator, Theodore Weld and the Dilemma of Reform*, pp 92–3.
5 Letter of John Philip to the American Board of Commissioners for Foreign Mission, published in *Missionary Herald*, November 1833.
6 Letter of John Philip to American Board of Commissioners for Foreign Mission.
7 Philip to Directors, 31 March 1846, SA Incoming Letters, Box 22, Folder 1.
8 *The Passionate Liberator, Theodore Weld and the Dilemma of Reform*, Chapter VI, *passim.*
9 Macmillan, *Bantu, Boer and Briton*, p 258.
10 *See* Martin Legassick, '*The Frontier Tradition in South African Historiography*'.
11 *See* C Van Woodward, *The Strange Case of Jim Crow.*
12 *Proceedings of the Conference on Opposition in South Africa.*
13 *See* the very supportive letter from Schultheiss, Superintendent of the Berlin Mission, to Philip on the issue of English settler antagonism towards the Cape Folk and the Xhosa, 1 September 1847, Africa Odds, Box 6, Folder 6.
14 V C Malherbe, 'The Life and Times of Cupido Kakkerlak', in *JAH*, Vol 20, No. 3, 1979, pp 365–78.
15 Philip to Tidman, 11 March 1845, S A Incoming Letters, Box 21, Folder 2.
16 Livingstone to W Thompson, 30 September 1852. Letter 44 in D Chamberlin, *Some Letters from David Livingstone.*
17 *Some Letters from David Livingstone.*
18 Livingstone to W. Thompson, 6 September 1845. Letter 43 in *Some Letter from David Livingstone.*
19 *Some Letters from David Livingstone*, Letter 44.

Bibliography

MSS SOURCES
The London Missionary Society Archives (School of Oriental and African Studies): South African Outgoing Letters, Boxes 1–10; South African Incoming Letters, Boxes 1–25; South African Odds, Boxes 1–6 and South African Journals, Boxes 3 and 4.
Philip Family Letters in the Library of the University of Cape Town.
Philip Family Letters and Fairbairn Family Letters in the Cullen Library, University of the Witwatersrand.
Pringle and Fairbairn Correspondence in the Library of Parliament, Cape Town.
Series C.O. 48 and 49 (Cape Colony) in the Public Record Office, London.

OFFICIAL PUBLICATIONS
British Parliamentary Papers
Report from the Select Committee on Aborigines (British Settlements): with the Minutes of Evidence, Appendices and Index (1836), VII(538).
Further Report for the Select Committee on Aborigines (1837), VII(238), (425).

Confidential Print
Summary of Correspondence relative to the Policy pursued towards the Native Tribes on the Eastern Frontier of the Colony of the Cape of Good Hope, including the Wars of 1835 and 1846.

NEWSPAPERS
The South African Commercial Advertiser.
Grahamstown Journal.
The Missionary Herald (Journal of the American Board of Commissioners for Foreign Missions, published in Boston).

BOOKS
R H Abzug, *Passionate Liberator: Theodore Dwight Weld and the Dilemma of Reform* (New York 1980).
J Backhouse, *Narrative of a Visit to Madagascar and South Africa* (London 1844).
A G Bain, *Journal of Andrew Geddes Bain*, (ed) M H Lister (Cape Town, 1949).
J Bird (ed), *The Annals of Natal: 1495–1845*, 2 vols (Pietermaritzburg 1888).
J M Bowker, *Speeches, Letters and Selections* (Reprint, Cape Town 1962).
J C Brauer, *Protestantism in America* (Chicago 1968).
J Bulloch, *Centenary Memorials of the First Congregational Church in Aberdeen.*
The Cambridge History of the British Empire, Vol. VIII (Cambridge 1936).
E Casalis, *My Life in Basutoland* (London 1889).
B Catton, *The American Civil War* (New York 1971).
D Chamberlin (ed), *Some Letters of Livingstone* (London 1940).
G E Cory, *The Rise of South Africa*, 5 Vols (London 1910–30).
P Curtin, *The Image of Africa* (Madison, Wisconsin 1964).
T R H Davenport, *South Africa, A Modern History* (London 1973).

C W de Kiewiet, *A History of South Africa: Social and Economic* (London 1957).

W A de Klerk, *The Puritans in Africa* (London 1975).

The Dictionary of South African Biography, 4 Vols (Pretoria, 1968–81).

A L Drummond and J Bulloch, *The Scottish Church, 1688–1843* (Edinburgh 1973).

M Duberman (ed) *The Anti–Slavery Vanguard* (Princeton 1965).

A du Toit and H Giliomee (eds), *Afrikaner Political Thought* (Los Angeles 1983).

R Elphick and H Giliomee (eds), *The Shaping of South African Society, 1652–1820* (Cape Town 1979).

D Eltis and J Walvin (eds), *The Abolition of the Atlantic Slave Trade* (Madison, Wisconsin 1981).

H Escott, *A History of Scottish Congregationalism* (Glasgow 1960).

G W Eybers (ed), *Select Constitutional Documents Ilustrating South African History, 1795–1810* (London 1918).

J J Freeman, *The Kaffir War* (London 1851).

J J Freeman, *A Tour of South Africa* (London 1851).

J S Galbraith, *Reluctant Empire* (Berkeley 1963).

R Godlonton, *A Narrative of the Irruption of the Kaffir Hordes into the Eastern Province of the Cape of Good Hope, 1834–1835* (Grahamstown 1836).

R Godlonton, *Case of the Colonists of the Eastern Province of the Cape of Good Hope, in reference to the Kaffir Wars of 1835–1836 and 1846* (Grahamstown 1846).

T F Gosset, *Race: The History of an Idea in America* (New York 1973).

D W Kruger, *The Making of a Nation* (London 1971).

B A Le Cordeur, *The Politics of Eastern Cape Separatism* (Cape Town 1981).

U Long, *Index to Authors of Unofficial and Privately-owned MSS 1812–1912* (Cape Town 1947)

R Lovett, *The History of the London Missionary Society*, 2 vols (London 1899).

W M Macmillan, *Bantu, Boer and Briton* (Oxford 1963).

W M Macmillan, *The Cape Colour Question* (London 1927).

A D Martin, *Dr Vanderkemp* (London 1931).

H Meikle, *Scotland and the French Revolution* (Glasgow 1912).

J Meiring, *Thomas Pringle: His Life and Times* (Cape Town 1968).

A K Millar, *Plantagenet in South Africa: Lord Charles Somerset* (Cape Town, 1965).

J S Moffat, *The Lives of Robert and Mary Moffat* (London 1886).

D Moodie, *The Record, or a Series of Official Papers Relative to the Condition and Treatment of the Native Tribes of South Africa* (Photostat reprint, Cape Town 1960).

J W D Moodie, *Ten Years in South Africa*, 2 vols (London 1835).

S D Neumark, *Economic Influences on the South African Frontier*, 1652–1836 (Stanford 1957).

J M Orpen, *Reminiscences of Life in South Africa* (Durban 1908).

J Philip, *Researches in South Africa*, 2 vols (London 1828).

P Philip, *A Fifeshire Family: the descendants of John and Thomas Philip*, 2 vols (Cape Town 1975).

J B Pieres, *The House of Phalo* (Johannesburg 1981).

T Pringle, *Narrative of a Residence in South Africa* (London 1835).

O Ransford, *The Great Trek* (London 1974).

R Robinson and J Gallagher with A Denny, *African and the Victorians* (London 1961).

R Ross, *Adam Kok's Griquas* (Cambridge 1976).

J Sales, *Mission Stations and the Coloured Communities of the Eastern cape, 1800 1852* (Cape Town 1975).

P Sanders, *Moshoeshow: Chief of the Sotho* (London 1975). C Saunders and R Derricourt (eds), *Beyond the Cape Frontier* (London 1974).

I Schapera (ed), *David Livingstone, Family Letters, 1841–1856*, 2 vols (London 1959).

A G L Shaw (ed), *Great Britain and the Colonies, 1815–1865* (London 1970).

W Shaw, *The Journal of William Shaw*, ed W D Hammond-Tooke (Cape Town 1972).

T C Smout, *A History of the Scottish People, 1560–1830* (Glasgow 1972).

T L Smith, *Revivalism and Social Reform*: *American Protestantism on the Eve of the Civil War* (Baltimore 1980).

G Sorin, *The New York Abolitionists* (Westport, Connecticut 1971).

A Stockenstrom, *The Autobiography of the late Sir Andries Stockenstrom, Bart*, 2 vols ed E W Hutton (Cape Town 1887).

G M Theal, *Basutoland Records*, 3 vols (Cape Town 1883).

L Thompson (ed), *African Societies in Southern Africa* (London 1969).

L Thompson, *Survival in Two Worlds*: *Moshoeshoe of Lesotho, 1781–1870* (Oxford 1975).

C Van Woodward, *The Strange case of Jim Crow* (New York 1974).

E A Walker, *The Great Trek* (London 1938).

E A Walker, *A History of Southern Africa* (London 1959).

M Wilson and L Thompson (eds), *The Oxford History of South Africa*, 2 vols (Oxford 1969).

PAMPHLETS

Robert Haldane, *Address to the Public concerning Political Opinions* (London 1800).

Robert Philip, *The Elijah of South Africa* (London 1851).

Ralph Wardlaw, *What is death? A Sermon delivered on the occasion of the death of Dr. John Philip* (Glasgow 1852).

ARTICLES

L C Duly, 'The Failure of British Land Policy at the Cape', *Journal of African History*, Vol 6 (1965).

H A Gaily, 'John Philip's Role in Hottentot Emancipation', *Journal of African History*, Vol 3 (1962).

J Lewin, 'Dr. John Philip and Liberalism', *Race Relations Journal*, Vol. xxvii (1960).

A Nash, 'Dr. Philip, the 'Spread of Civilisation and Liberalism in South Africa', *Conference on the History of Opposition in South Africa* (Johannesburg 1978).

C Saunders, 'James Read; Towards a Reassessment', Institute of Commonwealth Studies, *Collected Seminar Papers, Societies of Southern Africa*, Vol 7 (London 1977).

S Trapido, 'The Origins of the Cape Franchise Qualification of 1853', *Journal of African History*, Vol 5 (1964).

Index